BEYOND THE NATION?

Immigrants' Local Lives in Transnational Cultures

Beyond the Nation?

Immigrants' Local Lives in Transnational Cultures

EDITED BY ALEXANDER FREUND

UNIVERSITY OF TORONTO PRESS
Toronto Buffalo London

© University of Toronto Press 2012
Toronto Buffalo London
www.utppublishing.com
Printed in Canada

ISBN 978–1-4426–4278–2

Printed on acid-free, 100% post-consumer recycled paper with
vegetable-based inks.

Library and Archives Canada Cataloguing in Publication

Freund, Alexander, 1969–
Beyond the nation : immigrants' local lives in transnational cultures /
Alexander Freund.

Includes bibliographical references and index.
ISBN 978-1-4426-4278-2

1. German Canadians – History.   2. German Canadians – Social
conditions.   3. German Canadians – Social life and customs.   I. Title.

FC106.G3F74 2012   971'.00431   C2012-901841-4

This book was made possible by funding from the Social Sciences and
Humanities Research Council and the German-Canadian Studies
Foundation.

University of Toronto Press acknowledges the financial assistance to its
publishing program of the Canada Council for the Arts and the Ontario Arts
Council.

University of Toronto Press acknowledges the financial support of the
Government of Canada through the Canada Book Fund for its publishing
activities.

This book has been published with the help of a grant from the Canadian
Federation for the Humanities and Social Sciences, through the Awards to
Scholarly Publications Program, using funds provided by the Social Sciences
and Humanities Research Council of Canada.

In memory of Christiane Harzig

Contents

BEYOND THE NATION?

Immigrants' Local Lives in Transnational Cultures

Introduction

ALEXANDER FREUND

Migration scholars have argued for transnational perspectives in migration studies since the 1960s,[1] but they have nevertheless found it difficult to go beyond the national paradigm. Canada, immigration scholars have insisted, is 'a nation of immigrants,' and immigrants have made and shaped 'Canadian' history.[2] They have taken this tack in order to demonstrate 'that Canadian immigrant history is Canadian history.'[3] This is an important goal. Such a framework, however, makes it difficult to talk about immigrants' agency. Certainly, Canadian nation building structured immigrants' lives. They experienced both prejudice and privilege while participating – wittingly or unwittingly – in this state project. But this is not why they had come to Canada, and this was not the frame within which they saw themselves and the world around them. Rather, they acted both locally and transnationally.

Comparative and transnational studies from a Canadian perspective can demystify the national view from above by focusing on the migrants' local actions and following them along the paths of their transnational networks. Such studies, however, are rare.[4] This collection makes such an attempt. It is a story about an ethnic group's experiences of integration and incorporation within the larger national history that sees them outside a national master narrative. The authors of the chapters use post-national paradigms to tell comparative, transnational, transcultural, and diasporic stories. Their gendered narratives explore the realms beyond historians' narratives of the nation, but they also show how immigrants invented ethnicity under the conditions of Canadian nation building.[5] And they investigate migrants' collective memories and 'imagined communities' in their attempts to take immigration studies beyond the cultural turn.[6]

'German-Canadians' make for a compelling case study to probe the constraints and contingencies of the nation, national identity, and nationalism. Indeed, to speak of 'Germans in Canada' or 'German-Canadians' tells us less about the migrants themselves and more about researchers trying to make sense.[7] To think in national terms often seems 'natural' – which is exactly why nationalism has become a successful ideology. And certainly, throughout the modern period, the nation-state and national ideologies have shaped people's lives in powerful ways. Germans in particular, whether in Germany or abroad, have had a troubled and troubling relationship with various nationalisms;[8] migrations – theirs and others' – have often been a direct result of this complicated relationship.[9]

For the migrants, 'German' and 'Canadian,' or 'Germany' and 'Canada,' held little meaning. This was true for the time before the last third of the nineteenth century, when the two nation-states did not yet exist, and it is true for the late nineteenth and twentieth centuries. Throughout, 'German' migrants came to Canada from all over the world, and only from the 1950s to the 1980s did the majority come from the (West) German nation-state. Until the First World War, nearly 90 per cent of 'German' immigrants came from Eastern Europe and the United States. They had migrated to these countries since the eighteenth century (and sometimes as early as the twelfth century) and lived in German religious–ethnic enclaves, where they continued to speak the language (or rather, one of its many dialects) while maintaining some of the traditions of their homelands in Central Europe. They formed regional identities, for example, as Sudeten Germans, Transylvania Saxons, and Danube Swabians. Catholics, Lutherans, Mennonites, Moravians, and other religious groups migrated and settled in groups, not only in Eastern Europe but also in the United States. German-Americans with various, distinct religio-ethnic identities settled in Canada after the American Revolution and especially after land in Canada's West became more attractive at the turn to the twentieth century. In the interwar period, about 20 per cent of German immigrants to Canada came from Germany. Among the immigrants of the 1930s were Jewish Germans and Sudeten German Social Democrats fleeing Nazi persecution. After the Second World War, ethnic German refugees and expellees from Eastern Europe were among the first immigrants to Canada, but about two-thirds of the Germans who arrived in the 1950s were from West Germany. Since the 1990s, many of the German immigrants have been ethnic Germans from Kazakhstan who came to Germany after the disintegration of the Soviet Union and decided to move on to Canada.[10] Thus, for most of the time, religions, political convictions, cultural regions, and 'imagined communities' rather than nation-states have been the homelands of these diverse migrants.

German-Canadians make for a compelling case study also because their long and diverse migrations help us understand how men and women created local lives in transcultural and transnational settings. The immigrants came from diverse origins, and their destinations were similarly complex. Throughout the nineteenth and twentieth centuries, Europeans migrated to 'America' rather than Canada, to a 'story' rather than a reality. But they were, of course, not simply dreamers. The men, women, and children migrated to their brothers in Vancouver, their aunts in Winnipeg, and their friends in Halifax, who promised them initial housing, employment, and social and emotional networks; they migrated to prospective employers in Montreal, on church-organized schemes to households in Saskatchewan and sugar beet farms in Alberta, and on government schemes to mining towns across the country.[11]

The authors of this collection thus revisit core themes that migration scholars have explored over the past two decades. Within the framework of heterogeneous migrations over three centuries, they explore the concepts of transnationalism, transculturalism, and diaspora. They revisit the concepts of gender, ethnicity, and race as social constructions and cultural inventions. And they link the more recent work on collective memory and imagined communities to the study of migrants.

Over the last century, immigration scholars have used a variety of nation-centric concepts to understand how immigrants find and make their home in their 'new worlds.' 'Assimilation' dominated explanations until the 1960s, when academics began to reject the model's prescriptive assumptions, which depicted immigrants as social problems. Acculturation, integration, and incorporation seemed to be models to better explain that adaptation was a two-way street and that the receiving societies were changed by the new arrivals as much as they changed the immigrants.[12] More recently, migration scholars have pushed this idea of immigrants' agency further by describing not only immigrants' relationship with their new *host* society but also their ongoing relationship with their *home* society. In the late twentieth century, affordable and easy means of transportation and communication have made migrants' 'transnational' lifestyles more likely. Historians have pointed to pre-paid tickets, shipping lines' price wars, and a stable and efficient international mail system as the means of living transnationally even in the nineteenth century. Dirk Hoerder, at the forefront of critiquing the 'national' in 'transnational,' has pointed to the long nineteenth century: migrants did not move from one nation to another but from one *locale* or *region* to another, depending on their networks as well as on their dreams and imaginations. Thus it makes more sense to speak of 'transcultural' lives: of living in different cultures simultaneously and merging these cultures within oneself, one's family, and one's community. Several of the other contributors engage with this concept. Some also suggest the usefulness of transnationalism, even in the nineteenth century, when national borders were not yet as restrictive as they would become in the twentieth. Others find value in the concept of the nation from a diasporic and comparative perspective that connects experiences in Canada, the United States, and Europe.

Feminist scholars have been at the forefront of transnationalizing migration history, because it goes hand in glove with the goal of gendering the nation, which also means critiquing the nation as a public, political male sphere.[13] Several authors in this volume pay significant attention to women's experiences, and a few set out to gender German-Canadian Studies and thus transform the field in a fundamental way.

Unlike a decade ago, when scholars debated ethnicity from both positivist and constructivist perspectives,[14] the authors in this volume understand ethnicity as a construction and invention that changes over time and that is dependent upon political and economic contexts. Moving beyond the debates of who should be considered German or German-Canadian, they explore how migrants and their descendents reworked private and public identities, individual and collective images, in local as well as cross-border and transatlantic settings.

Similarly, Benedict Anderson's concept of nations as 'imagined communities' is adapted here to describe how ethnic German migrants thought of themselves in relation to a Germany they had never seen. This concept helps us understand how the migrants made sense of their experiences once they had immigrated to Germany and Canada respectively. Another form of 'imagined community' is the one we find in official histories and other forms of dominant collective memories. Several authors explore from historical and literary perspectives how migrants wrote themselves, and were written by others, into or out of such dominant national narratives. They document the mental and material consequences of migrants' inability to find themselves in master narratives or even smaller group stories. In all of this, the authors explore and document the migrants' agency in shaping their own lives and those of others in local and transnational settings.

The Chapters

The authors of the first two chapters in this collection suggest two major concepts for the study of migrants and ethnic groups: transculturalism and gender. Dirk Hoerder juxtaposes the nation-centred and at times nationalistic historiographies on both sides of the Atlantic with the many-cultured lives that migrants (and non-migrants) lived and crafted. He surveys the multiple cultural connections of sending and receiving societies and individual migrants and families. While the ideology of nationalism was powerful in imposing homogenizing pressure, scholars have not done enough to get out from under this national paradigm. Transculturalism offers a path away from this nation-centred investigation; it brings to light the diverse life strategies that migrants devised beyond and sometimes in opposition to the monocultural homogenization of nationalism. According to Hoerder, 'transculturalism denotes the competence to live in two or more differing cultures and, in the process, create a personal transcultural space.' Transculturalism also offers a new way of illuminating migrants' agency. Although their lives were shaped by national borders and ideas, they nevertheless based their decisions and actions on what they believed was best for themselves and their families. Often, this included an implicit (and sometimes explicit) rejection of the nation and its ideology. Migrants' life stories document that even in the heyday of monocultural nationalism, lives were lived transculturally – in, with, and across different cultures. We therefore need to study more carefully how people adapted, adopted, and mixed cultures in order to survive and create meaningful lives. Germans, coming from many cultural regions in the world, brought these experiences of transcultural lives with them to Canada.

Gender is a similarly powerful concept, as Christiane Harzig shows in her article on the gendering of migration history. She investigates how the prism of gender can decentre the nation and argues for a fundamental and systematic inclusion of gender in German-Canadian Studies. A mere inclusion of women won't do. How can German-Canadian Studies begin this transformation in research? Harzig casts a global historiographical net for answers. Canadian women's studies can guide us to understand how gender has created historically changing hierarchies and relationships of power. Parallel to this has emerged a constructivist interpretation of ethnicity that has gained much of its force from feminist theory. While most of the chapters in this collection embrace and sometimes even study ethnicity as a social and historical construct, many do not investigate gender. This must change, because gender allows for a fundamental unsettling of the national paradigm – a paradigm that has worked not only against the inclusion of women in Canadian stories about the past, but also against the inclusion of German and other immigrants. Feminist research has been a trailblazer in developing post-national conceptions of history, and scholars of German-Canadians are well advised to follow this lead. Studies of 'German women in the diaspora of North America,' and especially the United States, have shown the diversity of rural and urban experiences, especially in the late nineteenth and early twentieth centuries. Similar research into the experiences of German women in Canada is needed for comparative and transnational studies. German-Canadian Studies should also enter the discourse on race through critical whiteness studies. 'Race' as a category applies to everyone, including whites; they, too, are racialized. As studies of the Italians and the Irish in the United States have demonstrated, their 'whitening' could be a drawn-out, conflicted process. Research is needed to understand whether and how German men and women were ascribed whiteness and positioned in racial hierarchies. This would further complicate the multiple relations of power within which German migrants were historically positioned.

The authors in Part II look at the eighteenth and nineteenth centuries and the ways in which religion and politics shaped immigrant experiences. Kerstin Boelkow, using German-language documents previously neglected by historians of the Moravian mission to Labrador, examines the beginnings of this mission of German-language Protestants to the Inuit in the mid-eighteenth century. She carefully describes the lives of the female and male missionaries and their attempts to Christianize the Inuit. Although their duties were prescribed by the Church headquarters in Germany, infrequent communication forced the missionaries to rely on themselves to survive, thrive, and develop fruitful relations with Inuit men and women. Boelkow resists the pressure of previous German-Canadian historiography to press these people into an ethnic German-Canadian mould by postulating them as early German contributors to Canadian history and culture. It was religion, not any sense of Germanness, that guided the missionaries' thoughts and actions. This case study is a good example of Hoerder's concept of transatlantic connectedness. It exemplifies the experience of transculturalism, in which migrants – and those the missionaries were – crafted lives by using their transcultural knowledge. Similarly, the Church and its transnational networks allowed for fruitful if not always easy cooperation with institutions of the British Empire and the colony of Newfoundland.

Ross D. Fair re-examines the experience of the Pennsylvania Germans (Mennonites and Tunkers), who came to Ontario in the late eighteenth century, within a political rather than ethnic framework in order to show that the story of Loyalist migration from the United States to Upper Canada was not the simplistic narrative of refugees fleeing from American persecution to a British safe haven. It was their religious pacifism, rather than their German roots, that made them suspect in the eyes of Canadian officials, who placed many hurdles in their way to successful integration. Using the case of American Quakers for comparison, Fair effectively deconstructs the myth that Upper Canada's lieutenant governor, John Graves Simcoe, extended a special invitation to the 'Germans' and that they became his successful and loyal subjects. Rather, Simcoe invited everyone in the United States to settle in Upper Canada. Indeed, the Pennsylvania Germans' path to integration was more difficult than previously claimed. They migrated not because of a special invitation or the promise of military exemption in Canada, but rather because of high taxes and the threat of losing military exemption in the United States. For a long time, Simcoe was alone in proposing an open door policy; most British administrators were not eager to bring religious sects to Upper Canada or to exempt them from paying taxes. Especially when it came to paying militia fines and showing up for militia muster, there existed tensions between the three sects and the British administrators for several decades. This was particularly true in anticipation of and during the War of 1812. And it was only after 1828 that the pacifist immigrants were allowed to apply to become British subjects. Only in 1834 were the militia fines statutes relaxed, to be finally abandoned only in 1855. Barriers to civic integration were similarly high. All political participation required the swearing of oaths; Tunkers, Mennonites, and Quakers, however, by their religion, were not allowed to swear oaths. As long as they could not substitute an affirmation, they could not be elected to office, serve on juries, testify in criminal cases, or participate in many other aspects of civic life. Citizenship was similarly difficult to achieve. Indeed, 'for a time following the War of 1812, the future existence of the growing Mennonite and Tunker communities in the province had been in jeopardy.'

Barbara Lorenzkowski picks up the story of Pennsylvania Germans in dramatically changed circumstances. By 1871, they had been joined by a wide variety of other German immigrants, who had established Berlin (Kitchener) as their centre of business and culture. Setting out to answer why the German middle class in Berlin and elsewhere in North America turned to nationalism in the 1870s, she focuses on the transatlantic celebrations of Prussia's victory over France and the founding of a Prussian-led German empire in 1871. Through her carefully crafted analysis of discourses about ethnicity, nation, class, and gender, we follow middle-class ethnic leaders in Berlin and Buffalo, New York, in their attempts to stage Peace Jubilees that served their own purposes. They were fired not by ethnic and national solidarity (as implied by a *peace* jubilee) but by chauvinistic ethnic pride: the *German victory* over France. Although conscious of the need to show loyalty to Canada or the United States, they were unable to constrain themselves. Feelings of national triumph dominated the speeches and symbolism, which together strove to paint a picture of a homogenous German culture in North America. Gender was paramount in this construction of nation and ethnicity. According to contemporary commentators, 'masculine' Germany had defeated 'feminine' France. At the celebrations, this resulted in women's marginalization and relegation to the status of caretakers and icons. Like Catholics, Germans from Alsace-Lorraine, and much of the working class, women played extras in the celebrations of German unity, which were directed and performed by Protestant, middle-class men from the core lands of Germany. Despite all references to national pride, the ethnic elites nevertheless also depicted a transnational identity, in which Germans could also be American or Canadian. While ethnic elites in the United States were defensive about their loyalty to their new homeland, the Berlin elites were self-assured in their claims: they pointed to their contributions to Canada and attached a list of entitlements. Lorenzkowski's chapter is an excellent example of what Hoerder calls 'an analysis of the many-cultured connections of local societies.'

Angelika Sauer concludes Part II of this collection with an exemplary study that combines the conceptual interventions of Hoerder and Harzig. She explores the life of the German-born Canadian immigration agent Elise von Koerber, a pioneer for women's professionalization and participation in the migration business and a foremost example of transcultural working and living. Von Koerber, who remains a mystery on many levels, set herself the goal to establish a transatlantic migration network for female migrants and thereby, as Sauer writes, 'to create a new transnational gendered space, where women helped women migrate from one place to another.' Like the other authors, Sauer shows that people were often less interested in ethnicity than scholars of migration are. Class and gender shaped von Koerber's professional and private life more than a sense of national belonging. She moved transnationally among Canada, the United States, Germany, Great Britain, Switzerland, and other countries. She conversed transculturally in French, German, and English. Home was anchored not by geopolitical borders but by social relationships, and especially relations with women of all classes. Sauer's writing von Koerber into history also makes clear that we need to pay more attention to how history is produced: What we forget is as important as what we do remember. Why has von Koerber vanished from the national histories of Germany, Canada, and the United Kingdom? While pointing to an ethnic silencing is a useful approach, others must be considered as well: gendered silencing, class silencing, and national silencing. When historians pay attention only to those who are always there – in one nation – they exclude migrants. As such, they participate in the perpetuation of nationalism and the myths of social homogeneity. Von Koerber's story shows that people's lives sometimes contradict national historiographies. They present alert historians with challenges. Rather than making women and men fit national myths, migration scholars increasingly use life stories to expose the hegemonic claims of national stories. Elise von Koerber's 'unbound life' – a life spent not at home in one country, but on ships and in trains and carriages with brief stops at friends, partners, acquaintances, and relatives across North America and Europe – may have been exceptional in its intensity, but not in its underlying challenge to national(ist) historiography.

In Part III of this collection, we turn to the twentieth century and the experiences of German-Canadians as these were profoundly shaped by imperialist nationalism and two world wars. As is true for much historical research in Canada, immigrants' experiences in Quebec are researched separately from those in English Canada and are rarely integrated into a larger Canadian context. Manuel Meune's work on Germans in Quebec therefore is path-breaking. While his major work still awaits translation into English, in his chapter in this collection he not only gives an overview of German migrants' 'double integration' into Canadian and Quebec societies, but also develops a set of intriguing questions about German migrants' relationship to Canadian and Quebec nationalisms vis-à-vis German and especially Nazi nationalisms. In these complex negotiations of identity, Meune argues, German speakers in Quebec have developed multifaceted identities that have responded to their situations as Germans in Quebec and in Canada. Thus, he does at last for research on Germans in Quebec what the research of the 1990s did for Germans in English Canada – that is, raise critical questions about migrant identity vis-à-vis the concept of the nation.[15] But he takes this earlier set of questions into the twenty-first century, in which identity is seen as political and as critically linked to nationalism and cultural imperialism. Thus, multiculturalism from this perspective became not a simple vehicle of integration, but rather was used in multiple ways by Germans in Quebec to maintain views that ranged from right-wing, nationalistic, and even racist celebrations of multiculturalism as means of avoiding integration to left-wing, anti-nationalist, and anti-liberal (or anti-Liberal) critiques of multiculturalism as a policy hindering integration. Meune also moves the field into more recent studies of collective memory by investigating the German-Canadian historical consciousness of Germans in Quebec.

Patrick Farges addresses another 'blind spot' of German-Canadian Studies, namely, the experiences of the Jewish refugees from Germany who fled Nazi persecution in the 1930s. While Canada's abysmal record of barring most refugees from entering Canada is well known, we know little about the experiences of those who made it to Canada. Like several other contributors, Farges takes migration studies through a cultural turn that asks questions about the role of individual and collective memory in the process of acculturation. His thickly described case studies demonstrate that for the refugees, settlement became an unsettling experience, a process that required adjustments on different levels of identity. Family members tackled them in diverse ways. Adjustment was both complex and tragic, as it was shaped by multiple misunderstandings. Canadian Jews could not comprehend the refugees' nostalgia for Germany, and the refugees could not find a home in the Jewish communities of Canada, for they were religiously, socially, and culturally too different. They were in exile but knew there was no return. The non-Jewish German-Canadian communities failed to serve as a home for the refugees as well, for many reasons that are mostly unexplored. Anti-Semitism certainly was one major obstacle, but how widespread this was among German-Canadians is unclear. Although the German-Jewish symbiosis may have been more illusion than reality, there was no attempt to re-create it in Canada. After Auschwitz, the refugees' existence became nearly impossible and they were written out of the master narratives and out of everyday life. The refugees could not deal with their traumas because they had neither the narrative means nor the narrative stage to tell their stories. So acculturation and integration became more difficult, because the refugees believed – and Canadian Jewry concurred – that they could not speak of their own fates, especially after Auschwitz.

Exploring, like Farges, refugees' attempts of making a new home, Hans Werner's study of German migrants from the Soviet Union continues the focus on the cultural history of memory, narrative, and identity that illuminates, as he states, 'the contours of the Soviet German diaspora.' In his comparative study of Soviet Germans in postwar Canada and 1970s West Germany, Werner explores the concept of an 'imagined homeland' and asks how it shaped the migrants' experiences of integration. Werner's detailed look at homeland experiences and his comparative approach establish an important context for the study of migrants in the twentieth century. What appears unique when focusing on only one group and only the country of destination is shown to be a common experience across time, geography, and ethnicity. Thus, Soviet Germans experienced hostility in the Soviet Union, in Canada, and in Germany. The comparative approach also shows, however, that people made sense of such experiences in different ways, and that these ways of making sense were shaped by the place and time in which they lived. Soviet Germans in Canada found different answers to their questions about identity than their cousins in Germany. Thus, Werner fruitfully applies Hoerder's model of nineteenth- and early twentieth-century transculturalism with Sauer's call for a transnational perspective on the late twentieth century. His carefully crafted gender analysis of three women's and one man's narratives further reinforces the importance of Harzig's call for a gender analysis in German-Canadian Studies.

The phenomenon of trying to find oneself in various groups of potential allegiance without ever fully finding oneself at home is further explored by Pascal Maeder in his study of German expellees in Canada. At the end of the Second World War, twelve million Germans from across Eastern Europe as well as from Germany's eastern territories fled or were expelled to Germany. Some came to Canada. Although nearly half the expellees who came to Canada were from the eastern German provinces of East Prussia, Silesia, and Pomerania, they did not found any organizations. The so-called ethnic German refugees who had lived in Romania, Hungary, Czechoslovakia, and other places, however, established institutions that were based on their regional cultures of belonging. At the same time, they positioned themselves within a larger group of postwar European immigrants with shared experiences in Europe and Canada. Although expellees continued to protest against their expulsion, in Canada they never united in this struggle. Indeed, even within such small subgroups as the Sudeten-German refugees, internal divisions developed. Instead, the groups developed transnational connections with their parent organizations in West Germany and sometimes with sister organizations in the United States. This micro-study of the diversity of German-speaking postwar immigrants once again undermines the myth of a cohesive group of German-Canadians. At the same time, Maeder shows the development of shared experiences among postwar European immigrants, the development of a shared Euro-Canadian identity, and the potential if not the reality of cross-cultural solidarity. This raises questions about a multiculturalism policy that seems to undermine such solidarity by emphasizing the differences rather than the shared experiences of discrimination and exploitation as well as of discovery and excitement that many immigrants share.

In Part IV of this collection, we turn to spoken and written language. Grit Liebscher and Mathias Schulze continue Werner's exploration of language, but from a linguistic rather than a narrative perspective. Using examples of speech by German immigrants in the Kitchener-Waterloo region, they show how migrants acculturated through spoken language. Although linguistic analysis can seem abstract to readers unfamiliar with this scholarly discourse, the examples that Liebscher and Schulze quote make the diversity of acculturation immediately visible. The complex ways in which German and English are merged, morphed into each other, combined, confused, or creatively reinvented are apparent even to readers without knowledge of German. Rejecting nation-centred concepts such as 'language loss' and 'language death,' the authors instead propose the concept of language acculturation, which allows us insight into processes of acculturation and into migrants' constructions of identity. Thus, when immigrants mix up – intentionally and unintentionally – two or more languages, they create something new, which becomes part of and facilitates their new life and identity. Historians, literary critics, sociologists, and other scholars of German and other migrants would be well advised to use Liebscher and Schulze's analysis to uncover new meanings in the written and oral sources they use for their own research.

Finally, Myka Burke brings a literary perspective to German-Canadian Studies and takes the field through the discursive turn. She explores the meanings of identity by placing German-Canadian literature in the context of immigrant literature in Canada. As in Werner's and other authors' studies, Burke effectively uses comparison to dispel myths of German-Canadian uniqueness and thus again undermines the national paradigm. She takes the exploration of identity further by asking whether scholars' obsession with the question of who is German-Canadian may not be the wrong one to ask. Literature, Burke argues, should be seen not as a subfield within German-Canadian Studies, but rather as a practice that can inform the study of German immigrants and their descendants in Canada from a variety of disciplinary perspectives. Novelists and poets do not produce self-contained artefacts, but rather comment on the social worlds in which they live. At the same time, Burke emphasizes that literary studies must look beyond their discipline for insights, and she draws on Hoerder's and Harzig's theoretical models as well as the collection's other authors to weave a tapestry of meaning that pulls these essays together.

The chapters in this collection suggest the following for immigration and ethnic studies. First, a move beyond the nation as the major framework of research – the comparative, migratory, and transcultural aspects make immigration and ethnic studies an ideal field for the study of supra- and international, postnational, transnational, transcultural, and global phenomena. As such, the study of migration can serve as a critique of the national model. Second, the study of 'old' immigrant groups of white Europeans allows scholars insights into the subtleties of discrimination as well as into immigrants' negotiations of privilege and their participation in discrimination against others. While the study of immigrants' participation in colonization and the oppression of indigenous populations has begun, further research is needed and should be extended to the dynamics of power relations among various ethnic groups. Third, as both Harzig and Sauer make clear, gender should not be an optional category of historical analysis, but an integral one. Scholars of German-Canadians need to further investigate the experiences of women and men and the ways in which gender shaped their experiences of immigration and acculturation. Similarly, scholars will find an ideal case in German-Canadians for white race studies. Here, in particular, German-Canadians' long, complex, and ongoing relationships with Canada's indigenous peoples calls for more research.

In a volume about German-Canadians from 1998, the editors 'hope[d] to create a starting point for a new discussion and initiate dialogue with other areas of ethnic studies by opening up the boundaries of a closely guarded field.'[16] This collection attempts to connect to this discussion, which has been ongoing for over a decade in a rather scattered and disconnected fashion, and to create another vantage point in this discourse from which to survey past research and stake out future research. This transnational and transcultural vantage point promises to give us a better understanding of German migrants' experiences in Canada and their relationships with other ethnic groups; more than that, however, it promises to position those experiences within the larger transnational experiences of migrants worldwide.

NOTES

1 Frank Thistlethwaite, 'Migration from Europe Overseas in the Nineteenth and Twentieth Centuries,' *XIe Congrès International des Sciences Historiques Stockholm: Rapports,* vol. 5 (Göteborg: 1960), repr. with a new 'Postscript' in *A Century of European Migrations: 1830–1930,* ed. Rudolph J. Vecoli and Suzanne M. Sinke (Urbana-Champaign: University of Illinois Press, 1992), 17–49, 50–7.

2 Franca Iacovetta et al., eds., *A Nation of Immigrants: Women, Workers, and Communities in Canadian History, 1840s–1960s* (Toronto: University of Toronto Press, 1998); Marlene Epp et al., eds., *Sisters or Strangers? Immigrants, Ethnic and Racialized Women in Canadian History* (Toronto: University of Toronto Press, 2004); Gerald Tulchinsky, ed., *Immigration in Canada: Historical Perspectives* (Toronto: Copp Clark Longman, 1994); Elspeth Cameron, ed., *Multiculturalism and Immigration in Canada: An Introductory Reader* (Toronto: Canadian Scholars' Press, 2004).

3 Iacovetta et al., 'Introduction,' in *A Nation of Immigrants,* xi.

4 But see the work of several of this collection's contributors: Hans Werner, *Imagined Homes: Soviet German Immigrants in Two Cities* (Winnipeg: University of Manitoba Press, 2007); Pascal Maeder, *Forging a New Heimat: Expellees in Post-War West Germany and Canada,* (Göttingen: V&R unipress, 2011); Barbara Lorenzkowski, *Sounds of Ethnicity: Listening to German North*

America, 1850–1914 (Winnipeg: University of Manitoba Press, 2010). See also Bruno Ramirez, *On the Move: French-Canadian and Italian Migrants in the North Atlantic Economy, 1860–1914* (Toronto: McClelland and Stewart, 1991); Donna R. Gabaccia and Franca Iacovetta, eds., *Women, Gender, and Transnational Lives: Italian Workers of the World* (Toronto: University of Toronto Press, 2002); Mathias Schulze et al., eds., *German Diasporic Experiences: Identity, Migration, and Loss* (Waterloo, ON: Wilfrid Laurier University Press, 2008).

5 Kathleen Neils Conzen et al., 'The Invention of Ethnicity: A Perspective From the U.S.A.,' *Journal of American Ethnic History* 12, no. 1 (Fall 1992): 3–42.

6 Benedict Anderson, *Imagined Communities: Reflections on the Origin and Spread of Nationalism* (London: Verso, 1991); Victoria E. Bonnell and Lynn Hunt, eds., *Beyond the Cultural Turn: New Directions in the Study of Society and Culture* (Berkeley: University of California Press, 1999).

7 Angelika E. Sauer, 'The "Ideal German Canadian": Politics, Academics, and the Historiographical Construction of German-Canadian Identity,' in *A Chorus of Different Voices: German-Canadian Identities*, ed. Angelika E. Sauer and Matthias Zimmer (New York: Peter Lang, 1998).

8 Stefan Berger, *The Search for Normality: National Identity and Historical Consciousness in Germany Since 1800* (New York: Berghahn Books, 2003).

9 Klaus J. Bade, ed., *Deutsche im Ausland – Fremde in Deutschland. Migration in Geschichte und Gegenwart*, 2nd ed. (Munich: Beck, 1992).

10 Gerhard Bassler, 'Germans,' in *Encyclopedia of Canada's Peoples* (Toronto: University of Toronto Press, 1999); Jonathan F. Wagner, *A History of Migration from Germany to Canada, 1850–1939* (Vancouver: UBC Press, 2006); Alexander Freund, 'Germans,' in *The Encyclopedia of Manitoba* (Winnipeg: Great Plains Publications, 2007); Alexander Freund, 'Representing "New Canadians": Competing Narratives about Recent German Immigrants to Manitoba,' *Journal of Mennonite Studies* 30 (2012): 339–61.

11 Dirk Hoerder and Horst Rössler, eds., *Distant Magnets: Expectations and Realities in the Immigrant Experience, 1840–1930* (New York: Holmes and Meier, 1993); Alexander Freund, *Aufbrüche nach dem Zusammenbruch: Die deutsche Nordamerika-Auswanderung nach dem Zweiten Weltkrieg* (Göttingen: V&R unipress, 2004).

12 Donna Gabaccia, 'Do We Still Need Immigration History?' *Polish American Studies* 55, no. 1 (Spring 1998): 45–68.

13 Marlene Epp et al., 'Introduction,' in *Sisters or Strangers?*

14 Sauer and Zimmer, *Chorus of Different Voices*.

15 Ibid.

16 Ibid., x.

PART I

Approaches: Transculturalism and Gender

1 Local, Continental, Global Migration Contexts: Projecting Life Courses in the Frame of Family Economies and Emotional Networks

DIRK HOERDER

'Germans,' like all ethnocultural groups, develop self-images and at the same time are imaged, imagined, and labelled by neighbouring cultural groups: Germans are stolid and rooted in the soil; Germans have migrated afar and are superior to the host societies; Germany is not an immigration country – Germany needs guest workers. Such imaginings reflect predispositions, and in German public discourse, emigration and immigration have been particularly distorted. What little memory of emigration there is with few exceptions considers Germans abroad as a positive cultural influence. In contrast, migrants in Germany – whether Poles in the nineteenth century or Turks in the twentieth – are denigrated as culturally inferior. In this chapter, I begin by confronting the assumption that German-language men and women stuck to local roots and essentialist Germanness; I do so by analysing the many-cultured connections of local societies and by discussing the worldwide migrations of German speakers as well as the in-migrations of cultural Others. Then I turn to a discussion of the homogenization of diversity in the age of nationalism. After this, I discuss the many origins of German-language immigrants in Canada. Finally, I discuss the strategic competence of migrants to pursue their life projects in transcultural settings.

Local Lives as Part of Transcontinental Networks

Scholars, like public opinion, often juxtapose non-migrants – locals, persisters – with people moving to distant societies. But in fact, both may be part of transcontinental networks. Auguste Michaelis, daughter of a small Hamburg merchant couple, in the 1850s had two sisters who earned their living in England and a brother working with a French trading company in Saigon. As a widow in a small North German town in the 1890s, she had emigrant relatives in South Africa, and – through kin, neighbours, and friends – acquaintances in Nicaragua, Jamaica, Chile, Peru, Mexico, Switzerland, Sweden, the Tyrol, Paris, London, Kiautschou, Russia, Kattowice, Madeira, and America. She was well educated, but her interest in national politics was limited; occasionally she mentioned some European empress, but only with regard to her role as a mother. Still, her life was one of global connectedness. The Boer War affected her emigrant kin, and she cared for one of her South African–born nephews. She knew whether her acquaintances were succeeding in Kansas or died of an undiagnosed illness in Mexico. Would men and women of the lower classes be less transculturally connected? In these years, the newspaper *Der Sozialdemokrat* carried regular good-bye notices from working men departing for 'Amerika.'[1] Non-migrating female florists in Erfurt produced for export to metropoles around the world, and non-migrating male workers in Osterholz-Scharmbeck built boats for river trading on other continents or milled rice imported from Southeast Asia. From the founding of the Second German Reich in 1871 to the end of German mass migration from its territories in 1893, 2.4 million men and women emigrated out of a population of 40.8 million in 1870 – or one out of seventeen. Thus, in the era said to be the apogee of national belonging, the empirical data show high mobility. In rural and urban neighbourhoods, positioned in worldwide contexts, men and women lived locally as well as globally.[2]

To such local neighbourhoods, in-migrating men and women added their cultures. To North Germany came working men and women from many parts of Scandinavia, Swedes in particular. Hamburg's trade with South America was developed by Sephardic Jews, who, having been expelled from Iberia, had established a flourishing community in Amsterdam. Migrants from this community, excluded from Hamburg by the city's rigidly Protestant elite, had settled in the neighbouring but Danish-ruled, religiously liberal Altona. Through the Danish-Caribbean connection, manumitted slaves reached Hamburg via Copenhagen. They accepted baptism and married locally. The many Central European social spaces in which some dialect of the German language was the means of communication had always been social spaces of immigration and emigration at the same time.[3]

Such empirical data about people's lives in global contexts have not entered historical memory in *the Germanies*. Yet the essentialized

'Germany' has passed through many political forms and territorial extensions: the Central European (or Roman) Holy (or First) Reich, the hundreds of dwarf principalities, the northern cantons of Switzerland, the federations of the nineteenth century, the Second or Hohenzollern Reich of Prussian hegemony and (as its competitor) the Habsburg state of many peoples and of Austrian-German hegemony; then the Weimar Republic, the Third Reich, and the divided Federal and Democratic republics. The historians of (what they considered) the nation emphasized *missions to* the East, which was a twisting of the data, and *departures for* the West to an undifferentiated construct 'Amerika'; they pointed to achievements of settler colonies in South Africa and Australia and to grandiose schemes to populate the Reich's colonies in Africa. Such historian-ideologues decried the loss of 'blood' or *Volkskraft*, labelling emigrants 'fellows without a fatherland' and overlooking independently migrating women. Emigrant merchants, in contrast, were described as bridgeheads of German culture and economic expansion. Beginning in the 1880s and especially after 1918, nationalist ideologues conceptualized generic emigrants, who supposedly clung to their Germanness, as *Auslandsdeutsche* – and then instrumentalized them to increase the power of the German state. In early 1950s Germany-in-ruins, government labour bureaux (*Arbeitsämter*) were instructed to discourage able-bodied men from pursuing emigration but to encourage able-bodied women to go. The gender-stereotyped nationalist rationale implied a unitary German masculine *Volk*, which had to rebuild the economy and the nation; and it implied women who would remain deficient without husbands and who, after the mass destruction of German men on the battlefields of the war, would indeed often have had to remain single.[4]

Throughout the nineteenth and twentieth centuries, politicians, bureaucrats, and conservative voters were hostile to migration between cultures. The body of the people, *der Volkskörper*, was to remain intact. No Polish workers, no long-resident Germans of Judaic faith, no immigrant Ashkenazim ('Eastern Jews') speaking the Yiddish dialect of the German-language family, no Italian migrant workers were to penetrate or infect it. However, in contrast to the gatekeepers from the intellectual elites – that is, those with the power to define what would be retained in national memory – popular culture did take note of migration: *Hänschen klein* leaves for the wide world and, finally, returns from *Amerika* to his waiting and loving mother. Internal migrations of *Handwerksgesellen*, journeyman artisans, were the theme of 'Muss I denn zum Städtele hinaus und Du mein Schatz bleibst hier' and of many other popular songs.

Were rural populations less mobile? Did peasants cling to their land over generations? Each and every family with more than two children depended on selective emigration of some of their offspring to keep the family plot viable. Where landholdings were divided among children, as in the southern Germanies, the next generations might stay on ever more marginal plots, only to be forced to join the late eighteenth- and nineteenth-century mass emigrations. Inheritances had become too small to provide subsistence for the family – and ideologues of the soil could have understood this by a little arithmetic. Peasants must work the soil, so they experience its limitations: one emigrant expressed this by saying, 'take the soil in your hands.' People who must negotiate their lives are often far more sophisticated than intellectual elites in pursuit of such abstractions as nation, superiority, or masculine warfare.[5]

Memory, whether collective, familial, or individual, is central to the construction of identity. Thus societies that refuse the memory of emigration and immigration lack the competence to come to terms both with their history and with their future. Collective memory has long been found wanting in the Austrian, German, and Swiss education systems. In this regard, neither political nor educational strategies were developed to react (or 'pro-act') to the in-migration of 'foreign' workers around 1900 and of 'guest' workers beginning in the mid-1950s. Similarly undifferentiated is the memory of out-migration, of emigrants and their descendants.

Migrations in the History of German-Speaking Men and Women[6]

From the medieval and early modern period to the twentieth century, men and women speaking one of the many dialects of the German language were involved in artisanal, in rural–urban, and in interurban migrations as well as in circular moves that brought them back to their place of origin after working and experiencing other societies elsewhere. Even when migrants planned to establish a cultural enclave, as was the practice in dynastic states, they interacted with the surrounding society, whether as 'Germans' in the Slavic lands or as Huguenots in one of the German states. A survey reveals complex patterns of mobility and settlement. In the Middle Ages, a *rural* Balto-Slavic-German-Flemish mixed population emerged and the Transylvania 'Saxons' established themselves. Later, migrants established an East Central European and East European *urban* German-language culture based not on some generic German law, *ius teutonicum*, as nationalist historiography once pronounced, but on the laws of particular cities, *ius civitatum urbanum*. At the time, 'German' was not considered a useful designation. German-Jewish refugees and migrants established Ashkenazim communities and their *shtetl*-cultures in Poland, Lithuania, and Russia. Artisans migrated eastward to Novgorod and St Petersburg, southeastward via Ofen, Buda, and Pest to Alexandria, and westward to Paris and London. Their dialect became the *lingua franca* of Europe's craftspeople and, in the nineteenth century, of technological innovation – at the time, however, in competition with English.

In the eighteenth and nineteenth centuries, new eastward moves – the Danubian 'Swabians,' the Black Sea and Volga Germans, the Mennonites in East Prussia and South Russia, the workers in Russia's Polish towns – established many distinct cultures. Artisanal German was a means of communication, whereas the administrative German of the Habsburg and Hohenzollern bureaucracies was a means of *rule*, imposed on peoples who had no reason to consider their native language inferior to their rulers' alien one. After the Napoleonic wars, ever more migrants selected new directions: westward to North America, where there emerged settlements as differentiated as in eastern Europe, albeit in a nineteenth-century industrializing context; and southward to Latin America, South Africa, and Australia, where small islands of settlement developed. Between 1815 and the aftermath of the Second World War, some 7 million people left the territories of the culturally diverse and politically divided but geographically contiguous Central European German-language region that had become the Second Reich in 1871. To these, German-speaking migrants from other states and distant destinations of earlier migrations must be added.

Over the same centuries, the people in the German-language region accommodated in-migrants from many cultures. Traders from afar came, and as early as 1508, Albrecht Dürer painted an 'Ethiopian' clerk in one of Augsburg's mercantile houses. Why has this painting not entered collective memory? The Christian Church Europeanized the image of its Palestinian-born Jesus, even while the faithful venerated the African St Mauritius as well as Black Madonnas whose features had not been recast as white European. An African scholar taught at the University of Halle, and many rulers had men (and some women) of African origin in their entourages. Some of these married locally and, with their children, became part of society in the capital cities. After the Reformation's schism of 1517, German principalities generated masses of religious refugees and admitted co-religionists who had been sent fleeing from elsewhere, among them the French Huguenots. Religion rather than language or ethnoculture served as the marker of identity and belonging.[7] The many-cultured exchanges along the Rhine, across the Alps, in East Central Europe, and along the Baltic and North seas meant interaction, mixing, cultural creation – *métissage, transculturación*, multiculturalism, to use modern terms. The German language lacks terms for this process except for the word *Mischlinge* ('half-caste' or 'half-breed'), with its racist connotations. Though traditional nation-state master narratives never admitted this, German history and that of all European states is one of *métissage*, of the intermingling of peoples of different cultures by marriage, in their everyday lives, and through economic transactions. Urban populations were culturally mixed: the language of Hamburg's stock exchange was Flemish, Vienna had a Greek colony, Cologne its Jewish quarter. Along the littorals of the northern seas, sailors arrived from many cultures; courts called administrators and military officers from afar and hired soldiers wherever they could be had for comparatively low wages. Commercial and industrial development in the nineteenth century brought Italians, Poles, Swiss, Swedes, Dutch, and many others from their own internally diverse societies. By the 1880s, Germany along with Britain, France, Switzerland, the Netherlands, and the United States were the greatest importers of labour migrants. Industrial and societal development depended on migrants. The tens of millions of migrant men and women within Europe, transcontinentally, and across the Americas searched for better opportunities but hardly ever for unlimited ones.

In the history of out-migration from the territories in which one of the numerous variants of German was spoken, Canada was one of many destinations. At their many homes, these migrants reflected the diversity 'at home.' The so-called German-Canadians and their cultural neighbours, the Mennonite-Canadians, the Russian-German-Canadians, Yiddish-speaking men and women, as well as Austrian- and Swiss-Canadians, came from multiple backgrounds, some directly, some in secondary migrations, others by way of repeated and complex moves.[8]

Diasporas, Aliens, Fatherlands: The Homogenization and Hierarchization of Peoples

Migration to a new society involves cultural change for both the migrants and the receiving society. It also leaves the society of origin with less (wo)manpower, less talent, less potential, and less initiative.

Did the in-migrations bring about a multicultural Germany or the out-migrations a German-language diaspora? The concept of diaspora implies continued links to the culture of origin as well as between its segments.

Regarding outbound moves, within each of the separate Mennonite, Protestant, Catholic, or other small religious communities, ministers and priests maintained their links to the 'home' church and to other communities. But no interdiasporic network of relations emerged, nor did links from afar to the 'homelands.' Rather, individual migrants remained in touch with family and friends in their community of origin: family networks developed rather than a diasporic interconnectedness.[9]

A sense of a common Germanness emerged only in the second half of the nineteenth century. This homogenization was part of increasingly nationalist attitudes in the Western hemisphere. The homogenizing pressures of the new Second German Reich on its Polish-cultured citizens led to a national as well as a Catholic revival, a self-organization of Catholic Poles. In the Atlantic world, the newly invented political regime of 'nation-states' ended traditional ways of adhering to local, regional, or immigration cultures. Life in bloc settlements (e.g., Russian-German ones) or in urban enclaves (e.g., Huguenot ones) appeared anachronistic to host societies that had embraced concepts of national homogeneity and integrated bureaucratic rule. Immigrants who had not fully accepted the cultural ways of their host or new home society were seen as deficient, as alien to the state. Under the preceding dynastic regimes, diversity had been acceptable: in-migrants had been viewed as subjects, economically active and contributing to the society.

Based on such nationalist premises, the Hohenzollern and Habsburg empires attempted to impose on distant emigrant communities a sense of imperial belonging and duties to the two 'fatherlands.' This occurred when policies of national homogenization in the host polities – Russia and the Balkan states in particular – reduced the self-administration and cultural preservation (i.e., 'self-centredness') of the German-language ethnocultural and ethnoreligious communities. Such policies destroyed these groups' already tenuous internal cohesion as well as their positions in the host states. Among emigrants and their descendants, only some were proud of the growing power and reputation of their 'fatherland,' which had been politically marginal for so long. Such sense of a 'greater diasporic Germany' and the Reich's concept of '*Auslandsdeutsche*,' which was intended to counter emigrants' intercultural negotiation, imparted and imposed a unity from above that proved detrimental to coexistence in the society of immigration. At a time when the respective receiving society demanded Americanization, Russification, or Canadianization, the 'fatherland's' designs for imperial expansion began to instrumentalize the emigrants.

In-migrants to the German-language territories, too, had settled in distinct neighbourhoods or, if of Jewish religion ('race' in terms of the times), had been segregated. As everywhere, economic interaction of the immigrant generation with the host society and of the immigrants' children with their peer group resulted in adaptations of (parental) cultures to new exigencies – a process of intergenerational and intersocietal translation. Only sojourners, like the late-nineteenth-century Italian migrants to the southern Germanies, who returned home seasonally, retained more of their lifeways. Over time, the German societies integrated newcomers until their difference was rendered invisible. (Otherwise, who would remember that two German statesmen of the 1990s, Oscar Lafontaine and Lothar de Maizière, were of Huguenot origin?) In the borderlands, however – the traditional regions of cultural interaction between residents – the new power politics led to warfare and cultural imposition, be it in the Danish, Flemish, Alsatian, Styrian, Bohemian, Moravian, Silesian, or Polish territories. Nationalist demands for assimilation drew boundaries where people had lived parallel but economically interactive lives for centuries.

Around 1800, the 'spirit of the people' – Johann Gottfried Herder's enlightened as well as Romantic notion of equality of cultures – was transformed by a growing national consciousness, then replaced in the Atlantic world by powerful and well-armed states that perceived themselves as superior to other states. A state's inhabitants of other than the national culture were denigrated as resident minorities or, if newcomers, as immigrant aliens. While Prussia expelled Poles, Russia withdrew the privileges of German-language communities, and Americanizers in the United States racialized Slavic-origin immigrants as 'dark,' Italian-origin newcomers as 'olive,' and the Irish and the Jews as anything but white. Nationalist homogeneity precluded cultural groups' self-determination, and nation-state power ended respect for other cultures.

Of this Atlantic World, Canada was a part. Ontario's and the Maritimes' British-minded elites, and Quebec's nationalist yet Rome-oriented clergy, laboured for their two distinct versions of national chauvinism in imperial contexts. While this dualism prevented uniform cultural power politics, the state still needed to attract additional inhabitants. The policy of 'preferred' – or, more exactly, racially selected – immigration was no longer viable since industrialization in the British Isles and the Germanies had reduced the propensity to emigrate. Populationist strategies required that the definitions of race and of nation be changed. The federal government opted for a two-pronged approach. First, while in nation-centred political thought across the Western world, distinct rights for ethnocultural and ethnoreligious groups had become unacceptable, Mennonite, Icelandic, and Doukhobor settlers were given the right to (limited) self-administration. Second, the image of Slavs was remodelled to 'peasants in sheepskin coats,' thus alluding to English yeomen and circumventing current racializations. In the interest of population growth, Canada's statesmen relegated cultural homogeneity to the backstage.[10]

Around this time, migrations of German speakers from their many regions of settlement in Europe brought culturally diverse groups to the Dominion. German-origin immigrants to Russia, facing loss of their special position, headed for Canada in secondary migrations. A shortage of land in Pennsylvania induced secondary moves of Mennonites to Ontario. After 1918 came so-called *Volksdeutsche* from territories no longer part of the Weimar Republic or Austria. Neither outside labelling as 'German-Canadians' – neighbours of these immigrants could hardly distinguish between the many regions of origin – nor attempts at self-elevation to a culturally influential and politically powerful homogeneous German-origin group could hide the diversity. After all, Mennonites had left the Germanies because of persecution,[11] and so had High-German and Yiddish-speaking Jewish Germans. Germans from the state of Germany, *Reichsdeutsche*, felt different from and often superior to *Volksdeutsche*.[12] Internal hierarchization undercut ideological postulates of one unified German-Canadian community.[13] Another factor of diversity was rooted in gender hierarchies. In the Western or Christian World, women's cultural belonging was subsumed under that of their husbands. When German-origin men married outside their group, their Canadian-born wives of other cultures counted as German-origin in the census. Lived ethnic belonging is complex. Ascribed ethnic belonging is a disaster, both for those assigned to a group not of their choice and for scholars' data and categories that inform policy making.[14]

The postulated national identity, often racialized and geneticized, among migration historians brought forth the 'nation to ethnic enclave' paradigm: migrants were assumed to leave a nation, and since their genetically fixed nationality could not change, they had to enter an enclave, a Little Germany, a Little Italy, or a Chinatown. The ideologues of the nation-state could not come to terms with the agency of citizens, could not accept that people would leave disagreeable conditions and select a polity, society, and economy that better suited their interests and life projects. In people's everyday lives, borders of cultural groups are fuzzy, as British historian Robin Cohen has put it. Canadian sociologist Lloyd Wong has gone a step further, arguing that states compete for citizens: an attractive sociopolitical frame will draw people from repressive regimes.[15] From this perspective, many European states and their elites – the German ones in particular – proved unable to devise regimes sufficiently attractive to keep people from departing. For potential migrants, intergenerational life projects are far more central than political borders or ideologies of monocultural lifeways.

Transcontinental Life Courses in the Frame of Family Economies and Emotional Networks

Individual speakers of German dialects or High German came to Canada not only from different regions but also under different concepts of self-identification. They came from different stages of economic development and with widely varying means and experiences. Some chose to leave their hierarchical societies after the war against Denmark in the 1860s or after the rise of fascism in the 1920s and 1930s. These men and women were focusing on their lives and those of their loved ones rather than on visions of national grandeur, visions that too often were ending in death.

In the 1750s, for empire-building as well as religious reasons, the British government set out to attract Protestant settlers to Catholic, French-speaking Acadia, which had been renamed Nova Scotia in 1713. Some 1,500 'foreign Protestants' – still denominated by religion rather than region – came from British-ruled Hanover and Brunswick, but also from Switzerland and elsewhere. They established the town of Lunenburg and, because of this reference to Lüneburg, have often been labelled 'German.' Historical memory simplifies. That Catholic Acadians were deported in the very years of the Protestants' arrival is usually not part of the historical memory.[16] In 1832, Adolphus Gaetz from one of the southwestern German territories arrived in Lunenburg, by then a commercial hub with trade reaching as far as the West Indies. The newcomer, who was not conversant with the local customs of trade and society, wanted to become part of the community, so he married

Lucy Zwicker, who belonged to a prominent local family. She provided him with access to social networks and with business connections. In the nineteenth century, fewer women than men migrated, but resident women integrated immigrant men into receiving societies as marriage partners. Gaetz did not intend to remain 'foreign,' and he achieved respectability by joining the Anglican Church and holding numerous offices.[17]

On the far side of the continent, in what was to become British Columbia, John Sebastian Helmcken arrived in 1850. His family's trajectory had been complex: His northern German grandparents had moved to London, following an established route of skilled workers and entrepreneurs to sugar-making trades. He planned a career in the maritime realm that extended from the British capital to many colonized parts of the world. Via the Hudson's Bay Company's York Factory and Singapore, he reached Fort Victoria, where, much like Gaetz, he became a respected citizen.

Others did not choose respectability. Count Alvo von Alvensleben, from his Vancouver residence, which was meant to resemble a castle on the Rhine, cheated his own countrymen out of their funds in order to advance his own real estate schemes. Rather than generic 'German-Canadians,' these were individuals in the many colonies who adapted to local conditions rather than establishing a diaspora. They added their capabilities (or shortcomings) to societies in the making.

In the 1880s, German-language migrants moved in a social space that extended from the Volga to the Canadian Pacific coast along routes determined by where acquaintances and families happened to live. The complex migrations and cultural fusion of the nineteenth-century European and North American worlds may be illustrated by one group of three families. A refugee French Huguenot family, a Prussian army officer's family, and a family of Moravian origin met in the low-lying Warthe and Oder river wetlands, where the Prussian Grand Elector Frederick William (1640–1688) initiated colonization with the help of recruited Dutch drainage experts. The three families, sharing status as subjects of the elector, acculturated over two generations and intermarried. By the mid-nineteenth century, when land was becoming scarce for their offspring, some were exploring opportunities farther east in Polish-settled territories; others were migrating to urban occupations within the Germanies. Still others chose Minnesota and Wisconsin; and after 1900, some of these moved on to Saskatchewan. While ideologues of Germanness extolled national superiority and instrumentalized

'*Auslandsdeutsche*,' such families left the reach of constraining – and in view of further wars, life-threatening nationalist-chauvinist – frames of reference. They pursued life projects transnationally – projects that would provide economic security for the migrant generation and that would also provide prospects for their children. Families formed emotional as well as economic units.

Similarly, in the Kurtenbach family, which had moved to the Dakotas in the 1890s, several sons and daughters contributed to the family economy. When ready to form their own families and thus requiring land, the family reconnoitred possibilities in Saskatchewan and used its savings to move there in 1906. Their neighbours were German Catholics, Americans, English, and 'the whole world,' as they wrote home. To establish their position, the Kurtenbachs donated land for a church. To impress their self-determined lives on family and friends in Germany, they emphasized in their letters: 'We elect our officials ourselves.' Migrations were directed not merely toward cheap and fertile land but also toward self-determined lives and material security.[18]

By contrast, families and individuals with little means and without the resources to collect information had to settle on marginal lands or join urban labour markets. In addition, in the 1920s and 1930s, Canadian immigration policies became more restrictive and enforcement officers came to be feared. The worldwide economic depression imposed severe hardships on recent immigrants who had not yet secured themselves economically. No mutually supportive German-Canadian community emerged. For example, in interwar Montreal, *Reichsdeutsche* arrived with more means than *Volksdeutsche*. As Germans from the core, they felt superior to those from distant regions who spoke different dialects; thus two distinct groups emerged.[19] After the Second World War ended in self-reduction and immense loss of life – and, for those surviving, in loss of prospects – *Rucksack-Deutsche* (migrants with all their belongings fitted into a backpack) came to many cities, Winnipeg among them. When, in the times of West Germany's economic miracle (*Wirtschaftswunder*), a new type, 'container Germans' (migrants whose belongings fit into a shipping container), began to arrive, the two cohorts did not integrate either. If the language was the same, the experiences and expectations were different.

Transcultural experiences before and after migration remained the rule decades after nationalism had taken hold. Waiting for his steamer in Hamburg, John Grossmann met a group of emigrating Saxons, who would have liked to see the city but did not dare move about: they could not ask for directions because they did not understand the Low German spoken by people on the streets. Even in the 1920s, German dialects were mutually unintelligible. The Wicks family originated in Danzig-Gdansk, the bicultural Polish-German region, and settled in a cannery town on the Skeena River in British Columbia, among Asian-origin workers, First Nations fishing families, and a few European-origin families and single men. This integrated community experienced as 'foreign' the railway workers, whether their background was Swedish, Finnish, or French-Canadian. The 'we/them' dichotomy – settled and orderly families versus single transient and sometimes brawling men – held no ethnic connotation but depended on workplace, time of arrival, and patterns of living.

To understand social processes, we must revise nation-state histories. Societies emerged from the sum total of family histories, the agency of common men and women, and their efforts to provide their children with a hopeful future. A historian like Heinrich von Treitschke in Germany might have asked himself why millions of men and women left the state, which he saw as moving toward a glorious future and to which, in his way of thinking, the migrants were genetically bound. In Canada, historians like Donald Creighton might have looked beyond the achievements of a John A. Macdonald. In much of nation-state–inspired historiography – usually written by men who did not migrate – migrants have been conceptualized as 'uprooted' or 'in limbo' or 'lost between cultures.' Those who left memoirs and autobiographies mention difficulties, but only rarely do they seem to have been lost. In fact, they could negotiate lives in two cultures – or more.

The Strategic Competence to Pursue Coherence in Life Trajectories

Migrants carry their life experience with them, not as a piece of 'cultural baggage' as historians have phrased it, but as a personal set of norms and everyday practices. Whether settling in rural communities or in city neighbourhoods, they transculturally live both worlds by creatively fusing the regional cultures of origin and of arrival. Some move back and forth and remain able to function in both societies; they remain transcultural or, if defining themselves by state and nation, transnational. Most of those discussed in this chapter, at some point in their trajectory, became more Canadian than German. They engaged in a process of acculturation or accommodation or – if times were difficult – of insertion into a niche that provided economic survival. Many consciously attempted to come to terms with their new society. Others felt that they remained immovably German and did not realize that 'their' Germany was the one they had left long ago. Their minds registered neither subsequent changes in German society nor their own Canadian adjustments, be they unintended or not.[20]

'Transcultural' refers to societal spaces defined according to empirical observation. Thus, not only are political units dissolved or relegated to a secondary level, but also the concepts of borderlands and contact zones are expanded. People acted out their own ambitions or, at the very least, *re*acted on a day-to-day basis to circumstances, within the limits imposed by family, local community, regional society, and economy. This cultural region, the space of the immediate life world of a person, provided the frame for his or her agency in terms of specific everyday norms as well as opportunities or constraints. It permitted life projects; and sometimes it led instead to involuntary trajectories. People moved between cultural spaces within the structures and institutions of a state. If culture is a complex system that includes tools, spoken and body language, arts, and beliefs created by human beings who must provide for their material, emotional, and intellectual needs in order to survive, then transculturalism denotes the competence to live in two or more differing cultures and, in the process, create a personal transcultural space. Strategic transcultural competence involved conceptualizations of life projects in multiple cultures, as well as choice between cultures. Transculturalization is the process whereby individuals and societies change themselves by integrating diverse cultural lifeways into dynamic new ones. Subsequent interactions and transcultural lives will change again this new – and transitory – culture.[21]

Transculturalization may imply difficult adjustments, and those who did not succeed are often lost from memory. Those who were sent fleeing by oppressive governments – in the case of Germany, the fascist one in particular – had no option but to prepare for life in a different culture. Political refugees, too, rather than adjust, would often look back to Germany in hopes of making the country liveable again. Most 'voluntary' migrants, who came to their decision under severe economic constraints, neither went to a mythical 'America' of 'unlimited opportunities' nor headed for political systems called the United States and Canada, though they may have known about immigrant admission regulations. People lived transoceanic family lives, and they still do. From 1900 to 1914, 2.77 million immigrants arrived in Canada. Regarding the 13.4 million who arrived in the United States in the same period, statistics show that 94 per cent went to family (79 per cent) or friends (15 per cent).[22] They aimed for one particular address, and at that address they would find a place to sleep and informed help in finding work. The Atlantic World was one not only of international relations but also of intercontinental family networks. People going to nineteenth-century Canada hardly ever mentioned the federal government, but they knew about the political framework that provided options for their lives. The federal government's one important service was the post office, which provided the communication link to the family left behind.[23] For sequential migration of kin and friends, women's letters about developments in the family were far more important than men's proud – and usually well-founded – listings of achievements.[24] Knowledge of Canada's political institutions was of no help in finding a job, but knowledge of local ways of life was indispensable.

After the First World War, when the various worldwide systems of migration contracted, insertion in a different culture was particularly difficult. Those from Weimar Germany had lived through the war and the inflation. The Krommknecht couple, unable to earn a living as workers in 1920s Berlin, attempted to eke out a living on a small plot allocated by the German government in the eastern territories. The plan proved a chimera, and the population planners and high priests of healthy farming might have known this. Thus, the 'basic decision to go seemed to make itself,' they remembered. Ali came in 1928, and Phyllis arrived on borrowed money in 1929. Intent on establishing themselves, both improved their English quickly. Compared to Berlin, Toronto seemed 'small and provincial'; relative to Germany's incipient social security system, 'there was absolutely nothing' in Canada. Only when by 1930 both were out of a job again did a 'feeling of strangeness' engulf their lives – not when they had left Germany. During their transatlantic trajectory, they had felt that they belonged to local societies regardless of which state they were in. Only when the Great Depression jolted them out of even minimal levels of decent living and out of their self-willed acculturation did they consider themselves alienated. They would later establish a home in Vancouver and, perhaps to show that they had conquered adverse circumstances, would rename themselves Ritter ('Knight'). They struggled to remain in charge of their destinies and to pursue strategies that would keep their lives coherent.[25]

Of the immigrants who described the strangeness of their first days on a new job or, for children, the first days in school, most decided to come to terms, to learn, to remain in charge of their life courses. This required adaptability – that is, the capacity to quickly grasp new ways and to process the information both in terms of fitting in and in terms of adjusting the circumstances to their goals. When economic, social, or personal circumstances imposed roller-coaster changes from exhausting labour to unemployment, all people could do was to react, while clinging to the goal of proactively charting a life course. Flexible personal identities provided continuity, and strategic competence to recognize and grasp any option for improvement tided them over.

If human agency is the key to keeping in charge of life courses, children whose parents do not impart to them such strategic competence will have great problems in charting trajectories. People socialized into a monocultural way of life may hesitate uneasily at each crossroads, may hanker for stability imposed by outsiders, for a *Leitkultur* – a guiding or dominant culture. The competence of men and women from many cultures to act on behalf of their own life projects in their interactions with communities resulted in the creating of societies in nineteenth-century Canada as well as of newcomers' social spaces at the beginning of the twenty-first century. In countries with established, more or less rigid structures and institutions, like Germany, such agency will more slowly but still continuously reshape structures. States provide a framework for such agency, and regional societies mediate between statewide regulations and local practices. Participation in the society's and the state's affairs beyond the input of individuals or families requires common organization – out of many immigrants of diverse backgrounds, German-Canadian or Turkish-German associations emerge in a process of post-migration cooperation or, perhaps, homogenization. Thus ethnocultural groups contribute to society as a whole, but only by making their cultural ways of expression understandable to their neighbours, by engaging in a process of interaction, of translation, of transcultural agency. The history of ethnocultural groups is not one of cultural retention and inflexibility but of cultural adaptation and *métissage*.

APPENDIX

Autobiographical Writings of German-language Immigrants to Canada

Austrian
Kain, Conrad (1858–1934). *Where the Clouds Can Go.* Edited by Mon-

roe Thorington. New York: American Alpine Club, 1935. [Austrian
mountain guide; from 1909 in British Columbia; farming, hunting,
climbing]

Swiss
Stricker, Jakob. *Erlebnisse eines Schweizers in Kanada.* Zürich, Leipzig:
Orell Fuessli Verlag, 1935. [Swiss immigrant 1923–32, Quebec, Mani-
toba, British Columbia]
Ochsner, Traugott. *Ein schweizerisch-kanadischer Auswandererroman.*
Edited by Hermann Boeschenstein. 4 vols. Bern: Lang, 1992.

Mennonite
Baerg, Anna. *Diary of Anna Baerg 1916–24.* Edited and translated by
Gerald Peters. Winnipeg: CMBC, 1985. [Arrived in 1924 from Russia]
Dyck, Arnold. 'Aus meinem Leben.' I:461–515 of *Collected Works.*
Edited by Victor G. Doerksen et al. 4 vols. Steinbach: Manitoba
Mennonite Historical Society, 1985–90. See also, for his life in Russia,
Verloren in der Steppe, ibid. v-456, Engl. transl. by Henry Dyck, *Lost
in the Steppe*, 5 parts (1945–48).
Eby, Gordon C. *The Gordon C. Eby Diaries, 1911–13: Chronicle of a Men-
nonite Farmer.* Toronto: MHSO, 1982.
Epp, Jacob D. *A Mennonite in Russia. The Diaries of Jacob D. Epp, 1851–
80.* Edited and translated by Harvey L. Dyck. Toronto: UTP, 1991.
[Life in Russia]
Klippenstein, Lawrence, and Julius G. Toews, eds. *Mennonite Memories: Settling in Western Canada.* Winnipeg: Centennial Publications,
1977. [Mennonites in Manitoba and British Columbia, 1874 and
later]
Lohrenz, Gerhard. *Storm Tossed: The Personal Story of a Canadian Mennonite from Russia* (n.p.: Christian Press, 1976). [Arrived in 1925,
settled in Saskatchewan near Gilroy]
Schulz, Henry. *A New Frontier: The Canadian Chronicles of Henry Schulz.*
Campbell River: Ptarmigan Press, 1984. [Mennonite from Russia;
parents immigrated to Canada in 1925, son followed shortly after;
has also published *Snowborne: The Siberian Chronicles of Henry Schulz.*
Vancouver: Orca Sound, 1982]

German
Early travel accounts
Du Roy, Anton Adolf. *Tagebuch der Seereise von Stade nach Quebec in*

Amerika 1776 durch die zweyte Division Herzoglicher Braunschwei-gischer Hülfsvölker. Edited and translated by Gerhard Teuscher as *Journal of the Voyage from Stade to Quebec in America by the Second Division of the Duke of Brunswick's Auxiliaries.* Toronto: German-Canadian Historical Association, 1983.

Friesen, Gerhard, ed. 'A German-Canadian Rarissimum: Briefe von Aussiedlern im Huron Trackt, Canada [1830s–1840s].' *German-Canadian Yearbook* 10 (1988), 11–31.

Migrants arriving before 1945
'IX. German-Canadian Individuals: Biographies, Autobiographies, and Diaries. *German-Canadian Yearbook* 11 (1990): 292–308.

Bublitz, Dorothea E. *Life on the Dotted Line.* New York: Vantage Press, 1960. [Born 1895 in Madison, Wisconsin; arrived 1910 with family at Gull Lake, Saskatchewan]

Debor, H.W. 'Ein Lebensrückblick und Bibliographie der deutschkanadischen Beiträge.' *Canadiana Germanica* Occasional Papers no. 8 (1986): 1–13.

Doerfler, Bruno. 'Father Bruno's Narrative, "Across the Boundary."' *Saskatchewan History* 9 (1956): 26–31, 70–4; *Saskatchewan History* 10 (1957): 11–26, 55–62. [Travel in search of land for a Church-centred colony of Catholic Germans from Minnesota, 1902: St Peter's Colony]

Gaetz, Adolphus. *The Diary of Adolphus Gaetz* [1804–1873]. Edited by Charles Bruce Fergusson. Halifax: Public Archives of Nova Scotia, 1965. [German immigrant in Lunenburg, 1855–73, merchant]

Grossmann, John. 'Streiflichter vom Rande der Zivilisation. Die Erlebnisse eines deutschen Heimstätters im Peace-River-Gebiet.' *German-Canadian Yearbook* 1 (1973): 191–244; and 2 (1975): 193–246.

Helmcken, John S. *The Reminiscences of Doctor John Sebastian Helmcken.* Edited by Dorothy Blakey Smith. Vancouver: UBC Press, 1975.

Hinsche, Max. *Kanada wirklich erlebt. Neun Jahre als Trapper und Jäger.* Berlin: Neumann, 1938.

Knight, Phyllis. *A Very Ordinary Life [of Phyllis Knight]. As Told to Rolf Knight.* Vancouver: New Star Books, 1974.

Koeppen, Ebe. 'Ebe Koeppen's Story.' In *Stump Ranch Chronicles and Other Narratives.* Edited by Rolf Knight. Vancouver: New Star Books, 1977. 49–116.

Kurtenbach, Elisabeth, and John Kurtenbach. 'The Kurtenbach Letters: An Autobiographical Description of Pioneer Life in Saskatchewan around the Turn of the Century.' Edited by Karl A. Peter and Franziska Peter. *CES* 11, no. 2 (1979): 89–96. [Letters of German immigrants Elisabeth and John Kurtenbach, 1907]

Leibbrandt, Gottlieb. *Little Paradise. Aus Geschichte und Leben der Deutschkanadier in der County Waterloo, Ontario, 1800–1975.* Kitchener: Allprint, 1977. English translation: *Little Paradise: The Saga of the German Canadians of Waterloo County. Ontario, 1800–1975.* Kitchener: Allprint, 1980. [Includes reprints of letters and memoirs of Pennsylvania Germans coming to Canada, 1800–1975]

Lutz, Otto, *A Mother Braving a Wilderness: Told by her Son Otto Lutz.* Edited by Thomas Gerwing. Muester: St Peter's Colony Jubilee Steering Committee, 1977. [Written 1917–18, orig. serialized in *St. Peter's Bote*, 1919, under the title 'For Her Children's Sake, or, A Mother Braving the Wilderness'; arrived in 1895 in Nebraska, arrived in 1902 in Saskatchewan]

Meilicke, Emil Julius. *Leaves from the Life of a Pioneer: Being the Autobiography of Sometime Senator Emil Julius Meilicke.* Vancouver: 1948.

Nordegg, Martin. *The Possibilities of Canada Are Truly Great: Memoirs 1906–1924.* Edited and introduced by T.D. Regehr. Toronto: Macmillan, 1971. See also W. John Koch. *Martin Nordegg: The Uncommon Immigrant.* Edmonton: Brightest Pebble, 1997.

– . *To the Town That Bears Your Name: A Young Woman's Journey to Nordegg in 1912.* Translated by Maria Koch, introduction by W. John Koch. Edmonton: Brightest Pebble, 1995.

Otto, Max. *In kanadischer Wildnis: Trapper- und Farmerleben.* Berlin: 1923; 5. Aufl. 1924. See also his *In Kanadas Urwäldern und Prärien. Erlebnisse eines Trappers und Farmers.* Berlin: 1925, 4. Aufl. 1926. [German Herrenmensch, active for a '*Auslandsgeheimdienst,*' looks down on Russian Germans, Jews, all Germans not supporting Germany]

Parry, John. Various works for MHSO and University of Toronto Press, as well as talks given in 1991–2. [Great-grandfather came from Germany, leaving letters and diary, partly in English and partly in German, to the University of Waterloo archives; now being translated; was lieutenant governor of the province]

Peterson, John, Rev. 'The Peterson Diary.' Edited by A.E. Byerly. In *Canadian-German Folklore* 1 (1961): 110–13. Waterloo: Pennsylvania Folklore Society of Ontario. [Troubles of JP with his congregation, 1819–27].

Prechtl, Joseph. 'My Homesteader Experience [1902–9].' In *Take the Soil in Your Hands.* Edited by J.A. Prechtl. Saskatoon: Herrem, 1984. 5–26.

Seel, Else. *Kanadisches Tagebuch.* Herrenalb: Erdmann 1964. [diary, 1927–1950s; reminiscent of Traill and Moodie] Cf. Rodney T.K. Symington: 'Else Seel: Eine Biographie im Nachlaß.' *German-Canadian Yearbook* 3 (1976): 193–8]

Wicks, Walter. *Memoirs of the Skeena*. Saanichton: Hancock, 1976. [German mother with two sons coming in 1900 to Northern British Columbia; story continued into the 1920s]

Migrants arriving after 1945

Blumenfeld, Hans. *Life Begins at 65: The Not Entirely Candid Autobiography of a Drifter*. Montreal: Harvest House, 1987. [German arriving in 1955; active as architect in Toronto].

Fast, Karl. *Gebt der Wahrheit der Ehre, Dritter Teil*. Winnipeg: Author, 1952. [autobiographical novel; Polish-German in post-1945 Winnipeg]

Holzapfel, Renate. 'Ich bin halt ein Frankfurter Child' – Kanada-Auswanderer erzählen. Frankfurt am Main: Brandes, 1996.

Paquin, Grete. *Chino*. Kitchener-Waterloo: German Ethnic Cultural Association, 1977. [German grandmother c. 1958 to Canada; works as housekeeper; rev. *German-Canadian Yearbook* 5 (1979): 258–60]

Priebe, Eckehart J. *Thank You, Canada: From Messerschmitt Pilot to Canadian Citizen*. Vancouver: author, 1990.

Surminski, Arno. *Fremdes Land oder Als die Freiheit noch zu haben war*. Hamburg: Hoffmann und Campe, 1980; repr. Berlin: Ullstein, 1999.

Baltic-German

Keyserlingk, Robert Wendelin. *Unfinished History*. London: Hale, 1984. [autobiography; his Russian childhood; experiences in Russian revolution and Hitler's Germany; settlement in Quebec Province; politics and war]

Russian-German

Yedlin, Tova, ed. *Germans from Russia in Alberta: Reminiscences*. Edmonton: Central and East European Studies Society, 1984.

German-Jewish

Sekely, Trude. *Le temps des souvenirs*. St-Lambert: Editions Heritage, 1981. [German-Jewish woman; grew up in Munich in the 1920s; fled via Paris, 1932, Spain, 1940, Portugal to Canada, 1944; became author of books on childbearing; only one chapter about experiences in Montreal]

NOTES

1 Letters, 1894–1902, from Johanna Christiane Auguste Michaelis (1831–1912), private collection of D. Hoerder; Hoerder, 'German Immigrant Workers' Views of "America" in the 1880s,' in *In the Shadow of the Statue of Liberty: Immigrants, Workers, and Citizens in the American Republic 1880–1920*, ed. Marianne Debouzy (Vincennes: Presses Université Françaises, 1988), 17–33; 'Bremen und (von Emden bis Hamburg) umzu: Lokale Welten – Atlantische Welten – Vielfältige Migrationen,' in *Bunte Metropolen. In der Vielfalt liegt die Zukunft*, ed. Christiane Harzig et al. (Bremen: WE Migrationsforschung, 2001), 22–35; 'Historical Dimensions of Many-Cultured Societies in Europe: The Case of Hamburg, Germany,' in *Socio-Cultural Problems in the Metropolis: Comparative Analyses*, ed. Dirk Hoerder and Rainer-Olaf Schultze (Hagen: ISL-Verlag, 2000), 121–39.

2 Peter Marschalck, *Deutsche Überseewanderung im 19. Jahrhundert: Ein Beitrag zur soziologischen Theorie der Bevölkerung* (Stuttgart: Klett, 1973); *Bevölkerungsgeschichte Deutschlands im 19. und 20. Jahrhundert* (Frankfurt: Suhrkamp, 1984).

3 Klaus J. Bade, ed., *Deutsche im Ausland – Fremde in Deutschland. Migration in Geschichte und Gegenwart* (München: Beck, 1992); Dirk Hoerder with Jörg Nagler, eds., *People in Transit: German Migrations in Comparative Perspective* (Cambridge: Cambridge University Press, 1995).

4 Dirk Hoerder, *Geschichte der deutschen Migration vom Mittelalter bis heute* (Munich: Beck, 2010); Johannes-Dieter Steinert, *Migration und Politik. Westdeutschland – Europa – Übersee 1945–1961* (Osnabrück: secolo, 1995), 124–43.

5 In Quebec, the ideologues of *habitant* family life and *terroir*-rootedness might also have benefited from some simple accounting. Richard J.A. Prechtl, *Take the Soil in Your Hands* (Saskatoon: Herrem, 1984).

6 This section is based on Hoerder, 'The German-Language Diasporas: A Survey, Critique, and Interpretation,' *Diaspora: A Journal of Transnational Studies* 11, no. 1 (2002): 7–44.

7 For the multiple intra-European migrations, see the relevant entries in *Enzyklopädie Migration in Europa vom 17. Jahrhundert bis zur Gegenwart*, ed. Klaus J. Bade et al. (Paderborn/Munich: W. Fink/Schoeningh, 2007), with extensive references to further literature. As regards the small number of Africans, major research projects are under way. See, for example, Annegret Kuhlmann, 'Schwarze Europäer: eine transregionale Untersuchung zur Sozial- und Kulturgeschichte von "Hofmohren" im Alten Reich,' PhD diss., Universität Bremen, 2008.

8 Dirk Hoerder, 'German-Speaking Immigrants of Many Backgrounds and the 1990s Canadian Identity,' in *Austrian Immigration to Canada: Selected Essays*, ed. Franz A.J. Szabo (Ottawa: Carleton University Press, 1996), 11–31.
9 In contrast, Polish and Italian migrants did develop a diasporic connectedness. Adam Walaszek, 'Labor Diasporas in Comparative Perspective: Polish and Italian Migrant Workers in the Atlantic World between the 1870s and the 1920s,' in *The Historical Practice of Diversity: Transcultural Interactions from the Early Modern Mediterranean to the Postcolonial World*, ed. Dirk Hoerder et al. (New York: Berghahn, 2003), 152–76. From among German speakers, the Mennonites established links between settlements in Eastern Europe and the Americas, but for them no state of origin existed.
10 A fallacy was still involved: The government wanted rural families, men with stout wives and numerous children, at a time when industrial workers were needed in most cities of Canada's many regions. Single labouring men with their capabilities for organizing the working class remained unwanted. However, since the latter came anyway, this misconception did not operate to the detriment of Canadian society and economy.
11 When, during the 1940s, Mennonite women constructed themselves as 'German' to gain the protection of German troops from Stalinist persecution, it was not some cultural Germanness but the fascist Germanness, as Christiane Harzig has pointed out in an unpublished critical discussion of Marlene Epp, *Women Without Men: Mennonite Refugees of the Second World War* (Toronto: University of Toronto Press, 2000).
12 Secondary migrants from the Russian empire constructed themselves as 'Germans from Russia' rather than as Russian Germans.
13 This has been accepted neither by the 'we were there too' type of contribution history nor by nationalist versions of ethnic enclaves. Heinz Lehmann, *The German Canadians 1750–1937: Immigration, Settlement, and Culture* (St John's: Jesperson Press, 1986), translated, edited, and introduced by Gerhard P. Bassler from Lehmann's *Zur Geschichte des Deutschtums in Kanada* (1931) and *Das Deutschtum in Westkanada* (publ. 1939).
14 Dirk Hoerder, 'German-Speaking Immigrants [in Canada]: Co-Founders or Mosaic? A Research Note on Politics and Statistics in Scholarship,' *Zeitschrift der Gesellschaft für Kanadastudien* 14, no. 2 (1994), 51–65.
15 Robin Cohen, 'Fuzzy Frontiers of Identity: The British Case,' *Social Identities* 1, no. 1 (1995), 35–62, and *Frontiers of Identity: The British and the Others* (London: Longman, 1994). See also Lloyd L. Wong, 'Home Away from Home? Transnationalism and the Canadian Citizenship Regime,' in *Communities across Borders: New Immigrants and Transnational Cultures*, ed. Victor Roudometof and Paul Kennedy (London: Routledge, 2002), 169–181.

16 Winthrop P. Bell, *The 'Foreign Protestants' and the Settlement of Nova Scotia* (Toronto: University of Toronto Press, 1961).

17 See the appendix for the autobiographical writings cited.

18 See also the autobiographical writings of Dorothea E. Bublitz, Bruno Doerfler, Otto Lutz, and Joseph Prechtl.

19 Albert Moellmann, *Das Deutschtum in Montreal* (Schriften des Instituts für Grenz- und Auslandsdeutschtum an der Universität Marburg, no. 11) (Jena: Fischer, 1937), 88. This book was based on his 'The Germans in Canada: Occupational and Social Adjustment of German Immigrants in Canada,' MA thesis, McGill University, 1934.

20 A young German woman while visiting Canada in the 1970s was accosted by an elderly German Canadian, who disconcertedly demanded why she was not wearing plaits. In the mid-1990s, the author overheard a German immigrant in British Columbia bitterly complain that return to Germany was impossible because of the many 'foreigners' there. It never occurred to him that by that kind of reasoning, he was a foreigner in Canada.

21 For a discussion of the development of the concept, see Dirk Hoerder, 'Transculturalism(s): From Nation-State to Human Agency in Social Spaces and Cultural Regions,' *Zeitschrift für Kanada-Studien* 24, no. 1 (2004): 7–20.

22 *Reports of the Immigration Commission* (Dillingham Commission), 41 vols. (Washington: 1911), III:358–9, 362–5.

23 Immigrants of the 1970s and 1980s had access to new means of communication and thus could increase the transcultural aspects of their lives. Comparatively cheap air travel permits frequent visits home; the telephone provides a faster and more direct means to exchange information than letter writing; and, finally, the Internet permits regular access to newspapers 'at home' and thus the possibility of remaining *au courant* with events in the community where parents and other kin live. Eva-Maria Opitz-Black, 'Searching for Networks: German Immigrants in Today's Toronto, Canada,' MA thesis, Universität Bremen, 2002.

24 Wolfgang Helbich, Walter D. Kamphoefner, and Ulrike Sommer, eds., *Briefe aus Amerika. Deutsche Auswanderer schreiben aus der Neuen Welt 1830–1930* (München: Beck, 1988). English edition: *News from the Land of Freedom: German Immigrants Write Home*, trans. Susan Carter Vogel (Ithaca: Cornell University Press, 1991), 31–9.

25 Phyllis Knight, *A Very Ordinary Life: As Told to Rolf Knight* (Vancouver: New Star Books, 1974), 100–21. See also 'Ebe Koeppen's Story,' in *Stump Ranch Chronicles and Other Narratives*, ed. Rolf Knight (Vancouver: New Star Books, 1977), 49–116.

2 Gender in German-Canadian Studies: Challenges from across the Borders

CHRISTIANE HARZIG

In 1991, Donna Gabaccia argued in an essay titled 'Immigrant Women – Nowhere at Home' that the different methodological and theoretical trajectories of women's and immigration history had resulted in immigrant women being overlooked as historical agents. This was not because historians were unaware of the topic – mind you, this was the 1990s and not the 1960s – but rather because of different research agendas related to social class.[1] This void, of course, has now been filled after two decades of intensive research into gendered and ethnicized social and cultural history. However, I would like to make a similar argument about the history of German immigrant women in Canadian history. Where are they? Again, it is not for lack of interest that we know so little about them or that they seem invisible, but rather because they fall between the cracks of different research trajectories.

While carving out (new) contours for German-Canadian Studies and the elements of that research agenda is one of the objectives of this volume, I want to explore additional sources of intellectual inspiration from outside the field in order to lay out research trajectories, both for more gendered analyses in German-Canadian Studies and for the history of German women in Canada. Gender in German-Canadian Studies may be situated against four seemingly separate academic subfields: (1) Canadian women's history; (2) a globally constructed migration history, one that aims to be gendered or that demands to be; (3) studies on German women in the diaspora or North America; and (4) studies on the social and historical construction of whiteness.

I intend to demarcate some of the borders as well as the academic spaces underlying them. This may present challenges for the way gender is further analysed or inserted into German-Canadian Studies.

Eventually German-Canadian women will have to become part of the (new and diversified) Canadian master narrative or at least of Canadian historiography.

In a reflection on the 'Promise of Women's History' while 'Rethinking Canada,' Veronica Strong-Boag has summarized the research in Canadian women's history, pointing out that 'thirty years of sustained research have complicated the study of Canadian women's history.' She argues that when they started out in the 1960s and 1970s, historians of women 'tended to emphasize the experience of Europeans, assuming in the then prevalent notion of "global sisterhood" that their experience was coincident with others of their sex.' Thus the experiences of European women were taken as the 'universal' paradigm or vantage point from which to gender Canadian history. However, she does not specify which 'universal' European women came to signify; and the universal itself remains unspecific. This may well be its very marker, but it, too, remains untheorized. Today, she argues, women's history has become part of gender history's trajectory in studying how 'masculinity and femininity are mutually defined and redefined over time.'[2] A feminist-motivated research agenda should commit itself to exposing the workings of masculine powers and privileges. So the first task on the current agenda is to expose gendered power structures and hierarchies in historical relationships.

Strong-Boag's next key word is 'diversity': 'Three decades of inquiry have shown that there is no single, monolithic Canadian women's history.' And of diversities there are many: race, class, region, ability, and religion, in addition to sexual identity and preference, as well as age and generation, all determine women's perceptions of and reactions to historical changes and provide the contours for their own agency. Thus, there is no longer a single portrait of women's experience. In addition, the 'pattern of variety and the responses to them are not constant' either, so the time factor has a decisive impact on how women's experiences should be captured and analysed.[3]

Linda Kealey, after reviewing and summarizing the most recent publications about Canadian women historians, agrees with Strong-Boag in the intellectual necessity of acknowledging diversity in Canadian women's experience, but she also emphasizes the need to think reflectively about the categories we use when we write about women. The relations among the concepts and how they organize our analyses need to be constantly questioned and re-evaluated. As the most recent gendered histories show,[4] we must be constantly willing to engage with 'race and gender as variables that shape both history and the way historians think' about the historical issue under analysis.[5] Thus any gendered analysis of German-Canadian experiences over time will be well served by applying the analytical tools of power and diversity as well as by critically reflecting on the validity of time-honoured concepts such as 'homeland,' 'heritage,' 'culture,' 'identity,' and 'blood,' and whether they enhance or blur our understanding of the German-language past and present in Canada.

When investigating the second intellectual landscape – that is, migration studies – it may be helpful to recall some of the developments in migration historiography.[6] In the 1970s, migration history, under the sway of the American paradigm of exceptionalism, was perceived and written as *immigration* history. Though not necessarily conceptualized any more as filiopietistic contribution history, the focus of historians' research was the ethnic histories of individual immigrants and ethnic groups. Sometimes, these histories were written within the larger framework of urban histories – Philadelphia, Chicago, New York; other times, they focused on community building processes and the retention of ethnic identity. Motivating these studies was the desire to deconstruct a consensus-type history of triumphant American democracy and capitalism in which every immigrant evolved into a good American. The result of this focus on ethnic group history was a detailed knowledge of the functioning of ethnic identifying processes in modernizing urban (and to a lesser extent rural) America. Ethnicity had inscribed itself onto the American research landscape and become a conceptual category to be inserted into the analytical toolkit when American histories were being written.

In the 1980s, historians began questioning the key assumptions of the master narrative that had been developed around the melting pot paradigm; they began to think instead in terms of a multicultural United States, a nation of immigrants. These were not studies of individual communities but of ethnic *interaction;* a major focus now was studies revealing how 'local, regional, and national cultures and identities emerged through social practices.'[7] The analysis had shifted to changes in such things as family formation patterns, work habits and processes, resistance to exploitative practices, social demands and social services, and – to a lesser extent – religious practices. Historians now wanted to understand how ethnicity and culture shaped and influenced social processes and practices. In addition, analyses of ethnic identity formation revealed that ethnicity was fluid rather than static; it was something that was constructed and that evolved; it was often maintained by and in the service of an interested group of gatekeepers.

Though Canadian historiography shares many of the same social-historical concerns as American historiography, it was never, of course, cast in the 'exceptionalism' paradigm. Rather, the transcontinental nation-building process became the intellectual and conceptual space for immigrant insertion, albeit with a focus on (immigration) policy issues. The top-down approach, with the state as the major player in the narrative, structured interpretations of the relationship between the historian and the immigrant; thus the immigrants' varied stories were excluded from the metanarrative of Canada, which was historiographically perceived as a 'white settler society.'[8] This changed in the 1970s and 1980s, however, when historians on the left, in search of a 'usable past,' rediscovered traditions of protest and radicalism in histories of the 'other' (i.e., immigrant groups) rather than in 'mainstream' or standard Canadian histories.[9] In addition, multiculturalism, when it became a state policy in the early 1970s, encouraged and sponsored the writing of various ethnic groups' histories in Canada. Many of these were written in a filiopietistic and contributionist vein; nonetheless, they were important additions to immigration historiography. All of these were necessary steps in addressing the question of immigrants' impact and agency in creating Canadian society rather than merely influencing it.[10]

In the course of these historiographical developments, migration researchers engaged two insights: first, gender had become a more prominent category of analysis because of parallel developments in women's studies. In the 1970s and 1980s they pursued a somewhat bifurcated research agenda focusing, on the one hand, on working-class and family history, and on the other hand, on bourgeois women's personal and public experience. Second, ethnicity, though it remained a 'geschichtsmächtige' (historically relevant) category, was more and more perceived as socially constructed, one as malleable and as multifaceted as gender.

In the 1990s, immigration and migration studies were confronted with even more complex challenges. According to Gabaccia, a European school of migration studies had emerged, questioning the American paradigm of exceptionalism again, this time as it related to the United States being an exceptional 'nation of immigrants.' Migration scholars in Europe showed the diversity of European cultures, stemming from century-long migration experiences. In addition, the discerning and analysing of transnational, multisited migration systems led to a decentring of the nation as the principal unit of analysis. Systems that connect centres of production with marginalized regions via the mobility of labouring people function above and beyond artificially drawn borders. So do migrants, who instead follow their own dynamic of regional networks and relations. This concept of the decentred, deterritorialized or 'unbound' nation may be a useful tool of analysis in capturing German-Canadian migration systems.

At the same time, women's studies developed in new ways. The following methodological and theoretical issues became contested: the (wrongly framed) dichotomous positioning of cultural history (including the linguistic turn) versus a social history based on race, class, and gender; the (equally unnecessary) prioritizing of gender over women's history; and a (rightly posed) focus on how gender shaped transnational migration networks, household formation, exchanges among family members, and individual women's migration trajectories.

Thus, historiography moved from a nation-centred analysis of women and migration in the 1970s and 1980s toward transnational and gendered approaches to women and migration in the 1990s. Women's history took its own global turn by examining women as international travellers, as participants in empire building, and as social reformers on an international scale. Women's history also made demands on the research agenda of migration studies – specifically, by rewriting national histories as stories of ethnic interaction, and as gendered histories of transnational diasporas, or as global and world histories of women.

By entering the third academic landscape, I return to developments south of the border, in German-American studies regarding women and gender in the past twenty years.[11]

Results from fifteen years of (often feminist-inspired) research have provided us with a better understanding of how women's participation in rural life helped shape German-American agrarian communities, how women structured the urban labour market, and how their activities altered religious communities and provided cohesion for urban communities. We know now that they participated in the labour movement and were hesitant observers of the women's movement – though active, nonetheless, in building their own female ethnic public sphere. But most of all, this research has brought to light how gender became a strong marker for ethnic identity in the transcultural exchange.

Historians of German-American rural settlements, especially those with a feminist perspective, are often confronted with difficult interpretative decisions regarding how to assess and evaluate the position of women in an environment that seems to have been so obviously patriarchal and socially conservative. Yet historians have been able to see the important input women had in structuring and influencing the immigration project. Their emotional, financial, and most of all *physical* investment was often the difference between success and failure. Their input also made ethnic distinctiveness visible. To the casual onlooker of German-American farming methods between the 1840s and the 1920s, the most striking differentiating feature was that women worked the land alongside their men. It was, indeed, the labour input of women that enabled farmers to maintain yeoman farming methods longer than other groups. In addition, these farms raised poultry and cattle, cows for dairy products, and swine and sheep. Markers of German-American farmsteads included a diversification of crops and a stronger retention of subsistence production.

Using Chicago as an example, we may outline the contours of family life in German-American urban communities around the turn of the century. The most striking feature of these communities was their ethnic homogeneity and stability paired with patriarchal dominance. German-American women in Chicago were less likely than women of other ethnic groups to add to the family income by renting out to boarders. However, they were much more willing to take in family members who were not able to run their own households. Elderly widowed mothers, aunts, and grown-up daughters with children were often part of extended households. And while teenaged daughters tended to leave the household in order to find employment as domestics, grown-up sons remained in the household until they were able to form their own families. Thus, they added part of their income to the family economy while profiting from their mother's household skills and labour.

Adolescence and family formation produced experiences different from those in the home country. Young men and women in German-American Chicago were able to form their own families earlier than in the old country. The average marriage age for men was about twenty-six, for women twenty-two; in marrying young, they behaved according to the trend of American urban life. They were also able to decide for themselves when and whom to marry. The timing was not determined by inheritance of the farm, an appropriate dowry, a place of abode, or a suitable partner. Other factors such as the ability to work, steady employment and adequate income, health, and even love and peer group acceptance became important. German-American urban women also bore fewer children than their mothers and sisters in the old country, and the death rate among children was lower. In these aspects they had adjusted to the modernizing trend in urban environments.

Although German-American married women were seldom members of the paid labour force, their grown-up daughters, almost inevitably, went out to work. Outside employment was a very distinctive period in the course of their lives, situated tightly between school and marriage. Most of these young women worked as domestic servants, this being an occupation shunned by native-born white American women. For German-American women it was a respectable form of employment, because, as was argued, it prepared them for married life. Besides domestic service, they sought out employment in trade and industry, mainly in the many neighbourhood-based sites of production and trade such as tailor shops, bakeries, laundries, box factories, and dry goods stores. Although being a salesgirl, in one of the neighbourhood stores or in the fashionable department stores, ranked higher in the unwritten employment hierarchy than being a domestic or a factory girl, wages and working conditions did not warrant such an attitude. Their workdays were marked by long hours of standing on their feet, elaborate systems of fines and punishments, and high turnover rates.

At the turn toward the twentieth century, German-Americans were not among the rising, well-educated professional women of the American bourgeoisie, nor did they belong to the growing group of working wives and mothers becoming visible at that time. They also did not belong to the growing group of well-educated daughters who sought their chances in an expanding, and more diverse, female labour market. Nevertheless, they were well represented in the urban labour market. Their focus on family and work, first as supporting daughters and later as competent housewives and mothers, came to be an important ethnic marker for German-America.[12]

Unlike research on religious communities among the Irish or Italians, which often focus solely on Catholic communities, research on German-speaking immigrants must consider Protestant, Catholic, Jewish, and Mennonite contexts, to name only the larger groups. It has often been argued that the Church provided continuity and stability in migrants' lives; yet in fact, it was the separation of Church and State that imposed new structural forms on religious communities and that demanded an altered form of religiosity from German-speaking migrants. How these differences were played out over time has been studied by Irene Häderle. Her analysis of two Protestant communities in Ann Arbor, Michigan, shows that women's initiatives and activities eventually enhanced and fostered Americanization. This result is somewhat unexpected, since Lutheran communities were considered the fortress of Germanness in North America, and women were seen as the preservers of ethnic identity and as the gatekeepers of tradition. Here, however, they acted as agents of change. Women's aid societies, charity work, financial contributions to maintain and support the Church and community life (e.g., the pastor's salary), as well as the move from a pastor-centred church structure toward a community revolving around laypeople's activism were indicators of this Americanization process. All of these changes were rooted largely in women's activities.[13]

To recognize religious diversity to the extent that it includes the German-Jewish experience is a fairly recent development. It began with Sibylle Quack's study on émigré women from Germany during the Nazi period. Her narrative of pre-migration social and cultural situations, refuge, and adjustment to immigrant conditions in the United States (mainly New York) is based on information gained from social historical analysis and oral history. Quack conducted the interviews in the early 1990s, just in time to capture and chronicle the memories of this besieged group of women. Here, recollections of flight, coping, and adjustment were more prominent than the spirituality in or the functioning of the Jewish community. This, however, is at the centre of analysis of Tobias Brinkmann's study of the early Jewish (inevitably German-Jewish) community in Chicago. Unfortunately, Brinkmann chose to ignore any kind of gender analysis, so we learn little about women's engagement in this development.[14]

At the other end of the urban–rural spectrum, we find studies by Linda Pickle, Carol Coburn, and Kathleen Conzen that make use of the ethnoreligious paradigm.[15] Conservative Protestantism, the German language, and agrarian environment and modes of production blended together to create a way of life that was influential in shaping Midwestern agrarian society in more ways than is often acknowledged. However, it is not just the material signs that left their mark on the outlook of the Midwest that are of interest here. It is the broader concept of culture – 'the socially produced structures of meaning expressed in and engendered by public behaviors, languages, images,'[16] the interactions and negotiations among meaning and belief systems, social development, and environment – that has left its imprint on Midwestern society.[17]

These traditional patterns of meaning were influenced by the discursive construction of German women as cultural preservers and as carriers of ethnic identity. German observers of the United States together with German-Americans assumed they had the 'better class of women' and a superior understanding of family. American woman may have symbolized modernity and progress, as was often suggested, but it was the *German*-American woman who promised future development based on solid foundations, moderation, and wise judgment.[18]

German-American women, when they discussed issues of urban bourgeois womanhood, had a strong sense of their merits in a cultural environment that was perceived not as multicultural but as *bi*cultural. Their point of reference was the Anglo-American bourgeoisie. The various newspapers written and edited by women, addressing the female reader, did not necessarily express uniform opinions, but they nonetheless agreed on the central importance of the family. They also appreciated the more moderate forms and demands of the German women's movement and rejected the perceived radicalism of the American women's movement. Most important, they viewed themselves as the better housewives, promoting thrift and placing the family at the centre of their attention, while accusing American housewives of being wasteful and of neglecting their children. With visionary insight, they demanded economic recognition of the macroeconomic value of household labour, thus anticipating a debate on wages for household labour – a debate that would dominate the women's movement seven decades later.[19]

Despite all this inward-looking rhetoric – which focused on husband, children, and housework – not all German-American women acted accordingly. Women of the German-American bourgeoisie in Chicago, for example, actively constructed a female public sphere and thereby helped build a vibrant ethnic community. Women's groups within *Turn- und Gesangsvereine* (gymnastics and singing clubs), and charity organizations, were as much part of this female public sphere as were women's pages and women's newspapers. German women often formed auxiliaries that were responsible for the social aspects of club life. They staged festive events in honour of successful sporting and singing heroes; they also organized gymnastic groups for young girls and established all-female choirs. Women's clubs, which provided educational lectures and cultural entertainment, were usually organized around the desire to socialize with other women. To situate women firmly in the context of the family, as supporting daughters or as competent housewives and mothers, was an important discursive construction encouraged and discussed on women's pages and in bourgeois German-American newspapers.[20]

Charity work was the most important and successful aspect of the female public sphere. In rallying support for the various fund-raising efforts, women became important community builders and demonstrated the potential of ethnic groups. In Chicago, the charity ball that German-American women organized in support of the old people's home developed into the major social event for the elite. Here, the German-American upper class proudly presented itself to Chicago-at-large.[21]

So far, the research trajectory on German-American women in the United States has focused on social-historical analyses of urbanization and community development, agrarian structural changes, and family formation and changing work patterns as much as on cultural analyses of changing religious practices and women's positioning in the public sphere. It would be worth noting the different results of a similar research agenda that addresses Canadian developments. Markedly different insights might be generated as a result of differences in agrarian environments, farming practices, and market relations on the Canadian Prairies, the belated (1950s) insertion into urban space, a far more heterogeneous group of German-speaking people, and a more diverse receiving culture.

The final border we may want to cross is that of 'whiteness' or 'mainstream' studies. Whiteness, which since the 1990s has become one of the most challenging research paradigms in social-historical and cultural studies, poses a particular challenge for historiography and research in German-Canadian Studies. Ruth Frankenberg has defined whiteness as (1) a location of structural advantage, a race privilege; (2) a 'standpoint,' a place from which white people look at them/ourselves, at others, and at society; and (3) a reference to a set of cultural practices that are usually unmarked and unnamed.[22] In Canadian history, the relations among white, mainstream, and hegemonic cultures still need to be explored in more detail, but I think it is safe to argue that all three signifiers indicate entities that have much in common. These entities – which, for the time being, I treat as similar in that they are male dominated, female inspired, bourgeois, and white – are historically and socially constructed and contingent of time and space. Even so, they are generally considered the norm that need not be explained or justified; they appear to be unmarked, nameless spaces that consist of a number of subcultures. Despite their lack of distinction, they nonetheless have content: they generate norms, and they structure the way we think about history and culture and, by extension, about ourselves; they interrelate with other identifiers such as masculinity, femininity, and class, which are in turn implicated by them; and, most prominently, they are linked to dominance and power. Throughout history, some groups have been excluded from them on racist and cultural grounds (Asians, blacks, Jews); other groups have had the choice to join them or to remain outside (Irish,[23] Germans, Scandinavians), and their insertion or resistance has produced little social commentary. Other groups had such a strong outside presence (Ukrainians, Italians, Mennonites) that their relationship to the mainstream was noticed and they were, indeed, able to affect the way the mainstream was perceived; and some groups have to be 'discovered' as a distinct subculture and as different from the mainstream (English, French).[24]

Regarding 'Germans,' the chapters in this volume tellingly indicate the flexible operations of this hegemonic-cum-white culture in the Canadian nation-building process. Very early on, when it was in the interest of the British colonial power to allow the Moravian Brothers to pursue their missionary activities in Labrador, this mainstream culture seemed far away, yet its hegemonic features were clearly noticeable. As Kerstin Boelkow demonstrates, the cultural negotiations between the white European missionaries and their Inuit targets, though marked by egalitarian exchanges of knowledge and goods, were immediately turned into uneven power relations. The missionary mandate implied that the 'whites' (Germans) possessed superior knowledge and thus could relegate the converted (Inuit) to a 'helping' position. Five decades later, when confronted with the politically dubious pacifism of 'foreign' but productive settlers in Waterloo County, the British imperial habitus allowed, as Ross Fair shows, for a large degree of tolerance toward these Pennsylvania German immigrants. And Barbara Lorenzkowski's analysis of German cultural patterns in Waterloo County suggests to us that this inclusive version of hegemonic society also made room for pockets of distinctive cultural difference. However, while the hegemonic culture could be expansive on the material and even political level, it contracted when it came to gatekeeping memory and to forging the master narrative, as shown by Angelika Sauer's account of Elise von Koerber's activities.

As Elise von Koerber's fate in historiography shows, this kind of analysis needs to be pursued further. German women, so it seems, had choices in positioning themselves: they could build ethnic communities, or they could become part of the mainstream. Sometimes, the historical context – that is, the public memory of the Holocaust – might cast them as outsiders or as 'victims of ethnic stereotyping,' but more often than not they could move from immigrant to ethnic to mainstream more easily than most other immigrant groups, especially if their husbands were successful participants in an economic community. When looking at German immigrants or German-Canadians from a historical perspective, we have to dig deep for their gendered and racialized relationships, behaviours, and identities. We need to disentangle their relationship with the mainstream or hegemonic culture to see whether they were 'in' or 'out.' We need to know whether they opposed that culture by constructing and maintaining their separate ethnic and cultural identity or whether they actually participated in its formation. Also, their relations with other subcultures and ethnic groups have to be looked at, taking their respective gendered and classed positions into account, and acknowledging their inside/outside places. In short: Can you take the mainstream out of the German without taking the German out of the mainstream?

What is there to be gained from this venturing across the borders for the study of German-Canadian women? And how can they become a factor in Canadian history? In the most recent publication on immigrant women's history in Canada, edited by Marlene Epp, Franca Iacovetta, and Frances Swyripa,[25] all veterans to the field, several areas of inquiry are outlined. First, 'the traditional, and still important focus on the contribution of immigrant women to their families and communities, both in acculturation to Canadian society and in preservation of ethnic distinctiveness.' Second, issues of race and 'how ideals of "whiteness" and of white womanhood shaped the work of colonizers and the experience of immigrants.' Third, women's experiences within family and community and their relationship to society at large, including topics such as family violence and changing demands on equally changing gender roles. Three further areas of inquiry include the world of work and political activism; aspects of non-conformist behaviour (e.g., criminality and drunkenness); relationships to immigration policy issues, social services, and reception work; and last but not least, all issues related to transnationalism – that is, how pre- and post-migration experiences relate to each other and how pre-migration knowledge and practices impact post-migration lives.[26]

In future research on German-Canadian gendered and female experiences, we may pick up some of these suggestions. There is still a strong need for basic social-historical research on German immigration to Canada and for a better understanding of the contours of German-Canadian women's reality in Canadian (social) history. In the first instances, we know very little about the gendered aspects of community building and the change over time. In the Canadian context, different numbers are involved, and therefore community as a concept of analysis may take on a different meaning or may be defined differently as we look at regional differences and time sequences. In a second instance, we also know very little about German-Canadian women's impact on urban development, on agrarian structural changes, on religious life, and on family formation processes. For example, their presence does not figure yet in analyses of a gendered and ethnicized youth culture in Kitchener/Berlin before the First World War, or in the construction of social institutions on the Prairies in the 1920s and 1930s, or in the formation and retention of the various local religious (Church) communities.

And although there is very good research on Mennonite social reality in Canada, we should not take the Mennonite experience as the 'ethnic universal' for what is to be considered 'German-Canadian.' The prominence of Mennonites and research on them, however, has shown that there is no such thing as the genuine German-Canadian presence.[27] Unlike in German-American Studies, the concept of diversity has always been at the heart of German-Canadian Studies as much as the concept of the decentred nation is immanent, much more so in Canadian studies than in U.S. American-German history.

A second set of issues would address how larger social and cultural developments shaped and played out in specific locales and social institutions. This may range from (possible) participation in the women's movement (e.g., in the various locally based clubs that make up the National Council of Women), to participation in processes of domesticating politics, to working-class activism and religious and spiritual expressions.

A third set of questions could then relate to theorizing about the formation of what emerges as the centre, the mainstream, the dominant hegemonic narrative. What colour is 'white'? Until proven otherwise, I refuse to believe that 'white' is homogenous or that what constitutes the 'dominant' is uniform and monolithic. That is, how did German-Canadian women participate in the articulation of the margin *as well as* the mainstream? Did they become part of the dominant class? If they did, what was their impact? If they did not, what were they up against and how did they participate in the construction of a marginalized 'other'?

Research that is informed by theoretical and methodological negotiations between a social-historical research agenda and the discourse informed by post-colonial racialism and whiteness studies, with an added emphasis on and sensitivity for power hierarchies so prominent in Canadian women's history (and cultural historiography), will make German-Canadian women visible in Canadian historiography and history.

NOTES

1 Donna Gabaccia, 'Immigrant Women: Nowhere at Home,' *Journal of American Ethnic History* 10, no. 4 (1991): 61–87.
2 Veronica Strong-Boag, 'Rethinking Canada: The Promise of Women's History, 1986–2002,' unpublished manuscript, paper given at the annual conference Gesellschaft für Kanadastudien, February 2004.
3 Ibid.
4 Adele Perry, *On the Edge of Empire: Gender, Race, and the Making of British Columbia, 1849–1871* (Toronto: University of Toronto Press, 2001); Marlene Epp, *Women without Men: Mennonite Refugees of the Second World War* (Toronto: University of Toronto Press, 2000); Constance Backhouse, *Colour-Coded: A Legal History of Racism in Canada, 1900–1950* (Toronto: University of Toronto Press, 1999).
5 Linda Kealey, 'Review Essay: Race and Gender in Canadian History – Recent Contributions,' *Zeitschrift für Kanadastudien* 39, no. 1 (2001): 172–6 at 175.
6 Cf. Donna Gabaccia, 'Women, Gender, and Migration History: Bringing Globalization Theory "Down to Earth,"' unpublished paper presented at the SSHA, St Louis, 2003.
7 Ibid.
8 Franca Iacovetta et al., eds., *A Nation of Immigrants: Women, Workers, and Communities in Canadian History, 1840s–1960s* (Toronto: University of Toronto Press, 1998), ix.
9 Franca Iacovetta, 'Manly Militants, Cohesive Communities, and Defiant Domestics: Writing about Immigrants in Canadian Historical Scholarship,' *Labour/Le Travail* 36 (Fall 1995): 217–52.
10 How this may lead to a reinterpretation of the Canadian master narrative has been shown by Dirk Hoerder, *Creating Societies: Immigrant Lives in Canada* (Kinston and Montreal: McGill–Queen's University Press, 1999).
11 Cf. Christiane Harzig, 'Gender, Transatlantic Space, and the Presence of German Speaking People in North America,' in *Traveling Between Worlds: German-American Encounters,* ed. Thomas Adam and Ruth Gross (College Station: Texas A&M University Press, 2006), 146–82.

12 Linda Schelbitzki Pickle, *Contented among Strangers: Rural German-Speaking Women and Their Families in the Nineteenth-Century Midwest* (Urbana: University of Illinois Press, 1996).

13 Irene Häderle, *Deutsche kirchliche Frauenvereine in Ann Arbor, Michigan, 1870–1930. Eine Studie über die Bedingungen und Formen der Akkulturation deutscher Einwanderinnen und ihrer Töchter in den USA* (Stuttgart: Steiner Verlag, 1997).

14 Tobias Brinkmann, *Von der Gemeinde zur 'Community.' Jüdische Einwanderer in Chicago, 1840–1900* (Osnabrück: Rasch Verlag, 2002); Sibylle Quack, *Zuflucht America. Zur Sozialgeschichte der Emigration deutsch-jüdischer Frauen in die USA 1933–1945* (Bonn: Dietz Nachfolger, 1995).

15 Pickle, *Contented among Strangers;* Carol K. Coburn, *Life at Four Corners: Religion, Gender, and Education in a German-Lutheran Community, 1868–1945* (Lawrence: University of Kansas Press, 1992); Kathleen N. Conzen, *Making Their Own America: Assimilation Theory and the German Peasant Pioneer,* German Historical Institute, Washington, annual lectures series no. 3 (New York: Berg, 1990).

16 See Conzen, *Making Their Own America;* references are to Medick and Geertz.

17 See also Kathleen N. Conzen, *Germans in Minnesota* (St Paul: Minnesota Historical Society Press, 2003).

18 George von Bosse, *Das deutsche Element in den Vereinigten Staaten* (Milwaukee: 1908).

19 Clara Michaelis in the women's page of the *Chicagoer Freie Presse.* See Christiane Harzig, *Familie, Arbeit und weibliche Öffentlichkeit in einer Einwanderungsstadt. Deutschamerikanerinnen in Chicago um die Jahrhundertwende* (St Katharinen: Scripta Mercaturae, 1991), 238–42.

20 Harzig, *Familie, Arbeit und weibliche Öffentlichkeit,* chapter 6.

21 On the female public sphere in Chicago, see Christiane Harzig, 'The Ethnic Female Public Sphere: German American Women in Turn of the Century Chicago,' in *Midwestern Women: Work, Community, and Leadership at the Crossroads,* ed. Lucy E. Murphy and Wendy H. Venet (Bloomington: Indiana University Press, 1997), 141–57.

22 Ruth Frankenberg, *White Women, Race Matters: The Social Construction of Whiteness* (Minneapolis: University of Minnesota Press, 1993), 1.

23 The position of the Irish, as Brownen Walter argues, is determined less by choice than by hierarchical allocation. See her *Outsiders Inside: Whiteness, Place, and Irish Women* (London and New York: Routledge, 2000).

24 For the English, this has been argued by Pauline Greenhill, *Ethnicity in the Mainstream: Three Studies of English-Canadian Culture in Ontario* (Kingston

and Montreal: McGill–Queen's University Press, 1994); and the French-Canadian quest for a distinct society is part of today's Canadian political culture.

25 Marlene Epp, Franca Iacovetta, and Frances Swyripa, eds., *Sisters or Strangers? Immigrant, Ethnic, and Racialized Women in Canadian History* (Toronto: University of Toronto Press, 2004).

26 Epp et al., 'Introduction,' in ibid., 10–14.

27 Angelika E. Sauer and Matthias Zimmer, eds., *A Chorus of Different Voices: German-Canadian Identities* (New York: Peter Lang, 1998).

PART II

Eighteenth and Nineteenth Centuries:
Religion, Politics, and Culture

3 Success through Persistence: The Beginnings of the Moravian Mission in Labrador, 1771–5

KERSTIN BOELKOW

This chapter examines the contribution of the Moravian Church to Labrador history by describing the founding of the first Christian mission to the Inuit of what is now Canada, the missionaries' impact on the Inuit, and the Church's historical and continuing significance.[1] Few historians have written about the Moravian presence in Labrador, and their studies are based mainly on available English-language materials and focus on the English point of view. This chapter includes German archival sources[2] and looks at the Labrador mission from the German Moravian point of view.

After a brief survey of the Moravians' path to Labrador and the beginnings of the Moravian presence in Labrador in the eighteenth century, this chapter describes the establishment of a permanent Moravian mission along the Labrador coast, the early years of missionary work among the Inuit and the missionaries' experiences, and the reaction of the native people.

The Founding of the Moravian Mission along the Labrador Coast

The Moravian mission in Labrador was established on the basis of experiences the brethren had in founding the Moravian Greenland mission. In 1721 the Norwegian missionary Hans Egede founded a permanent settlement in Greenland under Danish sovereignty.[3] Egede wrote the first Greenlandic grammar, which the Moravians used to establish missions both in Greenland and later among the Inuit in Labrador.[4] During the eighteenth century the brethren founded many settlements along the west coast of Greenland, some of which exist to this day.

Wishing to expand its mission among the Inuit, the Church's executive governing body in Herrnhut, the so-called Unity's Elders' Conference or UEC (*Unitaets-Ältesten-Konferenz*), set its eyes on Labrador. This had become possible after the British parliament recognized the Church as an 'ancient Protestant Episcopal Church' in 1749.[5] However, the first mission, financed in part by Claude Nisbet and led by Johann Christian Erhardt, came to a disastrous end. After founding a one-house mission at Nisbet Harbour, which they named *Hoffnungsthal* (Hopedale), Erhardt and part of his crew died under mysterious circumstances; the surviving crew members as well as the four missionaries of Hopedale returned to Europe the same year.[6]

This first Moravian mission attempt failed for a number of reasons. Unlike the Greenland Inuit, the Labrador Inuit had had no contact with whites until the sixteenth century, when European fishermen began making regular visits to the southern part of the Labrador Peninsula. The Europeans traded goods with the Inuit, but because of language difficulties and distrust on both sides, quarrels arose.[7] These conflicts often led to bloodshed. The situation of the Labrador Inuit in the seventeenth and early eighteenth centuries was precarious. The white settlers forced them to retreat from southern to northern Labrador;[8] at the same time, the south was like a 'magnet' to the Inuit because there they could trade for European goods such as steel knives, cotton clothes, tobacco, and rum.[9] Taking into account these circumstances of contact, the killing of Erhardt and his companions seems less unusual.[10] To the Inuit, Erhardt must have appeared as just one more trader like the ones they had encountered in the south, and he was never able to correct this assumption because of his lack of language proficiency.

After the unsuccessful first attempt, the United Brethren Church did not try again to found a mission in Labrador until 1764, when the Danish carpenter Jens Haven (1724–1796) continued the work in Labrador. After missionary work in Greenland, where he learned the Inuit language, Haven set off for Labrador.[11] For this mission, he had received the approval and support of Newfoundland Governor Sir Hugh Palliser and the British authorities.[12]

Haven's work among the Inuit was much more successful than Erhardt's, because he spoke their language and wore their kind of clothing.[13] Over the course of several weeks, Haven visited the Inuit and told them about the crucified Lord. In October 1764, Haven returned to England, where he told the Board of Trade and other governmental organizations about his journey.[14] He received permission and support to continue his mission. His suggestion that a mission post be established in the north of Labrador, far from any European settlement or fishing camps, was approved by the British administration.[15] The UEC in Herrnhut then started finalizing plans for a mission outpost in Labrador. After further exploratory trips to the Labrador coast, in 1769 the Moravian Church received a land grant from the British government of 100,000 acres around Eskimo Bay.[16] During a third exploratory voyage, the brethren established a mission at Kauk Harbour, a place sufficiently protected, with good access for ships, not too far from the Inuit's gathering places, with a stream close by and fertile soil for agriculture.[17]

In the meantime, the UEC in Herrnhut had obtained financial support from the Society for the Furtherance of the Gospel Among the Heathen (SFG) to pay for the Labrador mission.[18] Because of the hostile environment, they did not expect the Labrador mission to be self-sufficient, as they did other missions. This one was going to rely on annual shipments of provisions.[19] The *Amity* left England in May 1771 with thirteen missionaries,[20] provisions for one year, equipment, guns and ammunition, trading goods, and a wooden house. For unknown reasons, the brethren settled at Unity Harbour rather than Kauk Harbour, as had been decided the year before. At Unity Harbour the missionaries built a house and named the place Nain, as the UEC had decided.[21]

The UEC had instructed the missionaries to form a community after the European model.[22] The lack of regular contact with the authorities in Germany, however, complicated the self-government of the Nain missionaries, because questions could not be asked nor problems addressed immediately. The only way to communicate with the 'outer world' was through the annual supply ship. The Brethren were used to the strongly hierarchical structure of the Moravian Church and wanted to ask the UEC for help and advice; but the long distance to the head office in Germany made this nearly impossible, which left the brothers and sisters at Nain to make their own decisions. The missionaries often walked on thin ice in deciding what they were *allowed* to do without the advice and consent of the UEC and what they *had* to do in order to survive in the hostile environment. Given the extraordinary circumstances at Nain – the geography, the climate, the solitude – the mission post could never be a precise copy of a regular community.

Nevertheless, the brethren tried to organize the Labrador community and their religious life in conformity with the European model. Hence the Nain community had a superintendent (*Helfer ins Ganze*), Brother Brasen, who kept an eye on the local community as well as on the Labrador mission. Brasen supervised the missionaries' duties according to the regulations of the United Brethren Church. He also held services, meetings, and Bible studies in rotation with the other brothers. When disputes developed among brothers and sisters, he served as mediator. In addition to these religious duties and his duties as a doctor, Brasen's practical duties included fishing, hunting, and working at the mission house or guarding the sheep.[23] The SFG had also assigned Brasen, who was a scientist, the task of examining Labrador's flora and fauna.

Like a regular brethren community, the Labrador mission established 'conferences,' which had decisive powers within the small community. Nain had an Eldest Conference (EC), a Choir Helper Conference, and a House Conference, but in contrast to Germany, no other official conferences, such as the *Gemeingericht* (common court), the *Dienerkonferenz* (servants' conference), or the *Handwerkskonferenz* (trades conference). No other committees were needed at Nain because of its isolated position, the small number of missionaries, and the mission's constant and growing flow of brothers and sisters. Nevertheless, the few established conferences were vital to the community's functioning.

As the highest authority at Nain, the EC made decisions relating to the community (e.g., when liturgical meetings and the Holy Communion were to be held, what houses should be built, and who was to go hunting) and to the mission (e.g., should the brother get permission to visit the Inuit?) on the basis of majority vote. Only decisions relating to the founding of the mission, such as whether another mission post should be established, had to be determined by the UEC.[24] The EC was responsible for corresponding with the UEC as well as with the local government and authorities. The six brothers and three sisters who were voted from the UEC by lot into the EC had equal rights. In strong distinction from the eighteenth-century disregard for and suppression of women, the Moravian sisters had the same rights as their brothers: they were members of decision-making committees, had the right to vote, and held offices.[25]

At Nain, the duties of the three sisters consisted of cooking and washing. A Moravian principle was that both parents should educate their children, but because of the extraordinary circumstances at Nain, this task was carried out solely by the women. Children stayed at the mission post until age six and were then given to a pedagogical station in Germany. Parents often did not see their children for years. As strict as it seems, one must remember that the mission station was marked not only by privations but also by serious dangers for children: long, cold winters, the shortage of provisions, and diseases. Like the brothers, the sisters came into contact with the Inuit, but because of the sisters' limited linguistic knowledge, conversations hardly ever took place.[26]

The brothers, who were carefully vetted by the UEC and then 'chosen' by lot, had many different tasks. According to the order of the UEC to 'make use of every Brother according to his gift,'[27] each brother was deployed on the mission for specific tasks. Their main duties were to obtain food, to make crafts within the limits of personal requirements, and to carry out orders relating to the Inuit. The requirement that all brothers contribute to subsistence was more than a principle of the Moravian Church; in the hostile environment of Labrador, it was essential. The annual provisions from Europe were meagre, so when the missionaries wanted fresh meat or other fresh food they had to go fishing or hunting. Only in rare cases were the brothers able to barter for food with the Inuit. Most of the time, indeed, the Inuit could hardly spare anything. Cattle breeding and agriculture were possible only to a limited extent. Labrador was not 'full of animals,' as the UEC had promised the missionaries, and their hunting methods proved to be less than successful. Hunting during winter was even more difficult.[28] The UEC's belief that Labrador's inhabitants, environment, and climate were similar to Greenland's turned out to be erroneous.

Besides gathering food, the brothers' main tasks during winter were to collect firewood, cut timber, do necessary repairs, clean whalebone, and produce blubber. The brothers manufactured smaller things, such as lamps, knives, and iron arrowheads, to barter with the Inuit because self-sufficiency of mission stations was a Moravian principle.[29] During summers, the brothers built and repaired boats for the Inuit. That was not done for the small profit but rather to give the Inuit an incentive to stay in the north instead of moving south, where, the brothers feared, the Inuit would come in contact with guns and alcohol.

For the unity of the community in this remote region, daily religious practice was vital. The religious routine followed established rules. Daily meetings in the morning and in the evening were as common as liturgical meetings, sing-alongs, Bible lectures, community hours, and choir hours. Holy Communion was held once a month on behalf of the UEC.[30] Some practices were adapted to the local circumstances, such as singing liturgies in German and English. Feasts like Christmas and Easter were celebrated together with Inuit, who liked to attend the feasts silently.

As was the case with other Moravian missions to the heathen, the brethren at Nain hoped to integrate the natives into the religious life of the mission station as 'Inuit Helpers.' But the missionaries were confronted with a serious problem: the Inuit were nomadic people. During the summer they lived in tents at sites where fish, berries, and caribou were available, and during the winter they lived in houses near seal-hunting grounds. The missionaries wanted them to stay at Nain the year round so that a settled community of baptized Inuit could be developed. The missionaries were confronted with another problem as well: Nain was an Inuit summer gathering place, and during the winter, the Nain region did not offer sufficient seal-hunting opportunities. As a result of this miscalculation, not until 1779 did the first Inuit settle at Nain.[31] Thus the brethren had no Inuit Helpers for church services during their first years in Labrador.

The first years of the Nain mission, then, turned out to be more difficult than the UEC and the missionaries had anticipated. Cramped living conditions, isolation, and loneliness compounded problems among the brethren. Only a censure from the UEC and the SFG as well as a visit by UEC member Paul Eugen Layritz in 1773 improved the situation and the mood among the brothers and sisters. Visits by UEC members had long been an instrument whereby the authorities supervised the missions. The Layritz visit to Nain was important for the mission because as he became acquainted with the situation in Labrador, he was able to advise the missionaries and the UEC according to the circumstances. He made decisions that were vital for the continuation of missionary work in Labrador. The introduction of a so-called *Katechumen-Gruppe* (group of Inuit on the verge of baptism) made the mission easier. Over the following decades the catechumen became a fixed part of the Church organization, from which the missionaries chose their Helpers, who became the 'most important links between the missionaries and the population.'[32] The generally positive report from Layritz to the UEC gave the supreme authority better insight into the Labrador mission and served as a basis for future decisions. The report was forwarded to the English Admiralty and the Board of Trade, resulting in another guarantee of safety and support for the Moravian mission.[33]

The nomadic ways of the Inuit made it difficult for the brethren to bring together enough Inuit to form a baptized Inuit community. This led to a debate among the missionaries and the UEC as to whether Nain was the right place for a mission station. Layritz's visit bolstered the conviction that Nain was a good place for a mission post but a bad one for Inuit food gathering. So on returning to Germany, Layritz suggested to the UEC that more mission stations be founded in Labrador, since Nain on its own was never going to 'collect' enough Inuit to establish a community of baptized natives. In 1774 and 1775 the UEC ordered the missionaries to search for suitable sites for two further mission posts: one to the north, in the Kivertlok area, and one to the south, in the Arvertok area. The missionaries had explored the northern coast on an exploratory voyage in 1774 – a journey that had ended tragically for brothers Brasen and Lehmann. Even if more mission posts were established, Nain would still be the mission's centre.[34] In 1776 the Moravians established a new station north of Nain called Okkak,[35] after the Church had been granted a second land grant by the British government. This was followed in 1782 by a third station, Hopedale, south of Nain.

The Missionary Work of the Brethren in Nain among the Inuit

A systematic Moravian mission theology did not exist during the eighteenth century.[36] In addition to witnessing the telling and repetition of the Passion, the Inuit were able to ask the brethren religious questions whenever they wanted. The natives were also invited to participate silently in the brethren's daily religious meetings.[37] This practice was rooted in the understanding that the Moravians were a 'living example' of a Christian life. Even on feasts like Christmas and Easter, the Inuit were invited to participate silently. If an opportunity emerged, the missionaries illustrated religious matters with examples.

Singing and music making played an important role in the missionaries' work. Since the Inuit liked singing, they were willing to learn new songs and verses, but it is to be doubted whether they cared about the religious content of the songs. Therefore the missionaries taught the Inuit religious songs in Greenlandic, but also in English.[38]

Missionary work always meant enormous social and cultural change for the people who were being Christianized. The brethren never thought of the Inuit as 'personified savages' who were a 'dirty and evil raid- and murder-nation,' as contemporary historians called the Inuit.[39] Rather, the Moravians viewed the Inuit as 'poor Heathen inhabitants' because they did not know Jesus Christ. The brethren called the indigenous people of Labrador 'Eskimo' and sometimes 'Inuit.' The term 'savages' was resorted to only by the English brethren or the British government. Sometimes the missionaries called the Inuit their 'neighbours.'[40] Nevertheless, all missionary work was based on assumptions about the missionaries' superiority and on their presupposed right to judge other people and their customs and beliefs as culturally and morally inferior.

One Moravian principle was the prohibition on distributing alcohol and guns among the Inuit. During the first years of the Moravian presence in Labrador, this was practicable, but because of the continuing colonization of southern Labrador and the Inuit's growing demand for guns and ammunition, this principle was finally abandoned. Gifts from the Inuit were never to be accepted, at least not without giving something back. To be in anyone's debt was strictly forbidden. It was also forbidden to grant credit to the Inuit, but this turned out not to be practicable and would become a major problem over the following decades. Since the UEC did not know the particulars of Labrador, they could only offer the missionaries general principles.[41]

Baptism had a central place in the proselytism of the Moravians, who believed that a 'First Fruit' among the Inuit would be a 'useful tool' to convert the other Inuit. The goal was to establish a baptized Inuit community that would be able to govern itself without any help from the missionaries. The brethren prayed with the Inuit in their mother tongue, though Inuktitut differs from Greenlandic; hence the Moravians had to learn new words and pronunciations. The studies of the Greenlandic missionary Hans Egede and the grammars and dictionaries the missionaries wrote themselves were of great help. The only problem turned out to be that most of the religious words in German, which the Moravians used in their daily sermons, simply did not exist in the Inuit mother tongue. The brethren solved this problem by introducing new Inuktitut words. During the first years only three brothers could preach to the Inuit because they were the only ones who were fluent in the natives' language. The other brothers and sisters, who had the duty to learn the language, were also to seek contact with the Inuit, to whom they could 'preach' through exemplary behaviour.[42]

Usually the Inuit visited the Moravians at their station at Nain. There the brethren preached to them in the 'Eskimo house.' Depending on the number of Inuit staying at Nain, the brethren held sermons and meetings for them twice a day. The brothers also visited the Inuit in their tents during their stays at Nain.[43]

The Moravians also travelled to Inuit living, hunting, and fishing places, not only to preach but also to gather food and to get to know the country. For their own safety, they would accompany the natives on their sleds or hire natives as guides. Most visits were made in the winter, because during summers, the brethren were too busy working at the mission post. In between these two seasons, travel was not possible.[44]

Primarily, the Moravians were preachers to the Inuit, but like other missionary congregations, they were also negotiators, educators, and doctors.[45] These additional functions advanced their missionary work and encouraged the natives to accept their presence. At the same time, the brethren avoided any radical interference in Inuit society. They did notice problems such as the common exchange of women, polygamy, and violence against Inuit women, but taking sides would have endangered the whole mission – indeed, it would have jeopardized the missionaries' lives. So the brethren positioned themselves as moderate 'negotiators' in the background.

In the beginning, the main reason for the natives to come to Nain was to trade blubber and whalebone for European goods. It can be assumed that the mission station was nothing else for the Inuit than a well-placed trading post where they could get everything they needed. An Inuit told a brother: 'We are the only inhabitants of this country who have Europeans living alongside them and we are thankful for this, because we can buy here what we need.'[46]

The brothers always offered the Inuit a warm place to sleep, but the Inuit assumption that the brethren would also supply them with food was incorrect. Only in utmost need did the missionaries give them provisions, for they had little to spare. Besides, they did not think it advisable to accustom the Inuit to European food.

The Inuit were never forced to stay and listen to the missionaries. If the Inuit did not want to listen to sermons, they simply left the station. A missionary once asked an Inuit whether he had understood the preachers. The reply: 'I do not know what you want, but do you have a knife for sale? I have got two whalebones to trade.'[47] We can see that the Inuit cleverly used the missionaries for their purposes.

Officially, mission and trade were strictly separated. In Nain, brothers Wolfes and Frech were chosen to be the trading agents for the Ship's Company, a brethren-owned trading company formed in 1770.[48] Their task was to trade European goods with the Inuit. They had nothing to do with the missionary work of the other brothers and sisters. The offered trading goods were to be strictly utilitarian, for it would have violated the Moravians' ethics to distribute useless goods among the Inuit. For the same reason, alcohol was banned as a trade good.

The UEC could not avoid setting up a trading post, partly because the SFG and the Ship's Company needed the profits to support their mission, and partly because without one the Inuit would probably never have settled near the missionaries – instead, they would have travelled south to obtain goods they wanted from the regular traders, thus coming in contact with alcohol and guns and probably meeting the same fate that was already befalling their kinspeople in that area: swift extinction. Usually the Inuit came to the brethren to barter; most of the time they brought whalebone and seal blubber to exchange for European goods, for money was unknown to the natives.[49] The Inuit always wanted to trade first and then listen to sermons. Trading was conducted in Inuktitut, whenever natives arrived with the wish to trade.

 Beside trading, the missionaries manufactured goods for the Inuit. In part, this was to help fund the mission; in part, it reflected the Moravian principle that every community should be self-supplying. In exchange for artisanal goods (small boxes, axes, lamps, boats), the missionaries received food (caribou and seal meat, salmon, trout, dried fish) as well as eiderdown and furs for clothing.[50]

The division of trade would have worked out had the Ship's Company made enough profits, but during the first years the company made losses, and its debts increased over the years. In the coming decades, the rivalry with the missionary trade would lead to ongoing quarrels among England's SFG, the Ship's Company, and the German authorities. These conflicts eased in 1797, when the Ship's Company was taken over by SFG. Even then, the Ship's Company barely made a profit from the Labrador trade. Not until 1925 was the controversial link between mission and trade finally dissolved; that year, trading rights and trading stores were handed over to the Hudson's Bay Company for a term of twenty-one years.[51]

Prospects and Conclusion

Founding a Moravian mission in Labrador turned out to be more difficult than the Church had expected. The missionaries were confronted with unforeseen problems that had to be solved before a functioning community could be established after the model of a regular German community. Nevertheless, Nain could never become like a regular brethren community, for its practices had to be adapted to Labrador's harsh climate and scarcity of resources and to the nomadic lifestyle of the Inuit. The daily work of the brothers (barter, hunting and fishing, missionary work) and sisters (household and child care) determined daily routines, and religious life had to be adjusted accordingly. The Inuit helped the missionaries to survive in the hostile environment and to adapt their life to the circumstances. They served the brethren as guides as well as 'insiders' who knew and understood the land. So the missionaries learned from the Inuit.

The process of conversion was slow. In 1776, the missionaries celebrated the first baptized Inuit, Kingminguse, as a 'First Fruit,' only to brand him a backslider fifteen years later when he took a second wife. A breakthrough for the missionaries occurred in the early nineteenth century when a religious revival affected the Inuit, and by 1818 some 600 Inuit had been baptized at one of the mission stations. The Moravian Church expanded enormously during the nineteenth and twentieth centuries, and seven more stations north and south of Nain were established to serve the Inuit as well as the settlers who by then were migrating into Labrador.[52] Between thirty and forty missionaries, mostly Germans, served at the various mission posts along the Labrador coast. Most of the stations had to be closed for economic reasons or declining population; today, only Nain, Makkovik, Happy Valley, and North West River are still active Moravian congregations. In 1970 the Canadian government recognized the Brethren Church as the 'Moravian Church in Newfoundland and Labrador.'[53] 'Today, most of the people on Labrador's north coast are Moravian and the European missionary presence has given way to church administration by Labradorians.' The provincial government of Newfoundland and Labrador has taken over the Moravian schools, and the International Greenfell Association has assumed full responsibility for medical services along the coast.[54]

The Moravian mission had severe consequences for the Inuit way of life. Social, cultural, and economic changes in Inuit society were inevitable. During the decades of Moravian mission, the brethren introduced the Inuit to new technologies such as fishing nets and sealing nets, thus making hunting easier and more successful. The Moravians organized schools for the Inuit as soon as enough converts had settled around the mission posts. While speaking German at home, the missionaries taught the Inuit in their own tongue. When teaching mathematics, they had to improvise because the Inuit could only count on their fingers and lacked the words for any number above five except for one that meant 'many.' The brethren overcame this problem by introducing the Arabic numerals under their German names.[55] By the beginning of the twentieth century the Moravians had 'advanced' the Inuit to the point where they were the most literate people along the Labrador coast: the natives were able to read and write in their own language, and some of them even could speak a little English. This was important for the Brethren because the Inuit were now able to teach one another in the Christian faith. All in all, the Inuit learned from the Moravians.

NOTES

1 The chapter is based on my MA thesis, 'Am Rande der Zivilisation: Die Anfänge der Herrnhuter Brüdergemeine in Labrador 1771–75. Unter besonderer Berücksichtigung der Frage, wie sich die Missionsstation in Nain, Labrador, selbst verwaltete und von der obersten Direktion in Deutschland geleitet wurde,' University of Trier, 2002.

2 The archival sources are held in Herrnhut, Germany (Unitäts-Archiv, UA), in the United Brethren Archive, and at Queen Elizabeth II Library at Memorial University of Newfoundland, where most archival material has been preserved on microfilm.

3 Heinz Israel, *Kulturwandel grönländischer Eskimo im 18. Jahrhundert. Wandlungen in Gesellschaft und Wirtschaft unter dem Einfluss der Herrnhuter Brüdermission* (Berlin: Akademie-Verlag, 1969), 13; Friedrich Ludwig Kölbing, *Die Missionen der evangelischen Brüder in Grönland und Labrador* (Gnadau: H.F. Burkhard, 1831), 33–4.

4 David Crantz, *Historie von Grönland*, vol. 2. (Olm: Hildesheim et al., 1995 [1765]), 421.

5 Hans Rollmann, *Labrador through Moravian Eyes: 250 Years of Art, Photographs, and Records* (St John's: Special Celebrations Corporation of Newfoundland and Labrador, 2002), 6.

6 Alfred Gysin, *Mission im Heimatland der Eskimo* (Hamburg: Ludwig Appel, 1966), 5; Rollmann, *Labrador through Moravian Eyes*, 6–7; Karl Müller, *200 Jahre Brüdermission*, vol. 2: *Das zweite Missionsjahrhundert* (Herrnhut: Verlag der Missionsbuchhandlung, 1932), 147; James K. Hiller, 'The Foundation and the Early Years of Moravian Mission in Labrador, 1752–1805,' MA thesis, Memorial University of Newfoundland, 1967, 23. For Nisbet's report in German, see Müller, *200 Jahre Brüdermission*, 149.

7 Diamond Jenness, *Eskimo Administration*, vol. III, *Labrador* (Montreal: Arctic Institute of North America, 1965), 7.

8 Even if the retreat of the Inuit was not completed in the 1760s, it seemed that no Inuit were living south of Cape Charles by that time. See Hiller, 'Foundation,' 28.

9 Jenness, *Eskimo Administration*, 7.

10 It was never proven whether the killing was murder or manslaughter. The Moravian sources claim that Erhard and his companions were 'murdered.'

11 Auszug aus Bruder Jens Havens eigenem Aufsatz, von seinem Ruf und ersteren Versuchs-Reise nach Terra Labrador, seiner Ankunft darselbst, und ersteren Bekanntschaft mit den Eskimoern; von Anno 1764 bis 1770,' 5, Queen Elizabeth II Library, Memorial University of Newfoundland (in the following cited as Auszug Haven).

12 Auszug Haven, 15; William H. Whiteley, 'The Moravian Missionaries and the Labrador Eskimos in the 18th Century,' *Church History* 35, no. 1 (March 1966): 77; Hiller, 'Foundation,' 37.

13 Auszug Haven, 26–7.

14 Whiteley, 'The Moravian Missionaries,' 78.

15 John C. Mason, *The Moravian Church and the Missionary Awakening in England, 1760–1800* (Rochester: Royal Historical Society, 2001), 30.

16 Hiller, 'Foundation,' 46, 55; Order-in-Council, Bethlehem Collection (BC), Pennsylvania, reel 12, 15429 (on microfilm reel 512, Center for Newfoundland Studies, Queen Elizabeth Library, Memorial University of Newfoundland, St John's).

17 Mikak, an Inuit woman who had been taken to England and returned home, served as the missionaries' guide. It must be assumed that it came to a misunderstanding in 1770: when the Brethren asked Mikak to take them to 'Eskimo Bay,' the Inuit thought of a place where many Inuit gathered. Hence she took them to the Nuneingoak Region, where many Inuit gathered at that time of year. A 'contract' with the Inuit was completed, but it is to be doubted that the Inuit had the same idea of 'possessing land' as the Moravians. *Unitaets-Ältesten-Konferenz* (UÄK) Protokolle 10 January 70; Letter UÄK to Drachardt, Haven, Jensen 22 March 1770, BC, reel 4, 3579–82; Hiller, 'Foundation,' 71, 76–7; Helge Kleivan, *The Eskimos of Northeast Labrador: A History of Eskimo-White Relations, 1771–1965* (Oslo: Norsk Polarinstitutt, 1966), 28.

18 The costs of the missions were paid mainly from voluntary contributions and donations, as well as by special aid societies (*Hilfsgesellschaften*), which supported the missionaries with food and equipment. The SFG, founded in 1741 by James Hutten, supported the missionaries in Labrador.

19 UÄK Protokolle 29 September 1770, 17 January 1771, and 21 December 1770; Letter SFG to UÄK, 9 April 1771, Unitäts-Archiv Herrnhut (UA), R.15 Kb.17.a; Mason, *Moravian Church*, 46; Letter SFG to UÄK, 1 February 1771 (UA), R.15.Kb.a.45; Adolf Schulze, *Abriss einer Geschichte der Brüdermission. Mit einem Anhang, enthaltend eine ausführliche Bibliographie zur Geschichte der Brüdermission* (Herrnhut: 1901), 141.

20 The married couples Brasen, Schneider, and Haven and brothers Neisser, Jensen, Rhodes, Drachardt, Morhard, Turner, and Frech.

21 Letter Brasen to Petrus, n.d., 1771 (UA), R.15.Kb.17.a.74; Diarium Nain (DN), 26 September 1771.

22 Helfer-Konferenz Protokolle, 26 August 1772.

23 Instruktion, 23 March 1771 (UA), R.15.Ka.7c; Synodalverlass der Generalsynode, 1769, BC, 20431; letter Brasen to Petrus, 6 July 1771 (UA), R.15 Kb.17.a.60; Haus-Konferenz Protokolle, 19 July 1773.

24 Instruktion, 23 March 1771 (UA), R.15 Ka.7c; Verlass der Generalsynode 1769, BC, 20383.

25 Christian Hahn, 'Brüder-Unität,' in *Taschenlexikon Religion und Theologie* (Göttingen: Vandenhoeck & Ruprecht, 1974), 292. The Choir Helper Conference was subordinated to the EC and dealt with matters concerning Nain's small Unmarried Brother Choir and Married Couples Choir. The House Conference and the Helpers Conference were also subordinated to the EC (Synodalverlass Generalsynode, 1764, BC, 20196). The Helpers Conference dealt mainly with personal and internal matters related to the Nain community (Instruktionen an die Geschwister, 23 March 1771 [UA], R.15Ka.7c.) and kept an eye on the sisters' and brothers' 'heart condition' (*Herzenszustand*) (letter UÄK to Helfer-Konferenz, 20 February 1772, BC, reel 4, 3644). Meetings were held irregularly but at least two days before the next Holy Communion. In contrast, the House Conference met regularly once a week and decided more practical matters (ÄK Protokolle, 12 November 1772). It had nothing to do with the mission and determined things such as the division of the provision (Haus-Konferenz Protokolle, 11 November 1772), the acquisition of food through fishing and hunting (letter UÄK to Gemeine Nain 17 February 1772, BC, 3626), and daily tasks.

26 Verlass der Generalsynode, 1764, BC, 20231; Schulze, *Abriss*, 138; DN, 9 November 1771.

27 UÄK an die nach Labrador gehenden Missionare 1 March 1771, BC, 3626.

28 Instruktion, 23 March 1771, (UA) R.15 Ka.7c; DN, 28 September 1772; UÄK an die nach Labrador gehenden Geschwister, 15 March 1771, BC, 3620; ÄK Protokolle, July 1772; DN, 23 October 1772.

29 Haus-Konferenz Protokolle, 13 April 1773; ÄK Protokolle, 27 July 1773.

30 Instruktion, 23 March 1771 (UA), R.15 Ka.7c.

31 Schulze, *Abriss*, 154; Kleivan, *Eskimos of Northeast Labrador*, 29.

32 Ibid., 75.

33 Protokolle der ÄK in Nain, 1 September 1773, 193 (UA), R.15 Ka.11; UÄK Protokolle, 22 December 1773.

34 UÄK Protokolle, 28 December 1773.

35 UÄK Protokolle, 13 February 1775.
36 Nicholas Lewis Count and Lord of Zinzendorf and Pottendorf, who had given refuge to Moravian Brethren in Herrnhut in the 1720s and then led them in a renewal and revival, had never written a theory of missionary work. After his death in 1760, August Spangenberg started a Moravian mission theology, which focused on the crucified Christ. David A. Schattschneider, '"Souls for the Lamb": A Theology for the Christian Mission According to Count Nicolaus Ludwig von Zinzendorf and Bishop August Gottlieb Spangenberg,' PhD diss., University of Chicago, 1975, 63. Müller, *200 Jahre Brüdermission*, 303. The overall aim of the missionary work was to make the Inuit familiar with Jesus Christ, the 'creator and saviour' (Instruktion, 23 March 1771, (UA) R.15 Ka.7c.). Inculcation through repetition was the main method of the Moravian missionaries (DN, 2 March 1772; DN, 3 June 1772; DN, 5 January 1773).
37 For example, DN, 25 December 1771; DN, 26 April 1772; DN, 24 May 1772.
38 DN, 12 January 1772.
39 For example, Adolf Schulze, *Die Missionsfelder der erneuerten Brüderkirche* (Bethlehem: 1890), 64–5.
40 DN, 25 January 1772.
41 Letter, UÄK, an die nach Labrador gehenden Geschwister, 15 March 1771, BC, reel 4, 3619–22; Letter, UÄK to Brasen, 16 February 1772, (UA) R.15 Kb.16.a.
42 DN, 12 November 1771; Protokolle der ÄK in Nain, 4 September 1773, (UA) R.15 Ka.11 November; letter, Brasen to Spangenberg, 1 November 1772, (UA) R.15 Kb.17.a.118; letter, Brasen to Spangenberg, (UA) R.15 Kb.17.a.62; Instruktion, 23 March 1771, (UA) R.15 Ka.7c. The bases for the language studies were the studies of Hans Egede and the Greenlandic missionaries: letter, Brasen to Petrus, n.d., date 1771, (UA) R.15 Kb.17.a.74; ÄK Protokolle, 15 February 1773.
43 For example, DN, 8 November 1771; DN, 6 January 1772; DN, 14 April 1772; DN, 22 April 1772; DN, 4 May 1772; DN, 12 December 1772; Helfer-Konferenz Protokolle, 10 November 1771.
44 DN, 13 November 1772.
45 DN, 4 February 1772; DN, 1 April 1772; DN, 15 June 1772; DN, 29 December 1772.
46 'Wir sind die einzigen Einwohner dieses Landes, die Europäer bei sich wohnen haben und wir sind dafür dankbar, weil wir hier kaufen können, was wir brauchen.' DN, 19 January 1773; DN, 27 May 1772; DN, March 1773.
47 DN, Dezember 1773, DN, January 1774; Kölbing, *Missionen der evangelischen Brüder*, 58.

48 The Ship's Company or Labrador Company was founded in 1770. It was independent from the SFG, though most of the company's members came from the SFG. UÄK Protokolle, 29 September 1770, 17 January 1771, and 21 December 1770; letter, SFG to UÄK, 9 April 1771, Unitäts-Archiv Herrnhut (UA), R.15 Kb.17.a; Mason, *Moravian Church*, 46.

49 Jenness, *Eskimo Administration*, 18; DN, 27 May 1772: DN, March 1773.

50 DN, 3 June 1772; DN, 22 June 1772; DN, 23 June 1772; DN, 9 October 1772.

51 Hiller, 'Foundation,' 112; Jenness, *Eskimo Administration*, 19.

52 Hebron, 1830–1959; Zoar, 1865–95; Ramah, 1871–1908; Makkovik, 1895; Killinek, 1904–24; Happy Valley, 1954; North West River, 1960.

53 Hartmut Beck, *Brüder in vielen Völkern. 250 Jahre Mission der Brüdergemeine* (Erlangen: Verlag der Evangelisch-Lutherischen Mission, 1981), 274.

54 James Hiller, *The Moravian Church*, http://www.heritage.nf.ca/society/moravian.html, 27 June 2004; quote: Rollmann, *Labrador*, 10.

55 Jenness, *Eskimo Administration*, 22, 29, 38.

4 Model Farmers, Dubious Citizens: Reconsidering the Pennsylvania Germans of Upper Canada, 1786–1834[1]

ROSS D. FAIR

On 25 February 1831, Bishop Benjamin Eby, leader of the Waterloo Township settlement of Mennonites, stood before the County Registrar and declared: 'I do affirm that I have resided seven years in his Majesty's dominions, without having been during that time a stated resident in any foreign country, and that I will be faithful and bear true allegiance to the Sovereign of the united kingdom of Great Britain and Ireland, and of this province, as dependent thereon.'

He then picked up the registrar's quill and signed his name. By making this affirmation, Eby had finally become a British subject, though he had lived in Upper Canada for nearly twenty years. That same year, many other local Mennonites became British subjects as well. Between February and April alone, the registrar recorded the affirmations of some 140 adult male residents throughout Waterloo, Wilmot, Woolwich, and Dumfries Townships. Across the province thousands of other Americans, including many other Pennsylvania Germans, were naturalized under the terms of a law that had been passed by the provincial government in 1828.[2]

Historians of the Pennsylvania Germans in Upper Canada[3] have never mentioned or considered this important moment. Instead, they have focused exclusively on an earlier period, consistently portraying this immigrant group – composed of Mennonites and Brethren in Christ (known in nineteenth-century Upper Canada as Tunkers) – as Loyalist refugees who had arrived in the aftermath of the American Revolution, never having relinquished their rights and privileges as British subjects. Indeed, the American Revolution is consistently presented as the chief reason for the Pennsylvania Germans' departure for territory still governed by the British. The new republican government

of the United States, it is claimed, did not tolerate their pacifist religious practices, as had the colonial government of Pennsylvania, and
many Pennsylvania Germans chose to relocate to British soil in order
to regain such privileges as were promised them by British officials.
Because they have believed that the Pennsylvania Germans were British subjects, historians have seen no need to look for Pennsylvania-
German names among the lists of those naturalized under the terms
of the 1828 naturalization law, the aim of which was to secure British
rights and privileges for thousands of American settlers in Upper Canada. As I have argued elsewhere, the foundational myth of the United
Empire Loyalists, with its themes of loyalty and sacrifice, has provided
a valuable framework for interpreting the history of the Pennsylvania-
German communities of Ontario. The first published version of the
Pennsylvania-German immigrant narrative appeared in the 1890s, and
in the decades that followed, a focus on loyalty and sacrifice helped
protect these communities from being confused with the Germans
with whom Canadians were fighting in two world wars. More recently,
in modern multicultural Canada, historians have adjusted the narrative to identify these Pennsylvania-German immigrants as founders of
the wider German-Canadian community.[4]

The fragility of the Loyalist pedestal on which this immigrant group
has been placed is revealed when one pulls away the British flag in
which its immigrant experience has been wrapped. This chapter
describes some of the difficulties the Pennsylvania Germans encountered in their efforts to integrate their pacifist beliefs with those of
Upper Canadian society. A fresh examination of the political and
legal situation of the Pennsylvania Germans in Upper Canada is in
order; for as several other chapters in this volume make clear, there
is considerable interest in the Germanic communities that developed
around Ontario's original Pennsylvania-German settlements. If, as is
often emphasized, the Pennsylvania Germans provided the foundation of the wider German-Canadian community,[5] then it is critical that
we understand fully how that foundation was constructed. Only then
can we make connections between the integration of later Germanic
groups into Canadian society and the early experiences of the Pennsylvania Germans.

The principal barrier to their integration into provincial society was
not their Germanness. Rather, provincial administrators had to consider how prudent it was to extend tolerances to the pacifist sects, and
how far those indulgences might be extended under British law. This

study views the Pennsylvania Germans through the eyes of the provincial officials, who were rather cautious when it came to accommodating pacificist communities in the colony. It is crucial here to understand that Upper Canadian officials often bundled the Mennonites, the Tunkers, and the Quakers together when deciding whether to extend religious tolerances or to grant political rights. So this chapter explains how an understanding of the Pennsylvania Germans' integration into the colony must be achieved in tandem with an acknowledgment of the Quaker experience in Upper Canada.[6] To gain insight into this process of integration, this chapter will rely on legislative documents, communications among government officials, and the handful of communications that have been preserved between the pacifist sects and Upper Canadian authorities. Existing colonial documents indicate that Pennsylvania Germans, like most contemporary frontier settlers, did not record many thoughts about their place in the developing colonial society. For Upper Canada, petitions and other documents submitted to colonial authorities serve as rare glimpses into the moments when the Pennsylvania-German settlers felt compelled to defend the few religious tolerances that had been extended to them or to request additional tolerances and political rights. ·

This study has four sections. First, it examines the broadly accepted story that Upper Canada's first lieutenant governor, John Graves Simcoe, specifically invited the Quakers and Pennsylvania Germans to settle in his jurisdiction. Second, as that invitation included promises of religious tolerance for the peace sects, it examines the relationship between the provincial administration and the Mennonites, Tunkers, and Quakers with regard to the promise of exemption from militia service. Third, it takes a new look at religious rights in the province, for the issue of exemptions from militia service must be understood in the context of Church and State relations in Upper Canada. Finally, the paper examines the decade of the 1820s, when the dubious nature of the Pennsylvania Germans' citizenship was brought into sharp focus. Like thousands of other American aliens in the province, their future as residents of Upper Canada rested on the outcome of a debate that centred on the fundamental question of who in Upper Canada was entitled to the rights and privileges of British subjects. The Pennsylvania Germans were allowed to profess their allegiance to the Crown, but they were not made full citizens of the province until 1833, when the Upper Canadian government granted them civil rights and privileges equal to those of the other residents of the province.[7]

John Graves Simcoe as William Penn

In *The Trail of the Black Walnut* (1957), G. Elmore Reaman declares with confidence: 'The significance of the statement, "What William Penn was to Pennsylvania, John Graves Simcoe was to Ontario," can be easily explained.' He claims that Penn, in the late seventeenth century, had wisely invited the Palatinate and Swiss Germans to settle Pennsylvania 'as the right people to take over his lands,' and that Simcoe, a little more than a century later, was right to have invited Pennsylvania-German farmers to settle Upper Canada. The latter's interest in the Pennsylvania Germans, Reaman argues, stemmed from his service as a British officer during the American Revolution. Simcoe had been quartered for a winter in Philadelphia and 'realized what excellent farmers they were' for 'he had a close up view of the eastern counties of Pennsylvania as farmed by the Palatinate and Swiss Germans.' When Simcoe became lieutenant governor of the new territory of Upper Canada, Reaman continues, he remembered the farms he had seen in eastern Pennsylvania and was 'determined to invite those who farmed them to come to Canada.'[8] Although based on no more than two vague references offered by Simcoe in his correspondence, Reaman's claim has become embedded in the Pennsylvania-German narrative as *prima facie* evidence of the immigrant group's loyalty.[9]

Simcoe did spend a short time in Pennsylvania. He arrived from Boston with the 40th Regiment in 1777, was injured at the Battle of Brandywine Creek on 11 September, and was taken to Philadelphia to convalesce. A month later, he assumed command of the Queen's Rangers, who were camped outside Germantown northwest of Philadelphia; but he recalled his unit to Philadelphia, and it is quite possible that he did so without having travelled out from the city. Between mid-October and February 1778, he may have had contact with farmers outside Philadelphia, for the Rangers had been deployed to protect the local farmers who were bringing supplies into Philadelphia. In February the Queen's Rangers left Pennsylvania for good, and by 1781 Simcoe had returned to Britain. If he had been fascinated by German agricultural practices in southeastern Pennsylvania, he noted nothing in his otherwise detailed military journal or in his letters.[10]

When the old Province of Quebec was divided into Upper and Lower Canada in 1791, Simcoe left Britain to assume his new appointment in the upper province. Like many British officials, he believed that the American Revolution had been carried out by a radical minority and that the republican experiment would soon fail. Before leaving London, he had told his superior, Henry Dundas, Secretary of State for War and the Colonies: 'There are thousands of the Inhabitants of the United States whose affections are centred in the British Government and the British Name; who are positively enemies of Congress and to the late division of the Empire, many of their Connections have already taken refuge in Canada and it will be true Wisdom to invite and facilitate the emigration of this description of people in that Country.'[11] All that many Americans needed, he argued, was the right enticement. His supposed invitation to the Pennsylvania Germans must be analysed in this context.

While on his way to Upper Canada, Simcoe wintered in Quebec. In February 1792 he issued a proclamation offering two-hundred-acre grants of land to those willing to swear an oath of allegiance on their arrival to the province. Simcoe wanted his proclamation to be circulated as far and wide as possible, for he believed that his competitors were American land speculators, who would be trying to draw the same pool of prospective settlers to their lands along the western frontier of the United States. To prevent speculators from taking control of his province's frontier, Simcoe was offering free land solely to individual petitioners. Only at the lieutenant governor's discretion could an individual receive a grant larger than one thousand acres.[12]

Simcoe was proud of his proclamation and confident that it would succeed in its goals. Others, including Dundas, disagreed with Simcoe's open-door policy for immigration. Dundas was concerned that circulating the proclamation in the United States might heighten tensions between that country and Great Britain. So he strongly discouraged Simcoe from encouraging immigration to Upper Canada. If Simcoe's claims were correct, he argued, then a sufficient number of settlers would be arriving from the United States of their own accord. Population, he warned, was the result of a country's prosperity, but never a country's prosperity as such. An 'ingrafted Population, (if I may so call it), to a great extent and outrunning (as it must do), all those regulations, laws, usages, and customs, which grow up and go hand in hand with a progressive and regular Population, must I conceive in all cases be attended with a want of that regularity, and stability, which all, but particularly Colonial Governments, require.' Simcoe did not agree, pressing Dundas later in 1792 that the population growth of Upper Canada must 'not only be progressive and regular, but immediate and rapid.'[13]

Around six weeks after issuing his land proclamation, Simcoe received a letter from Charles Stevenson, the newly appointed Deputy Quartermaster General at Montreal. In it, Stevenson offered his opinions about the settlement of Upper Canada and reported on a Quaker who had once planned to settle some three thousand Quakers in the province. His specific information about Quakers in that letter suggests that he was replying to a request from Simcoe. Stevenson indicated that the Pennsylvania Quakers had been complaining recently 'of the present grievous taxes, with the prospect of their being increased, and the militia bill having passed that does not admit of religious scruples exempting from military duty.' He noted that Phineas Bond, Great Britain's Consul to the United States at Philadelphia, had suggested that 'with a little management' the Quakers would 'probably turn their thoughts to Canada.'[14] Stevenson's letter and Simcoe's subsequent actions suggest that the lieutenant governor was embarking on another of his many overly ambitious projects for Upper Canada.[15]

In his April 1792 letter to Dundas, Simcoe noted proudly that he would be sending a person to Pennsylvania to discuss the possibility of a 'large body of Quakers to emigrate.' Four months later, he informed Dundas that he had 'not hesitated to promise to the Quakers and other sects, the similar exemptions from Militia duties which they have always met with under the British Government.'[16] This latter report provides one of only two mentions by Simcoe of any sect other than the Quakers. The second came in the lieutenant governor's introductory letter to Bond in Philadelphia, which stated: 'Should any Society wish to emigrate, I should be happy to see those persons who should be authorized under mutual confidence for that purpose, and to give my best assistance to promote their views and establishment.'[17] At no time, however, did any British official ever name the Mennonites or Tunkers.

Indeed, more senior British officials continued to be wary of locating American Quakers on British North American territory, let alone other pacifist sects. They were also unclear as to what policy should guide the settlement of Quakers in the upper province.[18] In October 1793, Dundas sent Simcoe what appear to be the first unambiguous directions concerning the admissibility of Quakers as settlers in the province. In response to a circulated set of questions, Dundas agreed that 'every reasonable degree of encouragement should be given to the Quakers as they are perhaps of all others the most useful to an Infant Colony.' Exempting them from any taxes, however, would be 'impolitic if not impracticable,' and it might create discontent among other settlers of the province. The Canadas' Governor-in-Chief, Lord Dorchester, responding independently, agreed that Quakers were a 'useful People and of good example in a young Country,' but he too cautioned that 'exemptions may be carried too far.'[19] These responses from Dundas and Dorchester made no mention at all of other sects; but most important, they said nothing that would have actively discouraged Simcoe from enticing interested Quaker settlers. This, even though any invitation that might be extended to the peace sects of Pennsylvania would definitely *not* be in accordance with a clearly defined British policy.

Militia Laws

If Simcoe delivered any promise to the 'Quakers and other sects' at all, it was contained in this 1793 clause of Upper Canada's first militia act:

> [T]he persons called Quakers, Menonists, and Tunkers, who from certain scruples of conscience, decline bearing arms, shall not be compelled to serve in the said militia, but every person professing that he is one of the people called Quakers, Menonists or Tunkers, and producing a certificate of his being a Quaker, Menonist, or Tunker, signed by any three or more of the people (who are or shall be by them authorized to grant certificates for this or any other purpose of which a pastor, minister or preacher shall be one) shall be excused and exempted from serving in the said militia.[20]

In the first history written of the Mennonites of the Waterloo settlement, Ezra Eby – grandson of Benjamin Eby – made a direct link between this piece of legislation and the supposed invitation, claiming that 'the principal cause' of the Mennonite migration to Upper Canada 'may have been the great faith they had in the British Government in fulfilling their promise, made to them over one hundred years previously, in granting them exemption from military services and from taking the oaths.' Since the publication of his opinion in the 1890s, historians have consistently emphasized the ease with which the Pennsylvania Germans and their pacifist beliefs were integrated into Upper Canadian society through the exemptions granted to them, while consistently downplaying the financial burden of the exemption fines.[21]

Under the province's first militia act, adult males between sixteen and sixty who proved their membership in one of the three sects could avoid militia service by paying their local militia officer twenty shillings a year in times of peace and five pounds a year in times of war.

The act, rather than extending a friendly gesture of welcome, included a stern warning that an individual who did not pay his fine could have his goods and chattels seized and sold in order to raise enough money to pay the fine plus expenses. Only if the latter method of securing the fine was deemed 'oppressive' could the oppressed complain to the County Lieutenant or Deputy Lieutenant – the very same individual charged by the act with mustering the militia and securing payment from the objectors for non-attendance.[22]

Many Quakers, Mennonites, and Tunkers avoided paying their fines – or that, at least, was the perception among some provincial militia leaders. In 1801, Samuel Street, the Deputy Lieutenant of Lincoln County, thought it necessary to remind the three sects of their obligations to the militia. In his notice of the upcoming militia muster for Lincoln County, Street made it clear that the militia laws required members of the sects to do more than simply pay a fine. The process, reminded Street, required them to attend the muster 'with such certificates as the law requires, and pay the exemption money (if not sooner paid to the deputy-lieutenant of said riding) or expect to be proceeded against as the law in such case directs.'[23]

A few years later, John McGill, the Lieutenant of York County, reminded his deputy and Captain of the York Militia, William Jarvis, that Mennonites, Quakers, and Tunkers who did not pay their fines were to be considered with the same regard as any other individual who was absent from the militia muster. To Captain William Fummerfelt of the York Militia at Markham, where settlements of both Quakers and Mennonites were to be found, McGill issued a reminder that members of those communities who could not produce a certificate were 'to be considered as a part of the Militia and subject to attend all Parades and Musters.'[24]

On occasion, the provincial government imprisoned those who did not pay militia fines. In 1808, six Quakers in the York jail begged Lieutenant Governor Francis Gore for relief of their situation. Despite the prisoners' claims that they were men 'who cheerfully comply with every Law except that which oblidges [sic] us to contribute to the carrying on war,' Gore was unmoved. He informed the two members of the House of Assembly who had presented the prisoners' petition 'that he was well disposed to the Quakers in general and sensible of their industrious and peaceable pursuits, but that when the Laws were once made that they must be put in force and that it was a matter of conscience with him not to permit them to be disregarded.' Although the

Quakers 'might have been attached to the King's interest in the Revolutionary War,' he argued, any further exemptions extended to the Quakers 'should have been introduced when the Militia Law was passed.'[25]

Although this example pertains to Quaker males abiding by their faith, the wider context of the incident illustrates that it was a poor time for anyone to be shirking his militia obligations. By 1808, it was becoming increasingly clear that war was looming between Britain and the United States, and Upper Canada had good reasons to fear that the battle lines would be drawn along the border with the United States. As part of the preparations for defending the province, the government passed a new militia act in March that added provisions for a jail term of up to one month for those who did not pay their militia fines. And it altered the method of paying fines for the Quakers, Mennonites, and Tunkers. The previous law had required the male members of the sects to pay their fines to the leaders of the local militia muster; now they had to register their names with the local District Treasurer and offer him the annual fine prior to the first day of December.[26] Perhaps the government had noticed that it upset the peace sects that they had to pay their exemption fines to militia personnel for military purposes. More likely, however, the government's decision was based on the premise that District Treasurers could keep more regular accounts of the fines paid and of delinquent individuals than could the militia leaders.

The changes did not satisfy the Pennsylvania Germans. In February 1810, two petitions – the first signed by two preachers, two elders, and 'thirty-five members of the Society of Mennonists and Tunkers,' and the second signed by thirty-four individuals – were read in the House of Assembly. Tradition has it that the main advocate for changes to the militia laws in both 1808 and 1810 was Bishop John Winger, the leader of the Tunker community on the Niagara Peninsula.[27] He and the other petitioners protested the requirement that an individual belonging to either sect had to produce a certificate proving his membership when paying his annual fine. Both Mennonites and Tunkers practiced adult baptism, the petitioners noted, and many of their sons 'now under age and incapable of judging in matters of conscience, are not as yet actually considered as Church members, and cannot of course secure the necessary certificates.' Therefore, the petitioners requested that they might also be exempted from militia service 'by paying the commutation money until they arrive at the age of twenty-one, or until they be admitted as Church Members.' They also asked the government to consider reducing the amounts of the annual fines, after taking into consideration 'the many difficulties which poor people, with large families, have to labour under in new settlements.'[28] No reductions in fines were forthcoming, though the petitions did spawn legislation 'for the relief of Minors of the Societies of Mennonists and Tunkers' that freed Pennsylvania-German males between sixteen and twenty-one from militia duty on payment of the standard annual fine.[29] While this act provided a small degree of tolerance, an amendment to the militia act passed during the following year further emphasized the government's overall aims.

During the same 1810 session, the House of Assembly had requested information concerning the amount of fines paid to the government by members of the peace sects. Upset that the assembly's request could not be answered (presumably due to poor record keeping), David McGregor Rogers, who represented a riding of the province settled by Quakers, tried to shepherd a bill through the assembly aimed at altering the militia fines. Two things suggest that the mood of the assembly was not right for such a bill. First, Rogers himself agreed to pull the bill prior to its third reading.[30] Second, the bill the provincial parliament did pass during the subsequent session reflected an increasing interest in maintaining a strong militia as the United States and Britain drifted closer to war. It appears that the Upper Canadian government was growing tired of having to sell the belongings of Quakers in order to raise money equal to the fines. Under the new act, any money raised from the sale of a Quaker's chattels that exceeded the cost of the fine would no longer be returned to the Quaker in question. Instead, the money would be paid to the District Treasurer, to be kept for that individual's future payments toward his annual exemption from the militia.[31] Although the act was not directed at the Mennonites or Tunkers, the message to all Upper Canadians was clear: non-payment of militia fines was a serious offence. This was a tone far different from the supposed welcome that the militia laws had extended to the peace sects.

In his study of pacifism in Upper Canada, Peter Brock downplays the effect the militia fines had on the Mennonites and Tunkers. He suggests that, compared to the Quakers, the Mennonites and Tunkers adopted 'a much less aggressive attitude, and consequently there existed in their case fewer possibilities of confrontation between military obligations and sectarian conscience.'[32] However, the characteristics he ascribes to the Pennsylvania Germans seem to be based on his discovery of more Quaker than Mennonite or Tunker examples of conflict with the government over non-payment of militia fines, combined with an assumption that the enforcement of militia duty or the collection of fines was uniform across the province. This was certainly not the case.

When war did break out in 1812, provincial officials tried to keep a watchful eye on the activities of the Mennonites, Tunkers, and Quakers. At the end of 1813, John McGill, the Inspector General of the province, issued a circular to each District Treasurer requesting 'with the least possible delay' a return enumerating all such Quakers, Menonists, and Tunkers who had claimed exemption from militia service in 1812 or 1813, noting who had and who had not paid their fines.[33] By the following June, McGill was frustrated that such lists had not been supplied to him from each district, for the delay prevented him from knowing what money 'should have been paid into the hands of the Receiver General.' Accordingly, he issued a new directive that the District Treasurers furnish him with this information. There is no evidence that he was any more successful on his second attempt. District Treasurers did not appear to have been any better than militia officials at ensuring that every Mennonite, Tunker, and Quaker male paid his militia fines. Moreover, some were confused as to what they should do with the money they had collected.[34]

In 1814, the wartime government, under increasing pressure to maintain a functioning militia with both men and money, doubled the wartime exemption fine for Mennonites, Quakers, and Tunkers to ten pounds per year. Rules for seizing and selling chattels continued to apply to those who refused to pay; however, the government did offer some relief to those who tried to abide by the new laws yet who could not raise the entire fine. In specific cases, a justice of the peace could refer a case of non-payment to the local militia commander to allow the acceptance of a partial payment of the fine.[35]

Brock also claims that after the War of 1812, the 'military question lost much of its urgency for the Canadian peace sects.'[36] This is true, but he overlooks the fundamental reason for the decrease in concern among the Mennonites and Tunkers in particular. In 1816, reacting to the fear of American settlers in the province who had done little to support the British cause during the conflict, the provincial government passed new militia regulations that required militia duty only from each adult male between age sixteen and sixty who was 'a natural born subject of his Majesty naturalized by an act of the British parliament, or a subject of his Majesty having become such by the cession of Canada, or a person who has taken the oath of allegiance.'[37] The sudden loss of interest in militia matters among the Pennsylvania Germans did not stem from any tacit approval of the government regulations, as Brock suggests. Instead, many men who otherwise would have had to pay for their exemption from the militia were now exempt because they were not British subjects.

By 1815, some provincial officials had been singling out the Pennsylvania Germans among the suspicious body of American settlers in Upper Canada. Reverend John Strachan, the Anglican Archdeacon of Toronto, Executive Councillor, and a man emerging as one of the most influential voices among the Upper Canadian elite, asserted:

> No Quakers, Tunkards or religionists who refuse to bear arms to be admitted [into the province]. They have been a clog – leaning to the Enemy – hiding deserters obstructing the service by bad example & advice – holding back their produce or selling it at exhorbitant prices – refusing to transport stores – crying down the Government paper issue. Treat those well who have been admitted but our population is too small to allow a large portion to be non Combatants.[38]

For almost fifteen years, the question of what to do with the non-British residents of the province generated fiery debates in the provincial legislature. Not until 1828 did the Upper Canadian government agree on a naturalization act, allowing many of the illegal American residents to become British subjects. Accordingly, those who became naturalized were once again eligible for militia duty; hence, many Pennsylvania Germans were required to pay for their exemption once again. Not surprisingly, by the early 1830s leaders of the peace sects had restarted their petitioning for the elimination of the annual militia fines or at least a reduction of them.[39]

The Mennonites, Quakers, and Tunkers did not succeed in their endeavours until the 1833–4 parliamentary session. In response to the petition of twenty-eight Mennonites and Tunkers, the 1834 'Act for the relief of certain Religious denominations of persons called Menonists, Tunkers and Quakers' reduced the annual exemption fine from twenty shillings to ten shillings during peacetime, and the wartime fine to five pounds per year. Mennonites, Quakers, and Tunkers who suffered infirmities or who were aliens were not required to pay the fine. And fines paid would no longer be directed toward military purposes. Instead, the new law required that adult males of the three sects record their name and place of residence with the local tax assessor, who was now responsible for collecting fines and for turning the money over to the District Treasurer. The funds collected would be employed to complement the expenditures on 'Public Roads, Highways and Bridges' in the areas where the fines were collected.[40] Although the government had granted more lenient terms for exemption, it would take another twenty-one years for the Mennonites, Quakers, and Tunkers to secure free exemption from militia duty.[41]

Religious Disabilities

The subject of militia fines must also be placed in the wider context of Church and State relations in Upper Canada. Contrary to the standard claim that British officials welcomed the Pennsylvania Germans to the province with offers of religious freedoms, the immigrants arrived in a province that was anything but religiously tolerant. Whereas the U.S. Constitution had set forth the separation of Church and State, Upper Canada's constitution provided for the Church of England to be the established church of the province, with one-seventh of the land surveyed in every township reserved for its use. From the birth of the province, all denominations that were not Church of England were denied certain religious rights and privileges, and the Mennonites and Tunkers were among a diverse collection of denominations whose rights were thereby denied – a group that included Lutherans, Baptists, Congregationalists, Quakers, and Moravians. Among the non-Anglican denominations in the colony, it was Presbyterians, Methodists, and Roman Catholics who wielded the greatest political influence, for they were the largest and their growth was easily outpacing that of Anglican congregations. By the time the Pennsylvania Germans arrived, these denominations had begun a decades-long struggle to secure the right to perform marriages and to own church property. The Mennonites and Tunkers would owe much to these denominations for their integration into Upper Canadian society.

Following the commands of his superiors in London, Lieutenant Governor Simcoe had been determined to invest the Church of England with a great deal of religious control over the lives of the colonists. With the adoption of English civil law for the province during the first legislature of 1792, Upper Canada also aimed to adopt the requirement that Anglican clergymen validate all marriages.[42] An imperfect marriage act for Upper Canada came into effect in 1793, after the House of Assembly was 'prevailed upon to withdraw' its amendment to a Legislative Council bill 'giving power to Ministers of every sect and denomination [...] to solemnize Matrimony.'[43] It granted clergy of the Church of

England the sole right to perform marriages even though there were only two such clergymen in the province. Only where there was no Anglican clergyman within an eighteen-mile radius did the law allow for civil marriages to be performed without previous state validation in the form of a certificate issued by the Church of England.[44]

Not surprisingly, the province's various denominations did not agree with the new marriage laws. Simcoe recorded that on the first day of the 1794 session of parliament, 'Petitions from Mennonists, Tunkers & others [had been] brought forward praying that their Ministers might be authorized to solemnize Marriage with validity.' Their petition was disregarded, for offering one or two small religious sects an exclusion from the act would only enrage the much larger numbers of Protestant and Roman Catholic congregations throughout the province. In fact, no constructive discussion could be held on the issue in the provincial legislature because of the intense feelings it generated.[45]

The matter remained unresolved for another five years. Simcoe, facing increasing pressure from the non-Anglican denominations, devised a new plan in 1796 that would maintain the central authority of the Church of England by investing it with the power to grant licences to non-Anglican clergy, who could then perform legal marriage ceremonies.[46] New provisions allowed 'the minister or clergyman of any congregation or religious community of persons, professing to be members of the church of Scotland, or Lutherans, or Calvinists,' to perform marriages, provided that one of the individuals to be married had been a member of 'such congregation or religious community' at least six months prior to the ceremony. Eligible clergyman had to be recognized by the state and obtain the necessary marriage certificates from a justice of the peace.[47]

Mennonites and Tunkers were covered under this legislation, for they were viewed as Calvinists.[48] But there was a serious inconsistency in Upper Canadian law with regard to these two sects. The new law required clergymen to swear an oath of allegiance in front of a justice of the peace, something the Mennonite and Tunker faiths prevented their members from doing. A British law of 1749 allowed Quakers to substitute an affirmation for an oath in such cases, but Upper Canadian law would not extend that right to Mennonites and Tunkers until 1809. Therefore, technically speaking, the religious leaders of the Pennsylvania Germans would not be able to take complete, lawful advantage of the marriage act's provisions until after the 1809 law was passed.[49]

In many of the congregational and genealogical histories of the Mennonite, Tunker, and Quaker communities of Upper Canada, historians have highlighted the great faith of the early pioneers, who often donated some of their property for a church or a burial ground.[50] While such donations may certainly have been motivated by faith, prior to 1828 they were a necessity. Only congregations of the established Church of England had the legal right to possess land on which to build churches or rectories or to open burial grounds. All other denominations had to do so on privately donated land. Though little discussed in the history of the colony, thirty-four years of Upper Canadian development passed before the matter was resolved.

A bill 'to enable Societies professing Christianity to hold lands for certain purposes' was first tabled in the House of Assembly in November 1825. Although the assembly offered solid support for the measure, the Legislative Council treated it as it had been treating an increasing number of House of Assembly measures by completely rewriting the bill and returning it to the lower chamber. The assembly had agreed to a bill allowing all Christian societies in the province to own property; the bill that was returned by the Legislative Council itemized those eligible – Mennonites, Tunkers, Quakers, and Moravians were included – and limited each congregation of the denominations listed to five acres in any one township in the province. The amendments were unpalatable to the House of Assembly, and it set the matter aside.[51] Again during the following session, the House of Assembly passed a new bill 'to enable religious societies to hold lands for certain purposes.' The Legislative Council discussed the bill in committee on five different occasions and even formed a separate committee to consider the bill. In the end, however, the upper chamber simply discarded the issue.[52] A similar scenario emerged during the 1828 parliamentary session. Once again the Legislative Council disagreed with an assembly bill regarding denominational property rights and returned it with amendments. This time, however, two conferences with the Legislative Council were held on the matter, and the assembly agreed that while it did not concur completely with the amended bill, it was expedient to see the measure pass.[53] The act 'for the relief of Religious Societies therein mentioned' allowed any congregation of 'Presbyterians, Lutherans, Calvinists, Methodists, Congregationalists, Independents, Anabaptists, Quakers, Mennonists, Tunkers, or Moravians' to possess up to five acres 'for the site of a church, meeting house, or chapel, or burying ground.' Each of the peace sects could consider itself fortunate, for other denominations of Christians not listed in the 1828 act had to wait until 1845 to receive similar rights.[54]

Civil Disabilities

Hand in hand with the advancement of religious rights came the acquisition of political rights for the Pennsylvania Germans. The Protestant
denominations had led the fight for the former set of rights; it was the
Quakers who opened the path for Mennonites and Tunkers to become
more politically integrated with Upper Canadian society. During the
province's first parliamentary elections in August 1792, Philip Dorland,
a Quaker, had been elected to the House of Assembly by the voters of
his riding. However, the Speaker prevented Dorland from taking his
seat as a member of the assembly, for in accordance with his religious
beliefs, Dorland had refused to swear the prescribed oath of office. He
attempted to substitute an affirmation for the oath, but this was rejected
by both the Speaker and the other members of the legislature, and a
writ was issued for a new election in Dorland's riding.[55]

Simcoe, who wished to attract Quakers to the province, solicited the
advice of his superior, asking Henry Dundas whether an affirmation
could 'be considered as legal as an Oath and enable them to have a seat
in the Assembly, Legislative Council, &c.'[56] Dundas replied that under
British law, 'in most instances the Affirmation of a Quaker is equivalent
to an Oath.' Dundas doubted, however, whether the oath prescribed
by the Constitutional Act to be taken by all members of the Legislative Council and House of Assembly could be dispensed with in any
particular instance. Moreover, he was unsure whether a Quaker could
substitute an affirmation if one 'to the same tenor and effect' as the oath
were created. Dundas explained that the oath 'requires him to "defend
His Majesty to the utmost of his Power against all traitorous Conspira-
cies and Attempts, &c.," this obliges him to personal service and to use
force if necessary, whereas the Principles of Persons of his Persuasion
extend only to their being obedient to The King and the Government,
and not to the bearing of Arms in their defence.' On the basis of this
advice, as well as Governor Dorchester's opinion that 'Exemptions
may be carried too far,' Simcoe abandoned any plans to obtain rights
for the Quakers to hold office or to vote.[57]

The taking of oaths was a significant part of life in the British Empire,
for under British law, there were many occasions when legal oaths were
required.[58] Certain exemptions from swearing oaths by the addition
of affirmations had first been allowed by the Toleration Act of 1689.
Under its provisions, those who could not swear oaths of allegiance
and supremacy owing to religious beliefs could make a 'declaration of

fidelity.' Whereas an oath required the words 'I swear,' and 'so help me God,' an affirmation only required the statement 'I do solemnly profess and declare.' By 1749, legislation had been enacted that allowed Quakers to offer an affirmation whenever an oath was required, except in order to give evidence in criminal cases, to serve on juries, or to assume any government office or position.[59] In adopting British law through the Constitutional Act of 1791, Upper Canada adopted Britain's legal tolerance of Quakers, but that set of laws did not automatically cover the Pennsylvania-German sects.

Several years after Simcoe's departure from the province, the Quakers appeared again on the government agenda. During the legislative session of 1801, the assembly passed legislation granting 'indulgences' to Quakers, Mennonites, and Tunkers, but the Legislative Council refused to even give the bill a second reading.[60] Five years later, Thomas Dorland, the brother of Philip and an assemblyman who represented the Quaker settlements in his riding of Lennox and Addington, introduced a bill 'for removing doubts respecting the affirmation of the people called Quakers.' Although initially directed at Quakers alone, Mennonites and Tunkers were added to the bill's terms during debate, and it was renamed 'the Bill for relieving Dissenters of the Religious Societies of Quakers, Mennonites and Tunkers from certain legal disabilities.' Once again, however, the Legislative Council refused to be as liberal as the elected members of the lower chamber and discharged the bill from its agenda.[61] The only legal extension offered by the Upper Canadian government in the prewar years came in 1809, a time when more and more Pennsylvania Germans were arriving in the province. Only then did the government grant the Mennonites and Tunkers the right to use an 'affirmation or declaration' where an oath was required 'in the same manner and form as a Quaker by the laws now in force is required to do so.' To take advantage of this new tolerance, a member of either sect would have to affirm or declare that he was a Mennonite or Tunker. And the provincial parliament went no further than it felt obliged. As with the Quakers, this act did not allow Mennonites or Tunkers to 'be qualified or permitted to give evidence in any criminal cases, or to serve on juries in criminal cases, or to hold or enjoy any office or place in the government' in the province.[62] After the War of 1812, however, it became very apparent that many Pennsylvania Germans in the province had no claim to these legal rights at all, for they had been declared illegal aliens.

The lax attitude toward formalizing citizenship that had characterized Upper Canadian settlement prior to the War of 1812 became a serious issue for provincial officials in the aftermath of the conflict. First, Lieutenant Governor Gore tried in 1815 to enforce a more general restriction on all American immigration to Upper Canada by issuing an order to the local magistrates forbidding them to administer the oath of allegiance to individuals arriving from the United States. Then Lord Bathurst, Secretary of State for the Colonies, delivered his opinion in 1817 that the terms of Britain's 1790 settlement act did not qualify an American citizen to hold lands. That legislation had been directed solely at British subjects wishing to settle British territory, he claimed. An act passed in 1740 held precedent over the 1790 act, he argued, and under its terms a continued residence of seven years was an 'indispensable condition of being entitled to hold Lands.' Bathurst ordered a proclamation be issued in Upper Canada stating that 'no Foreigner will be permitted to hold Lands in the Province unless he shall inhabit or reside for the space of seven years or more in any of His Majesty's Colonies in America and shall not have been absent out of some of the said Colonies for a longer space than two Months at any one time during the said seven years.' He also ordered that the necessary legal proceedings be taken to dispossess 'those persons not entitled to the privileges of Natural Born Subjects who shall since the War have possessed themselves of Lands under any other circumstances than those admitted by the Law.'[63]

Although these orders launched the province into years of political turmoil, the restrictions posed little problem for the Mennonite families who continued to arrive in the Waterloo settlements from Pennsylvania each year between 1815 and 1829.[64] They were able to circumvent the new restrictions, for the lands on which they would be settling had been purchased through the Germany Company in Pennsylvania. Not having received individual land grants directly from the Crown, these Pennsylvania-German immigrants saw no need to affirm their allegiance in front of a government official before taking possession of their Upper Canadian lands. This course of action, however, would seriously jeopardize their right to maintain possession of their land.

Seven years after Bathurst's instructions, the awkward issue of who in Upper Canada was eligible to become a British subject was clarified by a British legal decision. In *Thomas vs. Acklam* it was ruled that every American-born person who had continued to reside in the United States following the Peace of Paris in 1783 had effectively relinquished British allegiance. Furthermore, any children of such a person born after that date were to be considered aliens under British law.[65] This new ruling, which affected about two-thirds of the province's population, meant that the only Pennsylvania Germans eligible to become naturalized as British subjects were those who had affirmed their allegiance after the passage of the 1809 law that allowed them to do so, and who had lived in the province continuously for more than seven years. For the next several years, the Pennsylvania Germans, along with thousands of other aliens in the province, must have held their breath for word that they would be able to retain their property and remain in the province.

Finally, in the spring of 1828, the provincial and imperial governments agreed on a method by which the many American aliens in Upper Canada could be naturalized. First, all those persons who had received a grant of land from the Crown, those who had held public office, those who had taken an oath or affirmed their allegiance, and those who had settled in the province before 1828 and had lived there continuously were 'admitted and confirmed in all the privileges of British birth.' Those who had not yet taken an oath or affirmation of their allegiance were required to do so. Furthermore, any person who was resident of the province on 1 March 1828 and who did not fall into the above categories could be naturalized after the period of seven years' continuous residence upon taking the oath or affirming his allegiance.[66] That many Mennonites, Quakers, and Tunkers living in Upper Canada – including Benjamin Eby – had not become British subjects prior to 1828 is witnessed by the list of those naturalized under the 1828 act compiled by the Canadian government in 1841.[67]

As the War of 1812 receded deeper into the past, and as the Pennsylvania-German settlements in the Niagara, Waterloo, and Markham regions developed into thriving farming communities, the Upper Canadian government viewed such immigrants with much less suspicion than suggested by Strachan's 1815 view. By 1827 a group of Mennonites in Pennsylvania had recognized the impending Naturalization Act's implications for the legal title of 'large portions of Land in the Townships of Waterloo and Woolwich' that they had purchased through the German Company. Unable to emigrate because they could not sell their property in Pennsylvania, they petitioned the Upper Canadian government in January 1828 for confirmation of the legal titles to their land in the province. The House of Assembly passed a bill in accordance with the petitioners' wishes. When the bill was sent to the Legislative Council for its approval, a select committee of that chamber considered the matter in detail and agreed that the Pennsylvania Germans should be offered the assistance they required, in part because their ancestors had immigrated to Pennsylvania before the Revolution, and in part because those who had already settled in Waterloo and Woolwich Townships were 'quiet, industrious, and inoffensive, inhabitants.' The Council passed the bill without amendment, giving the twenty individuals rights as if they were natural-born British subjects of Upper Canada.[68]

Shortly after the Naturalization Act offered a way for the Pennsylvania Germans to become British subjects, they received new political rights thanks in large measure to the British government's increasingly liberal attitude toward Quakers. In 1828 the British parliament had extended to Quakers and Moravians the rights of affirmation when it came to giving evidence in either criminal or civil cases, and the following year the Upper Canadian government brought its legal code into line by passing a law 'to provide for the admission of the evidence of Quakers, Menonists, Tunkers, and Moravians in criminal cases.' Notably, the act went no further than the British law required, continuing to exclude such individuals from serving as *jurors* in criminal cases.[69]

Five years later, word arrived in Upper Canada of the British government's passage of the Quakers and Moravians Act, which permitted an affirmation instead of an oath 'in all places and for all purposes where an oath is or shall be required.' The news arrived just as the Upper Canadian government was making its third attempt – this one successful – to remove the necessity of taking particular oaths and communion on assuming any provincial office. But candidates would still be required to take an oath of allegiance, and no option for substituting an affirmation had been extended in this case. This compromise solution, the product of much political squabbling, proved to be for naught, for news of the British statute required the Upper Canadian government to liberalize its laws accordingly.[70]

Benjamin Eby's naturalization in 1831 occurred during an era of important changes for the Pennsylvania-German communities of Upper Canada. By the late 1820s the Pennsylvania Germans had begun to shed their characterization as dubious citizens. Also, they could be naturalized as British subjects, thus securing title to the lands they occupied. By the early 1830s the Upper Canadian government had allowed for their more complete integration into provincial society by extending to them political rights and privileges equal to those of the province's other residents. As citizens, whose religious communities were now tolerated, they were also granted a reduction in fines for their exemption from militia service.

None of these gains can be appreciated unless we set aside the erroneous belief that the Pennsylvania Germans who immigrated to Upper Canada had been British subjects who accepted an official invitation to relocate to British soil following the American Revolution in order to live under a government that fully tolerated their religious beliefs. The Pennsylvania Germans gained their tolerances only after more than thirty-five years of pressuring the provincial government for change and with the vital assistance of other religious groups in the province. The religious beliefs of the Mennonites and Tunkers had posed a fundamental barrier to their integration into an Upper Canadian state that was not particularly tolerant of religious diversity. Moreover, as a result of a fundamental misunderstanding of the process whereby American immigrants could become British subjects and take possession of land in Upper Canada, for a time following the War of 1812, the future existence of the growing Mennonite and Tunker communities in the province had been in jeopardy. Bishop Eby's signature on a government list of naturalized persons was a strong signal that this serious threat had passed.

NOTES

1 Initial investigation into this subject was conducted with funding from an Edna Staebler Research Fellowship offered by the Joseph Schneider Haus Museum, Kitchener, Ontario.
2 Province of Canada, Legislative Council, *Journals*, 1841, Appendix 21, 'Schedule of the names of persons [...] who have taken the oaths of Allegiance.'
3 In this paper, the term 'Pennsylvania Germans' refers to the several thousand Mennonites and Tunkers (also known as Dunkers, River Brethren, and more formally as Brethren in Christ) who immigrated to Upper Canada from their communities in southeastern Pennsylvania between the 1780s and the 1830s. The few individuals and families who arrived in the 1780s crossed into the Niagara Peninsula and settled along Twenty-Mile Creek. A larger wave of migration followed 1800 with the purchase of the lands that would shape the Waterloo settlement. Chain migration continued to Waterloo until the mid-1830s, with individuals and families also

heading to a third destination, lands in Markham and Whitchurch Townships, north of the provincial capital of York/Toronto.

4 My detailed historiographical analysis of the Pennsylvania-German immigrant narrative from the 1890s to the late twentieth century is contained in '"Theirs was a deeper purpose": The Pennsylvania Germans of Ontario and the Craft of the Homemaking Myth,' *Canadian Historical Review* 87, no. 4 (December 2006): 653–84.

5 See, for example, Frank H. Epp, *Mennonites in Canada, 1786–1920: The History of a Separate People* (Toronto: MacMillan of Canada, 1974); Gottlieb Leibbrandt, *Little Paradise: The Saga of the German Canadians of Waterloo County, Ontario 1800–1975* (Kitchener: Allprint Company, 1980); K.M. McLaughlin, *The Germans in Canada* (Ottawa: Canadian Historical Association, 1985, Booklet #11).

6 Studies of Mennonite, Tunker, and Quaker migration from Pennsylvania to Upper Canada beg for comparison; however, they remain separate because authors emphasize individual community development, genealogical connections, or religious faith. See, for example, Arthur G. Dorland, *A History of the Society of Friends (Quakers) in Canada* (Toronto: MacMillan of Canada, 1927); Richard MacMaster, 'Friends in the Niagara Peninsula 1786–1802,' in *Faith, Friends, and Fragmentation: Essays on Nineteenth Century Quakerism in Canada,* ed. Albert Schrauwers (Toronto: Canadian Friends Historical Association, 1995), 1–11; Elizabeth Hovinen, 'Migration of the Quakers from Pennsylvania to Upper Canada 1800—1820,' MA thesis, York University, 1976; Robynne Rogers Healey, *From Quaker to Upper Canadian: Faith and Community among Yonge Street Friends, 1801–1850* (Montreal and Kingston: McGill–Queen's University Press, 2006).

7 In the British sense, 'subject' and 'citizen' are quite similar. The former denotes an individual who has the right to live in a particular country or colony governed by the monarch, while the latter denotes a member of a particular country who possesses rights and privileges because they were born in the country or were granted them upon naturalization. As will be shown in this chapter, the subtle difference becomes quite important in the case of the Pennsylvania Germans. They became British subjects through naturalization, but due to their religious beliefs, certain rights and privileges were withheld. Thus, they became subjects first and citizens later when additional rights and privileges were granted to them.

8 G. Elmore Reaman, *The Trail of the Black Walnut* (Toronto: McClelland and Stewart, 1957), 83.

9 Simcoe's invitation had been mentioned earlier in W.H. Breithaupt, 'First Settlements of Pennsylvania Mennonites in Upper Canada,' *Ontario His-*

torical Society Papers and Records 23 (1926): 8–14; and was mentioned in E. Morris Sider's contemporary article, 'Nonresistance in the Early Brethren in Christ Church in Ontario,' *Mennonite Quarterly Review* 31 (October 1957): 278–86. Reaman's interpretation has been repeated in several later studies of the Pennsylvania Germans in Upper Canada. See Epp, *Mennonites in Canada*, 99–100; Leibbrandt, *Little Paradise*, 6–7; McLaughlin, *The Germans in Canada*, 7; Peter Brock, 'Accounting for Difference: The Problem of Pacifism in Early Upper Canada,' *Ontario History* 90 (1998): 19.

10 Mary Beacock Fryer and Christopher Dracott, *John Graves Simcoe, 1752–1806: A Biography* (Toronto: Dundurn Press, 1998), 28, 36–8; John Graves Simcoe, *Simcoe's Military Journal* (1784. Reprint. Toronto: Baxter Publishing, 1962).

11 'Simcoe to Dundas,' London, 30 June 1791, in E.A. Cruikshank ed., *The Correspondence of Lieutenant Governor John Graves Simcoe*, vol. 1 (Toronto: Ontario Historical Society, 1923), 27. See also 'Simcoe to Dundas,' Quebec, 16 February 1792, *The Correspondence* vol. 1, 113.

12 'Proclamation,' 7 February 1792, *The Correspondence*, vol. 1, 108–09; 'Simcoe to Dundas,' Quebec, 28 April 1792, *The Correspondence*, vol. 1, 142.

13 'Dundas to Simcoe,' Whitehall, 12 July 1792, *The Correspondence*, vol. 1, 178; and 'Simcoe to Dundas,' Niagara, 23 November 1792, *The Correspondence*, vol. 1, 264. For the opinions of another contemporary who did not share Simcoe's belief in the numbers of individuals in the United States wishing to immigrate to British territory, see Duc De La Rochefoucault Liancourt, *Travels through the United States of America* (London: 1799), 231–2, 237–40.

14 'Charles Stevenson to Simcoe,' Montreal, 27 March 1792, *The Correspondence*, vol. 1, 124.

15 One of Simcoe's biographers has described Simcoe as an 'intellectual magpie' who promoted unfocused and inconsistent schemes for Upper Canada. S.R. Mealing, 'The Enthusiasms of John Graves Simcoe,' in *Historical Essays on Upper Canada*, ed. J.K. Johnson (Toronto: McClelland and Stewart, 1975), 314.

16 'Simcoe to Dundas,' Quebec, 28 April 1792, *The Correspondence*, vol. 1, 142; 'Same to same,' Niagara, 20 August, 1792,' *The Correspondence*, vol. 1, 198–9.

17 'Simcoe to Bond,' Quebec, 7 May 1792, *The Correspondence*, vol. 1, 154.

18 As early as 1788, Bond had expressed concern to his counterparts in London over the plight of the Quakers of Philadelphia. He had suggested, 'perhaps there never was a more favorable period…to encourage the introduction of settlers into Canada from hence; to which country a number of sober well-disposed persons among the Quakers have already

directed their views.' Bond noted that it was only the French land holding system, in particular the requirement of tithes to the French clergy within the Province of Quebec, that had discouraged the Quakers from emigrating. With the creation of Upper Canada, that problem had been eliminated, though no policy with regard to Quakers had been settled upon by the time of Simcoe's interest in the subject in 1792. 'Bond to Lord Carmarthen,' Philadelphia, 28 June 1788, *Annual Report of the American Historical Association for the year 1896*, vol. 1, 568. Also see 'Bond to Evan Nepean,' Philadelphia, 16 November 1788, 583–9; and LAC, MG 11, C.O. 42, vol. 18, 'Points to be decided previous to the departure of Sir Guy Carleton, [1786].'

19 'Lord Dorchester's remarks on Capt. Stevenson's suggestions,' Portsmouth, 4 August 1793, *The Correspondence*, vol. 2, 3; 'Dundas to Simcoe,' Whitehall, 2 October 1793, *The Correspondence*, vol. 2, 82–3.

20 Upper Canada, *Statutes*, 1793, 33 Geo. 3, c. 1.

21 Ezra E. Eby, *A Biographical History of Waterloo Township and other townships of the County: being a history of the early settlers and their descendants, mostly all of Pennsylvania Dutch origin, as also much other unpublished historical information, chiefly of a local character* (Berlin, Ontario: [n.p.], 1895), 9. For an extended analysis of this theme, see my article, '"Theirs was a deeper purpose."'

22 Upper Canada, *Statutes*, 1793, 33 Geo. 3, c. 1.

23 'Notice is hereby given,' *Niagara Herald*, 23 May 1801, 3.

24 Toronto Reference Library (TRL), Samuel Jarvis Papers, 'John McGill to William Jarvis, York, November 29, 1807'; Archives of Ontario (AO), Miscellaneous Collection 1807 #1, 'List of Names of Markham Militia and of those exempt, 1800–07.'

25 The two Members of the Assembly were David McGregor Rogers (Hastings and Northumberland) and Thomas Dorland (Lennox and Addington). LAC, RG 5 A1, Upper Canada Sundries (UCS), 'Petition of Sundry Inhabitants,' 5 March 1808, 2917–20.

26 Upper Canada, *Statutes*, 1808, 48 Geo. 3, c. 1.

27 Special Collections, Brock University Library, *Origin and History of the Tunker Church in Canada as Gathered from Authentic and Reliable Sources* (Ridgeway: M.V. Disher, 1918); E. Morris Sider, 'Nonresistance in the Early Brethren in Christ Church in Ontario,' *Mennonite Quarterly Review* 31 (1957): 281. J. Boyd Cressman claimed that the preachers and elders were from the Waterloo settlement. Cressman, 'History of the First Mennonite Church of Kitchener, Ontario,' *Mennonite Quarterly Review* 8 (July 1939): 159–86.

28 Upper Canada, House of Assembly, *Journals*, 8, 10 February 1810.

29 Upper Canada, House of Assembly, *Journals*, 10, 12, 15, 16, 20, 24, 26, 28 February and 12 March 1810; Legislative Council, *Journals*, 16, 17, 19, 20, 27 February and 12 March 1810; *Statutes*, 1810, 50 Geo. 3, c. 11.

30 Upper Canada, House of Assembly, *Journals*, 9, 11, 15 February and 1, 4, 5, 6 March 1810.

31 Upper Canada, *Statutes*, 1811, 51 Geo. 3, c. 7.

32 Brock, 'Accounting for Difference,' 27–8.

33 AO, Rogers Papers, 'Circular, Inspector Generals Office,' York, 18 December 1813.

34 LAC, RG 5 A1, UCS, 'John McGill to Robert Loring,' York, 22 June 1814, 8523–6; 'William Allan to Edward McMahon,' York, 3 January 1815, 9197–9; 'John McGill to Lieutenant Governor Gore,' 16 November 1815, 11001–5. See also the inconsistencies in the Adjutant General's report of 1829. This report gives a total of the money received from Mennonites, Quakers, and Tunkers in each district for the sixteen years between 1813 and 1829. UCS, 'Statement of the amount of Money …, March 19, 1829,' 51601–4; 'Statement of the amount of Money …,' enclosed in 'N. Coffin to Z. Mudge,' York, 19 March 1829, 51601–4.

35 Upper Canada, *Statutes*, 1814, 54 Geo. 3, c. 1.

36 Brock, 'Accounting for Difference,' 27–8.

37 Upper Canada, *Statutes*, 1816, 56 Geo. 3, c. 31.

38 'Remarks (extended if though necessary) to be sent to Sir George Murray if he answer my letter,' [1815], in George W. Spragge, ed., *The John Strachan Letter Book: 1812–1834* (Toronto: Ontario Historical Society, 1946), 92.

39 Upper Canada, House of Assembly, *Journals*, 11, 14, 15 January 1829. Though no bill was introduced requesting an elimination of the fines, the assembly was supplied with an account demonstrating that during the previous sixteen years, district treasurers had collected more than £7,300 in fines from Quakers, Mennonites, and Tunkers. The total was most certainly greater, for the account did not include the Waterloo settlements, as the Gore District treasurer had submitted no report. Furthermore, as reported to the Lieutenant Governor during the previous year, the Adjutant-General of the Militia believed there was a serious neglect in collecting the militia fines from the peace sects. LAC, RG 5 A1, UCS, 'Statement of the amount of Money,' enclosed in 'N. Coffin to Z. Mudge,' York, 19 March 1829, 51601–4; 'N. Coffin to Sir Peregrine Maitland,' 13 September 1828, quoted in Sider, 'Nonresistance in the Early Brethren in Christ Church,' 284–5.

40 See notice of petition in *Kingston Chronicle and Gazette*, 6 July 1833. Upper Canada, House of Assembly, *Journals*, 28, 30 November 1833, 2, 4, 9 Janu-

ary, 17, 18, 22 February, and 6 March 1834; Legislative Council, *Journals*, 19, 20, 21, 22 February and 6 March 1834. Upper Canada, *Statutes*, 1834, 4 Wm. 4, c. 13.

41 See Upper Canada, *Statutes,* 1838, 1 Vic., c. 8; 1839, 2 Vic., c. 9; Province of Canada, *Statutes*, 1841, 4 & 5 Vic., c. 2; 1846, 9 Vic., c. 28; 1855, 18 Vic., c. 77.

42 The original bill aimed at legislating this authority was withdrawn after its first reading, for it appeared that the bill, if passed, might invalidate all previous marriages conducted in the territory prior to 1791. The bill was subsequently sent to Great Britain for legal advice from the Imperial authorities. John S. Moir, *Church and State in Canada, 1627–1867* (Toronto: McClelland and Stewart, 1967), 140–2.

43 Moir, *Church and State*, 142; 'Simcoe to Dundas,' York, 16 September 1793,' *The Correspondence*, vol. 2, 53.

44 Upper Canada, *Statutes*, 1793, 33 Geo 3, c. 5.

45 'Memorandum respecting the Marriage Act,' *The Correspondence*, vol. 3, 4.

46 Moir, *Church and State*, 145; 'Opinion of the Attorney General,' 2 June 1796, *The Correspondence*, vol. 4, 287–8; 'Simcoe to the Duke of Portland,' 20 June 1796,' *The Correspondence*, vol. 4, 310–11.

47 Moir, *Church and State*, 146–7; Upper Canada, *Statutes*, 1798, 38 Geo. 3, c. 4.

48 William Riddell has suggested that the marriage acts of Upper Canada were of no concern to Quakers, for provisions under English law had made legal Quaker marriages in 1753. Great Britain, *Statutes*, 1753, 26 Geo. 2; c. 33. See William Renwick Riddell, 'Quaker Marriages in Upper Canada,' *Ontario Historical Society Papers and Records* 24 (1927): 507–11.

49 Great Britain, *Statutes*, 1749, 22 Geo. 2, c. 30 and 22 Geo. 2, c. 46. No doubt marriages were performed without state sanction, and justice of the peace records demonstrate that some had allowed Mennonites to substitute an affirmation of allegiance upon entering the province several years prior to the legislature granting them the legal right to do so: AO, RG 1–72, Surveyor General's Copies of Oaths of Allegiance'; and TRL, 'Oaths of Allegiance sworn before William Willcocks,' 7 October 1800–10 November 1806.

50 Thomas Casey, *First Missionaries and Earliest Quakers of the Bay of Quinte District* (Napanee: n.p., n.d.), 6. Also see information concerning Benjamin Eby's donation in E. Reginald Good, *Frontier Community to Urban Congregation: First Mennonite Church Kitchener 1813–1988* (Kitchener: First Mennonite Church, 1988), 34.

51 Upper Canada, House of Assembly, *Journals*, 16, 21, 24, November and 20 December 1825.

52 Upper Canada, House of Assembly, *Journals*, 5, 7, 12, 13, 15 December 1826;

Legislative Council, *Journals*, 18, 20, 22, December 1826 and 5, 9, 11 January 1827.

53 Upper Canada, House of Assembly, *Journals*, 25, 30, 31 January, 27, 28 February, and 10, 11, 14, 25 March 1828; Legislative Council, *Journals*, 1, 5, 6, 7, 11, 14, 18, 25 March 1828.

54 Upper Canada, *Statutes*, 1828, 9 Geo. 4, c. 2; Province of Canada, *Statutes*, 1845, 8 Vic., c. 15.

55 John Garner, *The Franchise and Politics in British North America, 1755–1867* (Toronto: University of Toronto Press, 1969), 149.

56 'Stevenson to Dundas,' *The Correspondence*, vol. 1, 412.

57 'Dundas to Simcoe,' Whitehall, 2 October 1793, *The Correspondence*, vol. 2, 81–2; 'Lord Dorchester's remarks,' *The Correspondence*, vol. 2, 3; Garner, *The Franchise*, 151–2.

58 For a full discussion of oaths and conscientious objection under British law, see Constance Braithwaite, *Conscientious Objection to Various Compulsions under British Law* (York: William Sessions, 1995).

59 Braithwaite, *Conscientious Objection*, 22, 24.

60 It is unknown what indulgences were being proposed, for no draft bill or legislative debates exist. Upper Canada, House of Assembly, *Journals*, 16, 17, 19, 20, 22, 23 June 1801; Legislative Council, *Journals*, 23, 24 June 1801.

61 Thomas had converted to Anglicanism. Upper Canada, House of Assembly, *Journals*, 9, 11, 12, 13, 14, 15, 17 February 1806; Legislative Council, *Journals*, 17, 19 February 1806.

62 Unfortunately, no legislative journals exist for 1809. Upper Canada, *Statutes*, 1809, 49 Geo. 3, c. 6.

63 'Bathurst to Smith, November 30, 1817,' in Arthur G. Doughty and Norah Story, eds., *Documents Relating to the Constitutional History of Canada, 1819–1828* (Ottawa: J.O. Patenaude, Printer to the King's Most Excellent Majesty, 1935), 5–6; Paul Romney, *Mr Attorney: The Attorney General for Ontario in Court, Cabinet, and Legislature 1791–1899* (Toronto: University of Toronto Press, 1986), 84.

64 Eby, *Biographical History*, 30–9.

65 Romney, *Mr Attorney*, 90.

66 Upper Canada, *Statutes*, 1828, 9 Geo. 4, c. 21.

67 Province of Canada, Legislative Council, *Journals*, 1841, Appendix 21, 'Schedule of the names of persons ... who have taken the oaths of Allegiance.'

68 Lieutenant Governor Sir Peregrine Maitland reserved Royal Assent in light of the bill's connection to the naturalization bill, however. Thus, it was not until October 1829 that the petitioners were secure in the title of their

land. Upper Canada, House of Assembly, *Journals*, 18, 21 January, 6 February, and 10, 20, 25 March 1828; Legislative Council, *Journals*, 11, 18, 19, 25 March 1828; *Statutes*, 1830, 11 Geo. 4.

69 Great Britain, *Statutes*, 1828, 9 Geo. 4, c. 32. Braithwaite, *Conscientious Objection*, 26; Upper Canada, House of Assembly, *Journals*, 22, 23 January, 2, 4 February, and 20 March 1829; Legislative Council, *Journals*, 5, 13, 16 February and 20 March 1829; Upper Canada, *Statutes*, 1829, 10 Geo. 4, c. 1.

70 Great Britain, *Statutes*, 1833, 3 & 4 Wm. 4, c. 48. Upper Canada, Legislative Council, *Journals*, 12, 19, 20, 22, 23 November and 17 December 1832; House of Assembly, *Journals*, 23, 28 November 1832 and 13 February 1833; *Statutes*, 1833, 3 Wm 4, c. 13; 'Copy of a Despatch from Viscount Goderich to Major General Sir John Colborne, dated Downing Street, 8th November 1832,' in Upper Canada, House of Assembly, *Journals*, 1835, Appendix no. 21, 'Seventh Report of Committee on Grievances.' Braithwaite, *Conscientious Objectors*, 26; Garner, *Franchise*, 152.

5 *Germania* in Canada – Nation and Ethnicity at the German Peace Jubilees of 1871

BARBARA LORENZKOWSKI

'Today was a public holiday as there was a great peace-jubilee in town,' Louis Breithaupt scribbled in his diary on 2 May 1871. In a few broad strokes, the sixteen-year-old resident of Berlin, Ontario, captured the festive air of the celebration that marked Germany's military victory over France in the Franco-Prussian War. The jubilee was ushered in by a salute of twenty-one cannon shots, followed by divine service 'in all the German churches of Berlin & Waterloo.'[1] Later, a procession wound its way to the courthouse, where orators celebrated Germany's 'righteous' triumph over France. As exuberant as the speeches were the ten thousand celebrants who clapped enthusiastically when an oak was planted 'as a truly German symbol.' In the evening, a torchlight procession marched down King Street, which was 'ablaze with illuminations, every house, workshop, factory, hotel and building being gracefully hung with Chinese lanterns, colored illuminations, devices in glass, and transparencies of every kind.'[2] With revellers singing German songs and loudly cheering at portraits of Emperor Wilhelm I, the celebration culminated in a fireworks display and the unveiling of an oil painting of *Germania* that symbolized Germany's newly attained national unity.

For three days, this town of fewer than three thousand residents became a focal point of German festivities, attracting celebrants from Toronto, Hamilton, London, Guelph, New Hamburg, and a host of other villages and hamlets in southern Ontario.[3] The influx of visitors led organizer Otto Klotz to exclaim that the jubilee represented a 'truly … national festival … considering that they had amongst them representatives from many other German associations, from the Province of Quebec, and also from the United States.' For Klotz, the presence of American revellers from Buffalo, New York, and Ann Arbor, Michigan, who marched in the Berlin parade seemed a living symbol of national unity.[4] Little did it seem to matter that Germany itself was still in the process of becoming. Germany was far from constituting a national entity on 18 January 1871, when the Prussian king was proclaimed German Emperor in Versailles; indeed, it would be several decades before German local, regional, and national identities merged into 'one representation of the nation.'[5] Yet viewed from a transatlantic distance, the newly created political entity had, almost instantaneously, donned the mantle of national greatness.

In paying tribute to Germany's newly attained national unity, the celebrants in Waterloo County were not alone. Across the United States, German communities staged elaborate festivals to honour Germany's ascent to the 'leading European people.'[6] No fewer than seventy-two communities, from New York to San Francisco, held jubilee celebrations, described in vivid detail in the pages of the *Berliner Journal*, Waterloo County's foremost German-language weekly.[7] Learning about celebrations in other North American towns and cities, the county's residents quickly concluded that they too had an obligation to organize a peace jubilee.[8] In May 1871 they added their own tune to the celebration of the nation and, shortly thereafter, snapped up the three hundred evening extras that the *Journal* had published the jubilee to proudly mail accounts of 'their' festival to family and friends in Germany. As the postmaster of Berlin reported, never before had he sent so many newspapers to Europe.[9] The fluid back-and-forth between the local and the (trans)national supports David Waldstreicher's assertion that 'celebrants of the nation took their cues from printed sources. They improvised upon events they read about and then publicized their own interventions in public life.'[10] Listening to stories of ethnicity and nation – and then enacting their own in the public street theatre that was the jubilee festival – celebrants became familiar with the idiom of a festive German culture that prided itself in unity, both the ethnic unity of German migrants in North America and the newly attained national unity of the German homelands across the Atlantic.

As expressions of group feeling, ethnicity and nationalism have striking similarities. Although only the latter aspires to state power and national sovereignty, both depend – in Matthew Frye Jacobson's compelling formulation – on 'ethnic consciousness (the sense of being "a people")' just as they 'fuel patriotism (the love of the country)' or may 'lapse into the flattering rhetoric of chauvinism (the claim of a group's superiority to other groups).'[11] In the context of festive culture in North America, the relationship between ethnicity and nationality assumes an added dimension. In telling stories about themselves in the public venues of streets and market squares, immigrants affirmed their folk culture and national heritage – two national constructs that, as historians have taken care to point out, were carefully crafted by an ethnic middle class that sought to harness the festive enthusiasm of the moment to overcome internal ethnic divisions and establish its own leadership in the community.[12] Organizers also aimed at weaving their stories so tightly into the national storyline of their host countries that the latter would come to concede the validity of cultural pluralism and dual loyalties.[13] Although they usually harboured these hopes in vain (for mainstream America, as Orm Øverland observes, did not care to listen), the plots and themes of the stories that immigrants crafted at ethnic celebrations, rallies, banquets, and picnics shared 'so many characteristics' as to constitute a genre of ethnic storytelling that was peculiar to North America.[14]

This study, too, regards ethnic celebrations as powerful forms of communication that projected messages about historical memory, national myths, and cultural identity both in non-literate, visual tableaux and in overtly didactic oratory. It analyses the symbolic universe in which the peace jubilees of 1871 unfolded by examining narratives of nation, by probing the rhetorical tropes of unity and diversity, and by delving into the world of myth into which the jubilee celebrations tapped. In addition, it directs attention to the intersections between print and performance, ethnicity and nation. As we shall see, the North American peace jubilees of 1871 were notable for lifting celebrants into a transnational space in which German-Canadian revellers took their festive cues from their 'German brethren' south to the border, while German migrants in both Canada and the United States looked across the Atlantic for the national imagery and festive symbols out of which to compose their own jubilee celebrations. Yet while transcending national boundaries, the peace jubilees also reaffirmed them; for when it came to inserting their stories of German grandeur and glory into the national narratives of Canada and the United States, rhetorical strategies began to diverge.

Why, out of myriad possibilities, have I chosen to focus on Berlin, Ontario, and Buffalo, New York? At first glance, it is difficult to imagine two historical settings more different. In the mid-1850s, Berlin was still a hamlet whereas Buffalo was the largest grain port in the world. The latter's ethnic composition constituted an 'American Pluralism,' to quote David Gerber. In 1865, German immigrants represented 45 per cent of the population, compared to Anglo-Americans (20 per cent) and Irish Americans (18 per cent). These figures, however, do not do justice to the regional diversity of Buffalo's German population. In 1870, 22,250 of the city's residents (19 per cent) had been born in Germany. While migrants from Bavaria and the southwestern states of Wurttemberg and Baden made up the majority of German-speaking migrants (46 per cent), they would soon be outnumbered by newcomers from Prussia and Mecklenburg (30 per cent), who began to wield their influence by the late 1870s. This regional split was reinforced by religious divisions between a predominantly Protestant north and an overwhelmingly Catholic south.[15] No comparable statistics exist for Canada, where the census lumped together immigrants from various German states. Yet census returns point to a town whose local mainstream was German, not British, and where German culture was firmly embedded in the structures of local community.[16] In 1871, 73 per cent of the Berlin's 2,000 residents were of German origin, and almost 30 per cent of the town's population had been born in Germany. In the county at large, German migrants and their descendants dominated townships and villages, except for the Scottish municipalities to the south.[17] Still, both communities formed part of a larger, interacting Great Lakes region in which ties of family, friendship, and business spanned the border and border crossings represented the rule, not the exception. In both communities, the peace jubilees spoke in a language of romantic nationalism of a distinctively German vintage, although the festive rhetoric was tailored to and shaped by Canadian and American national discourses. By studying the similarities and differences in the jubilees' festive scripts on the two sides of the Canadian–American border, we can thus learn which Canadian gown, if any, *Germania* wore in Canada.

Narratives of Nation

It was the medium of print that allowed the jubilee celebration to collapse boundaries of time and space. In creating 'fields of exchange and communication,' as anthropologist Benedict Anderson suggests, newspapers furnished both a festive vocabulary and a repertoire of national symbols that could be appropriated and adapted by readers in various national contexts.[18] With avid interest, Waterloo County's residents had followed the growing tensions in Europe that erupted in the Franco-Prussian War of 1870–1. So curious, in fact, were many subscribers to the *Berliner Journal* about the outcome of the latest battles that they travelled 'many miles on foot, or by vehicle, to procure their copy of the Journal at the press.'[19] Devoting its columns to accounts by German newspapers, the county's press chronicled the homeland's military triumphs and later its jubilant celebrations of 'peace,' thereby inserting its readers into a festive space that transcended national boundaries; for the very rituals celebrated by the 'German brethren' in the Fatherland could be re-enacted by German immigrants in North America.[20]

News of the Franco-Prussian War reached North America in July 1870 and almost immediately galvanized the representatives of organized *Deutschthum*.[21] In the United States, 'patriotic relief associations' (*patriotische Hülfsvereine*) formed to collect donations for the wounded, the widows, and the orphans of the war. Young men flooded the associations with requests to have their fares paid to Europe so that they could fight on Germany's side. Fearful that Americans might view such acts as unpatriotic, ethnic leaders routinely denied these requests. Humanitarian missions did not provoke the same misgivings. New Yorker relief societies sent forty-two physicians to Germany, where they worked in makeshift hospitals.[22] In Berlin, Waterloo County, German spokesmen like John Motz, the editor of the *Berliner Journal*, and Hugo Kranz, who would be elected to the House of Commons in 1878 as its first German member, spearheaded the founding of a 'German patriotic relief organization' that raised one thousand dollars for 'the wounded and widows and orphans of the German armies,' while Toronto's German community contributed two thousand dollars 'for the relief of the widows and orphans of the Fatherland.'[23] On both sides of the border, ethnic spokespersons were careful to highlight the humanitarian character of their donations, lest they be accused of disloyalty. Indeed, so concerned were some members of the New York City jubilee committee that a grand jubilee procession might arouse the ire of 'our American and Irish fellow-citizens' that they initially recommended avoiding any public demonstrations of national pride.[24]

The 'dear Fatherland' and the 'one Germany,' as it was described in the peace jubilee celebrations, evoked a feeling of belonging that transcended both time and space. 'What could it be that reunited us – we, who for years long have lived thousands of miles away from the old Fatherland or know the same only from our parents' accounts?' the *Canadisches Volksblatt* asked rhetorically. The answer, it held, was the realization of a long-cherished dream, 'the unity and power of the country of our descent.'[25] Across the border, in Buffalo, orator Edward Storck evoked the eternal ties that bound German migrants to the Fatherland. 'Upon such an occasion as this,' he said, 'we cannot forget that we are Germans; born perhaps in a different province of our country, but still bound by every tie of consanguinity to the Fatherland.'[26] What is striking about these descriptions of the imagined homeland, Germany, is the attempt to naturalize the bonds of nationality by likening them to family and kinship ties. The land of their fathers, orators held, was built upon ties of blood (the ties of 'consanguinity'), its memory kept alive by immigrants who faithfully handed down stories of the homeland to children and grandchildren. As another commentator suggested, the grand celebrations of Germany's victory provided ample proof that German-Americans represented 'a genuine branch of the magnificent trunk whose roots rest in the heart of Europe and whose strong branches reach further, year for year.'[27] Germany was represented not as a historical construction but as an organic entity whose branches reached as far as Germans had travelled to foreign lands.

As in other celebrations of immigrant communities in North America, the organizers constructed a narrative of German ethnicity that was meant to reassure Anglo-American and Anglo-Canadian audiences that their jubilee was compatible with mainstream cultural values. The middle-class organizers of the festival in Buffalo never grew tired of pointing out that were they assembled 'to sing praises to the Shrine of Freedom.' In the words of festival president Dr Storck, the city's leading German Republican, who had migrated to the United States after the failed 1848–9 revolutions in Europe and had established a popular medical practice, 'we meet as the votaries of peace, to celebrate the return of that happy state to our native Germany.' Storck's speech was listened to attentively by the members of Buffalo's Common Council, who had assembled in the Council Chamber before joining the peace jubilee procession.[28] In Berlin, Otto Klotz, a justice of the peace and the county's longest-serving school trustee, addressed a crowd of several thousand in front of the courthouse, reminding them that they were celebrating 'one of the noblest of public festivals – a peace festival.' The Germans of Ontario had assembled not to revel in the downfall of Paris but to express their 'joy and gratitude that at last an end had been put to the late terrible sacrifice of life and destruction of property.'[29] The conciliatory air of the festivities impressed English-language observers, who noted that the celebrants 'did not gloat over the sufferings of the French nor do anything by word or deed that could have pained the hearts of the most sensitive Frenchmen.'[30] Yet although the festivities were ostensibly peace jubilees, the rhetoric that permeated speeches and addresses served to subvert official tributes to the 'return of bounteous peace and the ending of a cruel and devastating war.'[31]

It was the laurel of the glorious victor, not the humble olive branch, that fired the imagination of orators in both Buffalo and Berlin. Ethnic group feeling, much like nationalism, depends 'on one group's defining itself *against* another (or others),' as Matthew Frye Jacobson has remarked.[32] In the case of the peace jubilees, this 'other' was France. Not, to be sure, the tiny minority of French-origin migrants who lived in Waterloo County and who represented 4 per cent of the county's population, or Buffalo's 2,232 French-born residents, who constituted a mere 2 per cent of the city's population, but the nation of France that had so arrogantly 'medd[led] in the domestic affairs of the Fatherland.'[33] In spite of official attempts to devise a festive script that was devoid of martial or nationalist overtones, orators tended to draw upon a historical narrative that pitted the noble nation of Germany against its jealous and frivolous 'old hereditary enemy.'[34] Ever since Napoleon's occupation of Germany and his subsequent defeat in the battle at Leipzig in 1813, the notion of France as the 'traditional enemy' of Germany had figured prominently at German national festivals.[35] When recounting the history of the war, immigrant orators, too, squarely placed the blame on the shoulders of France. James Young, the Member of Parliament for South Waterloo County, told a cheering crowd that France's 'jealousy ... at seeing Germany becoming one and united' had triggered 'the triumphant but bloody march from Berlin to Paris.'[36] Indeed, concurred orator Francis Brunck in Buffalo, Germany had done nothing to provoke the war.[37] Given that her 'most sacred rights had been violated,' even Anglo-American observers concluded that 'the quarrel out of which she [Germany] came so gloriously was forced upon her. The power that was the first to draw the sword has perished by the sword.'[38]

The orators did not stop at assigning blame. Their speeches also served a hefty dose of ethnic chauvinism that conjured the superiority of Germany over France. Dr Brunck told the crowd in Buffalo that the war had been 'a victory of justice over injustice'; Mr Schunck in Berlin pitted Germany's 'noble, prudent and brave conduct of war' against 'the revengeful, helpless and cowardly behaviour of the French.'[39] Unjust, jealous, frivolous, presumptuous, arrogant, insolent, barbaric, and criminal – this was the arsenal of adjectives that orators used to describe the beaten foe.[40] Little wonder, then, that they finished their speeches with literary flourish. 'In less than three months,' Dr Brunck concluded his address, 'proud France lay helpless under the foot of despised Germany, and had to beg for peace.'[41] These, clearly, were not words of conciliation but of triumph and righteousness that stood in marked contrast to the organizers' official agenda of holding a festival of peace.

In representing the nations of Germany and France to festive audiences in Berlin and Buffalo, orators and reporters drew upon gendered images. They celebrated the 'militarized masculinity' of Germany while reprimanding 'beautiful' France for its vanity and self-indulgence. 'The wickedness of her beautiful capital,' charged the Buffalo *Commercial Advertiser*, 'has culminated in an attempt at self-destruction. The fair city, like so many of those gay and guilty women of whom she is the prototype, has sought a suicide's grave.'[42] By intertwining conceptions of gender and nationality, immigrant commentators reinforced the notion that France itself was to blame for its humiliating defeat. Once renowned for its 'ideas, habits, and diplomacy,' the country had become entrenched in 'luxuries and pleasures.' 'Self-indulgence had become the law of the Parisian mind,' the *Buffalo Christian Advocate* wrote. 'There was no sense of duty to the family or the country ... The population were willing to forget their manhood.'[43] The thin veneer of civilization, a Berlin speaker suggested, only disguised a rotten core, for a country that ridiculed the sacred bonds of family was undermining its very own foundation.[44] Given the decadence and depravity of France, the *Christian Advocate* suggested, the Germans had acted merely as an 'instrument of punishment' and restored morality to European affairs:

> Whatever were the faults of the law, they were especially free from the vices of their Celtic neighbors. They peculiarly represent to the world a pure family life, a profound reverence for law, self-control under the sense duty ... Henceforth the thorough schooltraining of Prussia, the universal service of the nation, and her close discipline and drill, will be the model towards which other countries will aspire.[45]

Cast in gender terms, the Franco-Prussian War of 1870–1 appeared not as a battle for power and territory, but as a moral struggle in which 'feminine' France had been rightfully chastised by 'masculine' Germany. Political unity, of course, did not guarantee cultural unity, either within Germany or abroad. It remained to be seen whether the festive union of German-origin migrants, symbolized in the elaborate jubilee processions at Berlin and Buffalo, would translate into an ethnic identity that could transcend divisions of class, nationality, religion and gender.

Unity/Diversity

The spirit of community that suffused the festivities was perceptible to insiders and outsiders alike. 'We question very much,' the *Toronto Daily Telegraph* wrote, 'whether the Berlin of the Fatherland will exhibit more enthusiasm when the Kaiser and his men make their formal entry into the capital, than was exhibited by the Berlin of Canada today.' In fact, the writer could not conceal his surprise over the intensity of feeling he observed in Berlin; for 'it is a hard thing to become enthusiastic over a matter that happened three thousand miles away.'[46] In a similar vein, the *Buffalo Express* held that 'the spirit of nationality was rife and the sons and daughters of the Fatherland joined heart and soul in celebrating the return of peace to Germany.'[47] To these contemporary observers, the imagined bond with Germany and the more tangible community of fellow revellers merged in a whirlwind of enthusiasm.

The notion of ethnic unity was, indeed, central to the peace celebrations that were staged across North America. Typically, middle-class orators began their speeches by recalling the disgrace of the German people in the era before unification in 1871. The wretched provincialism, Georg Baltz declared in Buffalo, had allowed foreign armies to devastate the country. Its disunity, Otto Klotz in Berlin chimed in, bode poorly for the Franco-Prussian struggle of 1870–1. Yet as if to defy the boundaries of German principalities and kingdoms, the German people rose like one man to defend the country's integrity. 'The Prussian did not look with disdain on the Hessian or the Swabian,' Otto Klotz enthused, 'every one appeared in his place, from the sandbanks of the North Sea to the foots of the Alps. The whole people were united, and sacrificed willingly even more than they were asked to do.' Young and old, artisans and scholars, sons of day labourers and millionaires, Prussians, Mecklenburgers, Swabians, and Bavarians, republicans and monarchists all joined hands to fight against the arrogant neighbour to the West.[48] Out of their courage and unity, it was suggested, the nation was born. Hitherto, the editor of the *Canadisches Volksblatt* reflected, Germany had signified a geographical territory only. Now, it stood for a nation. At long last, he wrote, 'our dear, old Fatherland' occupied the position which it so duly deserved.[49]

From the triumphant cry 'They were all Germans,' it was a short step to declare that 'we, too, are all Germans.'[50] For German immigrants in Canada and the United States, basking in the glory of the newly created German nation-state, unity seemed a tangible goal. 'Germans, who now look with pride and joy upon united Germany,' Dr Storck in Buffalo declared, 'let us here, in this country, be united as our brethren beyond the ocean.'[51] Nowhere did the identification with the German Fatherland find a more public expression than in the massive peace jubilee celebrations, which were read by many as a visible sign of German unity.[52] Importantly, the pervasive rhetoric of unity that permeated the festivities represented less a description of what was than a prescription for what ought to be. As the anthropologist Victor Turner has noted, in ritual celebrations a social group does not merely celebrate an event; it 'celebrates itself.' It celebrates 'what it conceives to be its essential life.'[53] The very repetitiveness of newspaper accounts that conjured German unity and might should be read not as an objective description of the celebrants' intentions but as a rhetorical strategy designed to write into existence what presumably already existed.[54]

Evidently, the celebrations in Berlin and Buffalo took place on a very different scale. To an American observer, the peace jubilee in the neighbouring towns of Berlin and Waterloo on 2 May 1871 must have appeared charming in its simplicity. The procession that marched from the railway depot to the Berlin courthouse included – in no particular order – delegations from Hamilton, Toronto, and a host of other towns and villages, 'urged into quick time by several excellent brass bands' and headed by twenty-four adjutants on horseback.[55] Its one distinguishing feature was two wagons from Preston, carrying girls dressed in white and decorated with wreaths and garlands. Yet another wagon displayed a 'beautiful fair-headed girl,' *Germania*, surrounded by thirty-four others, representing the German states.[56] With Berlin decked in 'holiday attire' and more than eight thousand visitors cramming 'sidewalks, balconies, windows, and houses,' the procession passed the arches on King Street, breaking into enthusiastic cheers once it reached the portraits of Emperor William and Otto von Bismarck, 'as though they were anxious that they should be heard by the grim Chancellor all the way to the Fatherland.'[57]

In Buffalo as well, 'the enthusiasm generally expressed was as genuine as it was unrestrained.'[58] But the celebration had little of the ad hoc quality that characterized its Canadian counterpart. For weeks, the festival committee had elicited the participation of German associations, eighty-five of which marched in the three-mile-long parade. ('More

than anyone knew even existed,' the historian Andrew P. Yox quips.[59])
Festival marshal Richard Flach, a veteran of the Civil War, travelled
to New York and Philadelphia to learn first-hand of the work entailed in
organizing a peace jubilee. On 29 May 1871, Flach was instrumental
in dividing the multitude of organizations into seven divisions, each of
which was headed by an assistant marshal. Unlike Waterloo County's
three humble wagons, the Buffalo parade showcased float after float.
The cities' fraternal associations had engaged in a veritable competition to see who would assemble the most memorable display, while
local German industries seized the opportunity to demonstrate their
patriotism – and, the sceptic may add, to benefit from free advertising.[60]
Indeed, as historian Heike Bungert has observed in her study of German-American festivals in Milwaukee, the eagerness of participants at
the peace jubilee to use their floats to commercial ends 'seems to have
surpassed even the often derided "Yankee materialism."'[61]

Reminiscent of guild processions in early modern German and
Labour Day parades in nineteenth-century North America, German
workmen proudly put their skills on display on animated floats.[62]
Much admired by the thousands of Buffalo spectators, the blacksmiths
of Reiter's & Eager busily swung their hammers at a steam boiler, while
the float of the *Buffalo Telegraph* featured a printing press 'in full opera-
tion,' the printers tossing news sheets gratis into the crowd. 'A bakery
on wheels threw out hot rolls among the boys without regard to cost,'
while local butchers headed the seventh division, whose notable feature was a 'sausage factory.'[63] These displays could be read as admirable
signs of a German industriousness that found pride in its contributions
to building America, or, alternatively, as tributes to a 'mythical world
of craftsmen and farmers' that evoked a productive, orderly 'German'
past.[64] At the same time, the floats conveyed a message of social har-
mony and industrial paternalism as workers displayed their craft on
wagons bearing their employers' names.

The cosy feeling of unity that permeated the festivities could not dis-
tract from the tensions that surfaced over the course of the jubilees.
In Waterloo County, the beginning of the Franco-Prussian War pitted
German-origin immigrants from Alsace-Lorraine – then part of France
– against immigrants from the German core areas. These latent hostilities sometimes erupted into altercations and even fist fights, as the *Berliner Journal* reported in August 1870. One is left to wonder how those
'German-French,' as the newspaper called them, reacted to Otto Klotz's
endorsement of a policy of assimilation that would bring the provinces

back into the fold of 'German nationality' or how they viewed the ubiquitous banners that celebrated the return of Alsace and Lorraine to the
'Fatherland.'[65]

Religion, too, constituted a dividing line at the peace jubilees. In
both Buffalo and Berlin, the organizers invited all German churches,
regardless of their denomination, to offer divine services on the morning of the jubilee.[66] As historian April Schultz has suggested in her
analysis of the 1925 Norse-American Centennial, such requests may
have been motivated by the desire to add 'a sacred dimension' to a
secular event. 'An insistence on religious devotion,' Schultz wrote, set
celebrants apart from 'foreign radicalism' and proved them 'worthy
Americans' who demonstrated 'an abstract sense of religion and spirituality.'[67] But in the case of the German peace jubilees, this abstract
spirituality never translated into a central role for German churches,
which remained marginal to the festivities. In Buffalo, Evangelical
church groups joined the parade, as did members of Catholic associations; the latter, however, took pains to point out that they marched
not as religious representatives but as 'friends of the German cause.'
The Catholic German-language weekly *Die Aurora* failed to even mention the grand celebration.[68] The outbursts of patriotism of 1871 did
not resonate with a Catholic Church that presided over a community
of believers, not national groups. The prominent renditions of 'Nun
Danket alle Gott' (Let Us Praise Thee Lord) also held little appeal for
the Catholic hierarchy. Composed by Martin Luther, the father of the
Reformation, the chorus brought to the fore the secular Protestantism
that underpinned much of the festivities, thereby emphasizing that the
Catholic Church was central neither to the creation of imperial Germany, a country dominated by Protestant Prussia, nor to the peace
jubilees in North America.[69]

One group, finally, was so effectively denied a voice at the celebrations that its presence is easily overlooked. In the historical narrative
of the jubilee celebrations, women were relegated to the roles of either
cultural guardians or national icons.[70] While 'our brethren beyond the
ocean' had valiantly fought against the French foe, Dr Brunck said in
Buffalo, the country's women had fed and clothed the German 'warri-
ors.'[71] The work of political struggle was left to men, while women found
fulfilment in their roles as caretakers. At the peace jubilees, women had
to be content to decorate towns and market squares or, as in New York,
to organize 'lady fairs' in support of the widows and orphans of the
Franco-Prussian War.[72] If they entered the public sphere, it was as spec-

tators, not as actors, as icons, not as citizens. Embodying abstract principles such as the ubiquitous *Germania*, they were effectively excluded from the '*politics* of nationalism,' as Matthew Frye Jacobson has noted in his dissection of gender roles in immigrant parades.[73] The unity constructed during the course of the peace jubilees was thus a tenuous one. While no contemporary observer could deny the enthusiasm of the revellers, who celebrated their Germanness on a scale never before witnessed on the continent, divisions of class, nationality, religion, and gender persisted, only to be temporarily obscured in the exuberance of the celebration.

Myth

It was in the world of myth that jubilee organizers searched for the symbols and imagery with which to bind together German immigrants. These myths were suffused with romantic ideas of nationalism as they had been developed by the German philosopher Johann Gottfried Herder (1744–1803), who had located the 'nation's soul' (*Volksgeist*) not in the high culture of the elites but in the multitude of folk traditions. His was a nation defined not by political boundaries but rather by a shared ethnic descent and culture that had been profoundly shaped by the natural environment.[74] At the 1871 peace jubilees, the special closeness of the German people to their natural environment was evoked in two powerful symbolic gestures – the planting of an oak tree in Waterloo County and the odes to the Rhine as the mythical source of German identity.

By planting an oak tree in front of the courthouse, the Berlin festival committee drew upon a symbol that had formed part of the repertoire of German celebrations ever since the first German national festival of 1814, during which celebrants had adorned houses and streets with oak leaves, branches, and wreaths to commemorate the liberation of Germany from Napoleon at the Battle of Nations in 1813. The oak – 'an incarnation of fertility, steadfastness, and strength' – was thereby transformed into a metaphor for the German nation itself.[75] More than half a century later and a continent away, jubilee president Otto Klotz saw in the young oak, which had been imported from Germany for the occasion, a symbol of historical continuity. 'The old Germanic tribes,' he said, 'regarded the oak as the forest's foremost tree; in oak groves they preferred to assemble to make decisions on war and peace, to hold court and divine service; for the old Teutons honoured god not in temples but ... in the grand temple of sacred nature.'[76] Reminiscent of Tacitus' *Germania*, which had contrasted German authenticity with Roman decadence, Klotz projected onto the German tribes an image of noble savages whose inner strength and forthright morals were as admirable then as now.[77] The oak not only reached far into Germany's past – back to its ancient roots, so to speak – but also served as a reminder for future generations. 'May this oak,' the orator's voice told the audience, 'always remind us and our descendants of the great German accomplishments, be it a memorial of the virtues of the old Teutons.'[78] Although the oak failed to prosper in later years, its meagre growth a poor testimony to German greatness, its memory would be carved out in stone more than a quarter of a century later. In 1896, Karl Müller, the president of Berlin's singing society Concordia, suggested that a memorial plaque be erected to replace the oak that the celebrants of 1871 had planted and that had long since withered away. When donations began to exceed expectations, ambitions soared. The singers now set their sights on erecting a fourteen-foot memorial to the late German Emperor Wilhelm I, which was unveiled in Victoria Park on 13 August 1897.[79]

If the oak symbolized the inner qualities of the German nation, it was the Rhine that demarcated its outer boundaries. A 'myth of spatial origins' is, of course, central to nationalist narratives.[80] In the case of the German Fatherland, the Rhine symbolized the nation's 'natural' boundary to the west. For centuries, the Rhine had inspired poets and historians, who perceived that majestic stream – lined by 'authentic' German villages and 'ancient' castles such as Ehrenbreitstein, Stolzenfels, Sonneck, and Rheinstein – to be an embodiment of the nation's past. In more recent historical memory, the Rhine had captured the national imagination as the pivotal symbol of the Franco-Prussian War. 'As soon as Germany resounded with the war trumpet,' Georg Baltz declared in Buffalo, 'a whole nation arose in arms to guard the old and sacred watch of the Rhine, and with might and main to ward off the frivolous and wanton war with all its terrors from the fields of the Fatherland.'[81] So powerful was the image of the Rhine that it was thought to constitute the particular property of Europe's 'Germanic' tribes, a term broad enough to encompass both the Dutch and the Swiss.

If the jubilees portrayed Germany as an organic, immutable entity, embodied in nature itself, they also offered personifications of the German nation in both Hermann the Cheruscan and the allegorical figure of *Germania* who presided over a newly unified nation. In topical floats – grand in Buffalo, modest in Berlin – they told a tale of German history whose very timelessness framed the experience of migration in terms of historical continuity. As early as the 1850s, *Germania* had made her appearance in Germany in 'increasingly belligerent portrayals,' in which she wielded her sword aggressively, her feet caressed by the waters of the Rhine, her eyes turned to the West. In 1871, this metaphor for the German people underwent yet another change by representing the German empire as a political entity just as she had previously projected a longing for national unity. The irony that the German nation was being depicted as a woman – 'a member of the group most completely excluded from the nation as a political community' – was replicated at the peace jubilees in Berlin and Buffalo, where women represented the German nation but were otherwise refused a public voice.[82] Dressed in white, a symbol of moral purity, thirty-four 'young ladies' at the Berlin parade personified the German states, with 'Miss E. Hoffman, a flaxen haired Saxon lass of fifteen years of age, representing Germania.'[83] Observers readily agreed that only the solemn unveiling of the oil painting *Germania* in the evening, accompanied by the tune 'Die Wacht am Rhein,' could rival this sweet tribute to German unity.[84]

In Buffalo, too, *Germania* was celebrated, but in far more extravagant fashion. A display that had dazzled Manhattan spectators at the New York *Friedensfest* in early April 1871 was brought to Buffalo by the central committee. 'Drawn by six horses, each led by a footman arranged in costume of the olden time,' the float left Buffalo celebrants visibly impressed.[85] 'The central tableau was illustrative of the 'Watch on the Rhine,'' the *Buffalo Express* reported:

> Germania seated upon a massive rock, about the base of which the famed and lovely river was pictured in its winding course. At different points old castles might be seen rearing their towers and battlemented walls, and there was everything to complete the scene and make perfect the allegory. There were other figures also, arranged and costumed in harmony to represent the arts, the sciences, and the avocations of peace. This feature of the procession was truly superb, and was a centre of great admiration.[86]

Markedly absent from the display were any references to the defeated foe. Instead, *Germania* surrounded herself with symbols of a romanticized Germany whose greatness lay not in its martial triumphs but in its cultural accomplishments. By vaguely alluding to a grand cultural heritage, the tableau reflected the pervasive influence of romantic nationalism that believed nations to be defined by their language, customs, and cultural attributes, a message reiterated in the speeches at the peace jubilee.[87] *Germania* personified Germany's newly attained national unity while anchoring it in a nebulous past where myth and history merged on the banks of the Rhine.[88]

If *Germania* presided serenely over a unified nation, another float at the Buffalo *Friedensfest* delved deeply into collective historical memory. It commemorated a battle between the Romans and the Teutons in AD 9 in which Hermann (Arminius), the Cheruscan, defeated a Roman army in the Teutoburg Forest.[89] As a popular historical myth, which would be memorialized in stone in the *Hermannsdenkmal* nearby Detmold in Germany in 1875, the Cheruscan prince admirably suited the larger narrative of the peace jubilee; for Germany's victory in the Franco-Prussian War mirrored the military founding act of the Germanic tribes.[90] In addition, the dramatic contrast between the 'audacious … and energetic' Teutons and the 'lethargic, cynical, and weak' Romans – a trope first devised by Tacitus – found its parallel in the alleged differences between the pure and noble German nation and the decadence of France.[91]

To suggest that the Hermann-float at the Buffalo peace jubilee was embedded in a mythical German context is not to say that this myth was consciously evoked by the festival's organizers. Indeed, it is doubtful whether Friedrich Erstling, upon whom had fallen the honour of representing Hermann, paid much attention to a creation myth as he balanced uneasily on a giant globe, always in danger of stumbling unceremoniously as the float hit one pothole after another.[92] Rather, this is to suggest that the peace jubilee in Buffalo drew upon national myths that had evolved historically in Germany and travelled to North America as part of the popular culture of German-speaking migrants, memories of which were rekindled in the elaborate printed accounts of peace jubilees, published in the spring of 1871. Yet even if the spectators in Buffalo were only dimly aware of the mythical subtext underlying the display, they would have been hard pressed to miss the float's principal message. Connected to 'Hermann' with golden chains 'sat eleven young ladies dressed in white representing Prussia, Bavaria, Saxony, Baden, Wurtemberg [sic], Mecklenburg, Hesse, Brunswick, Bremen, Hamburgh [sic], Alsace and Lorraine,' who together symbolized 'the union of the German States in one great Teutonic Empire,' as the *Buffalo Commercial Advertiser* put it.[93]

Although the organizers of peace jubilee celebrations made use of a festive vocabulary that had been developed at national celebrations in Germany, they did add symbols of their own that corresponded to their experience of migration.[94] The globe on which Hermann struggled precariously for his balance bore two clasped hands 'indicating the union of Germans in Germany and America and the countries themselves through them,' as one observer noted. Even the most German of displays thus paid tribute to the migrants' adopted homeland. The image projected by this gesture of friendship and mutual respect was one of dual identity. To be German in 1871 Buffalo, it implied, was not mutually exclusive with being American; on the contrary, the feelings of fidelity and loyalty displayed at the peace jubilee revealed a measure of character that befit any American citizen. Even the *Commercial Advertiser*, a paper prone to nativist overtones in the 1850s and 1860s, acknowledged that in 'Herman [*sic*], standing upon the globe and overlooking all, was symbolized that, as Germans when in distant countries still look back to the Fatherland, so does it look on them with pride.'[95] This realization did not trouble the *Commercial Advertiser*. Like other English-language papers in the city, it published lengthy reports on the jubilee that cast Germany's victory in the Franco-Prussian War as beneficial both for 'the nations of Europe' and for mankind at large.[96]

Judging from the coverage of the jubilee celebrations, the symbols of dual loyalty that permeated the festivities were as ubiquitous as they were persuasive. As the *Buffalo Express* observed appreciatively, the *Germania* float featured 'trappings of crimson and gold, medallions with coat of arms, and the colors of Germany and America interwoven in all directions.'[97] From buildings fluttered the German tricolour in red, black, and white alongside 'the glorious stars and stripes.'[98] If the celebrants intoned Luther's chorus 'Nun Danket Alle Gott' and burst into enthusiastic renditions of 'Die Wacht am Rhein' (The Watch on the Rhine), they ended their ceremony with 'The Star Spangled Banner.'[99] Similarly, across the border, the Union Jack was as prominent as the German tricolour.[100] And just as in Buffalo, the revellers in Berlin bowed their heads to their adopted homeland; only upon the rendition of 'God Save the Queen' did the crowds disperse and the public celebration end.[101]

Ethnicity and Nation

The vivid historical tableaux that the peace jubilees carried onto the streets of Berlin and Buffalo were 'read' not only by the thousands of onlookers and celebrants, but also by the audiences of German- and

English-language newspapers. As the one and only peace jubilee in Canada, the Berlin event attracted much attention in the province's English-language press. On 18 May 1871 the local *Berliner Journal* reprinted, with evident pride, excerpts from eighteen newspapers that had reported on this 'splendid celebration' and had praised 'the biggest and most successful demonstration which has ever taken place in Canada.'[102] Clearly, the elevation of Waterloo County to Ontario's German heartland did not go unnoticed in the English-speaking press, whose reports in turn reinforced the association of 'Waterloo County' with 'German.' Ethnicity, of course, is always constructed in a dialogue between immigrants and the host society. Yet not always did the conversations about ethnicity and national belonging garner such publicity as they did during the peace jubilee celebrations of 1871, during which the organizers self-consciously addressed Anglo-American and Anglo-Canadian audiences. As the orators placed their ethnicity in a specifically national context, the stories of Berlin and Buffalo began to diverge.

In the United States, the Forty-Eighters, who had long dreamed of a unified Germany that would grant civil liberties to its people, viewed the country's unification initially with mixed emotions. Carrying to the United States the German liberal tradition of the revolutions of 1848, the Forty-Eighters had been 'deeply concerned over the rapid rise of Prussia into a powerful military state,' as Carl Wittke points out in his classic study of the German-language press in America. These misgivings gave way to mounting pride as the German-American press enthusiastically chronicled the Prussian victories against France and even sent 'special correspondents abroad to cover the news.'[103] Although Germany's victory over France fuelled the fires of national pride in the German-American press, it soon became apparent that Chancellor von Bismarck had no intention of granting either responsible government or freedom of speech and assembly.

Could the former radicals, many of whom had carved out a comfortable niche in American middle-class society, rejoice in unity without liberty? Most of them did. To be sure, a radical New York paper, *Die Arbeiter-Union* (The Workingmen's Union) folded after its circulation declined – an unmistakable reproof of the paper's critical stance toward Bismarck. There were also those Forty-Eighters, like Karl Heinzen and Friedrich Hecker, who criticized the absence of civic liberties in the newly created German nation-state. [104] More typical, however, was a feeling of fraternal unity that engulfed both 'Grays' and 'Greens.' In

Buffalo, for instance, Francis Brunck and Edward Storck, prominent representatives of the city's pre- and post-1848 migration waves respectively, shared the speakers' podium at the peace jubilee. Together they conjured the 'thrill of patriotic gladness' that welled in every German's heart after national unity had been attained.[105] Ironically, it was Buffalo's most radical German society, the gymnasts (*Turner*), who had first suggested that a peace jubilee be held and who marched proudly in the parade's first division.[106]

If freedom was mentioned at all, it was as an afterthought, coyly hidden in a stream of patriotic declarations. Perhaps, speculated Brunck, the democratic form of government was suited only for those people who had slowly grown accustomed to it. Rather than demanding the immediate introduction of civic liberties in Germany, he encouraged German migrants 'to preserve, with all our might, the Republic in North America.'[107] Even the city's German Republican paper, the *Freie Presse*, only once hinted at Bismarck's moral obligation to pay the German people in the currency they so duly deserved: freedom and civil liberties.[108] It was not freedom that dominated the German-American discourse on the Franco-Prussian War, but a curious mixture of pride and defensiveness. Finally, ethnic spokesmen concurred, Americans had become aware of the sizeable German element in their midst. Just as important, Americans had publicly recognized German diligence and dignity, industry and intelligence – in short, the German gifts to America.[109] But even while orators at peace jubilees basked in the overt admiration, they noted with dismay that some nativists persisted in questioning German loyalty.[110] 'They maintain,' Brunck said in Buffalo, 'that these demonstrations are not in accordance with our duties as citizens of the republic; that we cannot at the same time bear love and fidelity to our native land and this republic.' To refute this 'very narrow minded idea,' he evoked a popular metaphor that would run as the proverbial red thread through the proclamations of ethnic intellectuals in future years: 'If a young man chooses a wife and leaves his father's house, does he cease to be faithful to mother and father because he ardently loves his wife and is faithful to her? We have chosen this republic as our bride, but love not less our native land.'[111] A cultural allegiance to Germany, the mother, did not interfere with political loyalty to America, the bride. This message would be reiterated in the following decades whenever calls for the assimilation of all foreigners gathered force.

In Waterloo County, where German-speaking migrants represented the majority of the population, neither newspapers nor orators dared question the loyalty of 'the Germans of Canada.'[112] Instead, speaker after speaker lauded 'the German character – naturally quiet and unobtrusive, obedient to the laws, patient under extreme suffering, possessed of dauntless bravery,' as Charles Magill, the Member of Parliament for Hamilton, put it.[113] The very presence of dignitaries, who included members of the House of Commons and the Ontario Legislature, the County Court Judge, the bar of the county, the town council, and neighbouring county officials, indicated that the jubilee was a celebration of Waterloo County's cultural mainstream, which enjoyed the support of the local establishment. The éminence grise of the jubilee, Otto Klotz, sought to translate the festive exuberance into political claims. 'We Germans, here in Ontario,' he said, 'should occupy in this country the position to which we are entitled as sons of the grand, enlightened Germany.' He then proceeded to map out both the entitlements and the obligations of Canada's German citizens: the preservation of German customs, the cultivation of excellent schools, and the promotion of commerce, arts, and science.[114] His confidence was palpable. Evidently, Waterloo County's collective memory did not harbour stories of nativist attacks or even native resentment. As a local charter group, German-speaking settlers had cut the forest and cultivated the land. As pioneers, they claimed a place at the centre of the nation's narrative, not at its margins.

In what was one of the most remarkable characteristics of the peace jubilee, this place was readily conceded to them. Members of the House of Commons who climbed the speaker's platform in Waterloo County emphasized 'the bonds of sympathy between the German and British Empires.'[115] Here, one is reminded of Matthew Frye Jacobson's assertion that 'assimilation *is* world politics ... insofar as it requires the reconciliation or integration of competing national mythologies.'[116] In a very real sense, the perceived closeness of the German and British empires shaped the discursive universe in which the peace jubilee unfolded. Because the emphasis was on the ties of kinship that bound together Great Britain and Germany, the expressions of German patriotism could be cast as unthreatening. James Young, Member of Parliament for South Waterloo, told the attendees that 'while the German people took natural pride in the success of the Fatherland, they loved the Queen of England, and the glorious constitution under which they lived.'[117] Nowhere was this image of an essential union between the German and British peoples more powerfully captured than in an address by local English-speaking citizens, presented to the organizers of the jubilee:

You can hardly fail to remember that the bond of union between your Fatherland and our Motherland is one that has been cemented by relationships the most tender and sacred possible, that in the hatred of oppression and aspirations after true liberty, the genius of our fellow-countrymen in both lands is the same; and that in reverence for truth, morality and religion, the observance of law and order, and respect for constituted authority, as well as in the cultivation of all the graces of every day national life, the people of Germany and Britain have long been in mutual accord.[118]

It was in the Dominion of Canada, the address continued, that German and British citizens had joined forces to build a 'Great Canadian nationality.' In the New World, these two great peoples were merging 'as Canadians and Colonists relying upon the same rights, civic and political, animated by the same principles and aims.' In fact, so similar were their character and mission that the 'English Residents of Berlin' were proud to assert that 'we are so much one with you in everything as it is possible for any two peoples to be.'[119] A more public endorsement of the centrality of German migrants to the project of Canadian nation building is hard to imagine.

As early as 1871, the German ethnicity that the peace jubilees brought to the fore had thus acquired a distinct American and Canadian tinge. German migrants in the United States framed their identity in the language of republicanism. Keenly aware that Bismarck's German Reich refused to grant civil liberties, yet smitten by Germany's unification and by its newly achieved national greatness, Forty-Eighters toned down their calls for German democracy and instead expressed their appreciation for the freedoms available in the great American republic. Drawing upon the 'doctrine of immigrant gifts,' a notion first developed during a wave of anti-Catholic nativism in the mid-nineteenth century, they emphasized German contributions to the project of nation building, but never quite succeeded in shedding their defensive air.[120] They revelled in the public tributes to German character and culture as published in the English-language press; yet one critical comment seemed enough to evoke the spectre of nativism that had haunted German migrants in the 1850s. In Canada, by contrast, a self-confidence permeated the speeches of the German orators. Living in a heartland of German-origin migrants where the cultural norm was German, not British, speakers revelled in the entitlements of German-Canadian citizens without betraying the slightest fear that changing political circumstances might affect their position. English-speaking dignitaries, in turn, confirmed the privileged role that German migrants held in Canadian society by pointing to the close ties between the German and British empires. When Louis Breithaupt told the Ontario legislature many decades later that 'German Canadians are devoted to the British crown and, therefore, nobody will blame them for preserving, in their hearts, a strong affection for the old Fatherland,' he reflected the customs of a local charter culture that celebrated the birthday of Queen Victoria alongside the birthday of Kaiser Wilhelm I.[121] In reconciling competing national mythologies, Waterloo County's German residents skilfully highlighted the perceived closeness of the German and British empires, whereas their 'German brethren' across the border expressed both their pride and their defensiveness.

As the historian Thomas Bender has argued, to reimagine the history of the nation and rethink national narratives means to explore 'a spectrum of social scales, both larger and smaller than the nation and not excluding the nation; social worlds interacting with one another and thus providing multiple contexts for lives, institutions, and ideas.'[122] The German peace jubilees of 1871 provide an example of one such social world that was firmly embedded in the national contexts of Canada and the United States – indeed, one that aspired to rewrite the national narratives of both nations by highlighting the seminal contributions of the ethnic group while simultaneously transcending national boundaries in a new festive space that was infused with German myth and ritual and steeped in the rhetoric of romantic nationalism. In the medium of print, Waterloo County's German middle class carved out a space that encompassed no less than three nation-states, affirmed social and symbolic ties with fellow Germans in both the United States and Germany, and introduced German migrants to the language of nationalism in which they would frame grievances and celebrate achievements in the years to come. Pressures to conform to a national norm appeared greater in the United States, where cultural difference was viewed with suspicion. In Canada, by contrast, German migrants did not seem to feel threatened by the cult of Anglo-Saxon superiority; for were they not the proud descendants of the 'Saxon' who formed the other half of the Anglo's soul?

The peace jubilees of 1871, with their joint celebration of nation and ethnicity, added a new layer of identity to both the self-image and the public image of German migrants in North America. This is not to argue that the language of nationalism became the central or even the sole idiom in which immigrants expressed their identity, their hopes, and their anguish; nor is this to deny the special appeal that cultural nationalism held for the ethnic middle class as it vied for cultural and political power within the ethnic group as well as within the nation-state it now called home.[123] Rather, this is to suggest that immigrants became increasingly well versed in the language of nationalism and that the festive spark provided by the peace jubilees could ignite an ethnic tradition of remarkable longevity. In Waterloo County, the peace jubilee of 1871 was the catalyst for the first German-Canadian singers' festival of 1874. In 1873, buoyed by the success of the peace jubilee in Berlin, the German choral societies in Berlin, Waterloo, Preston, Toronto, and Hamilton founded the *Deutsch-Canadischer Sängerbund* (German-Canadian Choir Federation), which was dedicated to the cultivation of 'German nationality in language, customs, and traditions.' Although the federation would fade in and out of existence in the decades to come, the tradition thus invented carried over in the twentieth century. Between 1874 and 1912, the German residents of Waterloo County celebrated eight singers' festivals that drew upon a rich local tradition of music making and that carried on a (musical) conversation about what it meant to be German in Canada.[124] The dialogue between the migrants and the host society, which had assumed such a public dimension in the peace jubilee of 1871, would continue to unfold along much the same historical trajectory. Cloaked in the language of tradition, the dialogue pursued an inherently modern rationale by affirming the place of German migrants at the very centre of the Canadian nation.[125]

NOTES

1 University of Waterloo, Doris Lewis Rare Book Room, Breithaupt Hewetson Clark Collection, 'Diaries of Louis Jacob Breithaupt,' 2 May 1871.

2 *Toronto Daily Telegraph*, 3 May 1871; *Canadisches Volksblatt*, 10 May 1871; *Berliner Journal*, 4 and 11 May 1871.

3 *Toronto Daily Telegraph*, 3 May 1871; *Berliner Journal*, 18 May 1871.

4 *Berliner Journal*, 11 May 1871, *Canadisches Volksblatt*, 10 May 1871; Buffalo *Demokrat*, 30 May 1871.

5 Alon Confino, *The Nation as a Local Metaphor: Württemberg, Imperial Germany, and National Memory, 1871–1918* (Chapel Hill: University of North Carolina Press, 1997), 212.

6 See the reports on the Buffalo Peace Jubilee in the *Buffalo Christian Advocate*, 27 April 1871, and *Buffalo Daily Courier*, 30 May 1871.

7 For a summary description of German Peace Jubilees in the United States, see *Die Deutschen in Amerika und die deutsch-amerikanischen Friedensfeste im Jahr 1871: Eine Erinnerungs-Schrift für die Deutschen diesseits und jenseits des Oceans* (New York: Verlags-Expedition des deutsch-amerikanischen Conversations-Lexikons, 1871).

8 *Berliner Journal*, 9 March 1871; *Canadisches Volksblatt*, 26 April 1871.

9 *Berliner Journal*, 18 May 1871.

10 David Waldstreicher, *In the Midst of Perpetual Fetes: The Making of American Nationalism, 1776–1820* (Chapel Hill: University of North Carolina Press, 1997), 11. See also David Waldstreicher, 'Rites of Rebellion, Rites of Assent: Celebrations, Print Culture, and the Origins of American Nationalism,' *Journal of American History* 82, no. 1 (June 1995): 37–61.

11 Matthew Frye Jacobson, *Special Sorrows: The Diasporic Imagination of Irish, Polish, and Jewish Immigrants in the United States* (Cambridge, MA: Harvard University Press, 1995), 16.

12 Ellen M. Litwicki, '"Our Hearts Burn with Ardent Love for Two Countries": Ethnicity and Assimilation at Chicago Holiday Celebrations, 1876–1918,' *Journal of American Ethnic History* 19, no. 3 (Spring 2000): 3–34; Heike Bungert, 'Demonstrating the Value of "Gemüthlichkeit" and "Cultur": The Festivals of German Americans in Milwaukee, 1870–1910,' in *Celebrating Ethnicity and Nation: American Festive Culture from the Revolution to the Early Twentieth Century*, ed. Geneviève Fabre and Jürgen Heideking (New York: Berghahn Books, 2001), 175–214; Orm Øverland, *Immigrant Minds, American Identities: Making the United States Home, 1870–1930* (Urbana: University of Illinois Press, 2000), 175, 193; April R. Schultz, *Ethnicity on Parade: Inventing the Norwegian American through Celebration* (Amherst: University of Massachusetts Press, 1994). See also the influential cultural-anthropological accounts on the role of national imagery by Benedict Anderson, *Imagined Communities: Reflections on the Origin and Spread of Nationalism* (New York: Verso, 1991); Eric Hobsbawm, 'Introduction,' in *The Invention of Tradition*, ed. Eric Hobsbawm and Terence Ranger (Cambridge: Cambridge University Press, 1983), 1–14; and, more recently, Kirsten Belgum, *Popularizing the Nation: Audience, Representation, and the Production of Identity in Die Gartenlaube, 1853–1900* (Lincoln: University of Nebraska Press, 1998).

13 April Schultz, '"The Pride of the Race Had Been Touched": The 1925 Norse-American Immigration Centennial and Ethnic Identity,' *Journal of American History* 7, no. 4 (March 1991): 1265–95 at 1280–3, 1292; Øverland, *Immigrant Minds*, 2–4, 20 20; Fabre and Heideking, 'Introduction,' in *Celebrating Ethnicity and the Nation*, 13; Litwicki, '"Our Hearts Burn ... ,"' 6.

14 Øverland, *Immigrant Minds*, 192, 8–9.

15 David A. Gerber, *The Making of an American Pluralism: Buffalo, New York, 1825–60* (Urbana: University of Illinois Press, 1989). As Andrew P. Yox has pointed out, these figures are estimates, based on the 1865 manuscript census schedules. As the U.S. census classified American residents according to birthplace, not ethnic origin, American-born children of German migrants were categorized as 'Americans,' which resulted in a massive undercalculation of the German population. Only by turning to the manuscript census is it possible to determine the approximate size of Buffalo's German population. See Yox, 'Decline of the German-American Community in Buffalo, 1855–1925,' PhD diss., University of Chicago, 1983, 115, 165–70, 385.

16 Waterloo County thus represented a prime example of what the historian Kathleen Neils Conzen has called 'the localization of an immigrant culture.' Conzen, 'Mainstream and Side Channels: The Localization of Immigrant Cultures,' *Journal of American Ethnic History* 11, no. 1 (Fall 1991): 5–20.

17 *Census of Canada*, 1871. In 1871, 55 per cent of Waterloo County's 40,252 residents were of German cultural origin. For excellent historical accounts of the German presence in Waterloo County, see Elizabeth Bloomfield, *Waterloo Township through Two Centuries* (Waterloo: St Jacobs Printery, 1995); John English and Kenneth McLaughlin, *Kitchener: An Illustrated History* (Toronto: Robin Brass, 1996); and Geoffrey Hayes, *Waterloo County: An Illustrated History* (Kitchener: Waterloo Historical Society, 1997).

18 Anderson, *Imagined Communities*, 44.

19 Herbert Karl Kalbfleisch, *The History of the Pioneer German Language Press of Ontario, 1835–1918* (Toronto: University of Toronto Press, 1968), 89.

20 *Berliner Journal*, 17 March 1867, 21 July 1867, 12 and 28 July 1870, and 2 February 1871. See also *Canadisches Volksblatt*, 12 and 19 April 1871 and 17 May 1871.

21 France had declared war on Germany on 19 July 1870. The war ended with the capitulation of Paris on 28 January 1871.

22 *Die Deutschen in Amerika*, 3–4.

23 *Berliner Journal*, 25 August 1870; 15 September 1870; 20 October 1870; 27 October 1870; 17 November 1870; 1 December 1870; *Buffalo Daily Telegraph*, 3 May 1871.

24 *Die Deutschen in Amerika*, 29, 23.

25 *Berliner Journal*, 16 April 1896; *Canadisches Volksblatt*, 10 May 1871.

26 *Buffalo Express*, 30 May 1871.

27 *Die Deutschen in Amerika*, 1–3, 23.

28 *Buffalo Express*, 30 May 1871; Gerber, *The Making of an American Pluralism*, 230–1.

29 *Toronto Globe*, 3 May 1871.
30 *Toronto Daily Telegraph*, 3 May 1871. See also *Hamilton Daily Spectator*, 4 May 1871; *Toronto Globe*, 3 May 1871; *Buffalo Daily Courier*, 30 May 1871; *Buffalo Express*, 27 and 30 May 1871; *Buffalo Commercial Advertiser*, 29 May 1871.
31 Buffalo *Express*, 27 May 1871.
32 Jacobson, *Special Sorrows*, 18.
33 *Buffalo Daily Courier*, May 30, 1871.
34 Ibid. See also Bungert, 'Demonstrating the Values,' 178.
35 Dieter Düding, 'Das deutsche Nationalfest von 1814: Matrix der deutschen Nationalfeste im 19. Jahrhundert,' in *Öffentliche Festkultur: Politische Feste in Deutschland von der Aufklärung bis zum Ersten Weltkrieg*, ed. Dieter Düding, Peter Friedemann, and Paul Münch (Hamburg: Rowohlt Taschenbuch Verlag, 1988), 76–7, 84.
36 *Toronto Daily Telegraph*, 3 May 1871.
37 *Buffalo Demokrat*, 30 May 1871.
38 *Die Deutschen in Amerika*, 1; *Buffalo Commercial Advertiser*, 29 May 1871.
39 *Buffalo Demokrat*, 30 May 1871; *Berliner Journal*, 4 May 1871.
40 See, for instance, *Toronto Daily Telegraph*, 3 May 1871; *Toronto Globe*, 3 May 1871; *Buffalo Christian Advocate*, 1 June 1871; *Buffalo Daily Courier*, 30 May 1871; *Buffalo Commercial Advertiser*, 29 May 1871; *Die Deutschen in Amerika*, 1–2, 11–12.
41 *Buffalo Daily Courier*, 30 May 1871.
42 *Buffalo Commercial Advertiser*, 29 May 1871.
43 *Buffalo Christian Advocate*, 27 April 1871.
44 *Berliner Journal*, 11 May 1871.
45 *Buffalo Christian Advocate*, 27 April 1871.
46 *Toronto Daily Telegraph*, 3 May 1871.
47 *Buffalo Express*, 30 May 1871.
48 See the speeches by Georg Baltz and Otto Klotz, quoted in the *Buffalo Demokrat*, 30 May 1871 and in the *Berliner Journal*, 11 May 1871. See also *Die Deutschen in Amerika*, 1.
49 *Canadisches Volksblatt*, 10 May 1871, 2–3.
50 Otto Klotz, as quoted in the *Toronto Globe*, 3 May 1871 and in the *Berliner Journal*, 11 May 1871.
51 *Buffalo Daily Courier*, 30 May 1871.
52 *Die Deutschen in Amerika*, 1, 22–3.
53 As quoted in Schultz, '"The Pride of the Race,"' 1282. For a point of comparison, see Manfred Hettling and Paul Nolte, 'Bürgerliche Feste als

symbolische Politik im 19. Jahrhundert,' in *Bürgerliche Feste. Symbolische Formen politischen Handelns im 19. Jahrhundert,* ed. Manfred Hettling and Paul Nolte (Göttingen: Vandenhöck & Ruprecht, 1993), 18.

54 In making this connection, I am indebted to David Waldstreicher's study 'Rites of Rebellion, Rites of Assent,' 49–51. See also Fabre and Heideking, 'Introduction,' 14; and Roger D. Abrahams, 'An American Vocabulary of Celebration,' in *Time Out of Time: Essays on the Festival,* ed. Alessandro Falassi (Albuquerque: University of New Mexico Press, 1987), 180.

55 *Toronto Daily Telegraph,* 3 May 1871; *Toronto Globe,* 3 May 1871.

56 *Berliner Journal,* 4 May 1871.

57 *Toronto Daily Telegraph,* 3 May 1871.

58 *Buffalo Express,* 30 May 1871.

59 *Buffalo Christian Advocate,* 1 June 1871; Yox, 'Decline of the German-American Community in Buffalo,' 129.

60 *Buffalo Demokrat,* 4 May 1871. In this context, see also *Die Deutschen in Amerika,* 42; and Schultz, *Ethnicity on Parade,* 71–2.

61 Fabre and Heideking, 'Introduction,' 19.

62 Bungert, 'Demonstrating the Values,' 177; Craig Heron and Steve Penfold, 'The Craftmen's Spectacle: Labour Day Parades in Canada, the Early Years,' *Histoire sociale / Social History* 29, no. 58 (November 1996), 371–3.

63 *Buffalo Christian Advocate,* 1 June 1871; *Buffalo Express,* 30 May 1871; *Buffalo Demokrat,* 30 May 1871.

64 This interpretation was advanced in the souvenir booklet of the peace jubilees in the United States, *Die Deutschen in Amerika,* 23. See also Brent O. Peterson, *Popular Narratives and Ethnic Identity: Literature and Community in Die Abendschule* (Ithaca: Cornell University Press, 1991), 224.

65 *Berliner Journal,* 25 August 1870 and 11 May 1871. See also *Toronto Globe,* 3 May 1871.

66 *Toronto Daily Telegraph,* 3 May 1871; *Buffalo Freie Presse,* 27 May 1871.

67 Schultz, *Ethnicity on Parade,* 82–3.

68 Yox, 'Decline of the German-American Community in Buffalo,' 131; *Buffalo Freie Presse,* 13 May 1871.

69 *Buffalo Demokrat,* 2 May 1871; *Toronto Daily Telegraph,* 3 May 1871. See also Andreas Dörner, 'Der Mythos der nationalen Einheit: Symbolpolitik und Deutungskämpfe bei der Einweihung des Hermannsdenkmals im Jahre 1875,' *Archiv für Kulturgeschichte* 79, no. 2 (1997): 401.

70 For a point of comparison, see Bungert, 'Demonstrating the Values,' 177.

71 *Buffalo Demokrat,* 30 May 1871.

72 *Buffalo Demokrat,* 13 May 1871; *Die Deutschen in Amerika,* 67.

73 See Jacobson, *Special Sorrows*, 80.
74 Vicki Spencer, 'Herder and Nationalism: Reclaiming the Principle of Cultural Respect,' *Australian Journal of Politics and History* 43, no. 1 (1997): 1.
75 Düding, 'Das deutsche Nationalfest von 1814,' 76, 68.
76 *Berliner Journal*, 11 May 1871.
77 Simon Schama, *Landscape and Memory* (Toronto: Random House of Canada, 1995), 87, 96–7.
78 *Berliner Journal*, 11 May 1871.
79 Karl Müller-Grote, 'Onkel Karl: Deutschkanadische Lebensbilder,' *German-Canadian Yearbook* 15 (1998): 226–9; *Berliner Journal*, 16 July 1896 and 19 August 1897; *Hamilton Spectator*, 14 August 1897.
80 Anthony D. Smith, 'National Identity and Myths of Ethnic Descent,' *Research in Social Movements, Conflict, and Change* 7 (1984): 101.
81 *Buffalo Daily Courier*, 30 May 1871.
82 Patricia Mazón, 'Germania Triumphant: The Niederwald National Monument and the Liberal Movement in Imperial Germany,' *German History* 18, no. 2 (2000): 169–71.
83 *Toronto Daily Telegraph*, 3 May 1871; *Toronto Globe*, 3 May 1871. See also Jonathan Sperber, 'Festivals of National Unity in the German Revolution of 1848–49,' *Past and Present* 136 (August 1992): 119.
84 *Berliner Journal*, 4 May 1871.
85 *Buffalo Express*, 30 May 1871; *Geschichte der Deutschen in Buffalo und Erie County, N.Y., mit Biographien und Illustrationen hervorragender Deutsch-Amerikaner, welche zur Entwicklung der Stadt Buffalo beigetragen haben* (Buffalo: Reinecke und Zesch, 1898), 40; *Buffalo Commercial Advertiser*, 29 May 1871.
86 *Buffalo Express*, 30 May 1871.
87 *Toronto Globe*, 3 May 1871; *Buffalo Express*, 30 May 1871; *Buffalo Demokrat*, 30 May 1871; *Buffalo Daily Courier*, 30 May 1871.
88 For the role of myths in creating community, see Smith, 'National Identity,' 95; Pierre Nora, 'The Era of Commemoration,' in *Realms of Memory: The Construction of the French Past*, ed. Pierre Nora (New York: Columbia University Press, 1998), 632–3.
89 Dörner, 'Der Mythos der nationalen Einheit,' 395.
90 Ibid., 397.
91 Schama, *Landscape and Memory*, 102.
92 *Buffalo Demokrat*, 30 May 1871.
93 *Buffalo Commercial Advertiser*, 29 May 1871.
94 See Dieter Düding's discussion of the 'matrix of German national holidays' in 'Das deutsche Nationalfest von 1814,' 67–88.

95 *Buffalo Commercial Advertiser*, 29 May 1871.

96 *Buffalo Daily Courier*, 30 May 1871. The headlines in Buffalo's English-language press announced, for example, 'The Great German Peace Jubilee – A Memorable Day in Buffalo – One of the Grandest Demonstrations Ever Witnessed in the City.' Buffalo *Daily Courier*, 30 May 30, 1871. Or they advertised, in big, bold print, 'The Jubilee – Grand Peace Demonstration Yesterday – The Germans Out in Full Force – Splendid Procession and Interesting Exercises.' Buffalo *Express*, 30 May 1871, 4.

97 *Buffalo Express*, 30 May 1871.

98 *Buffalo Evening Post*, 30 May 1871.

99 *Buffalo Demokrat*, 26 May 1871.

100 *Toronto Globe*, 3 May 1871.

101 *Berliner Journal*, 4 May 1881.

102 *London Advertiser* and *Galt Reformer*, as quoted in the *Berliner Journal*, 18 May 1871.

103 Carl Wittke, *The German-Language Press in America* (New York: Haskell House, 1973), 164.

104 Carl Wittke, *Refugees of the Revolution: The German Forty-Eighters in America* (Westport: Greenwood Press, 1970[1952]), 345–52.

105 *Buffalo Express*, 30 May 1871; *Buffalo Daily Courier*, 30 May 1871.

106 *Buffalo Demokrat*, 27 and 30 May 1871.

107 *Buffalo Daily Courier*, 30 May 1871.

108 *Buffalo Freie Presse*, 29 April 1871.

109 *Die Deutschen in Amerika*, 2–5, 25–6. See also *Buffalo Daily Courier*, 30 May 1871; *Buffalo Express*, 30 May 1871; *Buffalo Commercial Advertiser*, 29 May 1871; *Buffalo Evening Post*, 30 May 1871.

110 *Die Deutschen in Amerika*, 9.

111 *Buffalo Daily Courier*, 30 May 1871.

112 *Toronto Globe*, 3 May 1871.

113 *Hamilton Daily Spectator*, 5 May 1871.

114 *Berliner Journal*, 11 May 1871.

115 *Hamilton Daily Spectator*, 5 May 1871.

116 Jacobson, *Special Sorrows*, 216.

117 *Toronto Daily Telegraph*, 3 May 1871.

118 Kitchener Public Library, Grace Schmidt Room of Local History, Waterloo Historical Society, Manuscript Collection 15.1c, 'Address of the English Deputation to the Managing Committee of the German Peace Festival, 1871, Berlin, Tuesday, May 2, 1871.'

119 Ibid.

120 Kathleen Neils Conzen et al., 'The Invention of Ethnicity: A Perspective

from the U.S.A.,' *Journal of American Ethnic History* 12, no. 1 (Fall 1992):
13. The defensive tone of the jubilee celebration in Buffalo is even more
noteworthy if we consider the 'colonizing vision' that imbued German-
American ethnic leaders, who aspired to transplant culture and sophis-
tication to a presumably culturally barren American landscape. See
Kathleen Neils Conzen, 'Phantom Landscapes of Colonization: Germans
in the Making of a Pluralist America,' in *The German-American Encounter:
Conflict and Cooperation between Two Cultures, 1800–2000*, ed. Frank Trom-
mler and Elliott Shore (New York: Berghahn Books, 2001), 11.
121 See, for example, *Berliner Journal*, 26 May 1887, 15 March 1888, 10 May
1888, 31 May 1888, 28 June 1888, 1 May 1890, 29 May 1890, 2 April 1891.
122 Thomas Bender, 'Historians, the Nation, and the Plenitude of Narratives,'
in *Rethinking American History in a Global Age*, ed. Thomas Bender (Berkeley: University of California Press, 2002), 8.
123 Litwicki, '"Our Hearts Burn ...,"' 11. For more cautious appraisals of
the long-term impact of ethnic celebrations, see Kathleen Neils Conzen,
'Ethnicity as Festive Culture: Nineteenth-Century German America
on Parade,' in *The Invention of Ethnicity*, ed. Werner Sollors (New York:
Oxford University Press, 1989), 71; and Dirk Hoerder, who, in his contribution to this volume, questions the significance that the nationalist
idiom might have held for migrants whose transnational lives defied
neatly drawn national boundaries.
124 Barbara Lorenzkowski, 'Border Crossings: Making German Identities
in the New World, 1850–1914,' PhD diss., University of Ottawa, 2002),
132–76.
125 On the 'affinities of ethnicity and modernity,' see Werner Sollors, *Beyond
Ethnicity: Consent and Descent in American Culture* (New York: Oxford
University Press, 1986), 240–5; and David A. Gerber, 'Forming a Transnational Narrative: New Perspective on European Migration to the United
States,' *History Teacher* 35, no. 1 (November 2001): 61–77.

6 A Weak Woman Standing Alone: Home, Nation, and Gender in the Work of German-Canadian Immigration Agent Elise von Koerber, 1872–84

ANGELIKA SAUER

Elise von Koerber was a lonely forty-five-year-old woman when she died in a hotel room in London, England, in the spring of 1884. The Canadian government's representative in Britain had to arrange and pay for her funeral, but that was only fair, since she had once been a salaried civil servant, one of the first female employees of the Canadian state. At the time of her death, German-born Koerber was a widow. Her Austrian husband had worked as a civil servant in the pre-Confederation Department of Crown Lands but had died in 1870 or 1871, leaving his family all but destitute.[1] After his death, Elise's health was fragile, and she periodically succumbed to spells of severe illness that she herself described as 'nervous and brain fever'[2] but that might well have been bouts of depression or exhaustion. A mother of four, she lost one of her teenage sons in 1877 to illness in Germany. Her daughter Matilda (born in 1861 in Ottawa) found employment in Somerset, England, as a governess. Another son may have been studying forestry in Germany. Her few remaining friends were in Montreal and Ottawa; she had acquaintances in Geneva, Stuttgart, and New York. In the last decade of her life she crossed the Atlantic no less than thirteen times, shuttling back and forth between Europe and North America at a frantic pace. Her peripatetic life came to a seemingly random end in Britain.[3]

The early history of Canada after Confederation is full of individual stories, and social and cultural historians have attempted to fit them into the national historiography, thus redefining and interrogating the very idea of nation. What poses an obstacle in nation-oriented historiography in the case of a person like Elise von Koerber is that so much of her life was lived elsewhere and that so much of her role in Canadian history is removed from Canadian territory, mostly visible in imagined and historiographical spaces that straddle borders and oceans. Immigration historians have been at the forefront of a trend to 'deterritorialize' history to address this problem of 'unbounded' lives. In this volume, Dirk Hoerder proposes a theoretical framework of transcultural lives to allow us to see both migration and national identity formation in their global context. Transculturalism, according to Hoerder, 'denotes the competence to live in two or more differing cultures and, in the process, create a personal transcultural space.' Other scholars prefer the term 'transnationalism' to acknowledge the undeniable power that national states, cultures, and elites possess in delineating the parameters of multisited social spaces and their meaning.[4] Transnationalism, defined as 'a social process whereby migrants operate in social fields that transgress geographic, political and cultural borders'[5] (or simply: living across national spaces), provides a new analytical framework for questions about immigrant integration as well as nation building.

There is no doubt that Elise von Koerber lived a transnational life. Born in the Grand Duchy of Baden in 1839, well before the formation of the German imperial state, she married an Austrian subject in the 1850s. Their subsequent immigration to the British colony of Canada rendered her legal status of belonging multilayered and confusing. Her sense of identity seemed to have been equally confounded. She was clearly fond of her adopted country Canada and lived there for most of her adult life, but she left this 'adopted home' in 1882 in middle age after a falling out with friends. Rather than returning to the place of her birth, Baden, or claiming German citizenship, she moved to Britain. Koerber read, wrote, and spoke German, English, and French; she naturally slipped into the language of her audience. Her sense of identity, as far as one can tell from her public writings, was based not primarily on ethnicity or nation but on gender and class. In the way she described her life and conducted her travels, there was no sense of 'leaving' and 'returning' and no steady national vantage point. Rather, her perspective seemed changing and circumstantial. Her 'home' was neither 'here' nor 'there' but in a place that she attempted to create through her work with female immigrants.

In this chapter, we look at Elise von Koerber in her function as an individual with a transnational sense of self who became involved in immigrant recruitment as an agent for the Canadian government. Her immigration work in the 1870s and early 1880s, especially in the field of female migration, is not well known although it clearly pioneered much better-publicized efforts that were later undertaken by British

and Anglo-Canadian organizations. These organizations were oper-
ated by women on a volunteer and charitable basis, yet the salaried
immigration agents in post-Confederation Canada were men. Therefore, Koerber's role as one of the first female salaried civil servants in
Canada adds a further dimension to this study. In the official letters that
Koerber wrote during the last twelve years of her life, as well as in several published speeches in German and English, we encounter a high-
strung, single-minded, assertive woman who chafed at the constraints
imposed on her by gendered definitions of duty. Her case reminds us of
the importance, alluded to by Christiane Harzig in this volume, of gendering the concepts of citizenship, transculturalism, and transnationalism and of questioning the gendered meaning of home and nation.

I

Immigration became an element of Canadian nation building shortly
after Confederation, in September 1872. A federal–provincial immigration conference identified the recruitment of immigrants as a crusade of
national importance that would require an effective system of federal
immigration agencies in Britain and continental Europe. Irish-born William Dixon was installed as the first permanent agent in London at the
modest salary of $1,000 annually.[6] Until his death in October 1873, Dix-
on – with two small rooms, two clerks, and a messenger at his disposal
– was in charge of overseeing subagents in Britain as well as temporary,
special agents sent from Canada to carry out additional recruitment
drives.[7] There was no coherent approach in Ottawa to choosing these
temporary agents. Indeed, the choice of immigration agents was considered by many one of the worst examples of civil service patronage.[8]
Much of the work of recruiting immigrants was left in the hands of
commercial agents who worked for various shipping or land compa-
nies. Many viewed this as little more than human trafficking.[9]

Elise von Koerber joined this motley, ill-favoured crew of immigration agents in the fall of 1872. What motivated a young, middle-class
widow and mother to choose immigration agency as her profession?
And what enabled her, a disenfranchised woman, to enter the ranks
of salaried civil servants during the high time of political patronage
appointments? Both questions take us beyond existing studies of female
immigration activists in the British Empire, studies that accurately portray their protagonists as women of means pursuing volunteer work
out of philanthropic sentiments.[10] Elise von Koerber did not fit this cat-

egory and was well aware of it: 'Some people are so fortunately situated as to have both the good will to do useful work and the necessary means to do so combined; others have only their intense desire and the courage of sacrificing time, energy, talent and life's best comforts. I possess but the latter qualification.'[11]

Her most obvious motivation for immigration work was entirely practical: after the death of her husband, she needed paid employment to support herself and her four children. 'I had to fill the place of father to my children, and therefore I had to work myself into a position which would ultimately bring me a salary,' she explained in a speech to the Toronto City Council at the end of the decade. Her unapologetic pursuit of paid employment, although dressed up in the appropriately gendered language of being a 'father' to her children while performing her work in 'a very quiet, unassuming and womanly way,'[12] suggests a resourceful and astute woman who challenged the boundaries of her prescribed gender role out of duty to her family. Her status as a well-connected widow may provide the answer to the second question. As Leanne Dustan's work on women in the early Canadian civil service[13] shows, very occasionally a widow could be awarded the position of her late husband; alternatively, the acquaintance of a well-connected male friend could lead to a female patronage appointment. Koerber's late husband had been a draughtsman in the Lower Canada Surveys and Patent Branch of the Department of Crown Lands, and the Koerbers seem to have been known to French-Canadian politicians and civil servants.[14]

For Koerber, the death of her husband, however tragic, seems in fact to have been an opportunity to escape the confines of her traditionally defined place in a gendered home that did not allow her to pursue rational economic or intellectual interests. She confessed to a long-standing fascination with the possibility of improving services for immigrants: 'I have been watching the progress of emigration for years, and have been wishing for an opportunity to become active in this line and to try and [sic] improve some points in connection with it.'[15] During her early years in Canada, she recalled, there were few provisions in place for the reception and settlement of immigrants. When people approached her and her husband for advice and help, she began to realize that a more systematic management of migration and settlement was needed.[16] However, there was nothing that she, a woman, could do. On the basis of this personal experience, she developed a desire 'to help emigrants in every way possible by guiding them according to certain rules, giving them special advice, caring for them with constant watchfulness, and at the cost and sacrifice of all my time, and all my thought.'[17] Both paternalistic and professional in her motives, Koerber was at the cutting edge of thinking about the role of the modern civil servant and well beyond accepted thinking in her ideas about women's contributions to building a nation-state. Widowhood provided her with the opportunity to leave home and enter the male world of managing, directing, and organizing, in addition to women's watching and caring.[18]

Once Koerber was able to leave the private, unpaid life of the traditional home, it became obvious that she wanted to leave home in more ways than one. By 1872, despite being in poor health, she seemed determined to travel to Europe to work in the field of immigrant recruitment. It would be easy to see this move as a desire to return to her 'real home' in Baden and perhaps her family of origin. However, Koerber's movements after leaving Canada in October 1872 defy this explanation. With an initial contact address in Aix-la-Chapelle, she proceeded via London to Alsace and Switzerland with only a brief stop in Karlsruhe, Baden. From there she travelled extensively in the Austrian Tyrol and in parts of southern Germany, especially Wurttemberg, with frequent excursions to Frankfurt, Berlin, and London. Her main country of residence for much of the 1870s was in fact Switzerland, but she also returned to Canada three times in 1873–4 alone.

Elise von Koerber did not locate herself in a home after 1872. Some of this unbounded life – at least, her failure to return permanently to Baden – may be explained by the hostility she encountered, both among the authorities, who considered her a foreigner and threatened to arrest her for illegal immigrant recruitment, and also among her own former friends, who considered her unpatriotic and possibly a white slave trader. Koerber's response was to shrug off the accusations and to suggest that immigration would no longer seem frightening as soon as one had dared to cross the borders of one's fatherland. For Elise von Koerber, leaving had become a normal way of life.[19]

At the same time it would be false to suggest that Koerber rejected her duties to her family, although she encountered many obstacles in her attempts to be a provider and a caregiver. At a time when the Canadian government had appointed two men, Jacob Klotz and William Hespeler, at full salary to organize immigration from Germany to Canada,[20] Koerber had to struggle to be recognized as the breadwinner of her family. She took a considerable risk. As she testified in the

House of Commons in 1880: 'I had no salary and no expenses; I paid everything myself. ... By degrees, however, my position was made an official one.'[21] Until the end of 1874, she was paid a per capita commission of two dollars for each immigrant she recruited, and she had problems simply getting reimbursed for regular Atlantic crossings, having to rely instead on free trips provided by the Allan Line and on financial support from the Ontario government's Emigrant Office.[22] In 1875 she obtained her first contract appointment, but for half the salary that male agents received for their work. Koerber was greatly annoyed by this obvious discrimination, pointing out that she had to cover not only personal expenses but also the education of her children.[23] Throughout 1875 and 1876, she demanded to be 'placed on the same footing with other agents, as regards the salary, for what I receive now does not suffice to cover my most indispensable daily wants for myself and my four children in countries where the living is so expensive.'[24] Her persistence paid off for 1877, when her salary was finally raised to $100 per month – the sum paid to male immigration agents at the time.[25]

A woman who redefined the meaning of home, Koerber also began to negotiate the idea of national belonging. Through her work she felt implicated in the nation-building projects of two countries at the same time. She approached immigrants as a European, calling them *emigrants* more often than *immigrants*. She saw well-regulated emigration as a necessary social policy for the landless proletariat of the German empire, defining emigration as 'the only way to social reform, the only rational means of assisting our masses, saving them.'[26] At the same time, she argued that Canada had an absolute need for immigrants: 'Immigration is the all-important point for the promotion of the welfare of this country.'[27] She recommended that the Canadian government use more effective recruiting methods, especially in German-speaking Europe,[28] and that it rely on educated bureaucrats with expertise in the language, culture, and political conditions of the country.[29] Koerber, then, thought that the state's main function was to protect those who could not protect themselves, and to erase antagonistic class tensions and create conditions for economic and social equilibrium. If a government was responsible for giving 'paternal protection to its subjects,'[30] then the educated middle class would serve a crucial function as experts and managers.

As a middle-class woman and as a German immigrant, Koerber designed for herself an active role in the future of Canada and of Germany. This point leads us to the crux of her motives for getting involved in Canadian government immigration work: she had an agenda – or, as she called it, her 'pet plan.'[31] Although she ostensibly went to Europe in 1872 to recruit Swiss settlers for Northern Ontario and Tyrolean dairy farmers for the Eastern Townships of Quebec, she in fact carried with her an idea that quickly evolved into a grand scheme: the creation of an international system of women's societies dedicated to the management and protection of women's migration. Her initial detour into general immigrant recruitment was necessary because she had to establish a professional reputation and gain the confidence of her superiors. For several years, she worked as a recruiting agent while pondering the problems surrounding women's migration. She then constructed plans for an elaborate international network of protective and control measures, provided by women for women. Through her work, she intended to create a new transnational gendered space, one in which women would help other women migrate from one place to another.

II

In developing a system of protection for transnational women, Elise von Koerber encountered numerous obstacles, created by gendered national discourses of bureaucracy, citizenship, and belonging, that stood in the way of her work and her life goals. From her public statements, it is not entirely clear whether, by the late 1870s, she had begun to envision a long-term future for herself as quasi-diplomatic representative of the Canadian government in Europe or whether she was committed to the management and control of female migration.[32] However, we may safely assume that Koerber was resourceful and that she negotiated her role according to circumstances, whatever her innermost wishes and desires. Initially, she considered her general migration work a means to the end of exploring the conditions and requirements of women's migrations. While it became increasingly clear that her work with female migrants was more acceptable to those in power, both as a gender-appropriate field of employment in the Canadian civil service and as a legal area of migration work in Germany, Koerber also discovered the appeal of power herself by associating with high-ranking European officials and by supervising male employees. Her choices eventually reflected the limitations she faced in the world of the 1870s and 1880s.

During the initial phase of her work in 1873, Koerber hoped to identify potential demand for her system of women's migration in the new German Reich. She falsely assumed that the German government's well-known antagonism toward foreign recruiters was limited to those promoting the emigration of military-aged males; she herself intended 'to promote female Emigration in this country, against which they surely can have nothing to say.'[33] She started by educating the general and philanthropic public on the issues as she saw them. Accompanying several Swiss families and single girls to Canada in June 1873, she observed closely 'all that passed on land, as well as on sea' to find evidence for her claim that better protections were needed.[34] She then published her thoughts on the organization of female emigration in a brief notice that she distributed during her extensive travels throughout Baden, Wurttemberg, Bavaria, Hesse, and Saxony as well as the Tyrol and Switzerland, hoping 'to create interest among the different unions of ladies and the authorities to favour the introduction of a system by which to control and protect female emigration from Europe.'[35]

Koerber did not question the premise that women had to emigrate and that they had to do so other than as part of a family unit. Like the proponents of the leading bourgeois feminist programs in both Germany and the Anglo-Saxon world, she was well aware of the structural problem of women's underemployment, underpayment, and undereducation. But she did not primarily worry about middle-class women like herself. Rather, observing the profound social transformations in Germany that had followed German political unification, she pointed out that 'there are thousands of women who have not received an education, who have to make a living.' Rapid modernization and industrialization left poor country women with few choices other than the degradation of unemployment and city life.[36] To Koerber, emigration seemed 'a most desirable means to relieve poverty and indigence, and to better the condition of many a poor woman,' especially if one contemplated 'the great want of females in transatlantic countries.'[37]

The necessity of single female migration firmly established in her mind, Koerber tackled the thorny issue of how to make such a process safe for *respectable* middle- and working-class women.[38] In all her reports and letters she proceeded from one starting point: 'Female emigration is perhaps more abused than that of men & families, at any rate to much more terrible purposes ... It is, in thousands of cases, a terrible curse.'[39] Her information led her to believe that existing commercialized recruitment had simply created a lively transatlantic sex trade. Many women supposedly 'leave their country, allured to do so by worthless characters, who lead them to destruction, and ... this fearful evil is carried to a terrible extent.'[40] Koerber claimed to have heard 'tales of shocking abuse' about the 'traffic ... which is made with women as purchasable merchandise ... Secret agents are continually traversing the Continent engaging women for evil purposes.'[41] She collected data that supposedly proved that German women were particularly vulnerable.[42] Koerber vividly evoked the potential evil that lurked at every corner of a transatlantic voyage: 'Females, alone and unprotected and inexperienced, are there [in lodging houses] thrown together with all kinds of people, sometimes the very scum of populace, and there it is that dangerous acquaintances are formed. I have seen things and people which made me shudder.'[43] The danger was perhaps greatest aboard ships and in immigration sheds, where women constantly mixed freely with men. The consequences of such 'unnecessary exposure'[44] could then be found in North American maternity wards, shelters for prostitutes, and police stations.

In Koerber's opinion, any transnational system of female migration had to be based on two premises: that every respectable woman had a right to freedom from sexual exploitation in separate and distinct women's spaces; and that there had to be close moral surveillance of those girls who, due to their age and class, could not be trusted to make respectable choices for themselves. Older, educated women like herself could seemingly observe sexual conflict from a detached place, unaffected by sexual oppression and seduction. They were capable of serving as protectors and guardians in mixed spaces – for example, as matrons aboard ships.[45] Wherever possible, however, separation was preferable to mixed spaces. Immigration sheds had to provide separate rooms because, as she remarked, existing arrangements in Toronto 'would not at all do for respectable women.'[46] Aboard ships, there should be strict rules 'that no women are allowed in the men's cabin after tea time, and that after 10 o'clock in the evening no women are allowed to be on deck.' These points, Koerber insisted, 'are all fundamental necessities for the importation of *respectable* female immigration.'[47] Furthermore, there should be a female reception agent. The best interest of the country would be served 'if womanly influence could gain ascendancy over the mind of the young women the moment they arrive ashore.' In her opinion, it was the moral protection of female immigrants, not *numbers* of female immigrants, that represented 'the greatest material service' to the country.[48]

Koerber's plan to address the problem of respectable female migration was premised on the principle of reciprocity. No single person, association, or country could bear such a momentous burden; success depended on the sharing of responsibility among all the countries of emigration and immigration. After several years' study of European conditions and the workings of philanthropic organizations, Koerber settled on the model of the Red Cross Alliance to describe her own system of organization and protection: a uniform system of national entities, rallying around the main principle (and directed by international headquarters), but each free to adapt to local circumstances and views.[49] The main point was coordination; if the matter of female migration was treated 'as a whole' and internationally (or as she initially said, 'universally'), the goal of comprehensive protection could be achieved. Women's migration had to be acknowledged as 'a system of its own' separate from the gendered, national interest expressed by the state.[50]

However, before a neophyte like herself could acquire the credibility to build such a system, she would have to prove her value in the field of immigration work to the Canadian government. Things did not go smoothly at first with her superiors, and Koerber recognized that the difficulties she had in her professional work were due to her gender. She resented the lack of encouragement for her ideas and complained about 'the general distrust as to a woman's capacity and judgment in public matters.' She challenged her detractors to allow women to contribute their special talents to the nation-building project: 'The true and high-minded men of our time recognize in various ways that the gifts of self-devotion, energy, enthusiasm and moral courage are to be despised in no one, and that the cases where women rendered considerable services, even to the State, are worthy of record and recognition.'[51] Unfortunately, the servants of patriarchy in both Europe and Canada continued to disparage her efforts. In 1875, the report of a Swiss delegation to Canada expressed 'surprise that the Government of Canada would have laid the interest of the country into the hands of a woman.'[52] Her supervisor accused her of indiscrete conduct[53] and recommended that her work in Switzerland be placed in the hands of a francophone 'gentleman.'[54] In relation to this matter, the author of a thesis on Swiss immigration to Canada has suggested that Koerber's informal approach to her work and her bypassing of bureaucratic formalities created enemies, and he may well be right.[55] Koerber resented the bureaucratic chain of command and relied on social networking and personal appeals to powerful men.[56] She wanted to work in a man's world but not by men's rules.

In some ways, this personal approach worked well with the European public. By the end of 1874 she had indeed raised 'beaucoup

d'intérêst dans différents circles [sic] officiels et autres'[57] and had established contacts with existing European organizations dedicated to the
welfare of women. In the fall of 1874, she was invited to a conference
of the Universal Alliance in Frankfurt and met the Grand Duchess of
Hesse (Queen Victoria's daughter Alice) in Darmstadt. German royalty
may have been well disposed toward her plans, but the German federal
and state governments were not. Nationalist resentment against foreign
promoters of emigration on German soil, and issues of a migrant woman's citizenship, became the next obstacles in the path of her transnational efforts. After Koerber returned from a trip to Canada in August
1874, she was suddenly 'ordered to leave the territory of Baden' as a
result of an inquiry from Berlin that 'had its reason in the law, which
only permits subjects of the Empire to work in emigration matters.'[58]

If Koerber wanted to continue her work in German territory, she
would have to sort out her official badge of belonging, her citizenship.
This turned out to be more complicated than she could have possibly
imagined. The authorities in Baden told her that 'as I have been living
in Germany 1 ½ years nearly, I have a right to claim my subjectship and
shall do so forthwith.'[59] However, the widow of an Austrian, naturalized in the colony of Canada before Confederation and born in Baden
before the German empire had been formed, found out that it seemed
impossible to ascertain whether she was a British, Austrian, or German
subject. Koerber truly was, as she said, 'a person ... who enjoyed the
protection of no country.'[60] She was not legally German, but neither was
she under the diplomatic umbrella of the Canadian or British governments as long as she was on German soil. It is no wonder, then, that she
created in her mind alternative forms of belonging. Since the nation-
states with which she associated herself had failed to provide the crucial protection she felt was owed to the individual by the government,
she appealed to a different authority. Addressing a German women's
organization, she declared her new allegiance: 'I come after what I have
done, as a weak woman standing alone, to solve the difficult questions
... Arriving at a point at which I feel I cannot go further alone, I put
myself under the protection of the ladies of Germany, trusting for their
assistance in carrying out what I have begun.'[61]

From this point forward, Koerber's energies increasingly went into
female migration work while she cleverly delegated general emigrant
recruitment to male colleagues or new acquaintances. In Switzerland,
she supervised and trained Johann Tanner; in southern Germany, she
found in Wurttemberg lawyer Otto Hahn a trustworthy man who did

not object to working with a woman and relying on her help.[62] In her women's work she shifted to the philanthropic model. During a temporary health-related sojourn in London in early 1875, she studied 'what the English Emigrant Societies have, as yet, achieved; what is their mode of working; if it could be adopted as a model to German societies; and if communication could be established between English and German societies.'[63] Koerber resolved to concentrate her practical efforts in Switzerland until her legal problems in Germany could be resolved. The time had now come to move from the information-gathering and networking stage into the phase of organizing committees that would oversee the selection of single women for emigration and issue letters of recommendation. Throughout 1876 she held drawing-room meetings in various Swiss cities, where she succeeded in tapping into an existing sentiment of protective philanthropy as well as existing organizational and international gatherings, such as the congress that had established the *Union Internationale des Amies de la Jeune Fille* in 1877. Switzerland was clearly receptive to the kinds of ideas that Koerber espoused, and she enjoyed considerable popularity.[64] In Lausanne, a committee was formed under her guidance that would later select a number of young servant girls, whom Koerber herself accompanied to Canada for placement in Kingston and Ottawa.[65]

The Swiss success notwithstanding, Koerber's heart was set on initiating similar committees in Germany. She pursued cooperation with the *Lette Verein*, founded in 1866 for the education and training of women.[66] The association enjoyed the patronage of the German Crown Princess Victoria, Queen Victoria's oldest daughter, who was married to the Prussian Crown Prince,[67] and it was with the Crown Princess's interest in female welfare that Koerber's fondest hopes rested. To her delight, she received an invitation in early April 1876 to attend a conference of German women's associations in Hamburg that had on its agenda the question of protecting female emigrants. Since she had no official accreditation, she had to decline an audience with the Crown Princess. However, she sounded out the German Foreign Office in Berlin as to whether her work protecting emigrants, rather than promoting emigration, would be acceptable to the German government. The results were sufficiently encouraging to embolden her to indicate to her boss, the Canadian Minister of Agriculture, that 'my female emigration scheme has arrived at so important and interesting a stage that it is absolutely necessary for me to have a personal conference with you as soon as possible.'[68]

During her time in Canada in late 1876,[69] she received what she interpreted as the minister's semi-official encouragement for her female immigration scheme; she also began to lay the groundwork for the reception of female immigrants. She had established contacts with the YWCA in Toronto during earlier visits and had negotiated the use of their reception home in 1877. She also attempted to form 'Ladies' Immigration Protective Societies' in Montreal and Ottawa and have them officially recognized by the Canadian government. Unfortunately, the German side of things was moving much more slowly; many people were still not convinced that the emigration of women was necessary, as well as the protection of those who emigrated. Not until two years later, in the fall of 1878, did Koerber set out for another congress of the *Lette Verein*, this one in Wiesbaden. She renewed her acquaintance with the Grand Duchess of Hesse, and later expressed to the minister in Ottawa her hope that Alice would convince her Royal Sister Louise, wife of the Governor General, to place herself at the head of the ladies' committees in Canada: 'then our cause would be safe here [in Canada].'[70] Koerber then moved on to address a *Frauen-Fortbildungsverein* in Dresden in October and suddenly realized that the climate had changed: people were ready to talk openly about emigration. A committee was formed, which held out the prospect of sending many hard-working Saxonian women to Canada.[71]

Koerber had reached a turning point in her female emigration work. She went on to Berlin to see if the ladies there, after two-and-a-half years of deliberation, were ready to act, and found to her surprise and delight that they were. The Crown Princess granted her a personal interview and told her that 'well protected emigration is by far the most rational means of helping a portion of our sex.' Next, the Union of Patriotic Ladies informed her that Her Majesty, the Empress of Germany, had taken a lively interest in her plans, which she thought 'well worth being furthered.' Koerber was near speechless and confessed that 'my reception [in Berlin] has been a favourable one above all expectations.'[72] She began to contemplate finally taking out German citizenship, moving to Berlin, and having her children become German subjects.

Just at this moment, in a case of singularly bad timing, the newly elected Conservative government in Ottawa terminated her appointment in a general retrenchment initiative that cost several special agents in Europe their jobs. Koerber managed to stay on until a meeting on 6 January 1879, at which Lina Morgenstern, editor of the *Deutsche Hausfrauen-Zeitung*, spoke in front of German and Swiss press representatives. There, Baron Theodor von Bunsen, a diplomat from a famous Anglo-German family, was named the head of the newly appointed German Central Committee for female emigration. This was a moment of triumph: 'Letters of congratulation came to me from all sides, for those who understand the difficulties with which I have had, and still have, to battle can judge also the extent of my success.'[73]

After her return to Canada in 1879, things seemed to continue developing according to plan. She finally convinced a group of Ottawa philanthropist ladies and gentlemen to form the Central Committee for the Reception and Protection of Female Immigration and to ask for government aid and recognition.[74] A branch committee in Toronto constituted itself formally in late 1879 or early 1880;[75] a Montreal committee followed suit in 1881.[76] The wife of the Governor General indicated that, like her royal sister the Crown Princess of Germany, she took 'an individual interest in the effort you are making to get girls and women from Switzerland and Germany to Canada, to provide good homes for them on their arrival here.'[77] The model of royal patronage was extended into Canada. In the meantime, Koerber attempted to make herself useful to the Conservative government as a consultant in Ottawa on matters relating to continental Europe.[78] She never did become a German subject and reverted to representing herself as the widow of an Austrian naturalized in Canada.

In 1879 and 1880, Koerber was called twice to appear before the House of Commons Standing Committee on Immigration and Colonisation.[79] Now forty years of age and with several years of experience hobnobbing with European diplomats, politicians, and even royalty, she had shed her demure demeanour toward men in public positions. She criticized the Standing Committee in forceful language for the Canadian government's abysmal failure to deal with the Swiss and German governments on matters pertaining to immigration, claiming that she, single-handedly, had opened the diplomatic channels between Ottawa and Berlin and could keep them open: 'I have the means of approaching the German Government, and it is a pity you do not make use of them.' She explained that it was 'a matter of deep regret to me when I was obliged to break off my work of promotion owing to public opinion in this country.' Yet she stopped short of demanding an official appointment: 'My services having been discontinued, I think, perhaps, you may prefer a gentleman to a lady to do the work.' After summarizing her career in the civil service, she added: 'I would not consent to return on the same conditions, because I could not do it. I am into debt as it is and I could not consent to go further into debt for the Department of Agriculture, which I do not consider to be a charitable institution.' One is left wondering how empowered Koerber really felt; her forthright language and assertive attitude notwithstanding, she had learned that she could not make a living in the civil service or have the career she desired.

When in 1882 she was offered reinstatement as a general immigration agent, she declined. She no longer wanted to be involved in immigrant recruitment and 'was compelled to make a daring dash for my circumstances,' looking for 'other auspices under which I could create a wider field'[80] by placing her scheme 'on an entirely philanthropic basis and claim[ing] public support for it.'[81] Koerber also started to dream about expanding her international system of organization and protection into the United States.[82] After introducing her plans in New York, she returned to Europe in the spring of 1882. Her purposes were twofold. First, in England, she established contact with the new Women's Emigration Society (WES), founded in 1880 by a group of philanthropists under Lady Jane Taylor with the intent of encouraging single women of all classes to emigrate. By September she was in Liverpool, arranging for a public meeting that was to be attended by Lady Jane. The meeting, which was supported by several prominent gentlemen, successfully established a branch of the WES in the seaport city.[83] Her second purpose enjoyed some early success. In Germany in early 1883, she organized an arrangement with Mathilde Weber, executive member of the *Frauenverein*, for the selection of twenty 'respectable, capable' servant girls from Stuttgart and Tübingen to be sent to Montreal and Ontario. The Montreal Protective Immigration Society was willing to advance the fare of five pounds each for six girls. If the seedling movement worked out, there would be government assistance for the other women.[84]

But after mid-1883, things went badly wrong for Koerber and her plans for the international organization and protection of female emigration. First, her request for government funding for the German women 'with the view of giving them the same advantages as are offered to young women proceeding from Great Britain' was declined without comment.[85] Next she got into an argument with Lady Jane Taylor, as a result of which her cooperation with the WES came to an end, and the British press attacked the unpatriotic character of her international ideas. She desperately attempted to organize an English protection society that would work parallel to the WES's promotion work and even jettisoned her German plans for this, but the doors seemed to be firmly closed for her. At the same time, a Miss Richardson, originally hand-picked by Koerber and Lady Jane in England, made herself the spokesperson for female immigration in Canada and was not only appointed to a government position in Quebec City but also obviously enjoyed the endorsement and cooperation of the Montreal Protective Immigration Society. Competition had suddenly burst onto the scene, and Koerber found herself thoroughly marginalized and alone. She protested the 'encroachment on *my* territory,' listed her role in initiating the various efforts, and requested that her 'first claims upon the Department' be respected.[86] Sadly, nobody was listening any longer. Female migration work re-emerged in the mid-1880s exclusively as a work of the British Empire, and has been treated as such by historians since.[87] As for Koerber, her pleas to be put back on the government payroll were increasingly desperate yet unsuccessful. Her career in female migration management, and her life, ended ignominiously with the terse note by the High Commissioner's office asking for funds to arrange for a proper burial.[88]

III

Clearly, Koerber's ideas emerged in the context of a larger European debate, but many of her initiatives can distinctly be seen in later developments in Canada and Britain. A Reception Home opened in Montreal, even during her lifetime. Women's protection societies formed all over the country to receive, supervise, and control female immigrants. Female migration work started as philanthropy but was soon professionalized and bureaucratized, though without being defeminized. As Koerber had predicted and desired, it stayed in female hands. The position she had craved and worked for, that of Superintendent of Female Immigration, was created three years later, in 1887.[89] In Britain, the Women's Emigration Society, which according to Koerber had suffered from Lady Jane's lack of experience and ineffective organization, in fact disintegrated in 1884.[90] It was replaced by the British Women's Emigration Association, which implemented through organization in Britain and Canada much of the seamless, transnational protective system that Koerber had envisioned.[91] Stricter regulations were put in place in Canadian legislation to regulate behaviour aboard immigrants' ships. Moral reform became an integral part of nation building and state formation by the turn of the century.[92]

It is not surprising that Koerber, a product of her class and time, would choose women like herself as the only suitable providers of better protection and safer guidance for female migrants. Everywhere, she saw a distinct opportunity for women, organized in the semi-public philanthropic sector, to effect positive change. She appealed to women on both sides of the Atlantic to make service to their own sex, their own 'sisters,' their first priority and the equivalent of a patriotic duty. In close cooperation with one another, women's associations, and their royal patrons, would provide for the woman traveller disinterested advice, supervised hostels in the port of embarkation, ship matrons, letters of recommendation, reception homes, and recommended employment.[93] Moved along by a borderless chain of female hands, a single woman would never have to leave the protected, gendered space thereby created. Koerber did not doubt that the 'ladies' in different countries would 'work hand in hand in this enterprise.'[94] Seen in this light, migration was not only an issue of national importance but an international humanitarian issue: 'We are treating a purely moral question ... where national interests do not cross each other.'[95]

Despite her own at least partly liberating experience of leaving home and nation behind, Elise von Koerber represented the basic paradox, identified by Mariana Valverde, of a reformer claiming the right to move freely in public while demanding from other women purity through seclusion. Like many middle-class feminists, she further exacerbated that paradox by claiming for herself a powerful role while reducing working-class women to objects of philanthropic concern.[96] Bourgeois feminists like Koerber lacked a radical-democratic perspective, and their philosophy 'stood rooted in a class-bound patriarchal society.'[97] Koerber also used strategies that were not unusual for feminists of her time. Attempting to create an international campaign organized by women for women, she never hesitated to utilize the help of powerful men to achieve her goals. Yet her insistence that the international management of female migration be placed to female hands, and her attempts to create a paid position for herself at the centre of such an international network, were early steps along the way toward the professionalization of female social service.[98]

IV

A case study such as that of Elise von Koerber allows us to interrogate the subject of gender and migration from various angles. She represents the historical female transmigrant with transcultural competencies and a transnational identity. The concept of transnationalism has been appropriated by the social sciences as a central feature of globalization and its concomitant revolution in transportation and communications technology.[99] However, historians and anthropologists are now reclaiming the concept's historical dimensions.[100] Transnationalism provides a new analytical framework for historical questions about immigrant integration as well as nation building. Koerber's case reminds us not only that the concept of transnationalism must be gendered but also that a true departure from the nation-state framework of analysis requires the definition of transnational identity as multilocal rather than necessarily bilocal.

Although Koerber herself may have had a transnational identity, various gendered nation-building projects interfered with her transnational way of life. This case study may serve to pose questions of gender and political sovereignty or territoriality, a topic of increasing salience in the nation-building era of the late nineteenth century, when increased border enforcement and nation-states' control over entry and exit brought citizenship and its gendered construction into sharp relief. Koerber's own problems with ascertaining her legal status and obtaining protection from any one government, combined with her concern for the moral reputation of single migrating females, remind us of the historical importance of gendered immigration policies that targeted unattached women as prostitutes, that allowed immigrant men but not women to sponsor their spouses and fiancées, and that required both admission criteria (such as literacy) and official papers from men only. Similarly, her assumption that the German government was less concerned with the emigration of women than with that of military-age men hints at the conflicted gendered relationship between citizenship rights (i.e., the freedom to move) and male citizen's obligations to defend the national territory.

Koerber further prompts us to examine the gendered nature of political citizenship by investigating women as employees of the state. Leanne Dustan's work on the Canadian civil service points out that early appointments were almost entirely the result of patronage – a system that, she argues, could serve women only if they could draw on the weight of political votes represented by their male friends or relatives. However, the shift of civil services in English-speaking countries to merit-based selection and professionalism in the 1880s further served to shut out women or to ghettoize them in low-paid clerical positions and areas designated as 'women's work.' Koerber's case study allows us to investigate whether the pre-professional system of patronage and personal relationships did not in fact allow for a less strict separation of male (political) and female (voluntary) public spaces in fields such as immigrant care and thereby created a brief niche of opportunity for enterprising, educated women that laid the foundation for future roles of women in the state.

Koerber's strong sense of her social status and its importance to her work also points to the importance of including class in any historical analysis of gender and migration. In Koerber's understanding of migration, those who undertook the process outside the safety net of pre-existing social networks (be they family ties or pre-existing trajectories defined by other members of the home community) ran grave dangers of exploitation by commercial interests. She defined those dangers in an essentially gendered way and tied them equally to regional migration and migration across borders or across the Atlantic. In her view, women who left the social control of their immediate family and community of origin by migrating from the rural community to the city, from their home region to another European region, or from Europe to North America were exposed to the feminized moral danger of sexual exploitation. She targeted in particular the in-between stage, the process of moving from one place to another on trains and ships, as a dangerous space of uncontrolled male–female interaction across class boundaries; and she attempted to create a solution that was not just gendered but classed: the control of working-class women by upper-class women like herself.

The issue of class finally raises the question of economic citizenship as a topic to be included in discussions of gender and migration. If economic citizenship for women can be defined as the right to work in one's chosen pursuit and to be free of economic dependence on men, then Koerber's emphasis on transnational opportunities for women raises the option of economic belonging in a larger transnational community as a female alternative. When nation-building projects on both sides of the Atlantic defined women's work as temporary, life-cycle–related expedients for the unmarried female, transmigrants like Koerber attempted to create a gendered transnational space in which women like herself could belong, could be protected, and could exist securely and comfortably.

NOTES

1 Ontario Heritage Foundation, Historical Plaque, Centennial Park, Mag-

netawan, describes Koerber as a native of Baden who had lived in Canada for some sixteen years in 1873. In an interview with the *New York Times* she described herself as the 'widow of an Austrian officer who spent the last years of his life in the Engineer Department of the Canadian Government.' *New York Times*, 23 January 1882. In another public address she claimed that her husband had worked for the government of Canada for nearly twenty years. Elise von Koerber, Address on Continental Immigration, delivered before the City Council of Toronto, September 1879 (hereafter 'Toronto City Council speech'), 9. William Baron von Koerber worked as a draughtsman in the Lower Canada Surveys and Patents Branch of the Department of Crown Lands from October 1862 onward. *Sessional Papers* (1867), 47.

2 Report of Special Immigration Agent Madame von Koerber, 28 August 1875, LAC, RG 17, vol. 141.

3 For information on her daughter, British Census 1881. On her sons, LAC, RG 17 vol. 238, Koerber to Lowe, 19 December 1878. On her death and date of birth, England & Wales Death Index.

4 Donna R. Gabaccia and Franca Iacovetta, *Women, Gender and Transnational Lives: Italian Workers of the World* (Toronto: University of Toronto Press, 2002).

5 Caroline Brettell, *Anthropology and Migration: Essays on Transnationalism, Ethnicity, and Identity* (Walnut Creek: Altamira Press, 2003), 48.

6 Patrick A. Dunae, 'Promoting the Dominion: Records and the Canadian Immigration Campaign, 1872–1915,' *Archivaria* 19 (Winter 1984–5): 73–93, 75–6.

7 Gordon H. Skilling, *Canadian Representation Abroad: From Agency to Embassy* (Toronto: Ryerson Press, 1945), 3.

8 Dunae, 'Promoting the Dominion,' 78. One historian writes that an appointment as Canadian immigration agent was 'a mere matter of knowing the right kind of people' in order to be sent abroad 'on a holiday at public expense.' Norman Macdonald, *Canada: Immigration and Colonization, 1841 to 1903* (Toronto: Macmillan, 1966), 40.

9 Toronto City Council speech, 4, 9.

10 Julia Bush, '"The Right Sort of Woman": Female Emigrators and Emigration to the British Empire, 1890–1910,' *Women's History Review* 3, no. 3 (1994): 385–409 at 394. See also Lisa-Anne Chilton, 'Emigrators, Emigrants, and Empire: Women and British Migration to Canada and Australia in the 19th and Early 20th Centuries,' PhD diss., York University, 2003.

11 Toronto City Council Speech, 9–12.

12 Ibid.

13 Leanne Dustan, 'Locating the "Gentle Sisters" of the Civil Service,' paper

presented at the annual meeting of the Canadian Historical Association, 2005.

14 Koerber was first appointed by Deputy Minister Letellier de St-Just under Minister of Agriculture J.H. Pope, also from Quebec, and received her full salaried appointment under the Liberal government and Minister Pelletier. Koerber, testimony before the House of Commons Committee on Immigration and Colonisation, 19 April 1880, *Sessional Papers*, 1880.

15 Circular dated 12 September 1874, published in German and circulated in translation among Canadian ladies' societies. *Sessional Papers*, 1876, no. 7, item #8 app. 37, 163.

16 Address to the Dresden *Frauen-Fortbildungsverein*, 18 October 1878, included in Koerber to Lowe, 3 November 1878, LAC, RG 17, vol. 235 (hereafter: Dresden speech). The quotation is a translation of the German original by the author.

17 Elise von Koerber, Annual Report, December 1874, *Sessional Papers*, 1875, no. 8 item #40, app. 33, 142–5.

18 For an example of this interpretation of home as a confining rather than a sheltering space, see Laura Agustin, 'Still Challenging Place: Sex, Money, and Agency in Women's Migrations,' in *Women and the Politics of Place*, ed. A. Escobar and W. Harcourt (Bloomfield: Kumarian Press, 2005). For Koerber as a visionary, see Jonathan Wagner, *A History of Migration from Germany to Canada, 1850–1939* (Vancouver: UBC Press, 2006), 77–80.

19 Report on Female Emigration, 1 July 1877, *Sessional Papers*, 1878, no. 8, item #9, app. 39, 122. Quote about emigration in German from Dresden speech.

20 Angelika Sauer, 'Ethnicity Employed: Wilhelm Hespeler and the Mennonites,' *Journal of Mennonite Studies* 18 (2000): 82–115 at 82–94.

21 Koerber testimony before the House of Commons Committee on Immigration and Colonisation, 19 April 1880, *Sessional Papers*, 1880.

22 Koerber to Lowe, 24 October 1872, LAC, RG 17, vol. 74. The Assisted Immigration Registers of the Toronto Emigrant Office contain four applications from Koerber for domestic travel assistance, dated July 1873, May 1874, and June 1874. http://www.archives.gov.on.ca/english/db/hawke.aspx. Report by Koerber to Minister, 28 August 1875, LAC, RG 17, vol. 141.

23 Koerber to St-Just, 9 December 1876, LAC, RG 17, vol. 178, file 18403.

24 Koerber to Minister Letellier de St-Just, 14 May 1876, LAC, RG 17, vol. 158. Koerber to Minister, 6 December 1875, LAC, RG 17, vol. 147.

25 Department of Agriculture to Agent General, 7 December 1876, 14 December 1876, LAC, RG 17, vol. 177. Koerber to St-Just, 9 December 1976, LAC, RG 17, vol. 178. Koerber to Lowe, 20 January 1877, LAC, RG 17, vol. 180. See also Canada, Senate *Debates*, 7 March 1876.

26 Toronto City Council speech, 4, 7. Koerber to Jenkins, 4 December 1875, *Sessional Papers*, 1876, no. 7 item #8, app. 36, 153.

27 Toronto City Council speech.

28 'Reception and Protection of Female Immigrants in Canada,' delivered in Ottawa, spring 1879, LAC, RG 17, vol. 247 (hereafter: Ottawa speech); Koerber testimony before the House of Commons Committee on Immigration and Colonisation, 19 April 1880, *Sessional Papers*, 1880.

29 Koerber to Minister, 20 November 1872, LAC, RG 17, vol. 76. Koerber to Minister, 24 February 1876, LAC, RG 17, vol. 151.

30 Ottawa speech, 2.

31 Koerber to Minister of Agriculture, 31 December 1874, *Sessional Papers*, 1875 no. 8 item #40, app. 33, 142–5.

32 Koerber testimony before the House of Commons Committee on Immigration and Colonisation, 19 April 1880, *Sessional Papers*, 1880, and City Council speech directly contradict each other on whether female migration work was a means to an end or the end itself.

33 Koerber to Pope, 20 November 1872, LAC, RG 17, vol. 74.

34 Roxroy West has suggested that she used the girls as informers to provide personal testimony as to the weaknesses of the arrangements for female migrants. West, 'Canadian Immigration Agents and Swiss Immigration, 1870–1930,' MA thesis, University of Ottawa, 1978, 29.

35 Report by Special Immigration Agent in Switzerland, 31 December 1874, *Sessional Papers*, 1875, no. 8 item #40, app. 33, 144.

36 Circular dated 12 September 1874, *Sessional Papers*, 1876, no. 7, item #8, app. 37, 156–64; Koerber to Lette Verein, December 1875, *Sessional Papers*, 1878, no. 8 item #9, app. 39, 117–19.

37 Report of Special Immigration Agent, 28 August 1875, RG 17 volume 141.

38 Lisa-Anne Chilton, 'Women's Work: The Politics of Imperial Migration,' paper presented at the annual meeting of the Canadian Historical Association, 1999, 9. Chilton demonstrates that 'a central field for many of these [female emigration promoters] was to make single female migration safe and respectable.'

39 Koerber to Swiss Federal Council, February 1877, LAC, RG 17, vol. 182.

40 Report of Special Immigration Agent, 28 August 1875, LAC, RG 17, vol. 141.

41 Ottawa speech. 'White slavery' was apparently a special concern in Hesse, where she had done part of her work. E. von Philippovich, ed., *Auswanderung und Auswanderungspolitik in Deutschland* (Leipzig: Verein für Sozialpolitik, 1892), 182–8.

42 Dresden speech.

43 Circular dated 12 September 1874, *Sessional Papers*, 1876, no. 7, item,#8, app.,36, 156–64.

44 Koerber to British Board of Trade, June 1883, LAC, RG 25, A-1, vol. 31.

45 On the migrant ship as a landscape in which social relations were reproduced through spatial control, segregation, and surveillance, see Jan Gothard, 'Space, Authority, and the Female Emigrant Afloat,' *Australian Historical Studies* 112 (1999): 96–115.

46 Koerber to Lowe, 6 December 1876, LAC, RG 17, vol. 174.

47 Koerber to Minister, 16 August 1877, LAC, RG 17, vol. 198.

48 Koerber to British Board of Trade, June 1883, LAC, RG 25, A-1, vol. 31.

49 Koerber to Sir Charles Tupper, 10 September 1883, LAC, RG 17, vol. 382. Her first principle was 'that each country should be asked to do its own share in the work.'

50 Report of Special Immigration Agent, 28 August 1875, LAC, RG 17, vol. 141. Koerber to British Board of Trade, June 1883, LAC, RG 25, A-1, vol. 31.

51 Toronto City Council speech, 8.

52 West, 'Canadian Immigration Agents,' 26.

53 Jenkins to Ontario Treasurer, 29 January 1875, LAC, RG 17, vol. 127.

54 Annual report by Edward Jenkins, 31 December 1875, *Sessional Papers*, 1876, no. 7 item #8, app.36, 133.

55 West, 'Canadian Immigration Agents,' 30–1.

56 She did so, characteristically, in response to Jenkins's request to replace her in Switzerland by appealing to the Minister in Ottawa: 'It would be a crying injustice to see my faithful services rewarded by dismissal – I do not think you could do it, Honorable Sir.' Koerber to Minister, 24 February 1876, LAC, RG 17, vol. 151.

57 Koerber to Minister, 3 November 1874, LAC, RG 17, vol. 121.

58 Koerber to Lowe, 25 August 1874, LAC, RG 17, vol. 118. Annual report by Edward Jenkins, 31 December 1875, *Sessional Papers*, 1876, no. 7 item #8, app. 36, 133. Following Bismarck's suggestion and Prussia's lead, the government of Baden had withdrawn all licences for foreign agents in 1873 and become very hostile to any activities that actively promoted emigration among the population. Philippovich, *Auswanderung*, 152.

59 Koerber to Lowe, 25 August 1874, LAC, RG 17, vol. 118.

60 Report by Special Immigration Agent in Switzerland, 31 December 1874, *Sessional Papers*, 1875, no. 8 item #40, app. 33, 142–5.

61 Correspondence printed in *Sessional Papers*, 1878, no. 8 item #9, app. 39, 117–18.

62 Koerber testimony before the House of Commons Committee on Immigration and Colonisation, 19 April 1880, *Sessional Papers*, 1880.

63 Report of Special Immigration Agent, 28 August 1875, LAC, RG 17, vol. 141.

64 A publication commented on her respectable and modest acting on behalf of humanist goals. Friedrich Jaeggi-Enger, *Die schweizerisch-kanadische Auswanderungsfrage mit Rücksicht auf die Thätigkeit der Frau Elsie von Koerber* (Bern: Jebt & Reinert, 1876). Even the German Ambassador in Bern, General von Röder, commented that 'Madam von Koerber has during her stay here moved in the very best society in Geneva, Lausanne, Berne and Zurich.' *Sessional Papers,* 1878, no. 8, item #9, app.,39, 123.

65 Report of Special Immigration Agent, 31 December 1877, *Sessional Papers,* 1878, no. 8 item #9, app. 43, 169–70; Jenny de Lerber, *Le Bulletin Continental* 3 (October 1877).

66 She initially approached the Lette Verein in late 1874 with an introduction by Princess Alice of Hesse. Doris Obschernitzki, *"Der Frau ihre Arbeit!" Lette Verein: Zur Geschichte einer Berliner Institution 1866 bis 1986* (Berlin: Editon Heinrich, 1987). See also "Brief einer englischen Dame an die Vorsitzende des Lette-Vereins," *Deutscher Frauen Anwalt* (1879): 53.

67 Dorothee Arden, 'Kronprinzessin Viktoria, Kaiserin Friedrich,' MA thesis, University of Frankfurt, 2000.

68 Koerber to Minister, 4 June 1876, *Sessional Papers,* 1877, no. 6, item #8, app. 8.

69 She promised the minister that 'I shall acquire the German subjectship should the German Government make this condition an unavoidable one.' Koerber to Minister, 9 December 1876, LAC, RG 17, vol. 178.

70 Koerber to Lowe, 3 November 1878, LAC, RG 17, vol. 235.

71 Ottawa speech, 7.

72 Report on Female Emigration, 18 December 1878, *Sessional Papers,* 1879, no. 7, item #9, app. 34, 115.

73 Ottawa speech, 8. The meeting was reported in *Deutscher Frauen Anwalt;* see Obschernitzki, *'Der Frau ihre Arbeit!'* 85.

74 *Ottawa Semi-Weekly Citizen,* 10 April 1879.

75 Mrs L.J. Harvie, Toronto. Minutes of the two first meetings of the 'Committee for the Protection & Organisation of Female Immigration,' 17 February 1880, LAC, RG 17, vol. 272.

76 Mrs G.H. Mussen, Montreal. Resolution from 'Committee for the Organisation & Protection of Female Immigration,' 25 October 1881, LAC, RG 17, vol. 326; Barbara Roberts, 'Sex, Politics and Religion: Controversies in Female Immigration Reform Work in Montreal, 1881–1919,' *Atlantis: A Women's Studies Journal* 6, no. 1 (1980): 27–38 at 27.

77 Quoted in Ottawa speech, 9.

78 Koerber to Minister of Agriculture, 17 July 1879, LAC, RG 17, vol. 242. Koerber to Minister, 5 April and 26 April 1880, LAC, RG 17, vol. 278.
79 *Sessional Papers*, 1879 and 1880.
80 Koerber to British Board of Trade, June 1883, LAC, RG 25, A-1, vol. 31.
81 Koerber to Lowe, 9 June 1883, LAC, RG 17, vol. 376.
82 *New York Times*, 23 January 1882.
83 *New York Times*, 12 September 1882. James Hammerton, *Emigrant Gentlewomen: Genteel Poverty and Female Emigration, 1830–1914* (London: Rowman and Littlefield, 1979), 148–9.
84 Montreal Women's Immigration Society (Protective) to Pope, 5 February 1883, LAC, RG 17, vol. 361.
85 Galt to Minister, 8 February 1883, LAC, RG 17, vol. 361. High Commissioner's Office to Minister, 23 May 1883, includes HC to Koerber, 4 May 1883, LAC, RG 17, vol. 371.
86 Koerber to Lowe, 9 June 1883, LAC, RG 17, vol. 376; Koerber to Sir Charles Tupper, 10 September 1883, LAC, RG 17, vol. 382.
87 See Bush, '"The Right Sort of Woman"'; Chilton, 'Emigrator, Emigrants, and Empire'; Roberts, 'Sex, Politics and Religion.' Lisa Gaudet, 'The Empire Is Woman's Sphere: Organized Female Imperialism in Canada, 1880s to 1920s,' PhD diss., Carleton University, 2001.
88 HC to Department, 8 April 1884, LAC, RG 17, vol. 400.
89 Ninette Kelley and Michael Trebilcock, *The Making of the Mosaic: A History of Canadian Immigration Policy* (Toronto: University of Toronto Press, 1998), 86.
90 James Hammerton seems to agree with Koerber's criticism when he concludes that 'the society's control organization was never placed on a sound footing, however, and by 1884 it had disintegrated.' Hammerton, *Emigrant Gentlewomen*, 149. Julia Bush suggests that the WES 'remained deeply sympathetic to the middle-class emigrant' at a time when the dominions were clearly looking for working-class domestic servants. Bush, '"The Right Sort of Woman,"' 389.
91 Gaudet, 'The Empire is Woman's Sphere.' The British Women's Emigration Association was established as an outgrowth of the emigration work of the Anglican Girls' Friendly Society. Ibid., 259n3 and 276–7. Gaudet gives credit as 'pioneers' of a system of selection, commendation, supervision, and lodging to Ellen Joyce and Louisa Knightley.
92 Mariana Valverde, *The Age of Light, Soap, and Water: Moral Reform in English Canada, 1885–1925* (Toronto: McClelland and Stewart, 1991), 27–8.
93 Notes to the German government, 1878, LAC, RG 17, vol. 238.
94 Circular dated 12 September 1874, *Sessional Papers*, 1876, no. 7, item #8, app. 36, 156–64.

95 Koerber to Sir Charles Tupper, 10 September 1883, LAC, RG 17, vol. 382.

96 Valverde, *The Age of Light, Soap, and Water*, 29–30.

97 Bush, '"Right Sort of Woman,"' 396.

98 Seth Koven and Sonya Michel, 'Womanly Duties: Maternalist Politics and the Origins of the Welfare States in France, Germany, Great Britain, and the United States, 1880–1920,' *American Historical Review* 95, no. 4 (October 1990): 1076–1108.

99 Steven Vertovec, 'Transnationalism and Identity,' *Journal of Ethnic and Migration Studies* 27, no. 4 (October 2001): 573–82.

100 Gabaccia and Iacovetta, *Women, Gender and Transnational Lives*; Nancy Foner, 'What's New about Transnationalism? New York Immigrants Today and at the Turn of the Century,' *Diaspora* 6, no. 3 (1997): 355–75.

PART III

Twentieth Century:
Ethnicity and Nationalism

7 German-Quebecers, 'German-Québécois,' German-Canadians? The Double Integration of People of German Descent in Quebec in the 1990s

MANUEL MEUNE

In North American history, the blending of French, German, and English was a result of military action – with demographic implications, to be sure, given that after the American War of Independence, German mercenaries settled in French- and English-speaking Canadian territories. Though people of German descent represented only 1.3 per cent of Quebec's population in 1996 even after several waves of immigration, there were still more than 100,000 of them.[1] Some chose to immerse themselves in French-speaking Quebec; many opted to live in the English-speaking neighbourhoods of Montreal; all, however, were affected by the political upheavals of the 1970s, when the French language became Quebec's only official language. Although most German speakers nowadays have at least some French-language skills, they identify mainly with Canada and not with Quebec.

Between the 1950s and the 1990s, many German-Quebecers negotiated a 'double integration' into two cultural universes: the first was principally with the anglophone minority in Quebec, and by extension with the anglophone majority of Canada; the second, especially after the 1970s, was with the francophone majority in Quebec and thus with the French minority in Canada. This compels one to ask how their relationship with German history, and especially with Nazi history, influenced their perceptions of (English-)Canadian and Québécois nationalisms. Immigrants to Quebec confront more complicated questions of identity than is generally the case if they go to English Canada instead. Questions of identity are posed to them three times: in relation to the English-speaking majority in Canada, the French-speaking majority in Quebec, and the English-speaking minority in Quebec. And when an immigrant identifies with a Germany that has been fragmented and reconstituted, the situation in Quebec cannot but expose a very German problematic regarding the relationships between people and nation, between state and territory, and between ethnic and civic nation. Thus, in navigating their experience of German history and their perceptions of Quebec particularism and Canadian multiculturalism, German-speaking people in Quebec come to identify themselves as German, Quebecer/ Québécois and/or Canadian.

Language and Historical Context

The French language knows only the ambiguous term *Québécois*; the English language knows both *Québécois* and *Quebecer*. This highlights the tensions that arise with regard to the primary object of national identification: Will it be Quebec or Canada? *Quebecer* refers to all Canadians who reside in Quebec, whether or not they speak French; *Québécois* is reserved for those of French-Canadian descent. Is there, underlying these two terms, an intent to reify the frontiers of ethnicity or to exoticize the French-speaking population, or perhaps both? Do these two terms not suggest a refusal to engage with the complexity of the new *Homo quebecensis*, in rejecting the ambiguity of the English term? Or should we, in French, resolve the tensions between the ethnic and the civic definitions of the people of Quebec by using, alongside *Québécois*, a word like *Québécain* or *Québécais* to distinguish the 'native' from the other?[2] This, of course, would be to frustrate the desire of those who would like to see an increasingly territorial Quebec nationalism come into being, a nationalism better able to unite fidelity to tradition with an openness toward the cultural diversity that characterizes contemporary Quebec.

Faced with these sorts of linguistic nuances, should we, in English, use *German-Quebecer* or *German-Québécois* to name a group that German-Canadian Studies has yet to examine closely? Myka Burke, in her chapter in this volume about German-Canadian cultural identity, points to the troubling implications of the term 'German-Canadian,' on which are always already inscribed processes of U.S.-American, (English-) Canadian, and German identity formation. The naming of a special category of German-Canadians who live in Quebec is even more complex than this, given the national question in Canada, the unique ways that (French-) and (English-)Canadian identities are stacked, and questions about whether Canada should be considered a 'uni-multicultural' or a 'bi-multicultural' country – that is, as having not one but two mosaics, a predominantly anglophone one and a predominantly francophone one.

A solution might be to use *German-Quebecer* when referring to those who are invested in the English-speaking world and *German-Québécois* when referring to those who are more attached to the French-speaking world. But the term *German-Québécois*, besides sounding clumsy, seems to me inadequate, because a francophone Quebec (in the sense in which Ontario is anglophone) is less and less identifiable with the Quebec of those French-Canadian descendants to whom *Québécois* initially referred. Quebec nationalism has become increasingly de-ethnicized though it is still rooted in language and culture. *German-Quebecer*, then, is the only word that – like its French equivalent, *Germano-Québécois* – would apply to all Quebec residents of German descent, regardless of their primary identification. Indeed, this search for the right word speaks to the complexity of political and identity structures in Canada and in Quebec. But the question of whether we should say *German-Quebecer* or *German-Québécois* is perhaps not as relevant as the question whether German-Quebecers generally see themselves as *(German-)Quebecers* or as *(German-)Canadians*.

Language was an important factor in how German settlers became part of Quebec society. The first German settler, Hans Bernhardt, is said to have arrived in 1664. The impact of Germans on New France was not negligible. When the French and British battled for control of North America, both sides employed German soldiers. But the most significant influx of Germans to Canada happened when 1,400 mercenaries, who had been recruited by the British to fight in the American War of Independence, took up permanent residence among the French-speaking population. So it happened that the Schumpf family became Jomphe, that Bauer became Payeur, and so on. More important than the number of immigrants was the quality of their contributions to this society. Ex-officers, for example, played a vital role in the development of Canadian medicine.[3]

Throughout the nineteenth century, German farmers settled in Quebec, especially in the Ottawa Valley. The founding of the *Deutsche Gesellschaft zu Montreal* in 1835 points to the rootedness of a German community that was already having to confront its double allegiances. At the society's inaugural meeting, members sang both *A la claire fontaine* and *We Will March Against France*. And if its president, Louis Gugy, a one-time sheriff of Montreal, helped quell riots during the Patriot Rebellions, Ludger Duvernay, a member of the *Deutsche Gesellschaft*, was exiled for being a Patriot.[4] In 1850, Montreal boasted three hundred citizens of German descent. As a evidence of their integration, a number of these would enter politics. J.C.S. Würtele, for example, was Quebec's finance minister between 1882 and 1884. After 1918, once anti-German sentiment had subsided, German-speaking immigrants began arriving again, especially from Eastern Europe. The census of 1931 sounds the arrival of the mostly Catholic 'Danube Swabians.' The Germans from Germany, who arrived in the next wave of immigration, during the 1950s and 1960s, tended to distance themselves from the Swabians, who nevertheless were respected for their community spirit. Today, nothing remains to call attention to the old German quarter of Montreal – except two German churches, one Catholic and one Protestant – for social mobility drew these parishioners into the city's English-speaking suburbs.

As elsewhere in Canada, the Germans in Quebec are seen as having 'succeeded.' When their rapid integration is explained, the emphasis is generally placed on their professional qualifications and on their values; these two factors enabled them to approach if not surpass the average income of English-Quebecers.[5] In terms of language spoken at home, the most recurrent situations in the 1990s, as uncovered in our sample population,[6] were the exclusive use of German, followed by the use of both German and English. Also, the joint use of German, English, and French was more common than the use of German and French. Generally, the degree of multilingualism was high. But if English dominated, French was not insignificant.

Research has yet to show whether circumstances in Quebec favoured protection of the German language. The particular linguistic situation in Montreal – the lack of pressure to assimilate into *one* linguistic community, and the social diversity – can be said to have aided language retention. Yet use of the German language has declined in Quebec to such an extent that by 1996 fewer than one-quarter of those who identified German as their mother tongue still spoke it at home. This decline can be partly attributed to the 'saturation' of the linguistic 'marketplace' – that is, to an increase in French-language learning since the passing of Bill 101, which reinforced the status of French in Quebec.[7]

Canadian or Quebecer?

Studies have shown that Germans do not tend to identify themselves by ethnicity as strongly as other groups do.[8] Among our sample population, only 10 per cent said they felt exclusively German. Most tended, rather, to *add* to their ancestral identification the one they had articulated in North America, and to insist on one or the other depending on the context. Identification with Quebec was not absent – we will come back to this – but national identification tended to be mostly with Canada. The contrast between the devastation of Germany in 1945, and this land of Canadian plenty, seems to have instilled immediate feelings of loyalty. Immigrants who came to Montreal in the second half of the 1920s might have experienced a similar contrast, but they then had to struggle with the impact of the Great Depression. Canadian identity, for them, appears to have been the natural consequence of certain rituals, whether the filing of income tax returns or the pledging of allegiance. But if a relationship exists between 'legal' and 'emotional' loyalty, the identification process was not as simple as the acquisition of a new passport. Losing one's sense of German ethnicity was not always as rapid a process as some proud Canadians seemed to suggest; indeed, those who had chosen not to become Canadian citizens – often in order not to lose their German citizenship – continued to perceive themselves as just as Canadian as any other, and just as concerned about the society in which they were living. Many refused to choose between the separate aspects of their double or triple identity, remaining divided between their linguistic assimilation to English or French or both on the one hand, and their emotional ties to the language of their childhood, on the other.

When questioned about their Canadian ideals, German-Quebecers tended to remember Trudeau and his project for a centralized Canada founded on federal bilingualism. Some admitted that their 'Canadian dream' had been eroded by the constitutional debates, from the 'repatriation' of the Constitution in 1982 to the Meech Lake and Charlottetown accords. If for many French-speaking Quebecers, Expo '67 symbolized an opening to the world, it represented for many German-speaking Quebecers a pre-separatist Golden Age.

A number of German-Quebecers in our sample appeared to have accepted whole the English-Canadian press coverage that described separatists as pawns manipulated by cunning demagogues and that insisted on the gap between politicians and the 'people'; thus they seemed convinced that 'good people' had been misled in the Quebec referendums of 1980 and 1995. This simplistic premise was all the more familiar in that it tended to be applied to the history of Nazism. French-speaking nationalists, according to this theory, were a bunch of trouble

makers who were out to revenge imagined slights and who were playing on people's ungrounded fears of assimilation. Many recalled the
role played by the Catholic Church in the 1950s and had not updated
their image of Quebec but rather recycled the myth of the 'good French-
Canadian,' the jovial, unsophisticated, and docile body whose entrance
into modernity was still far off.

Many of our interviewees stated that English-Canadians were not
nationalistic. These respondents denied being 'Quebec bashers' and
offered similar reasons for their attachment to Canada (most typically,
that it protected civil liberties); and many of them, in the tradition of
Canadian nationalism, boasted of the greatness of this unique country
and could not imagine anyone seriously preferring the narrowness of
Quebec. Thus, when the Goethe Institute of Montreal organized a conference around the Italian-born German writer Franco Biondi in 1994,
the Montreal edition of the German-Canadian weekly *Kanada Kurier*
did not take into account the arguments put forward by the separatist
Italo-Quebecer writer Marco Micone: that it was not necessarily incon-
gruous that an immigrant should identify primarily as a Quebecer.[9] In
an article about Saint Patrick's Day, on the other hand, the columnist at
the *Kanada Kurier* described the variegated crowds that had come out
to celebrate diversity, in contrast to the ethnocentrism she encountered
during the Saint-Jean-Baptiste Day parades, which she hoped one day
would address all Quebecers and not just '*pure laines*.'[10]

The German-Quebecers, many of whom had arrived during the 1950s
and 1960s, carried the weight of Nazism on their shoulders, regardless
of what their views had been during that period, and they could not
help but see Quebec nationalism in the light of their own experience.
Besides often comparing the rhetoric of the separatist leaders with that
of Hitler, both one-time Nazi sympathizers and those who never held
such sympathies drew an analogy between German and Québécois
nationalisms. These German anti-nationalists expressed their sense of
déja vu, their feeling of unease when they encountered expressions of
Quebec nationalism. This appears to have been especially the case for
those refugees who arrived in Canada during the 1940s, many by way
of England; and for German-speaking Jewish refugees, whom Patrick
Farges has studied in a systematic way, since this category of Canadians has been a 'blind spot' in German-Canadian historiography.[11] These
former refugees – with the notable exception of McGill University theo-
logian Gregory Baum – often insisted that the germs of intolerance and
the strategies of victimization, which they saw in Quebec's situation,

recalled the cynicism of Nazi propaganda. Realistically, it was not a genocidal tendency that they feared but rather the development of new forms of extremism. Moreover, certain members of the postwar genera-tion made the point that Germans must perforce be 'post-nationalistic' and must be horrified by any nationalistic tendencies whatsoever.

When asked about the language situation and about the cultural insecurity felt by French-speaking Quebecers, more than half the respondents expressed understanding mixed with reservation; the rest expressed attitudes ranging from total incomprehension of to total agreement with those who supported the language laws. That is, while a certain cautious reserve predominated among them, the German-Quebecers in the 1990s were far from a monolithic entity.

In the 1950s and 1960s, few Germans had any knowledge of French when they arrived in Quebec, where they focused learning English, which in Montreal at the time was the language of economic success. Many remembered struggling with the language barrier, so that the hurdle of having to learn yet another language, in this case French, seemed insurmountable. Some pointed out that they had immigrated not to Quebec but to Canada, which had been presented to them, offi-cially, as an almost exclusively English-speaking country. Even if they succeeded in digesting the linguistic turn of the 1970s, they viewed the new regulations as a broken contract. If they sometimes out of respect made symbolic use of the French language, they had maintained a dis-tance from it, like other postwar immigrant groups, such as the Poles, the Greeks, and the Ukrainians – though unlike the Italians or the Por-tuguese, who more often had chosen French.[12]

Many criticized the language laws as counter to the Canadian ideal and, in the North American context and in economic terms, as self-defeating. Regarding the requirement that the children of immigrants attend French schools, a number of those who had railed against what they viewed as ethnocentricism did not themselves hesitate to ethni-cize 'native' French speakers, implicitly inviting them to remain among themselves and denying them the right to grow their own population by integrating new immigrants, as if only an English-speaking host society could be pluralistic. Or, if they admitted that a certain degree of 'frenchification' was necessary in order to maintain a dynamic French-speaking society, they tended to favour the bilingualization of the school system – an option that is still rejected by French-speakers, who often see this as nothing but creeping assimilation.

In the run-up to the 1994 provincial election in Quebec, at a time when a separatist victory and a new referendum were anticipated, it became apparent that many German-Quebecers identified with the English-speaking community. The gravity of the times prompted the Montreal columnist of the *Kanada Kurier* to take up a taboo political issue by alluding to the 401 (the highway that leads to Ontario) and to fears that independence would result in discrimination against English speakers.[13] Moreover, though German associations had generally refused to take a stance on political or linguistic matters, in 1969 the *Deutsche Gesellschaft zu Montreal* had condemned (in response to a questionnaire designed by Quebec's immigration ministry) any attempt to impose French schooling on the children of immigrants – a sharply political issue indeed.[14] There was no doubt, though, that parents felt proud when *their* children learned to speak French. Sometimes this was simply a matter of pride in their children's new skill, but mainly it was about their children improving their chances in the job market and did not necessarily signify stronger bonds with the French-speaking world or with Québécois culture.

Second-generation German-Quebecers, likewise, had several kinds of relationships with Quebec, Canada, and Germany. They all spoke of having suffered, more or less, from being stigmatized as Germans, and of having been made to question to what extent German history could belong to them – though in every case, they had a less emotionally charged relationship with the question than their parents had. Having to choose among three competing points of identification, most opted for a Canadian identity, which was seen to be more practical than either an artificial German identity or a reductive belonging to Quebec. If the 'frenchified' youth increasingly identified with Quebec – in the sense of primary national-cultural affiliation – this feeling was balanced by those 'anglicized' youth who felt that an identification with Quebec could only be based on language or ethnicity. Many spoke of not being *allowed* to feel they belonged and of not having the same opportunities as 'native' Quebecers – for example, in government employment.

Some of the 'children of Bill 101,' having more or less reluctantly learned to speak French in French schools though they spoke English otherwise, said they felt superior to unilingual French speakers, insofar as they were able to make friends on all 'three sides' and viewed themselves as having broader horizons than those who were content with a 'peripheral' culture. But this sort of praise for functional multilingualism did not always imply an engagement with Quebec popular culture, which they reduced to a few names; their literary and pop cultural references were mostly English. Thus, many spoke of feeling alienated when francophones sang 'their songs,' of being unable to include themselves in the 'we' of Quebec.

Identification with Collective Aspirations in Quebec

If most German-Quebecers were uneasy in the face of Québécois nationalism, many sympathized with a Quebec that could assert itself on the federal stage, and a few even seemed to accept the province's possible independence. Some 'German nationalists' anticipated at least some degree of sovereignty. They saw in Quebec separatism a clear contradiction with their idealized vision of Canada; even so, such an outcome was acceptable to them with regard to their notion of the cohabitation of nations, each of which must be allowed responsibility for its own jurisdiction.

But this sympathy for the logic of separatism was also encountered among some German anti-nationalists, who felt that a stronger dose of sovereignty was required to redirect the balance of power toward French speakers, who had long been made to feel like foreigners in their own city and who even, until recently, had felt oppressed by the scornful gaze of English-Quebecers. Rare were those who wanted total independence, though some felt that this would not be the catastrophe so often predicted. Rather, they considered legitimate any 'soft nationalism' that, by reinforcing the historical duality, would return to Quebec the place that was its due – Lévesque's sovereignty-association, or the 'distinct society' that seemed to them so self-evident that it should be counted as a given. Some did insist, however, that any claims made by francophones should not simply reproduce new kinds of injustice toward English-speaking minorities.

If the respondents did not all agree on the means for combating French-Quebecers' linguistic insecurities, half spoke of understanding them and of accepting the compromise of Bill 86, which, following a period during which English signage was strictly prohibited, authorized bilingual signs on the condition that French be predominant. One-quarter of respondents went so far as to speak of supporting whole-heartedly Quebecers' cultural claims. They questioned the 'linguistic oppression' of English speakers, describing them as a minority imprisoned by its own cultural and linguistic superiority complex, which had been too slow in adjusting itself to what in many 'normal' countries would have been the rule: the use of a common language,

the language of the regional majority. This acceptance was greater outside Montreal. But even certain residents of the anglophone West Island
described themselves as not overly annoyed by the language laws – so
long as they could continue to access certain municipal and provincial
services in English.

This underscores a possible convergence of opinion among Ger-
man- and French-speaking Quebecers. Some felt that a kind of German
congeniality brought them closer to French speakers than to English
speakers, and that not being English-Canadian attracted the sympathy of francophones. Those who had once been very poor remembered
the social proximity they had shared with French-Canadians relative
to their anglophone employers. And if they had not since learned to
speak French, this experience had led them to approve the decision of
francophones to demand what was rightfully theirs.

An understanding of the French speakers' sense of oppression was
much more widespread among those – rare though they might be –
who had chosen to come to Quebec. The feeling of belonging mainly
to Quebec was often associated with the experience of immersion in a
French-speaking milieu. These 'adopted Quebecers' found themselves
able to criticize those Germans who, be it in Montreal or in the Eastern
Townships, had never learned to speak French. And if some did not
identify mainly as Quebecers, it was because this term – despite the
rising tide of 'territorial nationalism' in Quebec – remained too closely
linked to the national struggle of the descendants of French-Canadians
for them to embrace it completely for themselves – the reference to Canada, in this sense, seemed less ethnocentric.

Among the generation of German-Quebecers born in Canada, the
more exclusive identification with Quebec was, likewise, increasingly common when the children had been socialized into a uniquely
French-speaking milieu. The 'frenchified' were often astounded that
their anglicized 'compatriots' could be so fundamentally anti-Quebec
and so ignorant of local culture. Some described themselves as nationalists, even as separatists, though the latter insisted on the pluralism
that, in their eyes, would characterize the new French-speaking state;
only rarely did they subscribe to any collective history that focused on
the Battle of the Plains of Abraham as the beginning of the struggle for
cultural survival – and, for the separatists, on the most recent catastrophe, the loss of two referendums. They contrasted the logic of Canadian
multiculturalism with the interculturalism of Quebec, in which rather

transitory communities were being invited to participate in a common cultural project that worked through the French language.

Some spoke of having discovered that they were Quebecers while travelling in Germany, where they had missed *their* Quebec. When asked to compare German and Quebec nationalisms, they tended to reject both the mystique of German blood and the ethnocentricism of Quebec, though they described themselves as quite at ease in a Quebec that was already as open as English-Canadian society, if not more so. In response to those Germans who projected onto Quebec judgments informed by the Nazi past, they described the people of Quebec as fundamentally pacific and as calmly following their own destiny. Such 'frenchified' German-Quebecers naturally saw themselves as belonging to the new, inclusive rather than exclusive 'we' of Quebec. They voluntarily claimed the role of intermediary; and without feeling themselves bound by too rigid solidarities, they embraced for themselves a highly flexible identity, Quebecer *or* Canadian depending on the context.

A Single, Double, or Multiple Nation? Reactions to Multiculturalism

The differences between such modes of identification call out an important question: Is Canada a uninational or a binational country (or even multinational, if the First Nations are taken into account)? The discourse of the most anglicized of German-Quebecers was coloured by a vision that is widespread in English Canada, where the tendency is to denationalize or even folklorize francophone culture. As figured by the television newsmagazine *The National*, the 'Canadian nation' is still often presented as singular and indivisible and is perceived as largely anglophone, regardless of its significant francophone minority. For Quebecers, the sense of nationhood refers instead to Quebec, whereas Canada is perceived as a 'supra-nation' composed not of thirteen provinces and territories but of two principal cultures that are equal in dignity. Where in reference to Canada, Céline Galipeau, in her *téléjournal*, speaks of the *pays* (country), Peter Mansbridge often speaks of the *nation*, conflating into a single entity Quebecers, Newfoundlanders, Ontarians, and Manitobans; and whereas the latter three may think that their province is just as 'distinct' as Quebec is, they are probably not always aware that many French-speaking Quebecers might not recognize themselves in this vision of the nation that, essentially, unites English Canada.

According to this same model, the German-Canadian press in the 1990s often talked of *one* Canadian culture. The idea of a dialectical movement between an initial biculturalism and a more current multiculturalism was largely absent. The *multiple*, being mistaken for the *singular*, permitted the rejection of the *dual*. The history of Canada – which in this case is not as different from the logic of the American *e pluribus unum* as many might like to believe – was presented as the story of the successful integration of immigrants into a singular, essentially anglophone community, rather than as the story of the progressive development of *two* host societies, two melting pots, or – according to the preferred metaphor – two multicultural mosaics.

This conflated individual immigration with a collective political foundation so that, except for First Nations people, all Canadians were considered 'immigrants.' The notion of Quebec being the agent and the heir (in one way or another) of New France was largely absent – for example, in the centenary edition of the *Kanada Kurier*. Questioning the two-poled notion of Canada espoused by francophones, and according to the logic that asserts the historical depth of one by minimizing that of other groups competing on the 'identity market,' some more or less explicitly placed French-Canadians/Quebecers and German-Canadians on the same level. Thus, some contended that Germans, by virtue of their contributions as pioneers, also deserved the status of a 'founding nation,'[15] especially if the criteria were ethnic rather than political. This perspective overlooked the fact that no colonial power had ever founded a 'New Germany' in North America.

Multiculturalism policy, which favoured the emergence of such discourses, had been criticized; even so, it remained an obligatory reference point for any official German-Canadian discourse, in which was praised that group's increased visibility. Politicians, the better to attract 'allophone' votes, praised the contributions made by New Canadians to the building of Canada, and did so in the English *and* German media; meanwhile, some German-Quebecers, to obtain their 'certificate of Canadian-ness,' adhered to the belief that to be a good Canadian patriot was now to be a contributor to a multicultural nation. Strengthened by the generations of German presence here, these German speakers had an interest in demonstrating that 'they' had long ago internalized the true nature of Canadian society and that 'they' had embodied the multicultural paradigm before the word even existed. As early as 1964, Herbert Debor, as a harbinger of current political tendencies, had been urging Quebec's Germans not to be afraid to develop their own collective historical consciousness, which would correspond so well to the very logic of 'the Canadian nation ... born of the mix of many peoples.'[16] Several years later, in 1985, the 150th anniversary of the *Deutsche Gesellschaft zu Montreal* had served as the occasion for an explosion of multiculturalist discourses. Strategies of self-assertion continued to make reference to the mosaic.[17]

Yet it is not clear whether most German-Quebecers approved of these multiculturalist tendencies. Respondents and interviewees were often cautious about multiculturalist discourse, and their critiques – both progressive and conservative – could be quite bitter. For many, multiculturalism did not bring about any change. It had come too late for German-Canadians, had done nothing to strengthen their assimilation, and had reflected only their inability to develop an effective lobby group. It was only partial compensation for the germanophobia that once had raged, and for the negative stereotypes that continued to fill the Canadian media.

According to some, only visible immigrants benefited from the 'anti-racist terrorism' that had usurped the rights of 'real,' long-established (i.e., white) minorities. Some did no more than denounce political correctness and the proliferating requests for particular recognition; others exposed the xenophobia that often also operates inside minority groups, suggesting that German contributions had been qualitatively more profitable than those of 'dangerous' and 'lazy' present-day immigrants. Some admitted that multiculturalism might in the short term help maintain some degree of social cohesion among German-Canadians but also feared that in the longer term it could not protect them from being dissolved into some shapeless, 'bastardized' society. The most racist among the interviewees emphasized that, short of being able to save the 'German race,' an effort should be made to unite the whites in defence against the Judeo-Masonic plots that had hatched such multiculturalist proliferations.[18]

Ironically, though, some fervent German nationalists were quite glad of multiculturalism – not for its universal opening onto the 'other,' but for permitting them to reconcile their German with their Canadian nationalism. Gerd Mittelstaedt, who had been active in Quebec's German community and who had written many letters to the *Kanada Kurier*, was one of them. He wrote texts in which one detected an obvious touch of anti-Semitism – even when the word *Jews* did not appear. For instance, in a letter where Steven Spielberg's film *Schindler's list* was called *Schundwerk* ('rubbish') and *Volksverhetzungswerk* ('incitement of the masses'), he stated that 'ein Volk, welches nicht für sein Land und seine Vergangenheit eintritt, muß sich nicht wundern, wenn es immer nur zahlt, sich bückt und sich in seinen Selbstanklagen übersteigert' (a people that does not stand up for its country and its past should not be surprised that it always only pays, stoops, and hypertrophies in self-accusations).[19] And the same writer delighted that multiculturalism protected German newcomers from sinking into some great assimila-tory mire, permitted them to function within closed ethnic circuits, and allowed them to develop a German-Canadian identity that was largely equivalent to German identity ('I'm German, and thus, German-Cana-dian'). If there is no explicitly problematic language in the following citation, one may still notice that the vision of multiculturalism Mit-telstaedt holds is decidedly different from the conception held by the defenders of intercultural dialogue:

> I was ready to become Canadian. But this quickly begged the question, 'Who is Canadian?' Are all the different tribes of Indians and Eskimos Canadian? What about the French, the English, the Scottish, the Irish, the Italians, the Ukranians, the Poles, the Chinese, the Japanese – to name only a few of the 70 different ethnic groups in Canada – are they Canadian? Whoever has ears to hear with, and eyes to see with, could not but notice that THE Canadian, as such, does not exist (with the possible exception of the natives). There is no such thing as an American style *melting-pot*, here. Numerous inhabitants of this vast country simply negotiate their social contacts in terms of their ethnic origins, within their own associations and their own communal spaces. I could not, and could not want to, impose myself upon any such group in the hope of belonging to them. Thus, con-fronted by such a situation, I became conscious of the fact that I am Ger-man, and thus, German-Canadian.[20]

Multiculturalism has been reduced in that passage to a strategy for shrouding a homeland nationalism (visible in letters to the *Kanada Kurier*) in a reified notion of German identity. Dialogue between cul-tural groups has been replaced by dreams of defensive moats, while under the cover of assertions of difference, segregation has become the most comfortable alternative.

Multiculturalism is far from as egalitarian as the ideal would have it; it does *not* solve the problem of hierarchized visions of ethnic groups. It was designed to promote common citizenship and to overcome the need to think in rigid national categories, but it has not succeeded in being an antidote to isolationism. Indeed, this sympathy for multiculturalism among German nationalists has reinforced another critique – this time from 'progressives' – that highlights the risk of the kind of ghettoization that has blocked the integration of immigrants into host societies. For this reason, many have rejected multiculturalism insofar as it has not permitted cultural exchanges, has privileged provincialism, and requires a constant identification with origins.

Many others in Quebec posit that multiculturalism has *become* problematic as a political institution, insofar as it is related to a desire to dissolve the national duality and to temper the nationalist zeal of Quebecers. They argue that the cult of multiculturalism has only strengthened the nationalist impulse in Quebec. They also reject any attempt to confound multiculturalism with multilingualism – a few respondents suspect their fellow German-Canadians in Western Canada of wishing to remove French as an official language since German isn't one. They argue that French is the language of a *national* minority, not an ethnic one that, even in the West, should be seen as much more essential to Canadian history than that of other minorities, who do not express the same kind of collective consciousness. They reject the idea that Germans be granted the status of a founding nation, and they highlight the fact that Germans, unlike French-Canadians, have never conceived of themselves other than in terms of their relationship to English Canada, or to their belonging to the German *Volk*.

Limited Interest for German-Canadian Identity

These arguments surrounding multiculturalism call out the question of how German-Quebecers of the 1990s could have a real interest in claiming ties to a distinct German-Canadian group. Judging by the response to our surveys, it would seem that such an interest was very weak and that the dialectic between two identifications, German and Canadian/Quebecer, was much stronger than any awareness of a German-Canadian identity discourse. The fusion of these two elements into the definition of an original cultural identity seems to appear only in historiographical or metadiscourses on identity. The emergence of a distinct German-Canadian history, and the problematizing of group existence during the 1980s, no doubt affected the identity question, but only rarely did this impact translate into the hope that a German-Canadian group might survive the cessation of massive waves of immigration. Collective acculturation was not seen as sad or hurtful evolution so long as one could be sure that within the family, individuals would preserve traces of their origins and continue to cherish particular symbols. Many restricted their ambition to the occasional participation in cultural associations, and to the private sphere, where ethnicity was reduced to a set of rituals.

When asked what they associated with German-Canadian history, respondents often referred to particular places. Toponymy, the traditional support of collective identities, served the recollection that Canada's origins were not simply French/British or English/American, but that Germans had participated on the Canadian 'frontier,' from Lunenburg to the Red River Colony. The more astute respondents named not only locations but also particular events and historical figures. Some knew that, by virtue of the ties between the royal families in Germany and Britain, Germans in Canada had been well received until 1914, and thus did they repossess, in the 1990s, a 'German-Canadian mythology,' as embodied, for example, in the German-Canadian press: from the myth of Germans sailing aboard Viking ships, to the legends of Prince Rupert, by way of the stories of the many Germans who had worked in many professions.[21]

Only the story of the eighteenth-century German mercenaries was repeatedly mentioned – an episode associated with the introduction of the first Christmas tree into Canada, in 1781, in Sorel south of Montreal. This story was recalled with particular pride as *the* symbol of the German presence in Canada. This reference – which united the Canadian fir tree, lost in the immensity of a forest that resists domestication, with the German fir tree, vector of *Gemütlichkeit* – enabled the fusion of two distinct imaginations, both of which were marked by a tree's sacred character. While this episode was known to most respondents, it remains a rather meagre harvest from which to deduce a solid German-Canadian historical consciousness. Efforts to define a sense of belonging that amounted to more than a back-and-forth movement among various points of identity – other than a sense of sharing in the traditional values of 'Germanness' (*Gemütlichkeit*, *Fleiß*, etc.) – such efforts would have represented a long-winded endeavour indeed. But most 'ordinary' German-Quebecers found that it was neither possible nor desirable to found a distinct group and remained less than interested in seeing themselves collectively represented. Their strategies of identity were satisfied by the possession of a particular historical sensibility, while many of those who sought mainly to be integrated on an individual level saw in the exaggerated attachment to ethnic communities an extension of *deutschtümelnd* ('teutomaniac') attitudes that belonged to the past.

The publication of Jean-Pierre Wilhelmy's book on the German mercenaries of Quebec was the occasion for their many descendents to express themselves. Had they developed a more self-assertive identity discourse than those Quebecers of relatively recent German descent? In their letters to Wilhelmy, many had spoken of the mystery that surrounded their family histories. Given the consonance of their names, as well as the impact of insults and scorn, many had been impelled to pursue the question. Some, in addressing themselves to Wilhelmy, spoke of 'our ancestors,' as if they were seeking by means of this delayed assertion to wipe away past humiliations. In the 1990s, only rarely had the awareness of such differences enabled the development of an ethnic identity that provided for their inclusion in a collective German 'we.' So we observed when we interviewed some of the descendants of the mercenaries. For the most part, genealogical interest in this episode had not radically changed their identity. They continued to speak of themselves primarily as Quebecers – or as French-Canadians, for the older generations.

At the end of the twentieth century, the question of inclusion in the collective 'we' of Quebec sparked the interest of some Quebec intellectuals of German descent, such as Heinz Weinmann. In his work on the history, literature, and cinema of Quebec, Weinmann criticized the mystifying arguments made by some nationalist historians in Quebec, who blackened the British regime rather than comparing it to other contemporary regimes in Europe.[22] Nevertheless, Weinmann had a great deal of empathy for Quebec, even for its most nationalistic tendencies. In time, the gaze of the objective observer became compassionate. He defended Bill 101, especially the fact that immigrant children would now have to go to French school, because it protected of the cultural dynamics of French-speaking America. In this, Weinmann found himself part of the collective 'we' of Quebec – 'our literature' – not an exclusive *we* ('nous-autres'), but a *we* that remained open to the other. He admired the bold course taken by Quebec society over recent decades, a course he compared to the rebirth of nation-states after the fall of communism in Europe.[23] If Weinmann's strategies here – to which we might add those of other intellectuals of German descent, such as Gregory Baum and Lothar Baier[24] – did not necessarily represent many immigrants' experiences during the 1950s and 1960s, they did show the extent to which German-Quebecers, whom we tend too often to speak of as invisible, had been able to participate in the debates that had given birth to modern Quebec.

If the collective memory of German-Quebecers in the 1990s, thin though it may be, seemed to reach back as far as to those eighteenth-century German mercenaries, this historical episode occupied less space in their consciousness than did the memory of the Second World War. In their identification strategies, German-Quebecers had been unable to escape the singularity of Nazi history, which had confronted them with many accusations from Canadians. Even in Canada, so far from Germany, they had to come to terms with their past, as Germans, and to deal with individual suffering and collective silence, in a country where the *Vergangenheitsbewältigung* – in the West German sense – had not really taken place. In this sense, the Canadian-ness that was stressed by so many obviously enabled them to escape from the complexities of German identity.

To explain Germans' easy identification with Canada, we might hypothesize that for them, identification with Quebec was difficult because the fall of New France in 1760 played, in some Quebec nationalist discourse, the same key role as 1945 did for German-Canadians. The two events are hardly comparable, yet there remained in both cases a hint of bitterness that had lingered for decades and even centuries. The parallels between certain 'martyrological' aspects of Quebec history and the victimization that marked some postwar German discourse impeded any real feelings of sympathy for Quebecers, everyone being occupied with his/her own sense of defeat. This insistence on victim status – indeed, some readers *had* been expelled from the 'eastern territories' after 1945 – was reflected in the German-Canadian press of the 1990s and hardly encouraged readers to ponder their own moral responsibility for Nazism. Their collective pain had hardly yet been heard, and they seemed therefore often less than interested in thinking through German history in terms of the suffering that Germans had inflicted.

For these immigrants, who yearned for a fresh start after the Nazi years, it seemed easier to identify with the Canadian 'winners.' Their Canadianization had been impeded by the fact that the Canadian mainstream media portrayed Germans as 'the' enemy and often equated them with Nazis in their reporting about the Second World War. One approach to erasing this Nazi stigma and becoming 'regular' (Canadian) citizens involved minimizing the Third Reich years and placing Auschwitz on the same level as the *Vertreibung* (expulsion from the East). This strategy was fairly obvious in letters to the editors of the *Kanada Kurier*, such as this one:

Während fast täglich die meist erlogenen Grausamkeiten der Deutschen im letz-
ten Weltkrieg in allen Medien angeprangert werden, ist derselbe Nachrichten-
dienst seltsam schweigsam, wenn es um Verbrechen geht, die an uns begangen
wurden.[25]

While the made-up atrocities of Germans in the last World War are denounced almost daily in all media, the same news service is strangely mute on the crimes committed against us.

Clearly, many who had come to Canada from a truncated and divided Germany did not wish to find themselves once again in the midst of a 'fragmented' country, or to encumber themselves with the conflictual identity of Québécois. German-Quebecers, though they had largely been integrated into the English-speaking minority, had generally accepted the new political and linguistic distributions – if only by not having left after the *Parti québécois* victory of 1976 – and had thereby become exemplary Quebecers. If their identification with a French-speaking Quebec had often seemed partial, it was because the acquisition of linguistic competence did not go hand in hand with an internalization of prevailing cultural codes, nor did it entail an 'owning' of that discourse which presented Quebec as (almost) a nation. Some had just as easily asserted their identity as Montrealers, insofar as the metropolis – the second-largest French-speaking city in the world, but also one of Canada's major English-speaking and multicultural cities – mirrored the ambiguities that characterized Canada and Quebec, thus permitting those who rejected the reification of this or that identity to evade easy categorization.

Quebec nationalism, when faced with a Canadian nationalism that is often represented as simply patriotic, continued to trouble many of those who had been burned by the experience of Nazism. But there did not seem to be any direct correlations between adhering to German and Quebec nationalisms, respectively. As we have seen, then, some German anti-nationalists rejected Quebec nationalism on the basis of the risks posed by *all* nationalisms, whereas others viewed it as a necessary step in the defence of collective rights. Conversely, some German nationalists rejected Quebec nationalism in the name of economic realism, whereas others approved of it insofar as it exemplified the desire of every people to control their own state or territory.

In another respect, the apparently massive rejection of Quebec nationalism by German speakers could also be linked to their strong presence in the Montreal region, whereas sympathy for sovereignty seemed less inconvenient elsewhere. Given that individuals tend to identify with the places in which they were socialized, and thus with the national discourse that surrounds them, social geography is the more relevant explanation of Germans' attitude toward Quebec nationalism – better, that is, than the notion that Nazism had 'cured' Germans of strong nationalist tendencies. The logic of identity was founded on successive experiences of socialization, so that in recent decades, strong ties to the German nation do not preclude the possibility of identifying with Quebec. If Germans' integration with the anglophone world did not prevent the persistence of certain clichés, their encounters with French-speaking Quebec have inspired a significant number of anglicized German-Quebecers, if not to opt outright for independence, then at least to understand, profoundly, the grievances of francophones and thus, finally, to live out – rather serenely – their own double integration.

NOTES

1 According to *Statistics Canada*, there were 102,930 Quebecers of German extraction in 1996; for 23,730, their origins were uniquely German. One-third of these were born in Germany and two-thirds in either Eastern Europe or Canada. They represented 3.7 percent of the German population of Canada.

2 The English language, which has produced such designations as *Ontarian* and *Manitoban*, has produced no *Quebecan*. *Quebecer* sounds more like the designation for the people of a city.

3 See Jean-Pierre Wilhelmy, *Les mercenaires allemands au Québec* (Sillery: Septentrion, 1997).

4 See Karin Gürtler, *Geschichte der Deutschen Gesellschaft zu Montreal, 1835–1985* (Montreal: Deutsche Gesellschaft zu Montreal, 1985), 6–8.

5 See Inge Vestweber, 'Les Allemands à Montréal,' in *Ethnicity in Canada: International Examples and Perspectives: Kanada Projekt III*, ed. Alfred Pletsch (Marburg: Geographisches Institut, 1985), 240.

6 The following analysis is taken from a study that constructs a typology of the cultural and identity behaviours of German-Quebecers. It is based on a close reading of the monthly newspaper for German speakers in Quebec, *Das Echo*, and of the Montreal edition of the *Kanada Kurier;* on 65 interviews (28 people strongly involved in German cultural and associative life, 22 'not affiliated' citizens, and 15 representatives of the second, Canadian-born generation). They were conducted between 1992 and 1995,

most of them in Montreal, but also in Quebec City and rural Quebec. The analysis is also based on questionnaires distributed in *Das Echo* (1992) and in several associations (1993–4). Eighty respondents answered the twenty, mostly open questions about culture, language, history, and identity. See Manuel Meune, *Les Allemands du Québec. Parcours et discours d'une communauté méconnue* (Montréal: Méridien, 2003).

7 Herfried Scheer, 'Deutsche Sprache und deutsche Kultur in der Provinz Quebec,' in *Deutsch als Muttersprache in Kanada. Berichte zur Gegenwartslage*, ed. Leopold Auburger and Heinz Kloss (Wiesbaden: Steiner, 1977), 7–13.

8 K.G. O'Bryan et al., *Non-official Languages: A Study in Canadian Multiculturalism* (Ottawa: Minister Responsible for Multiculturalism, 1976), 192.

9 *Kanada Kurier*, 15 December 1994, 19.

10 *Kanada Kurier*, 21 July 1994, 13; 30 March 1995, 14.

11 See Patrick Farges, in this volume.

12 Claire McNicoll, *Montréal. Une société multiculturelle* (Paris: Belin, 1993).

13 *Kanada Kurier*, 15 September 1994, 15.

14 Quoted in Gürttler, *Geschichte der Deutschen Gesellschaft*, 83–4.

15 See Gerhard Bassler, 'Problems and Perspectives in German-Canadian Historiography,' in *Probleme – Projekte – Perspektiven*, ed. Karin Gürttler and Friedhelm Lach (Montréal: Universite de Montréal, 1986), 1: 'The German-Canadian press and the newly founded German-Canadian Congress are wondering why German Canadians as one of Canada's founding groups have been denied recognition of their more than three hundred years of significant contributions to the opening-up and development of Canada.' See also Gerhard Bassler, 'Introduction,' in Heinz Lehmann, *The German-Canadians: Immigration, Settlement, and Culture*, ed. Gerhard Bassler (St John's: Jesperson, 1986), i–xxvi at xxvi. We should note, however, that Bassler no longer makes reference to this concept in 'German-Canadian Studies Tomorrow: A Historian's Perspective,' *German-Canadian Yearbook* 8 (1993).

16 Herbert Debor, *Die Deutschen in der Provinz Quebec* (Montréal: 1964), 39.

17 Gürttler, *Geschichte der Deutschen Gesellschaft*, 'Préface' and 92–4.

18 *Kanada Kurier*, 11 November 1993, 16; 22 September 1994; 10 November 1994, 17.

19 *Kanada Kurier*, 1 September 1994.

20 Gerd Mittelstaedt, 'Das deutschkanadische Hilfswerk,' *German-Canadian Yearbook* 7 (1983) (translation into English by Meune), 178.

21 Thus, a special edition of the *Kanada Kurier*, in 1989, sought to fill the 'gaps' that gape throughout the official histories, and to reinforce German-Canadian identity by listing the significant features of the German face

of Canadian history. See, for example, Hellmuth Reif, 'Die Vorläufer als geistige und tatsächliche Wegbereiter der Entdeckungen in Canada und Nordamerika,' *Kanada Kurier ,Unser Centennial'* August 1989, 9; Elisabeth Meyer, 'So haben wir begonnen,' in same, 12, 15.

22 Heinz Weinmann, *Du Canada au Québec. Généalogie d'une histoire* (Montréal: Hexagone, 1987), 279, 323; see also his *Cinéma de l'imaginaire québécois, de 'La petite Aurore' à 'Jésus de Montréal'* (Montréal: Hexagone, 1990).

23 Heinz Weinmann, 'Dépendance et indépendance comme stratégie culturelle du Québec de demain,' in Pierre Lanthier and Guildo Gousseau, *La culture inventée, les stratégies culturelles aux 19e et 20e siècles* (Québec: IQRC, 1992), 353–60.

24 Gregory Baum (1923-) was professor of theological ethics at McGill University. He worked on ecumenism and on the Church's relations to non-Christian religions, but also on social and political theology, for example in *Nationalism, Religion, and Ethics* (Montreal and Kingston: McGill–Queen's University Press, 2001). Lothar Baier (1942–2004) was an author, publisher, translator, and a specialist in the francophone world's literature and philosophy. He spent the last years of his life in Montreal, where he wrote *Anders schreibendes Amerika. Eine Anthologie der Literatur aus Quebec 1945–2000* (Heidelberg: Wunderhorn, 2000).

25 *Kanada Kurier*, 24 February 1994.

8 'What Church Do You Go To?' The Difficult Acculturation of German-Jewish Refugees in Canada, 1933–2004

PATRICK FARGES

The making of the modern Canadian nation is now being rewritten as the result of ethnic interactions shaped by migrations, and Canada is now considered a multicultural, ethnically diverse society. In this process, the 'mosaic' metaphor has often been used to describe Canadian diversity, and multiculturalism policy has established an institutional framework in which ethnic cultures can be granted recognition. Multiculturalism has thus enabled, so it seems, the promotion of the 'acculturation' paradigm over the 'assimilation' paradigm thought to prevail in the United States. Official multiculturalism, however, also leads to a paradox: a distinct 'culture' can only be recognized and gain visibility if it fits to some extent into the institutionalized and socially accepted multicultural framework. Thus, identities have become somewhat fixed, and there is little allowance for interstitial positions, for 'in-between-ness.' Consequently, 'hyphenated' ethnic historiographers have devoted their efforts to creating coherence within such a framework, leaving aside important 'blind spots,' as Angelika Sauer has labelled them with regard to a certain type of German-Canadian historiography that overemphasizes the existence of 'pure' ethnic enclaves.[1] Once we underscore and understand the interactions and frictions at the margins of ethnocultural group definitions, we find unveiled for us the mechanisms that lead to such imagined group formations. Hence German-Canadian studies must venture into adjacent fields. One of those 'blind spots' in German-Canadian historiography is the story of the German-speaking Jewish refugees, a story that falls between the cracks of the mosaic – in between German-Canadian historiography and Jewish-Canadian historiography.

The involuntary migration of German-speaking Jewish refugees from National Socialism – refugees from Germany, Austria, and Czech-oslovakia – brought to Canada a small but particularly complex wave of immigrants, despite Canada's reticence in the 1930s to let Jewish refugees in. This particular type of migration is often called 'exile,' especially in the German- and French-language literature. The term is somewhat unsatisfactory, however, because it implies a temporary situation, whereas the lived exile is often permanent. English-language literature mostly uses the term 'refugees.' But the latter term is also confusing, as it now refers to a status internationally defined in the 1948 UN Declaration of Human Rights. Nevertheless, I will mainly use the term 'refugee' to refer to those migrants who left Nazi Europe after 1933. According to the historian Annette Puckhaber, with the Nazis' ascent to power, between 4,900 and 6,000 German-speaking refugees came to Canada, most of whom were Jewish.[2] Some were able to enter Canada because they had relatives who could vouch for them; others settled as farmers; still others were able to demonstrate proficiency in a profession favoured by immigration officials. Never during the 1930s, however, did Canada have an official policy regarding refugees.[3]

In 1940, Canada also took in civilian internees from Great Britain, the 'Camp Boys.' This group comprised for the most part Germans and Austrians residing on British soil. In view of Nazi Germany's growing military successes, the fear of a 'Fifth Column' of saboteurs spread over the United Kingdom, reaching a peak in the spring of 1940. In response, Winston Churchill decided to register and categorize all 'enemy aliens' and to intern some of them.[4] Among the interned were many refugees from National Socialism. About two thousand male internees were then sent overseas to Canadian internment camps (others were sent to Aus-tralia), where they spent several months. After finally being released, they became Canada's 'accidental immigrants,' to use Paula J. Draper's term. About half of them returned to the United Kingdom after their release, while the others settled permanently in Canada and the United States. This episode was part of a more general practice of war intern-ment in Canada and abroad.[5]

Some research has been conducted on refugees from National Social-ism, but it all too often focuses on famous émigrés. For instance, 'exile studies' (*Exilforschung*) developed over four decades ago, mainly in Germany, France, and the United States, in order to document the tra-jectories of refugees from Nazi Europe. Taken as a whole, this branch of research is one example of a 'divergent migration research agenda' as defined by migration historian Nancy L. Green[6] – a focus on the various destinations of migrants who come from the same area. Many scholars in exile studies have focused on the emigration of high-profile intellectuals and scientists. German historian Wolfgang Benz's work on the extraordinary lives of ordinary people in exile (*Das Exil der kleinen Leute*, 1991), however, documented the story of those who had until then been overshadowed by the all too grand and fascinating fates of Thomas Mann or Albert Einstein. This new perspective in exile studies was ground-breaking. Attention has recently been paid to refugees' interactions with and integration into host societies, as demonstrated by the 2001 issue of *Exilforschung – ein internationales Jahrbuch*, which focused on 'assimilation, acculturation, and identity.' The present chapter furthers the theoretical renewal in exile studies by drawing still more on multidisciplinary approaches such as migration studies.[7]

Migrants' experiences are generally shaped by three dimensions that constantly interact: (1) the cultural baggage and socialization acquired before departure, (2) the voyage as a moment of transition and translation (i.e., as a change of geographical as well as mental settings), and (3) the never-ending process of acculturation. This experience is both individual and collective, both psychological and 'societal,' as underlined by Dirk Hoerder.[8] The purpose of this chapter is to show how the German-speaking Jewish refugees who came to and stayed in Canada after 1933 recomposed their individual identity; how they interacted with their sociocultural environment; and how (and whether) they created and transmitted a form of collective memory within the larger frame of the Jewish Diaspora. These different aspects can all be considered dimensions of acculturation as 'those phenomena which result when groups or individuals having different cultures come into continuous first-hand contact, with subsequent changes in the original cultural patterns of either or both groups.'[9] The definition is based on an anthropological definition of culture as a 'historically transmitted pattern of meaning embodied in symbols, a system of inherited conceptions expressed in symbolic forms by means of which men communicate, perpetuate, and develop their knowledge about and attitudes towards life.'[10] My understanding of the acculturation process is thus akin to Dirk Hoerder's concept of 'transculturalization' in the present volume, defined as 'the process of individuals and societies to change themselves by integration of diverse cultural lifeways into a dynamic new one.' But how can acculturation or 'transculturalization' be assessed and documented from a historical perspective?

My research was conducted in part as an oral history.[11] Besides interviews, sources included personal papers, testimonies, letters, memoirs, and autobiographical accounts found in archival or private collections, as well as archives pertaining to clubs and associations. Consequently, this project amounts to a qualitative study of mostly everyday acculturation, based on the interpretation of personal and largely narrative data, and the documents bear traces of dense 'face-to-face interactions' that decisively shaped the acculturation process.[12] This type of interaction is also informed by institutional processes in a constant and asymmetrical dialogue. In the informants' own accounts, it is this particular interface with the new environment that is relevant. To quote Hoerder again: 'The record of many lives [permits] a composite view of societies in the process of being created.'[13]

Wilma Abeles Iggers: 'Far From Where?'

Until recently, Wilma A. Iggers travelled a lot. With her husband Georg G. Iggers, the famous historian and historiographer, she used to live six months of the year in Göttingen, Germany, and the other six in Buffalo, New York. I interviewed her in both places, but the excerpts quoted here are from the Göttingen interview. Through Wilma, it was also possible for me to interview one of her sons in Toronto, as well as her cousin Minna in Lynden, Ontario. Wilma told the following joke:

> So our impression of Canada was very good, but my father kept saying: *'It's awfully far!'* Do you know the joke about 'Far from where?' Well – so there's someone who wants to emigrate – it's a very simple joke – and he's supposed to go to Brazil or something, and so the other one says: *'Oh, but it's awfully far!'* And the next question is *'Far from where?'*[14]

Wilma Iggers, née Abeles, born 1921 in Miřkov (Czechoslovakia), grew up in the newly formed Republic of Czechoslovakia – 'Masaryk's Republic' – with which Wilma and her cousin Minna still strongly identify to this day. Wilma and Minna are Jewish, and they belonged to the German-speaking bourgeoisie of Bischofteinitz (Horšovský Týn), a town in the Sudetenland, a border region in which there lived many ethnic Germans as well as German-speaking Jews. The Abeles and their relatives, the Popper family, were farmers, *Jewish* farmers – a counterintuitive fact for many, including most Canadian immigration officials at the time, and this particular point turned out to be beneficial in furthering the family's immigration process. Wilma recalls that they were 'lukewarm Jews'[15] who attended religious celebrations only on the High Holy Days: 'Three-Days-Jews' (*Drei-Tage-Juden*), so to speak. After the *Anschluss* – that is, the annexation of Austria by Nazi Germany – the threat came dangerously close to home.

Fortunately, the Abeles-Popper family had anticipated the worst and prepared an emigration scheme as an extended family. The group originally consisted of thirty-nine people. Some members of the group, including Wilma's father, had made previous inquiries about immigration to France and Canada. In the early summer of 1938, a Canadian Pacific Railway immigration representative visited the Abeles farm. He was favourably impressed and made arrangements in Ottawa to speed up the immigration process. The Abeles-Poppers were to take over abandoned farms in the Hamilton area (Ontario).

After the Munich Agreement – which led directly to the invasion of the Sudetenland by Nazi Germany – the family was no longer safe. On 15 September 1938, at 4:30 a.m., they were warned by a friend that anti-Semitic actions were planned for that day, and they found refuge at a friend's farm in inner Czechoslovakia. On 24 October, Wilma left her home country and boarded a flight to Brussels. From there she went to England, then crossed the Atlantic Ocean on a six-day voyage. On 11 November 1938, she finally landed in Montreal.[16] A totally new life was awaiting her.

In the rural area around Hamilton, the 'Czechopeople-Farm,' as it was soon named by locals, quickly became a curiosity, and the cultural and religious background of these immigrants remained a challenging puzzle to the community: 'The first question in Canada, or sometimes the second one, was always: "What Church do you go to?"' Wilma remembers how absurd this question sounded to her, who came from a mainly secular (and certainly non-Christian) background. All of a sudden, she felt a complete stranger who had to adapt to a new society that defined itself according to religious affiliations. She also recalls how the members of her group, which increased in size in the first year as relatives were brought over, reacted in different ways to their new environment: 'Many of our people decided to present themselves as Gentiles or even to formally convert to a Christian religion.' For others, on the contrary, 'who had earlier not wanted to be known as Jews, the desire to be part of the group became dominant, and they joined the rest of the crowd in synagogue on special occasions.' It seems that one way or another, the members of the group felt the need to align themselves with the identifying categories then available in Canada. In Wilma's own words, though, this process of acculturation and identification has failed in great part, as the members of this particular group have become 'assimilated Central European Jews, still not entirely trusting the Germans, with very few ties to the Czechs in Czechoslovakia, and still not feeling one with the Canadian Jews of Eastern Europe.'[17] She thus expresses a complicated and multilayered identity, as well as a hiatus resulting from displacement. She and her family do not seem to have been able to completely fit in: the identity framework of the old homeland has clashed with Canadian sociocultural categories.

Symbiosis, Stigmatization, and Rupture: German-Jewish Identity

Displacement, both geographical and cultural, is the common feature of migrant trajectories, and migrants' life narratives are retrospectively structured as 'before' and 'after,' 'there' and 'here.' Often, sometimes only implicitly, a comparative dimension is at the core of the migrant experience. The remembered rupture shapes one's life narrative, but it also shapes collective experience and memory. Similarly, *adopting* the new environment – or merely *adapting* to it – is partly a collective phenomenon. One's individual adaptation is at the very least *informed* by knowledge about a larger collective process. Through imagination and narration, both migration and acculturation become collective experiences.

For the psychoanalysts León and Rebecca Grinberg, who draw on their clinical experience with exiles in Argentina, the rupture caused by exile is a traumatic experience with no single traceable cause. They suggest that the traumas of migration (including language and culture loss) mirror the individuation process. Exile becomes, the Grinbergs argue, a true catastrophe and the agent of catastrophic change, setting off psychic defence mechanisms: 'The immigrant needs a potential space that he can use as the "transitional space" and "transition" period between the mother country/object and the new outside world ... If he fails to create this potential space, the continuity between self and the surroundings is broken.'[18] Thus it gives way to a complex and diffuse trauma, stretched over time, a 'belated' trauma bound to be lived over and over again in everyday interactions. In the case of the Jewish refugees from Europe, several successive ruptures interacted: being stigmatized as a Jew in Nazi Europe, leaving the *Heimat*, facing a foreign world, being set apart in the new country, or keeping an accent. The rapid implementation of anti-Semitic laws in Nazi Germany certainly led to such a diffuse trauma with multiple layers. Informants recall everyday incidents at school or in shops, and they vividly remember being 'marked' by the Nuremberg racial laws of 1935, which defined and indelibly fixed who was to be considered a Jew. They also recall the affixing of Jewish names such as 'Sarah' and 'Israel' to their own first names on official documents. For Edgar Lion, whom I interviewed in 2003, the most striking memory is what happened after the *Anschluss* in his school, the famous Viennese *Theresianum*:

> Anyhow, I was there for 8 years, and I finished my Senior Matric … under the Nazis! Because when the Nazis marched into Austria, they occupied my school and turned it into barracks for the SS and SA, you see. It became barracks. And I had some pretty grim experiences there, because these people, who were really animals – that's the only way to describe them, they were not human, they were animals – and because they had nothing to do, their pastime was in catching people and torturing them! And we were upstairs and we had to watch it, you know. And I saw some of these things and they are staying with me for the rest of my life! It was the most horrible thing I've actually witnessed in person. And the direction of the school told my parents that they could not guarantee my safety. You see, there were very, very few Jewish students in the school.[19]

Far from being shielded from anti-Semitism after escaping Nazi Europe, the refugees were confronted with hostility in the host countries. In Canada, they were often twice stigmatized, as 'Germans' (and thus 'enemy aliens') and as Jews. When, after being released from internment, Gerd Waldstein was refused a job in 1944, he did not know if it was because his name sounded German, because it sounded Jewish, or both. In any case, he decided to change it to Gerry Waldston and quickly found a job in the advertising field in Montreal.[20] In his memoirs, Eric Exton (born Erich Eckstein) recalls that his first Canadian boss suggested a name change in 1943: 'We're at war with Germany, so a German and Jewish sounding name just won't do, he said. How about something more Canadian, like, say, Elliott?'[21]

When the interned refugees (especially the younger ones) were given permission to leave the camp temporarily and meet with persons of the opposite sex at social events in nearby towns, the overall feeling was one of awkwardness, not only because they had been in an all-male environment for several months, but also because they made quite a bizarre impression. Interviewed by CBC journalist Harry Rasky in 1981, one of the young ladies present at the time confessed: 'We certainly thought of them as foreigners because of course most of them did have accents. Not only did they have accents but they had German accents for the most part which, you could imagine, we were at war with Germany … was a combination that we found difficult to deal with.'[22]

As Canadian historiography of immigration has recently shown, Canadian society was generally not welcoming toward those who did not approximate the dominant model – that is, who were not of 'native stock,' which at the time meant of British (or American) or French origin.[23] In English Canada, the main concern of 'nativists' who opposed immigration was that the British character of Canada might be seriously threatened by a massive in-migration of peoples who seemed to defy assimilation, especially 'Orientals,' 'Negroes,' and 'Hebrews.' Alfred Bader, who studied at Queen's University in the 1940s after being released from internment, recalls that 'a protracted discussion went on at the university's Board of Trustees meetings regarding the increasing number of Jewish students. Before the war, two or three per cent of the students were Jews, by 1944 this had risen to ten per cent. They came mainly from Montreal where McGill enforced a *numerus clausus*. Jews had to have higher marks than Christians to be admitted.'[24]

Rampant anti-Semitism at universities – still largely denominational institutions at the time – is confirmed by Wilma Iggers, who studied at the (then Baptist) McMaster University, where 'only active Christians [were allowed] to teach.'

As in many Western countries, anti-Semitism was strong in Canada in the 1930s. It is a well-documented and well-discussed fact that anti-Semitism was strong in Catholic Quebec, with newspapers (such as *Le Goglu, Le Miroir,* and *Le Chameau*) and political leaders (such as Adrien Arcand) diffusing hate propaganda. But anti-Semitism was not limited to Quebec. As Betcherman convincingly demonstrates, 'English-Canada … persisted in regarding [Swastika-clubs and fascist political parties] as totally alien to its democratic way of life (while quite at home in Quebec). But fascism west of the Ottawa River was not just an import. English-speaking Canadians themselves indulged to some degree in its main component – racism.'[25]

Anti-Semitism was a widely accepted, normal, everyday aspect of life in the late 1930s and 1940s, as one interviewee recalls:

But there was anti-Semitism in Canada, I'm sorry to say. They didn't employ a Jew in a bank, you couldn't live in certain parts … You couldn't go to certain lodges, you couldn't go to certain summer resorts, you couldn't belong to golf clubs … Well, I tell you: when I first came to Canada and the people I lived with were Jewish, and I couldn't understand that they separated themselves from the non-Jewish people, and I felt 'Gosh, here I came to this country because we were Jewish, and now they tell me that the Jews are not equal,' you know, it was a big shock![26]

When endorsed by immigration officials or civil servants, this would lead to a form of institutional anti-Semitism based on simple prejudice, as well as elaborately constructed economic and social theories intended to justify anti-immigration measures.

If in most cases, a feeling of gratitude toward Canada prevails, some informants still hold grudges against the hostility they initial felt in their new environment. When entering Canada, the refugees were burdened with the weight of their cultural and experiential baggage, which included racial stigmatization, estrangement, and – sometimes multiple – displacement. The preferred strategy for avoiding stigmatization was to blend in as much as possible, to disguise oneself. If one could not possibly hide a German accent, one could at least deny being Jewish. This explains why some refugees 'decided' – or rather were coerced by the societal framework – to adopt English-sounding names, to marry non-Jews, or even to convert.

More dramatically, even the 'home culture' could not unproblematically be referred to anymore, either to reject it or as a means of grounding oneself. The informants' recollections raise the difficult question of a 'German–Jewish symbiosis' and how it is perceived in retrospect: 'German Jew. Do you know what irritates me most? So – what I do in Germany, in Frankfurt – and I would do it again – is go to young people in schools and tell them, explain to them that before the Nazis, we used to be Germans, that there existed something like that. We were Germans, we were Jews, we were Germans. It's unimaginable today.'[27]

Half a million Jews – those who claimed to be Jewish and who understood themselves as a religious minority – were living in Germany in 1933.[28] In German and Austrian urban centres, the proportion of 'assimilated' and sometimes converted Jews was high, to the extent that Judaism was no longer, or only marginally, part of the family's social practice and identity: 'My family was totally German … My parents were Protestants and dissidents … and in my early childhood, I didn't know a single thing about Judaism.'[29] These assimilated Jews, who often looked down on more recent Jewish migrants – the 'Ostjuden' (Jews from the East) – 'were very much typical German burghers in outlook, in their sense of values and other characteristics'[30] – that is, in their culture.

German-speaking Jewish refugees often wax nostalgic of the situation before 1933. Their nostalgia is partly a way of feeling grounded in a pre-traumatic period of their life, but also the partial memory of a historical situation. It is a way of re-*membering* the past, of both recalling and restructuring it. For Wilma Iggers, the symbiosis occurred in Masaryk's Czechoslovakia: 'We were seen as Jews, everybody knew it … and in that sense, it was better in Czechoslovakia than in any other country I know about.' Her cousin Minna confirms: 'My girlfriends were not Jewish. There were only two Jewish families in this village where I lived. So all my friends were non-Jews. I didn't feel any difference. I felt it more here [in Canada] than I did at home [in Czechoslovakia].'[31]

W. Gunther Plaut, the former Rabbi of the Holy Blossom Temple in Toronto, who was born in Münster in 1912 and whose family had lived in Willingshausen (Hessen) since the 1750s, retrospectively underlines the illusion of such a symbiosis. He calls for a distinction between apparent and actual integration, between the practice of conformity and the marked visibility of difference: 'This was just one more paradox of Jewish life in Germany: all week Jews tried to blend inconspicuously into the life of the community, but on Saturdays their mode of dress proclaimed publicly "I am a Jew."'[32] In this he agrees with Enzo Traverso's analysis. Traverso calls the 'Judeo-German symbiosis' a 'historical irony' involving a 'vast misapprehension' – that is, the 'illusory dream of [a] possible acceptance.'[33]

The rupture between the old life and the new was felt especially vividly in the microcosm of Canadian internment camps. The internment, which lasted from several months to over three years, is a good example of transitional 'thickness' between 'there' and 'here.' During internment, lives were put on hold for a time and shielded from the world's horrors. Rediscovering his diary of internment on the occasion of its publication, the Viennese-Canadian writer Henry Kreisel remarks: 'Suspended in a kind of no man's land for more than eighteen months, I could look back at the horrendous events of the 1930s and see them in some kind of perspective.'[34]

As a group, the internees could not have been more diverse and fragmented. Besides the 'Germans' and the 'Austrians,' there were the 'Jews' and the 'non-Jews,' the 'kosher' and the '*traif*' (i.e., non-kosher). Rabbi Erwin Schild recalls:

We certainly had fun, Jewish religious fun. Our community included fervent Hassidim and coldly intellectual Mitnagdim; modern Westernized orthodox Jews rubbed shoulders – and sensitivities – with 'Ostjuden,' mutually suspicious and quaint; the 'Yekkes' with their stiffly formal, punctilious style of Jewish observance clashed in good-natured way with the informality of the Yeshiva spirit; there were Jews praying in Ashkenazi and Sefardi rites.[35]

The 'Germans' looked down on the 'Austrians,' the 'kosher' on the 'non-kosher,' and vice versa. However, separating Jews and non-Jews did not appear self-evident. Ex-internees remember how the camp administration tried various ways to subdivide the camps for reasons of morale and order, but there could be no logical subdivision along identity lines.

It is difficult to assess retrospectively the reality of a German–Jewish or Austrian–Jewish symbiosis. The symbiosis was a powerful dream, and at the same time it was a lived reality for some: a tragic foundational master narrative. Traverso argues that it was above all a 'Jewish monologue,' that this myth was never shared by non-Jews, and that a subtle but indelible distinction was maintained throughout, a distinction that was easily reactivated after 1933.[36] Nevertheless, it certainly corresponded to a deeply felt commitment to the Heimat, to its values, its high culture, and – most prominently – its language. What the refugees express in their testimonies is nostalgia not so much for a symbiosis that was placed in doubt as events took their course, as for the societal fabric in which they felt embedded and in which they had become political subjects and social agents. As one interviewee puts it: 'When you were older, a world, your Welt, somehow got destroyed.' This symbiosis cannot be called a mere illusion, for it was lived intensely by two – and sometimes three – generations of German and Austrian Jews and was not restricted to intellectual circles. And it cannot retrospectively be called an illusion because it left traces in life stories and testimonies. German-Jewish reality was an emotional capital that some refugees carried abroad and transmitted to their children as a heavy and historically tragic burden: 'Well, I am a Canadian of German origin – and of Jewish fate [jüdischen Schicksals] if you wish,' says Helmut Kallmann.[37] Bereft of their home culture, their 'Welt,' the Jewish refugees were left with only their 'Jewish-ness' as the most readily available identifying characteristic. However, 'Jewish-ness' was in most cases not a matter of observance: in the Canadian context, it became one of ethnicity. And the German-speaking Jews certainly did not fit into the framework of the local Jewish community.

A Strange Voice in the Community

The history of the Jewish community in Canada is quite different from that in the United States. The first Jewish settlers in Canada were Sephardic Jews from England, Spain, and Portugal. They founded communities in Quebec, Trois-Rivières, and Montreal. In the 1850s, Montreal already had a lively Jewish community, whereas the 1846 religious census listed only twelve Jews in Toronto. In the 1930s, 156,000 Jews were listed in Canada; of these, around 60,000 lived in Quebec. Unlike the United States, Canada did not receive significant numbers of German-Jewish immigrants in the wake of 1848; thus it was only marginally influenced by the Reform movement and its accompanying philosophy of emancipation.[38] 'Canadian Jewry,' Sarna argues, 'never experienced a "great German period" in the sense in which this term is used in the United States. For this reason, the community is both more homogeneous and more heavily East European than in the United States.'[39] There were, however, a few exceptions, such as the German-Jewish Shaar Hashamaym Synagogue (Gateway to Heaven) in Westmount, founded in 1859, and Hamilton's Jewish community, founded in the 1850s by immigrants from Germany. There is also Emil L. Fackenheim, the German-Jewish refugee who came to Canada as an internee, later became the Rabbi of the Anshe Sholom Congregation in Hamilton, and was one of the most distinguished scholars of Judaism in Canada.

Eastern European Jews came to both Canada and the United States between 1880 and 1914, but in Canada, they developed their own institutions and character without the fundamental influence of prior German-Jewish immigrant communities. American urban centres like Philadelphia, Cincinnati, and especially New York had been characterized by an ongoing contact/conflict between German-Jewish 'Uptowners' (earlier immigrants) and Russian-Jewish 'Downtowners.' In Canada, however, the small wave of post-1933 refugees bore almost alone the weight of the *other* tradition.

Rabbi Plaut had first-hand experience of the differences between Jewish culture in the United States and Canada. His first destination when he came to the United States in 1935 was the American Reform Seminary of Cincinnati, where he encountered modern Judaism, 'a movement which attempted to wed American and Jewish ideals'[40] and that embraced assimilation as both desirable and necessary. Before 1933, Germany was the centre of modern Jewish studies, and this tradition carried on in the United States. Plaut spent more than twenty-five years in the United States before moving to the Holy Blossom Temple in Toronto in 1961. There he was assisted by Heinz Warschauer, another German-Jewish refugee, who headed the religious school between 1945 and 1976. German-speaking Jewish refugees like Fackenheim, Plaut, Schild, and Warschauer would play an active role in reshaping the Canadian Jewish landscape.

In general, however, German-speaking refugees did not fit into a community that largely used to speak Yiddish and that embodied a culture they had looked down on in the old *Heimat*. Rabbi Erwin Schild recalls that he had to learn Yiddish in order to address his congregation at the Adath Israel Synagogue in Toronto.[41] The refugees were total strangers in the local community: well-educated, worldly, and sophisticated, they were assimilated Jews who spoke German – often along with French – and they clashed with a working-class milieu dominated by Polish and Galician Jews. In the sharp and ironic tone so characteristic of his writings, Mordecai Richler gives his personal rendition of the arrival of the refugees, as embodied by 'Mr. Bamberger':

> The war in Europe brought about considerable changes within the Jewish community in Montreal. To begin with, there was the coming of the refugees. These men, interned in England as enemy aliens and sent to Canada where they were eventually released, were to make a profound impact on us. I think we had conjured up a picture of the refugees as penurious *hassidim* with packs on their backs. We were eager to be helpful, our gestures were large, but in return we expected more than a little gratitude. As it turned out the refugees, mostly German and Austrian Jews, were far more sophisticated and better educated than we were. They had not, like our immigrant grandparents, come from *shtetls* in Galicia or Russia. Neither did they despise Europe. On the contrary, they found our culture thin, the city provincial, and the Jews narrow. This bewildered and stung us. But what cut deepest, I suppose, was that the refugees spoke English better than many of us did and, among themselves, had the effrontery to talk in the abhorred German language. Many of them also made it clear that Canada was no more than a frozen place to stop over until a U.S. visa was forthcoming. So for a while we real Canadians were hostile.[42]

Minna Loewith offers an anecdote about interactions with local Jews in the Hamilton area:

How did they see us? Well, I tell you. We, my parents virtually came only with suitcases, but there were some people that were able to get their furniture out, so they saw these big boxes, and one Jew that came here – he had a scrap business and he came here either from Russia or from Poland – he said: 'These immigrants come here with all kinds of money,' you know 'all kinds of money,' which wasn't really so, but this is how he felt compared to the way he came. 'And they call themselves immigrants!' You know – this is how he felt.[43]

From another perspective, some of the refugees recall being perceived as 'arrogant know-it-alls who were not properly grateful for the marvellous opportunity afforded them in the New World.'[44] Helmut Kallmann confesses: 'I guess everyone went through a little bit of "*zuhause war alles besser*" [everything was better at home] attitude, perhaps as a self-defence, even when you came from Nazi Germany!'[45]

For those refugees who had gone to New York, it was possible to reactivate German-Jewish 'local' traditions. They were given imaginary and narrative resources to come to terms with their own experience, simply because 'people like them' (from Frankfurt, Berlin, or Hamburg) had previously come to New York and co-founded several 'Little Jewish Germanies.'[46] But such a readily available identification did not exist in Canada. It seemed almost impossible to re-create some kind of a *Heimat* or sometimes simply to refer to it. And never could they seriously envision getting closer to the German-Canadian community either. The informants sometimes echo the idea that in the 1930s and even later, most German-Canadians were anti-Semitic and largely pro-Nazi. Wagner has convincingly demonstrated that pro-Nazi activities had in fact a very limited influence on the greater German community in the 1930s.[47] Yet Meune for his part has shown that within the 'German-Canadian community,' especially among immigrants from the 1950s, there existed a small but vigorous minority voicing tendentious ideas – in the newspaper *Kanada Kurier,* for instance.[48] With the exception of the German Society of Montreal (twice chaired by refugees from Germany in the past thirty years), there was and is no real common ground in Canada for a German–Jewish dialogue, much to the despair of those who existentially embodied the memory of such a dialogue.

Separated from the cultural environment in which they had been socialized, and already affected by a dense phase of transition, the German-speaking refugees in Canada were often not given adequate emotional and narrative tools to tell their story. Sometimes they were stigmatized twice, as Jews and as Germans, and they were remnants of an 'impossible' cultural heritage for which there was little understanding after Auschwitz. Taken as a whole, this generation of exiles – the last (lost?) generation that synthesized Jewish and German identities – could no longer be heard in Canada.

Acculturation and History: Narration as Necessity

So far I have underlined several ruptures the German-speaking Jewish exiles went through, such as persecution, loss of the homeland, and stigmatization. These ruptures brought about several layers of 'delayed' traumatic experiences. Creating strategies to overcome trauma largely depends on available collective scripts.[49] In the case of German-speaking Jewish exiles, however, the collective dimension was not easily constructed and hence could not be drawn upon as a narrative script. For a long time, the stories of those who had escaped the Nazi regime *before* the death camps could not be told, as they were incommensurable with horrors of the Holocaust. But annihilation definitely occurred in exile, too: annihilation of a mode of living together, annihilation of a shared history, annihilation of a social and cultural fabric.[50] Expressed bluntly, one could say that German-Jewish culture, annihilated by the Nazis, was then largely erased a second time – in its own memory – by the impossibility of referring to it and of *telling the story*.

Life courses are trajectories through social structure, and the feeling of identity depends on the legitimacy of one's story within the wider framework of history. This process also deepens an inner sense of coherence. Narrative coherence is created when individual stories match collective scripts, thus enabling individuals to rewrite their lived experiences. If acculturation is defined as changes in original cultural patterns resulting from first-hand contact with others, then modifications in narrative patterns are definitely part of the acculturation process. Acculturation then means it is possible to 'straighten up' one's story in the greater societal framework, that is, in interaction with other groups. But can the German-speaking Jewish refugees be considered a group with a collective experience, and does this collective experience reach beyond the fact that they *retrospectively* shared a common trajectory?

As I have shown previously, they certainly were considered a group in the representations that others had of them. Moreover, in the case of internment or group migration, these refugees shared an important portion of their lives. More significantly, however, the refugees generally knew, and know, *about* each other. Their own personal experiences are informed by those of others. To a certain degree, their lives are intermingled, at least on an imagined level. In the course of my research, this is how I managed to trace potential interlocutors. Despite repeated assertions that they did not really formally keep in touch, the German-speaking Jewish refugees generally knew what had happened to others, and this created informal networks and kept the story alive. Here are just a few examples of spontaneous commemorations: a number of intermarriages took place over time between different groups of refugees; in the past decade, Helmut Kallmann has been able to start a newsletter for ex-internees, and in 2003 his mailing list bore more than 180 names; and on a regular basis, the Abeles-Poppers and their extended family celebrate huge reunions.

In the early days after the war, the pressure to blend in after years of stigmatization was so strong that the refugees would only reluctantly admit to keeping what one interviewee calls 'old world clubs.' For instance, gatherings were used as legal tools for receiving compensation from postwar Germany, and as places where German could be spoken and familiar forms of sociability could be reactivated, much to the frustration of Canadian spouses. In Israel, this generation bears the name '*Yekkes*' (i.e., 'people so formal that they wear a tie and jacket [*"Jäckchen"* or *"Jäcke"* in German] all the time, no matter how warm the weather may be').[51] After attending the funeral of a German-Jewish refugee in Montreal, Chaim Vogt-Moykopf wrote a nostalgic article in the *Aufbau* about 'the last *Yekkes*' in Canada.[52] But even if this culture is now dying away with the passing of its bearers, some sense of a distinct identity has often been transmitted to the children and grandchildren.

In the postwar (and post-1948) period, a dominant narrative emerged within a Canadian Jewish community that was becoming increasingly centripetal. As Abella summarizes:

> The world had become too dangerous a place for Jews to allow themselves the luxury of internal dissent and divisiveness ... Jewish energies were now totally devoted to protecting the State of Israel, to welcoming the influx of Holocaust survivors and to breaking down the barriers in Canadian society. One Yiddish pundit labelled postwar Jewry the 'sha shtill' generation, literally the silent generation, afraid to rock the boat for fear of sinking with it.[53]

The homogeneity within the Jewish community seems to have been greater in Canada than in the United States, the community it most extensively compares with. Waller analyses the high concentration of financial means, information, and power within the community in the postwar period.[54]

Fixed collective memories emerge when practices and discourses are quoted and reproduced over and over again. Little by little, one prevailing memory crystallized within the Jewish community in Canada. One of its main characteristics was the rupture between Jewish and German memories (and later between Jewish-Canadian and German-Canadian historiographies), which contradicted some of the German-speaking Jewish refugees' deepest identification feelings, especially among the younger generation. In the realm of 'ethnic groups' in the Canadian mosaic, the Jews slowly merged into one. This struck some German-Jewish refugees as unimaginable within their own emotional frame of reference. Another prominent characteristic of this rupture was the symbolic boycott of things German and, beyond that, of things German-Canadian. As Plaut writes: 'I still will not drive a German car in Toronto ... My abstinence is symbolic, yet symbols do play a role.'[55] The impossible return to Germany is a recurrent theme, as well as the impossible dialogue with 'Germans,' in Canada or abroad. These themes have become narrative features of a collective memory. One question seemed to overshadow any interaction with a 'German': 'What were you doing during the war?' Behind each German, there could potentially be a former Nazi, which echoes the idea of a 'collective guilt' of the German people.

This, however, put German-speaking Jewish refugees, the heirs of a German-Jewish culture, in an untenable identity and memory position. Postwar Jewish memory in Canada did not allow for such an 'unspeakable' identification, which led to deep psychological rifts. When I interviewed Willie Glaser in Montreal, it struck me that despite his 'very broad German accent,' as he himself acknowledged, he did not speak 'good German' any more. Indeed, he struggled to find his words.[56] Yet at the same time, he enjoyed speaking the unspeakable language and felt connected to it. And when he referred to scenes he had witnessed in Germany, his German suddenly became fluent and idiomatic again. It was as if German, the impossible language that had marked him for life (in his thick accent), had become a means of re-enacting traumatic episodes of his past life.

Similarly, it was for a long time unfathomable – 'inconceivable' –

why Jews would want to return to Germany: 'The return of Jews to Germany was a source of never-ending questions. Why would anyone wish to come back to this land?'[57] The son of German-speaking Jewish refugees told me: 'You know, when people say to me: "How could your father go back," you know, "after what they did to the Jews," you know, after that, it's inconceivable, you know, it's crazy. I mean, I don't feel that way. I understand fully that my father at some level believes he is German and still feels connected.'[58]

Postwar Canada opened its doors to around twenty thousand Holocaust survivors.[59] Within the 'silent generation' alluded to earlier, the German-speaking Jewish refugees' voice could not but be even quieter. As one of the informants puts it, it is sometimes impossible to tell 'one's own story of suffering' in view of the suffering of others, yet it is extremely important that one's story be acknowledged by others. In reviewing Koch's book *Deemed Suspect*, which deals with the internment in Canada of 'enemy aliens,' Rabbi Erwin Schild expressed a deep feeling of guilt and of not having the legitimacy to speak:

> Why did it take so long for an ex-internee to tell the story? [...] How could you speak of suffering when you had escaped from the Nazi continent, when you knew only too well what your brothers and sisters were experiencing? And how could you help feeling guilty when your contemporaries were undergoing the agonies of a horrible war and the bombs were dropping on London, while you were enjoying the security and the abundance of Canada, even though confined?[60]

The Holocaust had a 'delayed impact' on Jews in Canada. In the 1970s and 1980s, it became a structuring memory for the Jewish community in Canada. According to Franklin Bialystock, 'by 1985 most Canadian Jews felt that the destruction of European Jewry was *their* loss as well': the Holocaust 'had now become an important marker of ethnic awareness in a multicultural society.'[61] This structuring memory was accompanied by a certain type of survivor's guilt. In postwar Germany, the returning political and intellectual exiles were often stigmatized because they did not 'suffer through' the whole experience. In a similar way, the Jewish refugees who survived in exile because they had left before it was too late were not considered 'real' Holocaust survivors, because in fact they were not. But their voice in the community should not have been less legitimate and audible because of that. Rabbi Schild writes: 'Our internment was *a minor event, dwarfed by the Holocaust.*'[62]

In postwar Canada as well as in the United States, a moral – and even mystical – undertone became attached to the 'quality' of one's survival. But then, 'why confer on extermination the prestige of the mystical?' Giorgio Agamben provocatively asks in *Remnants of Auschwitz – The Witness and the Archive* (1999).[63]

When, in the late 1970s and early 1980s, Eric Koch – himself an ex-internee – undertook the task of researching the internment of 'enemy aliens' in Canada, he encountered quite some reticence. One of his interlocutors justified his refusal to testify as follows: 'As the alternative [to internment in Canada], at least in my case, would have been either a gaz [*sic*]-oven or the Blitz in London, I always considered my 27 months of internment in Canada an *undeserved fortune* for which to be grateful – and *of no interest to anybody*.'[64]

Again, it is a feeling of illegitimate – of 'undeserved' – survival that is expressed here, a morally incomplete right to testify. This is also expressed in the very title of Schild's review of Koch's book: 'A Canadian *Footnote to the Holocaust*' (italics are mine). Here the dense and traumatic experience endured by German-speaking Jews who went to Canada is equated with a mere 'footnote' in history, an infra-paginal co-text to the master narrative of Jewish history in the twentieth century.

Concluding Remarks

The life stories, autobiographical testimonies, and narratives of self of German-speaking Jewish exiles in Canada bear traces of the changes in values, norms, and attitudes, as well as in everyday interaction, that stem from the initial displacement. This illustrates the extent to which individual acculturation is informed by collective processes. Even in the case of an involuntary migration like the exile from Nazism, rupture is hardly ever fully unprepared or fully unforeseen – with the important exception, however, of tragic accounts of desperation and last-minute escapes. The narrative data used here show that pre-exile history significantly shaped the actual *conditions* in exile. Migration and acculturation are both essentially individual *and* collective. They are also comparative in nature and should be approached as such, as several comparisons are implicitly or explicitly present throughout: 'before' vs 'after,' Canada vs the United States, and comparison with other exiled Jews within the Diaspora, to name just a few. The degree to which the German-speaking Jewish refugees can be considered as having lived through a group experience varies, but in their narration and in their imagination, they have definitely created some sense of a 'we.' Yet their identity often did not – nor does it still – entirely fit into the larger framework of the Canadian mosaic. By and large, there is a striking discrepancy between their overall economic integration and their personal sense of belonging. Whereas success stories abound (be it in academia, in the arts, in the construction business, or in farming), a feeling of 'being apart' is often expressed. From a macro perspective, the period between 1945 and 1974, in which the refugees were professionally active, is one of tremendous economic boom – that is, a period during which economic success stories abound *in general*. But a sharper lens shows that the refugees did not fit into the dominant sociocultural categories. They certainly represent a strange voice with a peculiar accent within the Canadian Jewish community. Rather than *adopting* Canadian culture, they *adapted* to it, showing 'tactical skills' (in Michel de Certeau's terminology) in inventing new 'ways of operating' in order to evade dominant categories in their everyday lives.[65] The sources I used here show that this specific memory has partly been transmitted to the children of the refugees – to the second generation.

NOTES

1 Angelika E. Sauer, 'The "Ideal German": Politics, Academics, and the Historiographical Construction of German-Canadian Identity,' in *A Chorus of Different Voices – German-Canadian Identities*, ed. Angelika E. Sauer and Matthias Zimmer (New York: Peter Lang, 1998), 228.

2 Annette Puckhaber, *Ein Privileg für wenige – Die deutschsprachige Migration nach Kanada im Schatten des Nationalsozialismus* (Münster: Lit Verlag, 2002), 12, 41.

3 Donald Avery, 'Canada's Response to European Refugees, 1939–1945: The Security Dimension,' in *On Guard for Thee: War, Ethnicity, and the Canadian State*, ed. Norman Hillmer et al. (Ottawa: Canadian Government Publications, 1988), 179–216.

4 Cf. Tony Kushner and David Cesarani, eds., *The Internment of Aliens in Twentieth-Century Britain* (London: Frank Cass, 1993).

5 Eric Koch, *Deemed Suspect – A Wartime Blunder* (Toronto: Methuen, 1980); Paula J. Draper, 'Accidental Immigrants – Canada and the Interned Refugees,' PhD diss., University of Toronto, 1983; Franca Iacovetta et al., eds., *Enemies Within: Italian and Other Internees in Canada and Abroad* (Toronto: University of Toronto Press, 2000).

6 Nancy L. Green, 'The Comparative Method and Poststructural Structuralism: New Perspectives for Migration Studies,' in *Migration, Migration History, History: Old Paradigms and New Perspectives*, ed. Jan Lucassen and Leo Lucassen (New York: Peter Lang, 1999), 69–71.

7 Cf. Caroline B. Brettell and James F. Hollifield, eds., *Migration Theory: Talking across Disciplines* (New York: Routledge, 2000).

8 Dirk Hoerder, 'From Migrants to Ethnics: Acculturation in a Societal Framework,' in *European Migrants – Global and Local Perspectives*, ed. Dirk Hoerder and Leslie Page Moch (Boston: Northeastern University Press, 1996), 211.

9 Melville J. Hershkovits, Ralph Linton, and Robert Redfield, 'Memorandum for the Study of Acculturation,' *American Anthropologist* 38, no. 1 (1936): 149, quoted in Hoerder, 'From Migrants to Ethnics,' 211.

10 Clifford Geertz, *The Interpretation of Cultures* (New York: Basic Books, 1973), 89.

11 Patrick Farges, *Le trait d'union ou l'intégration sans l'oubli. Itinéraires d'exilés germanophones au Canada après 1933* (Paris: Ed. de la Maison des Sciences de l'Homme, 2008).

12 Erving Goffman defines 'face-to-face interaction' as 'the reciprocal influence of individuals upon one another's actions'; *The Presentation of Self in Everyday Life* [1959] (London: Penguin, 1990), 26.

13 Dirk Hoerder, *Creating Societies: Immigrant Lives in Canada* (Montreal and Kingston: McGill–Queen's University Press, 1999), ix.

14 Wilma A. Iggers, personal interview, Göttingen, 17 February 2003.

15 Wilma A. Iggers, 'Refugee Women from Czechoslovakia in Canada – An Eyewitness Report,' in *Between Sorrow and Strength – Women Refugees of the Nazi Period*, ed. Sibylle Quack (Washington: Cambridge University Press, 1995), 125.

16 Wilma A. Iggers and Georg G. Iggers, *Zwei Seiten der Geschichte – Lebensbericht aus unruhigen Zeiten* (Göttingen: Vandenhœck & Ruprecht, 2002), 31–7.

17 Iggers, 'Refugee Women,' 125, 127.

18 León Grinberg and Rebecca Grinberg, *Psychoanalytic Perspectives on Migration and Exile*, trans. Nancy Festinger (New Haven: Yale University Press, 1989), 13–4.

19 Edgar Lion, personal interview, Montreal, 4 August 2003.

20 Gerry Waldston, personal interview, Toronto, 13 May 2004.

21 Eric Exton, *Zaidie Exton's Odyssey*, vol. 1 (Toronto: privately published, 1986), iii.

22 Harry Rasky, transcript of interview 39 [1981], LAC, MG 30, C192, Eric Koch Collection, vol. 3, 3.

23 Franca Iacovetta, *The Writing of English Canadian Immigrant History* (Ottawa: Canadian Historical Association, 1997).

24 Alfred Bader, *Adventures of a Chemist Collector* (London: Weidenfeld & Nicolson, 1995), 41.

25 Lita-Rose Betcherman, *The Swastika and the Maple Leaf – Fascist Movements in Canada in the Thirties* (Toronto: Fitzhenry and Whiteside, 1975), 45.

26 Minna Loewith, personal interview, Lynden, 28 April 2003.

27 Eric Koch, personal interview, Toronto, 22 April 2003.

28 Cf. Wolfgang Benz, ed., *Die Juden in Deutschland 1933–1945. Leben unter nationalsozialistischer Herrschaft* (Munich: Beck, 1988).

29 Gregory Baum, personal interview, Montreal, 25 March 2003.

30 Exton, *Zaidie Exton's Odyssey*, vol. 1, 2.

31 Iggers, personal interview; Loewith, personal interview.

32 W. Gunther Plaut, *Unfinished Business – An Autobiography* (Toronto: Lester and Orpen Dennys, 1981), 28.

33 Enzo Traverso, *The Jews and Germany – From the 'Judeo-German Symbiosis' to the Memory of Auschwitz*, trans. D. Weissbort (Lincoln: University of Nebraska Press, 1995), xix.

34 Henry Kreisel, handwritten notes about 'Diary of an Internment,' University of Manitoba Archives (Winnipeg), MSS 59, Henry Kreisel Papers, vol. 1, folder 1.

35 Erwin Schild, 'A Canadian Footnote to the Holocaust – A Review Essay of "Deemed Suspect – A Wartime Blunder,"' *Canadian Jewish Historical Society Journal* 5, no. 1 (Spring 1981): 36.

36 Traverso, *The Jews and Germany*, 33–9.

37 Helmut Kallmann, personal interview, Nepean, 10 April 2003.

38 Gerald Tulchinsky, *Taking Root – The Origins of the Canadian Jewish Community* (Toronto: Lester Publishing, 1992), xxi.

39 Jonathan D. Sarna, 'The Value of Canadian Jewish History to the American Jewish Historian and Vice Versa,' *Canadian Jewish Historical Society Journal* 5, no. 1 (Spring 1981): 20.

40 Plaut, *Unfinished Business*, 56.

41 Erwin Schild, personal interview, Toronto, 10 May 2004.

42 Mordecai Richler, *The Street* [1969] (Toronto: McClelland and Stewart, 2002), 58–9.

43 Loewith, interview.

44 Plaut, *Unfinished Business*, 58.

45 Helmut Kallmann, Letter to Eric Koch [22 January 1979], LAC, MG 30, C192, Eric Koch Collection, vol. 1.

46 It is ultimately some sense of 'belonging' that is conveyed by the testimonies collected by Hempel among refugees in New York. Cf. Henri Jacob Hempel, ed., *'Wenn ich schon ein Fremder sein muss ...'* – *Deutsch-jüdische Emigranten in New York* (Frankfurt: Ullstein, 1984).

47 Jonathan F. Wagner, *Brothers beyond the Sea* – *National Socialism in Canada* (Waterloo: Wilfrid Laurier University Press, 1981).

48 Manuel Meune, *Les Allemands du Québec* – *Parcours et discours d'une communauté méconnue* (Montreal: Editions du Méridien, 2003), 135–53; cf. also his chapter in this volume.

49 K. Anthony Appiah, 'Identity, Authenticity, Survival: Multicultural Societies and Social Reproduction,' in *Multiculturalism: Examining the Politics of Recognition*, ed. Amy Gutman (Princeton: Princeton University Press, 1994), 149–63.

50 Wolfgang Benz, ed., *Das Exil der kleinen Leute. Alltagserfahrungen deutscher Juden in der Emigration* (Munich: Beck, 1991), 10–11.

51 Erwin Schild, transcript of interview with CBC journalist Rasky, in Exton, *Zaidie Exton's Odyssey*, vol. 2, 6.

52 Chaim Vogt-Moykopf, 'Die letzten Jeckes – deutsche Juden in Kanada,' *Aufbau – deutsch-jüdische Zeitung* 9 (1999): 11.

53 Irving A. Abella, *Coat of Many Colours* – *Two Centuries of Jewish Life in Canada* (Toronto: Lester and Orpen Dennys, 1990), 226.

54 The Canadian Jewish Congress (CJC), for instance, grew to become the voice of the community. Founded in 1919, the CJC was only a weak and disorganised institution until the wealthy entrepreneur Samuel Bronfman became active in late 1938 and was elected president in 1939. From then on, the CJC was transformed into a credible and weighty voice of Jewish interests. Harold M. Waller, 'Power in the Jewish Community,' in *The Canadian Jewish Mosaic*, ed. M. Weinfeld et al. (Toronto: John Wiley and Sons, 1981), 151–69.

55 Plaut, *Unfinished Business*, 312.

56 Willie Glaser, personal interview, Montreal, 24 March 2003.

57 Plaut, *Unfinished Business*, 306.

58 Daniel Iggers, personal interview, Toronto, 24 April 2003.

59 Franklin Bialystock, *Delayed Impact* – *The Holocaust and the Canadian Jewish Community* (Montreal and Kingston: McGill–Queen's University Press, 2000), 42–67.

60 Schild, 'Footnote to the Holocaust,' 42.

61 Bialystock, *Delayed Impact*, 6, 13.

62 Schild, 'Footnote to the Holocaust,' 40 [italics are mine].

63 Giorgio Agamben, *Remnants of Auschwitz – The Witness and the Archive*, trans. D. Heller-Roazen (New York: Zone Books, 1999), 32.

64 Robert Langstadt, Letter to Eric Koch [4 January 1979], LAC, MG 30, C192 Eric Koch Collection, vol. 1 [italics are mine].

65 Michel de Certeau, *The Practice of Everyday Life*, trans. S.F. Rendall (Berkeley: University of California Press, 1984).

9 'German Only in Their Hearts': Making and Breaking the Ethnic German Diaspora in the Twentieth Century

HANS WERNER

In a 1999 interview, Susanna Koop lamented the difficulties her sister's family experienced adjusting to a new life in Germany. Her sister was married to a Volga German but the family spoke only Russian. Susanna, herself a Soviet-German Mennonite immigrant, suggested that they were 'German in their heart' but added that they spoke no German and had problems integrating into their new home.[1] Similar words were used by the leaders of Germany's *Landsmannschaft der Deutschen aus Rußland* (Homeland Society of Germans from Russia) at a 1998 meeting, where they assured members that the association was not abandoning those who were 'German only in their hearts' but stressed the absolute importance of their learning German and becoming 'fully' German.[2]

Soviet Germans who came to Canada in the 1950s also faced challenges to their sense of Germanness. William Sturhahn, a Baptist World Alliance immigration worker, noted in his 1976 history of Baptist immigration that 'the bonds with the "Old Country" are almost exclusively with near relatives.' With pride he claimed that ethnic Germans from the Soviet Union and Eastern Europe had become Canadians relatively easily. He noted that young immigrants had 'Canadianized' in that they had acquired a Canadian education and had adopted the ways of their new country.[3] The end of the Second World War marked the beginning of the Cold War and coincided with the exodus of Germans from the Soviet Union, first to Canada in the late 1940s and the 1950s and then to Germany in the 1970s. The trickle of immigrants to Germany in the 1970s became a torrent as the Soviet system began to disintegrate in the late 1980s. Susanna Koop's sister and William Sturhahn's Baptists are examples, respectively, of the reinforcement and loss of a sense of being German among immigrants who had only an imagined connection with Germany.

Soviet Germans developed their sense of Germanness in isolation from the cultural and social realities of the nation-state of Germany. Hence, during the years between the Bolshevik Revolution of 1917 and their emigration after the Second World War, they created their sense of being Germans as a diasporic identity. Soviet Germans developed this diasporic identity based, as Donna Gabaccia suggests, on a sense of loss.[4] When Soviet Germans lost their isolated ethnic and religious worlds in the Soviet Union they replaced them with an imagined new home in Germany. Diaspora implies an ongoing connection with a 'homeland,' a connection that often takes the form of economic and social ties but may also be only mental – a feeling of being in two places at once.[5] This notion of a mythic homeland is shaped historically and is a particular feature of forced migration and refugee displacement.[6] By implication, diasporic identities can lose their coherence over time and under the influence of subsequent historical events.

In response to the turmoil of revolution, war, and the repressive Stalinist regime, Soviet Germans had created a new, imagined homeland in Germany by the end of the Second World War. They were indeed 'German only in their hearts,' and their experiences during the Cold War enhanced or diminished their diasporic identities, depending on when they left the Soviet Union and whether they went 'home' to Germany or chose a new home in Canada. This chapter begins by tracing the developments that led to the creation of a diasporic identity among Soviet Germans between the beginning of the First World War and the end of the Second, and the enhancement or decline of that identity during the Cold War.[7] It then considers how the Second World War and life under the Soviets was remembered in the autobiographical writings of four immigrants, two of whom went to Germany and two to Canada. The discussion seeks to understand how the two receiving environments shaped their narratives and sense of being a diaspora. For those immigrants who ended up in Canada, the diasporic identity they had cultivated in the Soviet Union began to diminish as they abandoned Germany for a new home in Canada. Their diminishing sense of Germany as an imagined homeland was helped along by a settlement environment in Canada that featured a vibrant economy and a Cold War mentality that disparaged both Nazi Germany and the Soviet Union. The diasporic identity of Soviet Germans who were left behind or who were repatriated to the Soviet Union after the war was strengthened by continued labelling as fascists and traitors. For them, the need to enhance their Germanness grew even when they were already in the homeland of their imagination in the 1970s and 1980s.

Germans had responded in large numbers in the eighteenth century when Catherine the Great invited European settlers to her newly conquered domains in South Russia, as she called present-day Ukraine. Coming from a number of German lands, Germans established three major groupings in the Tsar's empire. Mennonites from West Prussia settled in the region of the Dnepr bend, while Black Sea Germans established villages in the Odessa region. The largest settlement, the Volga Germans, lived on both sides of the Volga River near Saratov. Germans in South Russia were at the forefront of Russia's belated modernization, and escaping from the proletarianization that accompanied industrial growth was easier for them than for their Slavic neighbours. They responded by establishing agricultural daughter colonies, some on the vast steppes of Central Asia, far from the original heartlands. Most of Russia's Germans remained relatively isolated both from the increasing suspicion of Russian intellectuals and from a dynamic Germany that was quite different from the country their ancestors knew. They were at home in their villages, comfortable with the social and religious strictures they faced, and secure in their mission to impart order and progress to the sea of Slavic peasants among whom they lived.[8]

For Russia's Germans the path to a diasporic identity began in the late nineteenth century in the context of what Dirk Hoerder refers to elsewhere in this volume as 'concepts of national homogeneity.' Russia sought to erase their alien Germanness; at the same time, they became subject to attempts by Germany to include them in an expansionist imperial identity. The First World War, in particular, would force Russia's Germans along the path of an increasingly political, national German identity. For the first time, the spectre of losing their land, the restrictions on the use of German, and the common label given to all German colonists gave them a shared experience that worked to break down their isolation and that unified them against a common threat.[9]

An intense re-evaluation of German colonists' identity accompanied the period between the February Revolution and the Bolshevik takeover in October 1917. During the war, persistent attacks on their loyalty by Russian intellectuals forced Russian Germans to re-examine their earlier perception that, even if they were not Slavs, they were still loy-al subjects of the Tsar and their Russian homeland. A common theme of intergroup conferences and in the German press after the war cen-tred on the need to strengthen German colonists' cooperation and to improve education in the German-speaking community. These confer-ences were also a forum for debate about new nationalist sentiments, one that reflected the heightened awareness of political options in the new environment.[10] Although Mennonites, Volga Germans, and Black Sea Germans felt the stresses of the First World War in their particular cultural contexts, for the first time they shared the common experience of being labelled German nationals and felt the tension of coming to terms with that label.

Having embarked on a project of reinforcing their German identity, those colonists who came under German occupation in the summer of 1918 were particularly vulnerable. They welcomed and embraced Ger-man troops, which contradicted their earlier professions of loyalty to the Russian state and justified the fears of Russian nationalists. It was not, however, surprising. It was a small step for them to attach their recently developed sense of German colonist unity to the identity of the occupying German state. German colonists experienced for the first time a sense of national belonging that was out of step with that of their Russian homeland. The arrival of the German state as represented by its army, its language, and its customs suited this rising nationalism. The result was disastrous when these armies left.[11]

The Bolshevik Revolution of October 1917 and the ensuing civil war began a painful period for German colonists. After the Bolshevik vic-tory in the civil war, there came a period of relative calm and renewed economic activity. The years of the New Economic Policy (NEP) in the mid-1920s permitted some return to normal life in the German colo-nies. But the repression of German speakers resumed with the collec-tivization of agriculture in 1929–30, and the terror of the 1937–8 Stalin purges completed the destruction of the way of life that Germans had known before the First World War.[12]

The interwar years under the new Soviet regime did not threaten the national aspects of Russian-German identity to the same degree as the tension-filled war years had. There were, however, challenges to other aspects of their ethnic identity. Religion, a pillar of Russian-Ger-man identity, was subjected to extreme pressure. The Soviet attack on religion was ferocious and unabated. The recognized representatives of organized religion were under attack everywhere in the new Soviet state, and almost all Lutheran, Catholic, and Mennonite religious leaders disappeared from their communities during the purges of the late 1930s.

The destruction of religion and the disruption of families caused by arrests and exile during the 1930s destroyed much of what comprised the German colonists' ethnic world, and many of the differences that had set the various communities apart from one another were no longer relevant. When *all* religious life was under attack, religious differences between Mennonites, Catholics, and Lutherans – the most salient boundaries that separated Russian-Germans from one another – seemed less important. The First World War had enticed Russian Germans toward a common identity; the interwar years now broke down the boundaries that separated them. The processes that converged to create a common identity for Russia's Germans would peak in the turmoil of the Second World War and its aftermath.[13]

The experience of Soviet and other East European Germans during the Second World War can be grouped along three major fault lines of experience. First, the Hitler–Stalin Pact of August 1939 called for mutual population transfers from a soon-to-be-conquered Poland and a powerless Romania. Under the terms of the agreement, Germans living in new Soviet territories could move to Germany's newly acquired territories in Poland, renamed the Warthegau, while the Slavic population living there had the option of being resettled on the new Soviet lands.[14]

A second group were those Soviet Germans who lived in territories that Hitler's armies occupied after Germany invaded Russia in June 1941. German colonists were accorded favoured status under the occupation regime, which touted them as the vanguard of the new German order in the east. German defeats on the battlefield, however, forced their evacuation to the Warthegau in 1943 and 1944 to join their predecessors.

A third group of Soviet Germans never came in contact with the Nazis but were drafted into Stalin's work army (*Trudarmija*) and performed forced labour as punishment for their common ancestry with the enemy. The deportation of the entire Volga German Republic in September 1941, involving more than 400,000 people, was the largest component of this Soviet policy. Other Germans to the east of the *Wehrmacht*'s deepest penetration, or those evacuated in advance of their arrival, also shared this experience. Many of these Soviet Germans were distinguished from their fellow *Trudarmija* labourers and campmates by the fact that they had not been touched directly by the experience of contact with the Nazi German state, its army, or ordinary German nationals.[15]

The Nazis' attack on their homeland and the resulting turmoil of the Second World War had a powerful influence on ethnic German identity. The four immigrant narratives examined here share stories of disrupted families, uprooting from homes and villages, and the trauma of war. Lucia Kaa and Katharina Krueger were repatriated from Germany to the Soviet Union and ended up at the prison work camps of Archangelsk. They were finally able to emigrate and settle in Germany again – Lucia in 1992 and Katharina in 1976 – where they told their stories. Helene Latter and Otto Mueller immigrated to Canada via West Germany shortly after the war and settled in Manitoba, where they told their stories long after overcoming the difficulties of establishing a new home.

The narratives chosen here are all autobiographical. All have been published, and all were written some time after the events they recorded. None of the authors were prominent figures in their communities. Autobiographical sources are characterized by their focus on 'concretely experienced' personal reality rather than broader historical accuracy.[16] Autobiography often sets out to make sense of the writer's memories of a crisis, usually some time after the fact, and may 'rationalize ... ambiguous experiences and actions.'[17] Unlike the other major form of life writing, the diary, autobiography is written for an audience. These features of autobiography generally are also important in the memoirs examined here. It would seem that these four immigrant narrators were attempting to explain their lives to family and known acquaintances, but also to a broader audience that might wonder why they had come to Canada or Germany. The narratives are to some extent apologies for choices made as well as arguments for the host society to accept their presence.

Lucia (Ehrstein) Kaa was born in a village in Bashkir but grew up in Zaporoshe, South Russia. She was twenty-one when the war ended, and she and her family – four sisters, one brother, and her grandmother – were repatriated from the banks of the Elbe River in Germany. The family had ended up at the point where American and Soviet forces met, and because they were Soviet citizens, they were sent to work in a sawmill in Archangelsk.[18] They had heard nothing of their father since 1941, when he left for the east with cattle ahead of the advancing German armies. Lucia's narrative is part of a volume published in Germany by an association of Russian Germans commemorating the experience of Soviet-German women in the gulag 'archipelago' after the war. Her story focuses on the years between 1945 and 1956 and ends rather abruptly with a brief account of her immigration to Germany. Lucia applied to immigrate as soon as she heard that it was possible, but she arrived in Germany only in 1992.[19]

Katharina Krueger was born in 1908 into a Mennonite family in Ukraine, where she and her husband were teachers when the Germans attacked in 1941. Soviet authorities took her husband away soon after, and she never saw him again. She found out later that they had executed him a few months after she last saw him. When the German armies occupied their area, Katharina got a job in the city of Zaporoshe, only to be evacuated to Poland in 1943 along with other Soviet Germans when the German armies retreated. Here she had planned to marry again, to a Yugoslavian German, but she found out he was already married and had a family. She had, however, become pregnant. When the Soviet armies reached Poland in 1945, she and her infant son became refugees and found themselves unable to stay ahead of the Soviet advance. She was repatriated to Archangelsk and suffered the fate of many Soviet Germans who became victims of the gulag system. In 1953, she was able to move to western Siberia. There, she was granted permission to emigrate in 1976. Her memoirs were published in Germany in 1991.[20]

Loss of family and home plays an important role in the narratives of Lucia and Katharina. As the German position in the east deteriorated and Katharina was confronted with the fact that she had lost all contact with her family, she took comfort in the anticipated birth of her child. As she puts it in her memoir, 'I had overcome the horrible status of being alone for the time being. I would now not be alone, but would have a child, my own child.'[21] Lucia's narrative tells of her gaining permission to return to Zaporoshe after undergoing a difficult interrogation by Soviet authorities. The knowledge that she would be returning to her Ukrainian homeland had provided some comfort in the face of the bitter disappointment of having to return to the Soviet system. But when she returned to her family, her hopes were quickly dashed, for she learned that other family members had just agreed to relocate to Alma Ata in Kazakhstan. The Soviet authorities who had interrogated them had refused them permission to return to Ukraine, their former homeland. Thus, she lost her homeland once again and was instead sent, not to Alma Ata, but to a gulag in Archangelsk in the far north.[22]

As the reality of a lost homeland sank in, the stories of what had been lost became important to her. During the long, cold nights on the train that took them to Archangelsk, Lucia's grandmother told them stories of their homeland. She told them about the farmyard of her parents, about their grandfather, and about their family. Lucia recalls that these stories absorbed them deeply and helped pass the time.[23] The sense of a lost home became even more acute for those who were able to return for visits to their former homes after 1956, when West German chancellor Konrad Adenauer's visit to the Soviet Union helped ease travel restrictions for Soviet Germans. Katharina conveys the intense disappointment of those who returned but who saw only ruined orchards, destroyed buildings, and unfamiliar faces. Gone was even the 'small wood at the end of the village that took you to a slight rise from which you had such a beautiful view of the land far into the distance.'[24]

The sense that they had lost their place in Soviet society aided the formation of a diasporic identity. Lucia Kaa's narrative juxtaposes her sense of being German with the loss of her legitimacy as a Soviet citizen. After the Soviet armies caught up with them, an officer inter-rogated her, making her acutely aware of the contradiction between her identity as a Soviet citizen and her membership in an ethnic group accused of having betrayed their country of citizenship. The officer accused her of being a 'whore to the Fascists' and therefore a spy; she maintained that she had been caught between the millstones of two warmongers and was innocent of betraying either her country of citi-zenship or the state of her ethnic origin. When she told another soldier there was too much luggage for them to carry to the train, he retorted that she should get the fascists to carry her luggage. Soviet authorities assured Lucia's family that their accommodations would have been be better if 'their' fascists had not destroyed everything; they experi-enced the fear of Germans harboured by the members of the collective at Archangelsk, who called them fascists and demanded they leave when they finally arrived at their destination. Lucia's account offers numerous other examples.

Katharina tells her story in a similar way. She highlights the animos-ity displayed toward Germans by their Ukrainian neighbours when their young men had to report for military duty while German men remained at home with their families.[25] She quotes the soldiers she met after falling into Soviet hands who cursed her Soviet-German identity, claiming that the 'cursed Russian Germans were to blame for the war.'[26]

She points out that Germans who had intermarried with Ukrainians or Russians were the first to be repatriated and could return to their homes, while they themselves waited for transport to the far north.[27] Her narrative excuses a local woman in Archangelsk who gave her rotten potatoes in exchange for her son's baby sweater by reminding herself that it was after all a 'betrayer of the fatherland who stood before her, this was the label they gave to us.'[28]

Among the scattered Germans in Central Asia and the far north, Germany as the homeland of their imagination assumed mythic proportions. Katharina relates how a night-time visit to the camp barracks by strangely dressed men touched off a rumour that the visitors had been German officials investigating how they were being treated and that soon they would be coming to take them home to Germany.[29] She also portrays the electric anticipation that accompanied the news that Soviet Germans could apply to immigrate to Germany. She sent two applications in case one went missing; others collected a large number of applications and sent them along with someone who would deliver them directly to Moscow.[30]

Both narratives respond to arriving in Germany, the homeland of their imagination, by telling their stories in ways that legitimize their inclusion in the German ethnocultural nation. Lucia and Katharina's narratives often refer to the authenticity of their Germanness. Lucia tells us that when a Soviet soldier confronted her mother at war's end regarding her identity, she assured him that she was from the Soviet Union but found it easier to speak German than Russian.[31] Her narrative emphasizes her German upbringing, an upbringing that Soviet Germans believed placed high value on religion and family. She tells us about her grandmother, who was deeply religious and took responsibility for her grandchildren's spiritual lives. When she died, her mother refused to stop their religious instruction despite the danger of being discovered, because in the event of their father's return, she did not want to be accused of having raised pagan children.[32]

Katharina tells the story of how occupying German soldiers would instinctively speak German to her in the city, where there were few Soviet Germans. When she asked how they knew she spoke German, they replied that they could tell just by looking at her.[33] Stories of life in the resettlement camps in occupied Poland mention the singing of German folk songs, songs that Katharina maintains had been 'faithfully nurtured in Russia, even during the time of repression and the banning of the German language and songs; we faithfully preserved them.'[34]

Katharina emphasizes her lifelong desire to be in Germany. When a German soldier on furlough who was billeted in their home told them stories about Germany, particularly of its natural beauty during peacetime, she writes that it 'fascinated me because I always had a longing to visit the homeland of my forefathers.'[35] Lucia was enamoured with Germany's physical beauty. Her story begins on the banks of the Elbe, a name she says she would never forget and a landscape seemingly 'created to be enjoyed.'[36]

Katharina's story is told in the context of West Germany's membership in the Western alliance during the Cold War, while Lucia's is told in the context of a seeming Western victory in that war. By the time she wrote, the Berlin Wall had come down and German reunification was a reality. However, the contest of mentalities that characterized the Cold War still dominates her narrative. Lucia's recollections of American soldiers are generally positive. Although they handed her family and others over to Soviet authorities, she remembers them as kind, handing out chocolate to the children and helping with loading some of the heavy baggage. Soviet soldiers are portrayed as dour, rude, and cynical.[37] She also tells the story of a woman with whom she struck up a friendship who blamed their misfortune on the Germans. In her mind, it was the Germans who had brought on the loss of homeland, youth, and family they now experienced. Lucia legitimizes her own identity by reassuring her readers that the woman admitted to being a communist and to having a relationship with a Soviet soldier.[38]

Lucia and Katharina's narratives respond to a need to explain their legitimate membership in a Germany they had only imagined. The struggles of the Second World War and its aftermath are cast in the context of proving they are German by having suffered for being German. In contrast, the narratives of Helene Latter and Otto Mueller in many ways seek to minimize the disadvantages they perceive to being German in the context of Cold War Canada.

Helene Latter was born in 1914 in the Mennonite village of Halbstadt in Ukraine. Her father died in 1917 of natural causes, and her mother died of pneumonia in 1936. Helene became an accountant and took up work in Zaporoshe in 1939, where she married a Ukrainian radio technician. The German Gestapo arrested and executed her husband in 1943, leaving her alone with her infant son. In September 1943, advancing Soviet armies forced her evacuation and she came to a camp in occupied Poland. When the Soviet forces arrived there in January 1945, she was unable to escape but was able to avoid repatriation. She was, however, expelled in 1946 and sent to a village near Hamburg. She immigrated to Canada in 1948, where she remarried. Her Canadian husband published her memoirs posthumously in 1988.

Otto Mueller was born in 1921 in a Black Sea German village. In 1929, his father refused to join the collective farm and was arrested, as was his sister. His mother and one brother tried to start a new life in Siberia in 1932 but returned to their Black Sea home a year later. Otto's father returned home, but his health had suffered during his imprisonment and he died in 1933. When the German advance crossed over their area in 1941, Otto became an interpreter for the German army; when the fortunes of war turned against the Germans, he joined his unit in combat. He was naturalized and formally conscripted in 1944 and was in Soviet territory when the war ended. In February 1946, he escaped to West Germany. In 1947 he married a widow from the Black Forest and with his young family immigrated to Canada, where Otto had an aunt. They arrived in Winnipeg in 1951 and moved to the West Coast in the 1960s. Otto published his memoirs in 1999.

Like Lucia and Katharina, Helene and Otto experienced the loss of homeland and family. In September 1943, two weeks after receiving notice of her husband's execution, Helene and other Germans in Zaporoshe were given two hours to pack up to be evacuated to an unknown destination. She recalls they were told not to 'attempt to resist this order or your children will be shot.'[39] Otto Mueller looked for his mother and sister in Germany after the war, but by the time he found their address they had been repatriated and were on their way to the far north. He finally got a letter from his sister in the Soviet Union in 1957.[40]

Otto and Helene portray their sense of and pride in being German. Helene recalls how her Russian superior commented on her German punctuality when she delivered important documents into his hands by the appointed hour.[41] Helene also experienced the tension that came with being of the same ethnicity as the invading Germans. When she failed to collect the quota of taxes assigned to her as part of her job, her Russian superior claimed that as a German she was already working for Hitler and would have done better if she were a 'true, loyal citizen of the Soviet Union.'[42] For Otto Mueller, Germanness meant the closeness of family, which he describes as being 'almost sacred.'[43] Otto confesses that when the German armies approached, he was 'torn between being afraid and being excited about their arrival.' He was not sure how their relationship with Germans would evolve. As he poignantly asks: 'Were they still our brothers?'[44] When it came time for naturalization, the family's retention of German ethnicity saved the day. They got their citizenship in a short time because of his mother's 'excellent, fluent German and her marvellous memory for things in the past.'[45]

Although there are fragments of pride in being German in Helene's narrative, she is generally sympathetic to the Soviet regime, even if critical of its excesses. She assures us, for example, that the intention of the Soviets had been to send trains back for family members when most men had to leave the collapsing front with farm animals and equipment in 1941.[46] It seems that her marriage to a Ukrainian and the subsequent loss of her husband at the hands of Germans conspired to erase connections to Germany and Germans. When she describes how she and her work colleagues discussed the impending German threat, she evokes patriotic images, claiming that the Russians had no option but to 'resolve to stand for [their] country.'[47] She rails at the German occupation forces, arguing that she 'was a Russian citizen' and that Germans had no right to be in her country.[48] When she and her sister are rudely removed from a train while being evacuated from the Soviet Union, her sister becomes frightened when Helene yells at the offending soldiers, calling them beasts and reminding them they had not wanted to leave their homes but had been forced to evacuate.[49] Once in Germany, Canada emerges as the new desired destination. Helene describes the roller-coaster of emotions they experienced during the processing of their application to immigrate to Canada: 'It is difficult to put into mere words what our feelings were. For over six years we had been herded here and there, sent to this place and that, suffered extreme cold, lived on very short rations of food and clothing and now it seemed that all our hopes for a new homeland were for nothing.'[50] But the Canadian doctor who conducted the final medical examination before she gained entry to Canada is portrayed as kind, the consul as persistent but ultimately fair, the departure from Europe well organized with wonderful food, and the first attempts at beginning a new life a little embarrassing but humorous in retrospect.[51]

In Otto's case, the loss of a diasporic identity is driven less by personal losses and therefore is less explicit. His being male also means that his story needs to address the issue of his possible complicity in Nazi atrocities. He casts his narrative much more in the style of portraying himself as the 'good' German, exploring in much greater detail his horror at the treatment of Jews and his attempts to assist Slavic prisoners of war while working for the Germans. Canada emerges as the new homeland, in part because of Otto's disillusionment with the American acquiescence to the repatriation of Soviet citizens. Otto claims he 'began to doubt them' and thought they were 'nothing more than a Russian satellite.' He could not believe that the 'Americans would not know what kind of destructive force Soviet Communism was' and 'swore never to go to the States.'[52] In his mind, Americans were also to blame for the slow process of emigration from war-torn Europe. Canada emerges as the preferred new homeland. Otto's aunt had assured him that 'anyone willing to work hard could find a job and make it in that country.' In his memory, it was the desire for a better life for his children, away from genocide and Bolshevism, that made Canada a 'fitting place' for him.[53] In contrast to Helene, Otto had a much stronger desire to retain German connections. He sought out the German Club when he moved to the West Coast because, in his words, he 'needed the closeness of the "old" fellow-countrymen, to share in conversation about old times and a chance to sing some songs.'[54] However, his daughter's graduation was 'celebrated in good Canadian tradition,' and he tells us that when he became a citizen in 1971, he finally 'had arrived home.'[55]

How Katharina, Lucia, Helene, and Otto used their memories offers a small window into new ways of exploring the German-Canadian immigrant experience. Comparing Helene and Otto's stories told in a Canadian context with Katharina and Lucia's stories from Germany illustrates more clearly how diasporic identities are created and dismantled by historical processes. Their stories also illustrate the importance of pre-migration experiences for how they created new Canadian identities and wrestled with who they had been before coming to Canada, or Germany.

The four narratives examined here suggest the contours of the Soviet-German diaspora. Clearly, the experience of repatriation to the Soviet Union after the war and the pariah treatment in Soviet society contributed greatly to their imagining Germany as a homeland for Soviet Germans. Those who escaped the clutches of forced repatriation were intent on fleeing as far as possible from Stalin's grasp, and for them, postwar West Germany was not secure or stable enough. For those who ended up in the gulags of the north, the isolation and the labelling as fascists and enemies of the state gave powerful impetus to creating Germany as a homeland, albeit a mythic one for most of the Cold War.

The Soviet-German diasporic identity also grew out of women's experiences of the war. Since women had survived the Stalinist repression and Second World War in greater numbers than men, it was women who created the memories necessary to reconstruct the Soviet-German past as a distinctly 'German' experience. They told the stories of hearth and home, maintained religious and family connections, and taught the language and songs that often became the only vestiges of a German past and the ticket to a German future. As Christiane Harzig suggests in this volume, the experience of German-Canadian women has not often been placed in global and transnational contexts. As the stories of Katharina, Lucia, and Helene illustrate, Soviet-German women were not only the preservers of an ethnic German past but also instrumental in creating and dismantling diasporic identities.

The way these narrators remember being German is, however, also a product of their vantage point. Committing one's memories to the printed page and a public audience results in a different story for those in Canada than it did for those who immigrated to Germany. Writers marshalled memories to justify their decisions to immigrate to Canada and to assure Canadian readers of the wisdom of choices made both by immigrants and by the country that gave them a new home. Soviet-German immigrants writing these narratives for a German audience reified their Germanness to prove the legitimacy of their claims to admission.

NOTES

1 Susanna (Regier) Koop, interview by author, Bielefeld, 28 January 1999.
2 'Die russische Sprache,' *Volk auf dem Weg* 49 (May 1998): 4.
3 William Sturhahn, *They Came from East and West ...: A History of Immigration to Canada* (Winnipeg: North American Baptist Immigration and Colonization Society, 1976), 287–8.
4 Donna Gabaccia, *Italy's Many Diasporas* (Seattle: University of Washington Press, 2000), 6.
5 Steven Vertovec and Robin Cohen, eds., 'Introduction,' in *Migration, Diasporas, and Transnationalism* (Cheltenham: Edward Elgar, 1999), xviii.
6 Gérard Chaliand and Jean-Pierre Rageau, *The Penguin Atlas of Diasporas* (New York: Penguin Books, 1997), xiv–xv.
7 This section of the discussion is adapted from Hans Werner, *Imagined Homes: Soviet German Immigrants in Two Cities* (Winnipeg: University of Manitoba Press, 2007).
8 See, for instance, James Urry, *Mennonites, Politics, and Peoplehood* (Winnipeg: University of Manitoba Press, 2006), 95; Roger Bartlett, *Human Capital: The Settlement of Foreigners in Russia, 1762–1804* (London: Cambridge

University Press, 1979), 213; and James Long, *Privileged to Dispossessed: The Volga Germans, 1860–1917* (Lincoln: University of Nebraska Press, 1988), 55.

9 David G. Rempel, 'The Expropriation of the German Colonists in South Russia During the Great War,' *Journal of Modern History* 4, no. 1 (1932): 53; and Adam Giesinger, *From Catherine to Khruschev* (Lincoln: American Historical Society of Germans From Russia, 1974), 248–9.

10 Ingeborg Fleischauer, *Die Deutschen im Zarenreich: Zwei Jahrhundert deutsch-russische Kulturgemeinschaft* (Stuttgart: Deutsche Verlags-Anstalt, 1986), 540–2.

11 John B. Toews, *Czars, Soviets, and Mennonites* (Newton: Faith and Life Press, 1982), 76.

12 Giesinger, *From Catherine to Khruschev*, 298.

13 For a discussion of the rise in Germany of awareness of and sympathy for the plight of Russia's Germans, see James E. Casteel, 'The Russian Germans in the Interwar National Germany Imaginary,' *Central European History* 40 (2007): 429–66.

14 For an overview of the Soviet-German experience with the Third Reich, see Ingeborg Fleischhauer, *Das Dritte Reich und die Deutschen in der Sowjetunion* (Stuttgart: Deutsche Verlags-Anstalt, 1983). A more specific study of the resettlement of ethnic Germans is Valdis O. Lumans, *Himmler's Auxiliaries: The Volksdeutsche Mittelstelle and German National Minorities of Europe, 1933–1945* (Chapel Hill: University of North Carolina Press, 1993).

15 Giesinger, *From Catherine to Khruschev*, 305–6.

16 Mary Cisar, 'Mennonite Women's Autobiography: An Interdisciplinary Feminist Approach,' *Journal of Mennonite Studies* 14 (1996): 142–52.

17 Dirk Hoerder, *Creating Societies: Immigrant Lives in Canada* (Montreal and Kingston: McGill-Queens University Press, 1999), 19.

18 'Repatriation' was one of the provisions of the Yalta Agreement, whereby the Allies agreed to Stalin's demand that all former Soviet citizens be repatriated to the Soviet Union after the war, regardless of their consent.

19 Lucia Kaa, 'Großmutter, Mutter, Tochter,' in *Alle Spuren sind verweht: Rußlanddeutsche Frauen in der Verbannung*, ed. Nelly Däs (Stuttgart: Kulturrat der Deutschen aus Rußland e.V., 1997), 12–31.

20 Katharina Krüger, *Schicksal einer Rußlanddeutschen* (Göttingen: Verlag Graphikum, 1991).

21 Ibid., 40.

22 Kaa, 'Großmutter, Mutter, Tochter,' 21–2.

23 Ibid., 24.

24 Krüger, *Schicksal einer Rußlanddeutschen*, 166.

25 Ibid., 13.

26 Ibid., 53.

27 Ibid., 55.

28 Ibid., 68.

29 Ibid., 94.

30 Ibid., 164.

31 Kaa, 'Großmutter, Mutter, Tochter,' 12.

32 Ibid., 30.

33 Krüger, *Schicksal einer Rußlanddeutschen*, 27.

34 Ibid., 32.

35 Ibid., 25.

36 Kaa, 'Großmutter, Mutter, Tochter,' 12.

37 Ibid., 12.

38 Ibid., 16–17.

39 Helene Latter, *I Do Remember* (Morden: Walter F. Latter, 1988), 70.

40 Yvonne Schmidhauser, *Otto Mueller: A Life between Hitler and Stalin, New Beginnings in Canada* (Nanaimo: Loonbook by Island Art Creations, 2000), 105.

41 Latter, *I Do Remember*, 38.

42 Ibid., 52.

43 Schmidhauser, *Otto Mueller*, 38.

44 Ibid., 64.

45 Ibid., 79.

46 Latter, *I Do Remember*, 52.

47 Ibid., 50.

48 Ibid., 64.

49 Ibid., 72.

50 Ibid., 120.

51 Ibid., 120–4.

52 Schmidhauser, *Otto Mueller*, 110.

53 Ibid., 116.

54 Ibid., 134.

55 Ibid., 134, 141.

10 Germans into Europeans: Expellees in Postwar Canada

PASCAL MAEDER

Fearing renewed ethnic conflict in postwar Central Europe, the victorious Allies sanctioned in the Potsdam Agreements of August 1945 the transfer of nearly seven million Germans from Poland, three million from Czechoslovakia, and several hundred thousand from Hungary to occupied Germany. In addition, a further two million Germans from Russia, Ukraine, Romania, Yugoslavia, and the Baltic either fled ahead of the Soviet Army in early 1945 or were expelled from those countries in the heat of the Allied victory. In all, roughly twelve million Germans from Central and Eastern Europe were forced to find new homes. Seven million settled in West Germany, four million in East Germany, and the rest mainly in Austria, France, the United Kingdom, and the Americas. In West Germany, expellees became a prominent bulwark against communism, building up powerful organizations and calling for their return to their native lands. Meanwhile, in East Germany, the communist regime banned expellee organizations and accepted *de jure* the expulsion of Germans from Central and Eastern Europe.[1]

By the late 1950s, at least 85,000 expellees resided in Canada.[2] In fact, they were twice as likely to immigrate to Canada as Germans born within West Germany's borders and thus fuelled what one scholar has dubbed Canada's 'postwar German immigration boom.'[3] Like other German immigrants who after the war arrived *en masse* in the land of 'milk and honey,' the expellees attempted to rebuild their lives. But in marked contrast to the multitude of publications that have been written on expellees in Germany, very few scholars have attempted to trace the development of expellee identities in Canada. In surveys or more specialized studies of migration, social mobility, and language maintenance, expellees have generally been folded together with other

German immigrants.[4] A number of works that shed light on expellee immigrants have focused on distinctive subgroups such as ethnic Germans, Sudeten Germans, Danube Swabians, German Balts, and Germans from Russia and Romania, as well as Mennonites and Baptists.[5] Only one oral history study explicitly examines the acculturation of expellees. It suggests that despite the growing importance of multiculturalism, expellees were unable to publicly express their identity as forced migrants.[6]

Historians, linguists, and sociologists agree that postwar German immigrants rapidly gained a foothold in Canadian society and enjoyed a comparatively high degree of upward social mobility; but they debate the nature of their acculturation. Some scholars take up the case for empirically verifiable German-Canadian identities, while others deny their existence. The most recent assessment certainly made no secret of the diverging views, observing a 'chorus of different voices.'[7]

This paper suggests a different perspective by situating the acculturation of expellees in the broader context of Canadian immigration – or, following historian Dirk Hoerder, within an 'interactive whole,' wherein societal hierarchies of power are regulated across generations and societal groups.[8] Expellees in Canada could hardly weave their identity into the Canadian fabric in the way that was possible for them in West Germany. After all, in West Germany nearly one-sixth of residents were expellees; whereas in Canada they constituted only a minority within a minority, and so had to assert their identity as forced migrants among a generation of immigrants from war-stricken Europe. From their perspective, immigrants from the Baltic, Italy, or the Netherlands shared with them the experience of war, destruction, loss, and hopes for a new beginning in the New World. It is clear that their experience of immigration supported this perception. They had crossed the ocean on the same boats, had worked under the same exploitative conditions, and had lived in the same dilapidated immigrant neighbourhoods. Eventually – or so this perception purports – this generation of war-torn European immigrants made its way up the socio-economic ladder and gained a place in Canadian society. Thus the expellees developed a Euro-Canadian identity yet were also able to situate their life histories within the widely celebrated 'Canadian mosaic.'

To reconstruct this identity, I have divided this chapter into two sections. In the first, I trace the various organized expellee groups and consider their size, scope, and activities. The expellees founded a number of vibrant organizations, but they were also small, and their members had come from distinct regions in Central and Eastern Europe. As such, these organizations reflected transnational diasporas anchored mainly in West Germany, and in Canada they had little contact with one another. Instead they independently celebrated traditions in commemoration of the lost homeland while denouncing what they believed to be unjustifiable expulsions. In the second section, I examine the formation of their Euro-Canadian identity on the basis of memoirs, diaries, and interviews conducted in the late 1970s and early 1980s. As these sources clearly show, expellees drew on their experience of immigration to develop an identity that allowed them to see themselves as Canadians marked by both the Old World and the New.

Canada's Expellee Organizations

A group of just over one thousand Germans from Czechoslovakia formed the first expellee organizations in Canada. Unlike most other expellees, they had arrived in Canada as refugees fleeing the Nazis. As socialists, they had fled Hitler's takeover of the Sudetenland and found refuge in the United Kingdom, Sweden, and Canada, where they arrived just months before the outbreak of the Second World War. On their arrival in Canada, they were settled on remote farms in northern Saskatchewan and northeastern British Columbia. Most of these refugees, who as party activists were not very adept at farming, expected to eventually return to Czechoslovakia and abandoned their farms, either joining the army or moving to Toronto, Hamilton, or Montreal. The exodus to the cities was, as one Sudeten-German refugee put it, 'halfway to home.'[9] But the end of the hostilities shattered their hopes. The Skoutajan family, for example, received from Czechoslovakia in August 1945 detailed accounts of the deportations taking place in their native Aussig (Ústí nad Labem). Disillusioned about European politics, the Skoutajan family decided to stay in Canada.[10] The Weisbach family was equally shattered by the letters arriving from across the Atlantic and refused to be 'repatriated' to occupied Germany. Like most other Sudeten-German refugees in Canada and elsewhere, they preferred to stay in their country of refuge.[11]

Immediately after the war, the Sudeten-German refugees sowed the first seeds of a transnational expellee diaspora. As former party officials, they knew how to mobilize the public and set up organizations. Franz Rehwald, who was one of them, held a key position at the centre of German-Canadian affairs. As editor-in-chief of one of the two

German-Canadian national papers, the *Nordwesten*, he used his ample influence to drum up support for an end to the expulsion of Germans from Central and Eastern Europe. Not surprisingly, the *Nordwesten*'s pages were filled with reports that exposed, for example, the expellees' plight 'in the Land of Death.'[12] Also, the Sudeten Germans immediately after the war worked resolutely to overturn the government ban on German immigrants and helped organize an alliance of German-Canadian organizations that eventually succeeded in securing the admission of close relatives. As early as March 1946, the Sudeten Relief Committee was distributing pamphlets promoting the immigration of 'democratic Sudeten Germans.'[13] Sudeten Germans were also instrumental in founding Canada's only secular aid organization for postwar Germany, the Canadian Society for German Relief, which specifically sought to help expellees.[14]

But the Sudeten-German refugees in Canada comprised two feuding camps. On the one side, the group around Willi Wanka established the Canadian-German Association in Tomslake, British Columbia, where half the refugees had originally been settled. Wanka had been a leader of Czechoslovakia's German Socialist Party. In 1939, as the party leader's personal secretary, he had been tasked with coordinating the relocation of the Sudeten-German refugees to Canada. In 1945 he played a key role in organizing relief for party members in Europe and in bringing Sudeten-German relatives to Canada. On the other side, the group around Henry Weisbach founded separate clubs in Hamilton, Toronto, and Montreal. These small clubs were mainly social in nature. But they also upheld European labour traditions such as May Day, distributed a mimeographed newsletter, and expressed their solidarity with expellees across the Atlantic. They also joined the local socialist movement as well as the Co-operative Commonwealth Federation (CCF).

The rivalry between the two camps went back to the divisions within the party in the late 1930s, when the 'Czechoslovakists' opposed the party leadership's nationalist course.[15] During the war, these differences led to a schism among Sudeten-German refugees, including in Canada, where Weisbach and others had briefly sympathized with the dissidents. After the war, these differences were exacerbated, which led to a sharp division within the organized Sudeten-German community. In 1956, Weisbach's group formed the Central Association of Sudeten-German Clubs and so took over the leadership of the majority of Sudeten Germans in Canada. Four years later, Wanka's group attempted to challenge this leadership, founding the Western Canadian

Working Community of the Sudeten Germans, although to no avail. By the mid-1960s, Weisbach's group clearly dominated, having gained the undivided support of the social democratic Sudeten-German organization in West Germany, the *Seliger-Gemeinde*. Meanwhile, Wanka's group drifted into the hands of a right-wing group, the Wenzel Jaksch Circle, which continued to demand the right of expellees to return and which refused to accept West Germany's new foreign policy toward Eastern Europe.[16]

Besides the Sudeten Germans, other expellee groups developed organizations in the wake of the 'German postwar immigration boom' – in particular, expellees from the Danube Basin, who by the 1960s had formed Canada's strongest expellee organization. During the 1950s they founded or revived a number of associations in Ontario and Quebec, their main area of settlement. These included clubs in Montreal, Kitchener, Toronto, Aylmer, Bradford, Galt, Leamington, and Windsor.[17] In 1960 these clubs established the Alliance of the Danube Swabians in Canada (ADSC) and vowed to uphold Danube-Swabian folk culture. The ADSC maintained ties with corresponding Danube-Swabian organizations in West Germany, Austria, France, and Brazil and used the monthly *Homeland Messenger* as its press organ. The *Homeland Messenger* was founded in 1960 as the *Swabian Messenger* before being renamed the following year.[18] In 1964, four years after being founded in West Germany, a Catholic group associated with the ADSC at St Patrick's Church in Toronto launched a pilgrimage to Marylake near Midland on the Georgian Bay in remembrance of the lost homeland and the expulsion of the Danube Swabians. That first year, 2,500 people attended the event, which was apparently led by children clad in white, followed by youth groups dressed in traditional costumes, grandmothers with black headscarves, and survivors of Yugoslavia's postwar anti-German persecution, who carried white crosses with the engraved names of individual detention camps.[19] The ADSC also organized an annual meeting, held in rotation by one of its member associations on Labour Day weekend. These gatherings, which drew as many as three thousand people during the 1960s, were an opportunity for Danube Swabians to meet old acquaintances. They typically included a main rally, a parade of brass brands, and folk dances.[20]

Expellees from Transylvania formed a similar homeland society in Canada, although it remained considerably smaller than the ADSC and represented only fifteen hundred to two thousand Transylvanian Saxons (*Siebenbürger Sachsen*).[21] Most of these lived in southern

Ontario, where they founded new clubs in Aylmer or joined existing Transylvanian clubs in Kitchener-Waterloo and Windsor. These latter two Transylvanian clubs had been founded as mutual aid organizations, offering members help in the event of illness. Canada's Transylvanian clubs were also home to choirs as well as to youth, women's, and folk dance groups. In 1960 they established the Homeland Society of the Transylvanian Saxons in Canada, headquartered in Kitchener-Waterloo, launching the *Homeland Herald* as its newsletter. Three years later, in 1963, the Transylvanian homeland society joined forces with its larger American counterpart to form, although only for three years, a continent-wide organization with links to Austria and West Germany. The homeland society also organized annual gatherings complete with speeches, folk dances, and parades. During the 1960s, these events attracted between eight hundred and one thousand attendants.[22]

In the 1950s a third group of newly arrived expellees from the Baltic revived the Canadian Baltic Immigration Aid Society (CBIAS), which had ceased operations in 1947. The first branch of the CBIAS opened in London, Ontario, and was soon followed by branches in Kitchener, Montreal, Toronto, Winnipeg, Edmonton, Calgary, and Vancouver. By 1968 roughly half of all German-Baltic immigrants were members of the CBIAS, which boasted 1,528 members in all.[23] As a homeland society, the CBIAS brought together German Balts who in Latvia and Estonia had formed an elite until the collapse of the Russian empire. It published a periodical and maintained regular contact with the small yet powerful German-Baltic homeland society in West Germany, whose leading figures, Georg von Manteuffel-Szoege and Axel de Vries, were prominent in the expellee movement.

Beyond these four groups – Sudeten Germans, Danube Swabians, Transylvanians, and German Balts – no other expellee group founded an organization on Canadian soil, except for a handful of smaller clubs with informal ties to West German expellee organizations and a number of congregations that accommodated expellee groups. In Kitchener, for example, a small group of immigrants formed the *Alpenklub*, which had ties to West German and Austrian homeland groups from Gottschee (Slovenia). Also in Kitchener, the Bethel Lutheran church brought together mostly expellees from Poznan (central Poland) and Volhynia (western Ukraine). In Toronto, St George's Lutheran Church accommodated many German-Baltic expellees, and in southern Manitoba and on the Niagara Peninsula, Mennonite churches hosted expellees from Russia who had retreated with the German armies in 1943–4.[24]

Quite remarkably, none of the expellee groups from Poland gained a foothold in Canada, even though expellees from the former German provinces of Silesia, Pomerania, and East Prussia represented – as in West Germany – the lion's share of the expellee population in Canada. Immigration regulations up to 1950 favoured German expellees from Russia, Romania, and the former Yugoslavia, but this can hardly account for the lack of *reichsdeutsche* homeland societies. After all, in the Canadian census of 1971, expellees born within the borders of post-1945 Poland alone made up 44 per cent of the expellee population.[25]

Most of these expellees seem to have joined – if they joined any group – German-Canadian clubs or associations. Clive von Cardinal, for example, was instrumental in setting up both the Canadian Society for German Relief and a German-Canadian umbrella organization, the Trans-Canada Alliance of German Canadians (TCA). An East Prussian, Cardinal immigrated to Canada in 1929 and after the war lobbied hard for Canadian aid to expellees in Germany. He adopted two expellee orphans and maintained close ties with expellee circles in West Germany, notably the influential Göttingen Research Committee (*Göttinger Arbeitskreis*), which agreed to publish the newsletter of the Canadian Society for German Relief.[26] Similarly, the TCA's secretary in the late 1950s and 1960s, Bernard Stopp, helped ensure that the German-Canadian umbrella organization supported expellees. Born in Breslau (Wrocław), he came to Canada in the early 1950s. Within the TCA, he backed Sudeten-German initiatives for West German compensation payments and co-authored the final version of one of the resolutions that called on the federal government to support compensation claims abroad on behalf of expellees in Canada.[27]

The first *reichsdeutsche* homeland group was founded only in the 1960s. It was formed in Toronto and drew together expellees from Silesia. Named after a mythic Silesian mountain spirit, *Rübezahl*, in the 1990s this club evolved into the Society for the German Heritage of Eastern Europe.[28] Several factors explain the lack of *reichsdeutsche* homeland societies in the 1950s. First, and above all, *reichsdeutsche* expellees saw themselves more as Germans than as Silesians, Pomeranians, or East Prussians. Unlike the ethnic German expellees from the Baltic, Romania, and Hungary, they held no strong allegiance to any regional culture. The Sudeten Germans, for example, had developed an acute sense of their regional identity in the interwar years as they campaigned for minority rights in newly established Czechoslovakia.[29] Similarly, the German Balts had reinforced their group identity as small and beleaguered minorities in newly independent Latvia and Estonia.[30] Without such strong regional identities, it took *reichsdeutsche* expellees longer to build up homeland societies. This was notably also the case in West Germany, where they organized in interest-based associations before building homeland societies.[31]

Second, there was no support in West Germany for *reichsdeutsche* expellees. Indeed, West German officials viewed with suspicion any articulation of expellee interests in Canada. For example, when in 1958 the TCA passed a resolution that called on the Canadian government to exert its influence in the United Nations for the compensation of expellees, the West German consular representative in Toronto vehemently opposed the move.[32] Similarly, *reichsdeutsche* homeland societies in West Germany avoided fostering affiliated organizations in Canada, focusing instead on mobilizing their members in West Germany and on deploring the mass departure of expellees overseas.[33] This stands in marked contrast to the Sudeten-German and German-Baltic homeland societies, which took a keen interest in the lives and organizations of their counterparts in Canada.[34]

Third, after the West German government passed war compensation legislation in 1952, *reichsdeutsche* expellees who had lost assets as a result of the war were able to apply for compensation and so had a less acute need for organized action. Ethnic German expellees, by contrast, often required further lobbying to ensure their eligibility. This was notably the case for the Sudeten-German refugees. Unlike most other expellees in Canada, they had never resided in West Germany and so were unable to apply for reparation payments under the terms of the 1952 legislation. This led them to form the Central Organization of the Sudeten German Clubs to lobby for compensation.[35] Similarly, a large number of Danube Swabians had come to Canada from postwar Austria and so also were ineligible for West German compensation payments. As a result, the Danube-Swabian homeland society lobbied for change in Canada, West Germany, and Austria.[36]

Contacts among Canada's homeland societies were limited. There were no group commemorations to celebrate the heritage of the lost homeland. Homeland societies also differed in terms of their relationship to German-Canadian associations. For example, Sudeten Germans worked closely with the TCA, whereas other organized expellee groups were more reluctant to do so. After making strong efforts during the late 1940s to help expellees in occupied Germany immigrate to Canada, the Sudeten-German refugees continued to play an important role in the 1950s and 1960s. In 1951, members of the Weisbach group helped establish the TCA. Weisbach himself drew up the organization's statutes and in 1967 became its president.[37]

By contrast, the German-Baltic homeland society avoided the TCA and had little contact with other German-Canadian organizations. Its self-imposed isolation led to a public controversy in the mid-1960s when the ethnic press criticized the CBIAS's lack of involvement in German-Canadian affairs.[38] The Danube-Swabian homeland society, meanwhile, had a more mixed attitude toward homeland societies and German-Canadian organizations. On the one hand, it maintained good relations with the Sudeten Germans, who strongly backed the Danube Swabians' compensation claims. And in Toronto the Sudeten Germans increasingly used Danube-Swabian venues to organize meetings and folk dances.[39] On the other hand, it was reluctant to join the TCA. Individual Danube-Swabian clubs such as the ones in Toronto and Kitchener joined the TCA, but the homeland society as such did not.[40]

What were the reasons for this vexed relationship between homeland societies and German-Canadian organizations? With regard to the TCA, one reason may have been the organization's high membership fees, which apparently kept smaller clubs away from the TCA.[41] With regard to the CBIAS, one may also hypothesize that the generally well-educated German Balts, who most often came from middle- if not upper-class backgrounds, avoided social interaction with groups that were mostly of peasant background (such as the Danube Swabians) or of working-class background (such as the Sudeten Germans).

Equally, Nazi Germany's dire legacy may have encouraged some homeland societies to avoid German-Canadian associations. This, at least, was what German-Baltic expellees suggested in defence of their homeland society's lack of involvement in German-Canadian affairs.[42] A Canadian official who attended the TCA's annual general meeting in 1960 noted how Nazi Germany's legacy influenced relationships between homeland societies and German-Canadian organizations. According to his report, the head of the Danube-Swabian homeland society apparently claimed that his organization could not join the TCA because of the funding it received from the West German government to finance German-language schooling in Canada. Danube Swabians, he argued, had 'burned their fingers in the past' by joining organizations sponsored by German agencies and did not wish to repeat an experience that had led to carnage and deportation.[43]

Thus, all in all, expellees founded only a handful of organizations in the postwar years. These were small, and they developed no channels for working together. Moreover, all of them represented groups whose roots were in the former Austro-Hungarian and Russian empires. Thus, a variety of factors accounted for the lack of *reichsdeutsche* homeland societies. Besides there being a weaker regional awareness among Germans from Silesia or Pomerania, the powerful *reichsdeutsche* homeland societies in West Germany paid no heed to expellees in Canada, focusing instead on mobilizing the local members. The fact that expellees such as the Sudeten-German refugees had never held German citizenship also played a role. Ineligible for West German compensation payments, the Sudeten-German refugees founded their own organization and lobbied for the same rights that *reichsdeutsche* expellees had obtained.

'Euro-Canadians'

As victims of forced migration, expellees in Canada enjoyed no special status. On the contrary, they were exposed to homogenizing stereotypes that depicted Germans as relentless warmongers and that barely differentiated between expellees and other German immigrants. One Sudeten-German refugee tried to inform Canadians about the expulsion of Germans from Central and Eastern Europe and was told that after all, expellees were Germans too.[44] Another Sudeten-German refugee observed a similar lack of appreciation for the fate of expellees and felt disparaged as German.[45] Not surprisingly, the TCA repeatedly contested the bigoted nature of media broadcasts and declared the work it did for its members mere 'German rabble-rousing' (*Deutschenhetze*).[46]

That said, German stereotypes seem to have upset expellees only to a limited degree, and none of the homeland societies launched campaigns of the sort conducted by the TCA. During interviews held in the late 1970s as part of a project to record Ontario's multicultural heritage, few interviewees expressed concerns about such stereotypes. The views of Otto Leib, originally from Silesia, were typical of a generation of expellees who realized full well that Germany's Nazi past continued to resonate in Canadian society. In his interview he said he understood the reasons for disparaging remarks about his German heritage, especially when they were voiced by people who had lost friends or family members in Europe. He stressed that he had encountered little prejudice even though in Toronto he had lived, at first, in the Jewish quarter.[47]

Yet while most interviewees showed some understanding, they also objected to being assigned collective guilt for atrocities they believed they had nothing to do with. Ethnic German expellees distanced themselves from the crimes committed by Nazi Germany because they had typically held German citizenship for only a limited time – or in the case of the Sudeten Germans who arrived in 1939, not at all. They persistently used a strategy that German-Canadian community leaders had been deploying since the end of the war to remove ethnic Germans from possible association with Hitler's National Socialism. Lucy Amberg, a Danube Swabian from Hungary, during her interview plainly opposed collective accusations based on her German heritage. As she put it, she had not even stepped foot in Germany until after the war. Like Adolf Fischer, a Sudeten German who arrived in Canada in the early 1950s, she emphasized her roots in the 'East' as an ethnic German or *Volksdeutsche*. Amberg, Fischer, and others, in insisting on this distinct identity, distanced themselves from the presumably more culpable Germans from Germany.[48]

In Canada, the expellees aligned themselves with the masses of newcomers who had arrived from war-torn Europe in search of a brighter future. They remembered sharing the voyage across the Atlantic with other people from West Germany, the Netherlands, or Latvia who were equally keen to leave behind the rubble of the old continent. One expellee from the Baltic noted in his diary: 'There is a great collegiality among emigrants ... It seems that with growing distance to Europe many of the continent's bad habits disappear.'[49] In effect, they perceived the trajectories they followed upon departure from West Germany as typical experiences of postwar European immigrants. They recalled how they and other immigrants from the European continent had entered the Canadian workforce through schemes that had first been designed for displaced persons (DPs), which tied them to jobs as farm labourers or miners until they had reimbursed the costs of their transatlantic passage one or two years later. This was especially the case for ethnic German expellees who came to Canada in the late 1940s. Either they had travelled with the International Refugee Organization (IRO), which facilitated the transatlantic movement of DPs, or they had come under the auspices of the Canadian Christian Council for the Resettlement of Refugees (CCCRR) – the Canadian substitute for those ethnic German expellees who were ineligible for transportation with the IRO.[50]

As indentured farm labourers, lumberjacks, miners, or nurses, the expellees developed the sense that they were part of a common immigrant experience. Placed as they were in remote and inhospitable regions, they felt marked by the trials of underpaid work. In the interviews they recalled, for example, how they and other new immigrants from Europe had been dealt with in bulk, uncertain where the number tags they were given on arrival would take them. As one interviewee put it: 'They only knew the type of work they had signed up for.'[51] They also recalled working shoulder to shoulder with DPs and other European immigrants, thus breaking down barriers in a way that in Europe would have been inconceivable. In West Germany, for example, DPs were looked down upon as foreigners, tramps, and criminals.[52] In Canada, by contrast, expellees recalled relying on advice from DPs, most of whom had arrived a year or two before. One expellee, who landed in 1952 on a farm near Ottawa, noted how he had enjoyed the company of a Yugoslav DP who had helped him look for new work.[53]

Prejudice against immigrants exposed expellees to alternative categorizations that partly erased the Nazi stigma. Indeed, as a wave of xenophobia washed over immigrants in the postwar years, singling out DPs in particular, the expellees remembered how they were looked down upon as *immigrants* regardless of their ethnic background. In her memoirs, an expellee from Latvia who arrived in Canada from Austria under the auspices of the IRO remembered well the repeated defamations to which she was subjected as a DP. She felt disparaged by Canadians, and fifty years after her arrival, she recalled trying time and again to explain to Canadians that she was in fact a 'Delayed Pioneer.'[54]

Others felt that they had been discriminated against as newcomers. When applying for jobs, they had heard the same negative comment as other immigrants had received – namely, that they lacked 'Canadian experience.' This had forced them to take jobs in subordinate positions such as cleaning, construction, and farm labour. They also felt that as 'New Canadians,' they had to conform to socially accepted norms. These expectations included, as an expellee immigrant explained, 'in actual fact everything' from learning English or French to conducting oneself in a socially acceptable manner at work and in contact with Canadians outside the workplace. 'Every Canadian that immigrants meet,' he noted, 'must get the impression that immigrants are grateful for their admission to Canada and that immigrants as future citizens of the country will spare no efforts to settle and work for their new homeland.'[55]

Living conditions likewise impressed on expellees a sense of common fate as postwar immigrants from Europe. Lacking significant means, expellees had first resided in immigrant neighbourhoods, sharing rooms and apartments. In search of cheap accommodation, they had learned to cohabitate with immigrants and had lived in what one expellee called a 'Little Europe.'[56] In boarding houses they had shared rooms with other immigrants from across Europe, and decades later recalled how they had learned to get along with Latvians, Poles, and Ukrainians. One expellee from Pomerania, for example, noted in his memoirs his first encounters with a group of Poles. After a rough night revelling, he had passed out and fallen asleep. As he wrote: 'I never thought that a double bed could hold seven people nor did I ever think I could fall asleep next to a Pole. But here in Canada I could sleep with six of them and this in the same bed!'[57]

Also, the ability to speak German with other postwar immigrants from across Europe fostered a sense of common immigrant identity. Most Europeans had picked up some German during the war, in particular DPs who had been conscripted for the Nazi war industry. As a result, expellees, who had little or no knowledge of English, were able to speak German in order to get by in immigrant neighbourhoods. One expellee recalled going to a Polish corner store where she could do her purchases in German. Another expellee, who had opened a shop in the Jewish quarter, remembered how he had relied on the local residents' German linguistic skills to sell his products and services.[58] Thus, as a *lingua franca*, German had effectively bound expellees to their fellow 'New Canadians' and so had helped forge a sense of European immigrant identity.

Expellees felt a sense of achievement as they settled down in Canadian society. They attributed their success to immigrants' general social mobility and endurance in the postwar years. In their minds, they had worked their way up, found better jobs, obtained official credentials at evening schools, and eventually landed positions that gave them some security alongside European immigrants of other ethnicities. Both at work and in night classes, expellees had met Germans, Poles, Slovaks, Italians, and Jews who were eager to improve their lot or their English. They were 'hardworking people'[59] who had saved for down payments and had taken in lodgers to alleviate the financial burden of mortgages. They were proud of how their children had obtained university degrees and professional qualifications – things that for them had been out of reach.

Above all, expellees prided themselves on the contributions they had made to Canadian society. Within a single generation they had seen dramatic social and cultural changes attributable, according to them, to the vast influx of European immigrants. They felt that they had helped transform a seemingly parochial society anchored in the British Empire into the modern and vibrant 'Canadian mosaic.' They had seen the construction of highways, suburbs, and skyscrapers. They maintained that the marked liberalization of Canadian culture in postwar decades had been in part their achievement. For example, they believed that they had been instrumental in removing the prohibition against shop window displays on Sundays. Similarly, they took credit for the easing of liquor laws, which had finally allowed restaurants to serve wine to families with Sunday lunch. One expellee from Czechoslovakia certainly had no doubts: in the postwar years, European immigrants had radically changed the face of Toronto. From the British 'city of churches' that he first encountered in the early 1940s, he had seen the city transformed by immigrants into a sprawling metropolis complete with theatres, nightclubs, and opera houses.[60]

Conclusion

This chapter has shown that expellees founded only a handful of relatively small organizations in Canada. In all, four homeland associations emerged during the 1950s compared to more than twenty in West Germany. All four traced their origins to outside the prewar borders of Germany: to Czechoslovakia, the Danube Basin (Hungary/Romania/Yugoslavia), Transylvania (Romania), and the Baltic (Estonia and Latvia). Besides mutual assistance, these organizations provided members with places to share a common heritage and to speak the language or dialect of the homeland. In doing so, they were effectively based on what historian Roberto Perin has referred to as 'intense localism.'[61] That Canada's organized expellee groups were exclusively of ethnic German heritage from the former Austro-Hungarian and Russian empires is no mere coincidence. Similar to the Italian *contadino* who immigrated to North America before and after the war, these ethnic German expellee groups from Eastern Europe were still strongly marked by their peasant background and by their loyalty to the local community. What is more, except for the Sudeten-German groups, Canada's expellee organizations supported no political programs akin to the diasporic nationalism of their West German counterparts. This is particularly striking in the case of the German Balts, who focused on social and cultural activities. By contrast, the Sudeten-German refugees were a highly politicized group who knew how to 'do' politics. Thus, not surprisingly, in Canada they took a leading role in defence of expellees.[62]

Evidence from personal accounts and memoirs suggests that expellees developed a strong identity as immigrants. Parallel to the allegiance to their homeland – an allegiance that they basically expressed in private or through homeland groups and societies – they fostered an identity rooted in more common experiences such as a transatlantic passage, indentured work, and the primitive accommodations in boarding houses. Their gradual establishment in Canadian society sustained this perception. Looking back, they believed that postwar immigrants from war-torn Europe had generally been able to find secure jobs and buy homes. Ultimately, they felt they had lived the lives of a generation that started from scratch and that overcame the challenges of immigration. Their mixed feelings about their German heritage must be seen in this context. Expellees clearly faced disparaging remarks about their ethnic background. Lacking 'Canadian experience,' they were also more generally put down as immigrants. The fact that in the late 1960s and 1970s the notion of Canada's 'third force' gained wide currency among ethnic groups suggests that expellees were not the only newcomers in Canadian society to construct a distinct immigrant identity. On the contrary, like expellees and German immigrants in general, Ukrainians, Poles, and Italians took pride in their achievements and supported the idea of the 'Canadian mosaic,' which led to Trudeau's multiculturalism policies of the 1970s. In this way expellees as much as other immigrants were able to assert their heritage and gain a sense of belonging.

NOTES

1 English-language publications on the fate of Germans from Central and Eastern Europe in the aftermath of the Second World War are few. For a good overview, see Pertti Ahonen et al., eds., *People on the Move: Forced Population Movements in Europe in the Second World War and Its Aftermath* (Oxford: Berg, 2008); In German, see Andreas Kossert, *Kalte Heimat: Die Geschichte der deutschen Vertriebenen nach 1945* (Munich: Siedler, 2007); Arno Surminski, intro, in *Flucht und Vertreibung: Europa zwischen 1939 und 1948 mit einer Einleitung von Arno Surminski* (Hamburg: Ellert and Richter Verlag, 2004); Erik K. Franzen and Hans Lemberg, *Die Vertriebenen: Hitlers letzte Opfer* (Munich: Propylaen, 2001); Wolfgang Benz, ed., *Die Vertreibung der Deutschen aus dem Osten: Ursachen, Ereignisse, Folgen*, 2nd rev. ed.

(Frankfurt am Main: Fischer, 1996); and the two government-funded, dated, but still indispensable standard works: Theoder Schieder et al., eds., *Dokumentation der Vertreibung der Deutschen aus Ost-Mitteleuropa*, 5 vols. and 3 supplements (Bonn: Bundesministerium für Vertriebene, Flüchtlinge und Kriegsgeschädigte, 1953–1961); and Friedrich Edding and Eugen Lemberg, eds., *Die Vertriebenen in Westdeutschland: Ihre Eingliederung und ihr Einfluss auf Gesellschaft, Wirtschaft, Politik und Geistesleben*, 3 vols. (Kiel: F. Hirt, 1959).

2 For expellee statistics in West Germany, see Gerhard Reichling, *Die Deutschen Vertriebenen in Zahlen*, 2 vols. (Bonn: Kulturstiftung der deutschen Vertriebenen, 1989); for Canada, see Pascal Maeder, Forging a New Heimat: Expellees in Post-War West Germany and Canada (Göttingen: V&R unipress, 2011), 251–65.

3 Ronald E. Schmalz, 'Former Enemies Come to Canada: Ottawa and the Post-war German Immigration Boom, 1951–57,' PhD diss., University of Ottawa, 2000.

4 More recent publications include Alexander Freund, *Aufbrüche nach dem Zusammenbruch: Die deutsche Nordamerika-Auswanderung nach dem Zweiten Weltkrieg* (Göttingen: V&R unipress, 2004); Gerhard P. Bassler, ,Germans,' in *Encyclopaedia of Canada's People*, ed. Paul R. Magosci (Toronto: University of Toronto Press, 1999), 587–612; Andrea Koch-Kraft, *Deutsche in Kanada: Einwanderung und Adaptation mit einer Untersuchung zur Situation der Nachkriegsmigration in Edmonton* (Bochum: Universitätsverlag Brockmeyer, 1990); Manfred Prokop, *German Language in Alberta: Maintenance and Teaching* (Edmonton: University of Alberta Press, 1990).

5 Among the most important publications are Patrick Farges, *Le trait d'union, ou, l'intégration sans l'oubli: itinéraires d'exilés germanophones au Canada après 1933* (Paris: Maison des Sciences de l'homme, 2008); Hans P. Werner, *Imagined Homes: Soviet German Immigrants in Two Cities* (Winnipeg: University of Manitoba Press, 2007); Annette Puckhaber, *Ein Privileg für wenige: Die deutschsprachige Migration nach Kanada im Schatten des Nationalsozialismus* (Münster: Lit, 2002), 124–71; Willi Wanka, *Opfer des Friedens: Die Sudetensiedlungen in Kanada* (Munich: Langen Müller Verlag, 1988); Mathias Kuester, *Bricks and Mortar to a History of the Baltic Germans for Canadians* (Edmonton: private publication, 1997); Fritz Wieden and Michael Benzinger, *Canada's Danube Swabians* (Windsor: St Michael's Church, 1992); Fritz Wieden, *Kanadas Siebenbürger Sachsen* (Stuttgart: Institut für Auslandsbeziehungen, 1986); Marlene Epp, *Men without Women: Mennonite Refugees of the Second World War* (Toronto: University of Toronto Press, 1999); William

J.H. Sturhahn, *They Came from East and West: A History of Immigration to Canada* (Winnipeg: North American Baptist Immigration and Colonization Society, 1976).

6 Sylvia Brown, 'Voices from the Borderlands: The Problem of "Home" in the Oral History of German Expellees in Canada,' in *Refractions of Germany in Canadian Literature and Culture*, ed. Heinz Autor, Sylvia Brown, and John Considine (Berlin: Walter de Gruyter GmbH, 2003), 33–57.

7 Angelika E. Sauer and Matthias Zimmer, eds., *A Chorus of Different Voices: German-Canadian Identities* (New York: Peter Lang, 1998).

8 Dirk Hoerder, *Creating Societies: Immigrant Lives in Canada* (Montreal and Kingston: McGill–Queen's University Press, 2000), 301.

9 Julius Scharing, "'Montreal, die Halfway Station,"' *Forward* 16, no.: 4 (September 1964), 7.

10 Hanns F. Skoutajan, *Uprooted and Transplanted: A Sudeten Odyssey from Tragedy to Freedom, 1938–1958* (Owen Sound: Ginger Press, 2000), 191–212.

11 Henry and Hermine Weisbach, interview, 2 and 13 April 1984, Multicultural History Society of Ontario (MHSO), German Collection.

12 *Nordwesten*, 13 August 1947.

13 Willi Wanka, *Twice Victims of Munich: The Tragedy of the Democratic Sudeten Germans* (Tupper Creek: private publication, 1946).

14 Clive von Cardinal, interview, 9 November 1986, LAC, Audio Collection, 1987–0157 C 5864; Gottlieb Leibbrandt, *Canadian German Society: 25 Jahre caritative und kulturelle Arbeit des Hilfswerks der Deutsch-Kanadiers* (Waterloo: private publication, 1972).

15 See, notably, Nancy M. Wingfield, *Minority Politics in a Multinational State: The German-Social Democrats in Czechoslovakia, 1918–1938* (New York: Columbia University Press, 1989).

16 Wieden, *Sudeten Canadians*, 190–202.

17 Wieden and Benzinger, *Canada's Danube Swabians*, 58.

18 *Heimatbote* 2, no. 8 (June 1961): 1.

19 *Heimatbote* 5, no. 44 (June 1964): 8; Wieden and Benziger, *Canada's Danube Swabians*, 64–6.

20 Waldheim to Auswärtiges Amt betreffend Tag der Donauschwaben in Toronto am 5. und 6. September 1959, Politisches Archiv des Auswärtigen Amtes (PAAA), Referat 305/IIA6, B 32, vol. 50; *Heimatbote* 3, no. 23 (September 1962): 1.

21 Wieden, *Kanadas Siebenbürger Sachsen*, 14.

22 Ibid.; Bassler, ,Germans,' 602.

23 Kuester, *Bricks and Mortar*, 82.

24 Anton Pleschinger, interview, 30 November and 14 December 1977; Rev.
Helmut Pruefer, interview, 24 June 1977; Hans-Jürgen and Mita Kumberg,
interview, 21 February 1978, MHSO, German Collection; Dankadresse der
Mennonitischen Gemeinde an die Bundesregierung, Oktober 1963, PAAA,
Referat 305/IIA6, B 32, vol. 198.

25 Maeder, 'Forging a New Leimat,' 241.

26 Clive von Cardinal, interview, 9 November 1986, LAC, Accession, 9 and 11
November 1986.

27 Zentralvorstand TCA, Sitzungsprotokoll, 22 February 1959, LAC, Trans-
Canada Alliance of German Canadians, MG 28 V 4, vol. 1, file 9; Boeschenstein to Stopp, 13 October 1959, and Stopp to Boeschenstein, 14 October
1959, MG 28 V 4, vol. 4, file 11, part 2.

28 Information provided by Chris Klein, a Silesian and current president of
the Society of German Heritage of Eastern Europe.

29 Rudolf Jaworski, 'Die Sudetendeutschen als Minderheit in der Tschecho-
slowakei,' in Benz, *Die Vertreibung*, 33–44.

30 Lars Bosse, ,Vom Baltikum in den Reichsgau Wartheland,' in *Deutschbalten,
Weimarer Republik und Drittes Reich*, vol. 1, ed. Michael Garleff (Cologne:
Böhlau, 2001), 297–387.

31 Bernd Sonnewald, ,Die Entstehung und Entwicklung der ostdeutschen
Landsmannschaften von 1947 bis 1952,' PhD diss., FU Berlin, 1975, 44, 68;
Johannes-Dieter Steinert, *Vertriebenenverbände in Nordrhein-Westfalen, 1945–
1954* (Düsseldorf: Schwann, 1986), 210; Pertti Ahonen, *After the Expulsion:
West Germany and Eastern Europe, 1945–1990* (New York: Oxford University
Press, 2003), 24–38.

32 Von Waldheim to Stopp, 13 February 1959, LAC, Trans-Canada Alliance of
German Canadians Papers, MG 28 V 4, vol. 15, file 9.

33 *Ostdeutsche Zeitung / Stimme der Vertriebenen*, 14 May 1950.

34 Rückel to Lodgman von Auen, 6 March 1956; Rückel to Eichler, 18 April
1956; Eichler to Rückel, 6 June 1956; and Bundesverband der Sudetendeutschen Landsmannschaft to Peckert, 23 October 1957, Sudetendeutsches
Archiv, Nachlass Rudolph Lodgman von Auen, CV/1a IX 20; *Baltische
Briefe* 10 (October 1950): 4; *Baltische Briefe* 2 (February 1957), 3.

35 *Forward* 8, no. 10 (March 1957): 2; Henry Weisbach, 'Why the Sudeten
German Central Organization,' n.d. [circa 1957], LAC, External Affairs
Records, vol. 8382, File 10935-H-1–40; Wieden, *Sudeten Canadians*, 187–91.

36 *Neuland*, 22 February 1964.

37 Minutes of the Founding Assembly of the Canadian-German Alliance, 1
April 1951, LAC, Trans-Canada Alliance of German Canadians Papers, MG

28 V 4, vol. 1, file 5; on the TCA, see also Fritz Wieden, *The Trans-Canada Alliance of German-Canadians: A Study in Culture* (Windsor: Tolle Lege Enterprises, 1985).

38 *Nordwesten*, 22 October 1963, 31 March 1966, and 26 May 1966.

39 *Forward* 15, no. 6 (November 1962): 14.

40 Ibid.

41 Konsulat Toronto to Auswärtiges Amt, 28 February 1961, PAAA, Referat 305/IIA6, B 32, vol. 119.

42 *Nordwesten*, 22 October 1963, 31 March 1966, and 26 May 1966.

43 Stanley Zybala, 'Canadian Germans and Their Integration,' working paper given at the National Staff Conference of the Canadian Citizenship Branch, 20 October 1963, LAC, External Affairs Records, vol. 10112, file 20–18–1-13, part 1.

44 Kutscha to Jaksch, 23 August 1945, LAC, Emil Kutscha Papers, MG 30 C 132, vol. 3, file Correspendence Treuegemeinschaft Sudetendeutscher Sozialdemokraten, 1942–48.

45 Skoutajan, *Uprooted and Transplanted*, 187.

46 See, for example, the note of protest to the Canadian Broadcasting Corporation in 1957, CBC Resolution, 16 June 1957, LAC, Trans-Canada Alliance of German Canadians Papers, MG 28 V 4, vol. 4, file 11, part 2.

47 Otto Leib, interview, 5 October 1978, MHSO, German Collection.

48 Lucy Amberg, interview, 22 March 1979, MHSO, Danube-Swabian Collection; Adolf Fischer, interview, 16 November 1977, MHSO, German Collection.

49 Jürgen E. Kroeger, *Start am anderen Ufer: Erinnerungen aus den Jahren 1945–1972* (Lüneburg: Nordland-Druck, 1975), 47.

50 The former consisted primarily of Mennonites from the Ukraine and Russia as well as Danube Swabians who had come to Austria. The latter were ethnic German expellees whose German ethnic heritage excluded them from IRO. See Angelika Sauer, 'A Matter of Domestic Policy? Canadian Immigration Policy and the Admission of Germans, 1945–50,' *Canadian Historical Review* 74, no. 2 (June 1993): 226–263; Ted D. Regehr, 'Of Dutch or German Ancestry? Mennonite Refugees, MCC, and the International Organization,' *Journal of Mennonite Studies* 13 (1995), 7–25.

51 Hans-Jürgen and Mita Kumberg, interview, 21 February 1978, MHSO, German Collection.

52 Wolfgang Jacobmeyer, *Vom Zwangsarbeiter zum Heimatlosen Ausländer: Die Displaced Persons in Westdeutschland, 1945–1951* (Göttingen: Vandenhoeck and Ruprecht, 1985), 210–15.

53 Peter Hessel Diary, 3 August 1952, 112, LAC, Peter Hessel Papers, MG 31 H 178, vol. 1, file Diary February 1952–October 1952.

54 Barbara Redlich, "'"Ich nehme die Nummer 8!"': Ein baltischer Lebensweg," *Jahrbuch des baltischen Deutschtums*, 43 (2001):, 110.

55 Informationen für Canada-Auswanderer zusammengestellt von Herbert von Hahn, September 1951, Bundesarchiv Koblenz (BAKo), Axel de Vries Papers, N 1412, vol. 18, file German-Baltic Homeland Society. Canadian expectations included in particular also gender roles. S, see Franca Iacovetta, "'Making '
"New Canadians'Canadians": Social Workers, Women, and the Reshaping of Immigrant Families," ,' in *A Nation of Immigrants: Women, Workers, and Communities in Canadian History, 1840s–1960s*, ed. Franca Iacovetta, Paula Draper, and Robert Ventresca, eds. *A Nation of Immigrants: Women, Workers and Communities in Canadian History, 1840s–1960s* (Toronto: University of Toronto Press, 1998), 482–513.

56 Interview Helga Andresen, interview, 22M March 22, 1978, MHSO, German Collection.

57 Jost von der Linde, *The Uprooted Linden Tree* (Vancouver: private publication, 1995), 141.

58 Leib, interview, 5 October, 1978, Helga Andresen, interview, 22 March 1978, MHSO, German Collection.

59 Franca Iacovetta, *Such Hardworking People: Italian Immigrants in Postwar Toronto* (Toronto: University of Toronto Press, 1992).

60 Ludwig Loewit, ,Toronto im Wandel der Zeiten,' *Forward* 19, no. 4 (April 1967): 4.

61 Roberto Perin, "'Writing about Ethnicity," ,' In *Writing about Canada: A Handbook for Modern Canadian History*, ed. John Schultz, ed. *Writing About Canada: A Handbook for Modern Canadian History* (ScarboroughToronto: Prentice-Hall, 1990), 211.

62 Except for the Sudeten group, the German-Baltic, Danube-Swabian, and Transylvanian homeland societies continue to exist. In Toronto the Sudeten group now gathers in the social club Friendship (*Freundschaft*), formally the successor organization of the CCF Sudeten Club Toronto. The Society for the German Heritage of Eastern Europe also is still in existence, based primarily in the Toronto/Kitchener area.

PART IV

Language and Literature

11 Language Acculturation: German Speakers in Kitchener-Waterloo

GRIT LIEBSCHER AND MATHIAS SCHULZE

The migration of groups of people often leads to contact between languages, and this contact almost inevitably leads to language change. Within linguistics, a rich body of literature on language change exists, spanning from language contact phenomena related to the language structure to factors of language maintenance and loss. Researchers with such interests are commonly associated with the disciplines of contact linguistics and bilingualism. The current chapter draws on insights from these two disciplines in analysing interviews conducted with German-speaking[1] immigrants to Canada who were born in German settlements in southeastern Europe or very soon after their parents' arrival in Canada. In order to situate the results of our linguistic analysis in a sociocultural context, we will sketch the cultural and linguistic background of the communities of our speakers. We provide this background because it illuminates the discussion of our data, especially considering that all of the speakers and/or their families come from German-language islands outside of mainland Germany. The speech communities there maintained the German language for centuries, but our interview data point to a very different sociolinguistic situation after their arrival in Canada. We would also like to emphasize that the linguistic processes discussed – transfer, code switching, and code mixing – are typical of the German spoken by bilingual German-Canadians, independent of their dialects and cultural backgrounds.

Within current research on language contact and bilingualism, our data can be interpreted in several ways, some of which we find appropriate while others have to be rejected. Below, we highlight that the analysis of individual examples often allows for several alternative interpretations, as is not uncommon with this kind of analysis. However, there are also a number of concepts and terms that we will not use in our analysis and interpretation. Among the latter is 'language death.' Language death, which was made popular by Dorian,[2] implies that a language is dead when there are no more native speakers of that language. Most linguists would agree that this concept does not apply to language islands, which are outside the main area(s) in which the language is still spoken, and it is therefore not the process in which we can situate our data. For languages disappearing over time in language islands, the term 'language loss' is commonly used.[3] We abstain from framing our analysis in terms of language loss for three reasons. First, while it is likely that the influence of English on the language(s) of our participants has increased over the years they have been living in Canada, we have not actually measured this increase but can only observe the outcome at the time of the interview. Second, the term 'language loss' carries negative connotations and it is surprising that there is no equivalent such as 'language gain,' which is how one could easily interpret the influence of one language on another. Third, language loss as well as language death are usually used in reference to an entire group rather than individuals. In describing an individual's gradual loss of his or her first language, 'language attrition' is commonly used. The concept of attrition as it is currently used in the literature seems problematic considering that the deeper linguistic repertoire, including the range and breadth of the lexicon, appears to remain untouched by any systematic process of 'erosion' or 'attrition' – that is, what may be affected is only a speaker's actual and momentary control of the language.[4]

Considering the interplay of language use and social integration leads us to Kachru's concept of language acculturation. He connects two processes that underlie sociolinguistic diversification: acculturation and nativization.[5] Language acculturation focuses on the acquisition[6] and use of the transplanted language[7] – in our case German – in an environment that has a different majority language – in our case English. Acculturation in this sense refers to both the change in a particular language and the change in how this language is used by its speakers. Such processes are thus indicative of general acculturation processes the speakers undergo. Thus, in our discussion we focus exclusively on linguistic phenomena – how language is used – rather than on the speakers' references to their acculturation experience – what they say. Kachru's second process – nativization – is further evidence for continued acculturation. The term nativization describes processes that result in 'the approximation of a language to the linguistic ... characteristics of the ... dominant language of the area into which it has been trans-planted.'[8] Language acculturation and nativization manifest them-selves in text through very similar surface phenomena (e.g., transfer and code switches). Their gradual difference is not particularly impor-tant to us because these two processes can be located on a continuum.

We looked at the interviews by five speakers (see the section on inter-view data and methodology for more details): four are first-generation immigrants, and the wife of one of these speakers is from the so-called 1.5 generation, since she came to Canada with her parents before puberty. These five chose to converse in German, whereas all others – of the second and third generations – used English as their language of choice. The first group is more interesting from a linguistic point of view because of their 'location' on the acculturation end of the con-tinuum, whereas the English-language interviews of the second group are clearly evidence of nativization only.

The language used by our interviewees looks at first sight like an arbitrary mix of German and English. This is sometimes referred to as *Denglisch* – a rather pejorative term. We, however, see these speakers as competent bilinguals who construct their bicultural, acculturated iden-tity among other things through their bilingual language use.[9]

Linguistic phenomena that are evidence of language acculturation are at the centre of the analysis of our German-language interviews. First, we discuss important features of the participants' language accultura-tion in structural terms (e.g., transfer) and then in functional terms (e.g., code switching). The overall goal is to draw attention to ways in which language constructs individual identities and social meaning. Since the immigration background of our German-Canadian participants is an important factor in this discussion, the section that follows discusses the two immigrant groups relevant for the participants, with a focus on pertinent historical and sociolinguistic aspects of these two groups and on relevant immigration issues for speakers of German to Canada. Examples from our analysis are presented in subsequent sections.

Two Immigrant Groups: Danube Swabians and Transylvanians

The Danube Swabians are a group of German-speaking colonists in the Danubian Basin. After the end of the occupation by the Ottoman Empire, these areas were devastated and largely depopulated. The Habsburg Empire encouraged German-speaking, mainly Catholic farmers, but also Serbians, for example, to settle there for economic (agricultural) reasons as well as for military and political ones (defence of the borders against the Turks). This colonization process became known as the three Great Swabian Migrations (1718–37, 1744–72, 1782–87).[10] Although there were very few Swabians among the colonists, they came to call themselves Swabians (*Schwaben/Schwowe*) in informal conversations, and they often refer to their dialect as Swabian (*Schwowisch*). Their neighbours adopted this practice (cf. *svevi* [Latin], *sváb* [Hungarian], *svaba* [Serbian]). After the First World War and with the end of the Habsburg Empire, the 1.5 million German speakers came to live in three different countries: Hungary, Romania, and Yugoslavia. In 1944 the Tito government revoked the citizenship rights of the German minority and declared them enemies of the people, using as its main argument that many ethnic Germans had sided with the fascist authorities when Germany occupied Yugoslavia.[11] This led to the 'almost complete disappearance of Danube Swabians from the West Banat, whereas a small population remained in East and North Banat.'[12] The German minority in Yugoslavia shrank by about 88 per cent between 1931 and 1953.[13] Danube Swabians have been migrating to Canada for more than one hundred years. With the two great influxes of the 1920s and the 1950s, it has been estimated that altogether about 65,000 Danube Swabians have come to Canada.[14]

The German minority in Transylvania (*Siebenbürgen*) has an even longer history. The first German-speaking settlers arrived there at the invitation of the Hungarian king Géza II (1141–62). The most likely explanation why these people, who came from a wide variety of German dialect regions, are called Saxons (*Siebenbürger Sachsen*) is the use of Latin (*Saxones*) in official communication in mediaeval Hungary.[15] The area later belonged to the Habsburg Empire and became part of Romania after the First World War. 'By 1966 the German minority [of Romania] was about one half of the size it had been in 1940, totalling only some 375,000 people.'[16] Today it is estimated that there are still 50,000 Germans in Romania.[17]

German speakers from these areas speak several other languages, including Serbian, Hungarian, and Romanian. When the Danube Swabians were under the influence of the Hungarian part of the Habsburg Empire, the official language (Hungarian) became the 'high' one. 'When both Hungarian and German were taught at schools, the children often did not know either language well, and the parents began to demand more Magyar instruction.'[18] In the interwar period, Serbo-Croatian was used in all domains of social activity.[19] It was mainly Hungarian, the high-prestige language at the time, that influenced Danube Swabian. Contact languages such as Slovene, Serbian, Croatian, Slovak, and Romanian never played a significant role for Danube Swabians.[20] Transylvanian Saxons, on the other hand, lived somewhat isolated in their communities.[21] They were often bi- and tri-dialectal[22] in German; beyond that, only Romanian played an increasingly important role for them.[23] Examples of borrowings of grammatical structures are often cited in the literature.[24] These groups of German speakers were thus not monolingual, but multilingual speakers.

The language use of both Danube Swabians and Transylvanians was, at least until the Second World War, characterized by diglossia – that is, the rule-governed separation of languages according to domains of use, for example, the exclusive use of German in the home and in church and the exclusive use of the majority language for work and trade. The continuance of this diglossic situation over centuries resulted in a relatively stable bilingual situation and thus the maintenance of the German language at least up until the end of the Second World War.

Many Danube Swabians and Transylvanians fled their homelands in central and southeastern Europe at the end of the Second World War; others were expelled, sent to Soviet labour camps, and then returned to (East) Germany and/or Austria. A number of them later immigrated to Canada. Canada's postwar immigration policy has been described as cautious and reluctant.[25] It was not based simply on demographic and economic considerations; humanitarian motives also played a part, particularly in terms of accepting displaced persons from Europe.[26] Between 1946 and 1961 at least 200,000 European refugees immigrated in Canada, about 165,000 between 1946 and 1952 alone.[27] Many of these immigrants shared the common experiences of the Second World War and the postwar years in Europe. Until 1950 it was difficult for German nationals (*Reichsdeutsche*) to gain entry; the number of immigrants from Germany peaked in the 1950s.[28]

This can also be seen in the Kitchener Metropolitan Census area. Up until the First World War, three-quarters of the population of Berlin, Ontario (renamed Kitchener in 1916), claimed German ethnic origin. Though the absolute figures continued to rise after that, the size of this ethnic group has been shrinking ever since in relative terms.[29] In 1948 the last large influx of German-speaking immigrants began coming to the area, first from German-speaking areas outside Germany and Austria and later also from those two countries.[30] The *2001 Census of Canada* confirmed that German was the 'leading non-official mother tongue'[31] in the tri-city area (Kitchener, Waterloo, Cambridge), but it added that speakers 'with Spanish and Chinese as mother tongues were relatively young, and those with German and Portuguese were relatively old.'[32] Those with German as their mother tongue represented 17.8 per cent of Kitchener's allophone population, a drop from 21.2 per cent five years earlier. The population with German as a mother tongue represented 4 per cent of Kitchener's total population in 2001. Less than 2 per cent of the population reported speaking German most often at home.[33] The census numbers provide us with some overall impression of the language acculturation of speakers in the area. The following section provides a more detailed discussion of language acculturation through an analysis of language use.

The Interview Data and Methodology

The data for the present study come from a larger corpus of interview and conversational data collected at the University of Waterloo. Lori Heffner[34] interviewed members of three extended families of German-speaking background, each represented by three age groups (grandparents, children, grandchildren). Only the three interviews with the grandparents, conducted in German,[35] are analysed here. The linguistic–ethnic background of the five participants in the three interviews is as follows: A. Meier[36] (born in 1932) comes from Yugoslavia, describes the language he speaks as Swabian, and states that his family originated in Alsace. His wife, B. Meier (born in 1930), is from Austria. They both came to Canada in 1961. C. Schmidt (born in 1932) came to Canada in 1949 from Yugoslavia via Czechoslovakia, Austria, and Germany. D. Schmidt was born in Canada in 1933, four years after her parents arrived in Canada, and considers German to be her mother tongue; her parents are Danube Swabians. F. Bauer was born in Transylvania, Romania, in 1929 and came to Canada via Russia and Austria in 1951. Three of the five interviewees were thus born in German-speaking communities in Transylvania or the Danube Basin in non-German-speaking countries. Historian Dirk Hoerder argues that until 1945, the majority of German-speaking immigrants to Canada did not come directly from Germany.[37] The same applies to Austrian immigrants after the Second World War, many of whom originated from other countries, notably Yugoslavia, Romania, and Hungary.[38]

In the analysis of the participants' language use in the interviews, we focus on sentence structures and individual words that cannot be described within the language system of standard German or within a system of a regional variety. The interviews were conducted in standard German, the variety spoken by the interviewer, who did not speak either Danube Swabian or Transylvanian Saxon. This limited the occurrence of genuine dialectal constructions in the discourse, which facilitated our analytical focus on bilingual language contact phenomena. These (as well as the processes that lead to them) will be subsumed under the term transfer.[39] Thus, we are interested in how the German-Canadian speakers employ the two codes – German and English – in these predominantly German-language interviews. Thus, in our examples below we focus on individual speakers' turns in which both languages are present. An attempt is made to interpret these phenomena as textual representations of language acculturation. However, when analysing language use we have to consider the discrepancy between what speakers are able to say (linguistic competence) and what they actually do say (linguistic performance). We refer to these as problems in 'online processing' – when ideas and messages are turned into audible speech signals – and they arise for monolingual as well as bilingual speakers and are sometimes accompanied by a 'repair' and sometimes not. The result is that speech does not necessarily reflect the real ability of speakers and their knowledge of the language. Example 1 illustrates such an online problem. F. Bauer most likely knows the correct form of the participle of *bleiben*, but fails to produce it in this instance.

Example 1

F. Bauer: Aber die haben Rumänen geheiratet und die sind dann dort **gebleiben**.

After discussing typical transfer phenomena that were common to all three interviews, we will note some apparent differences among the German-Canadian speakers in the interviews in terms of their language acculturation. Three of them are first-generation immigrants from German-language islands outside of Germany (A. Meier, C. Schmidt, F. Bauer); one is a first-generation immigrant from Austria (B. Meier); and one is a second-generation German immigrant (D. Schmidt). The language use has to be discussed in the conversational context in which the data were recorded – that is, in the context of an interview with an English-German bilingual speaker who is in the third generation of a German-speaking immigrant family. This means she is recognized as a member of the same speech community as the interviewees. However, as a Master's student working on her thesis, she was most likely also perceived as a representative of the university – by interviewees who have no university education. This is to say, phenomena different from or additional to the ones described here may occur when participants talk in other conversational contexts, for example, with other German Canadians. However, two complex phenomena – transfer and code switching / code mixing – are typical of the language used by bilingual speakers. We focus on these in the next two sections, in which we discuss examples from our analysis.

Transfer Phenomena: A Structural Perspective

Transfer occurs at all language levels: sounds, word and sentence structures, meaning, text, and context. As will become apparent in our discussion of the data analysis, transfer at one level is often combined with transfer at another level. 'Bilinguals and trilinguals make their languages more similar (convergence) – and ... having done this, try to differentiate them in a particular way (divergence).'[40] Our speakers display a wide variety of transfer phenomena in the three interviews. The most salient and frequent of these is a lexical transfer.

Example 2

a) Meier: Die **boys** kaum was. (in answer to the interviewer's question: Was machen Ihre Kinder jetzt mit ihren Deutschkenntnissen?)

b) C. Schmidt: **Displaced persons** haben alles umsonst gekriegt.

c) B. Meier: Ja, **but** lesen können sie ja nicht so gut, wenn's Bücher sind.

Example 2 shows that individual content words (retaining their morphological and phonological features) can be transferred (2a), but this also occurs with larger units such as phrases (2b). *Displaced persons* is a cultural borrowing from English into German – a word or a phrase that is borrowed together with the concept – whereas *boys* is a core borrowing – a loanword that was adopted even though a word for the concept existed in German.[41] Not only content words are affected by these processes, but also functional words (c). Often the latter are discourse markers (such as 'but' in c) – that is, word-like elements that are used to structure the talk rather than to express meaning by themselves, and that signal 'the speaker's potential communicative intentions.'[42]

In other cases, the English sentence structure is transferred and filled with German words. However, several aspects must be considered in order to distinguish language contact phenomena from linguistic phenomena, which may originate in other variables of the communicative situation. First, spoken language differs from written language, but very often transcripts form the basis for an analysis. This tempts the analyst to project written-language rules onto the data. For example, speakers do not always utter sentences from start to finish as they would in written discourse. Oral discourse is full of unfinished sentences, ellipses, and repair phenomena. This can mean that words are arranged in an order that differs from written standard language, which makes it difficult to interpret the deviation of the German word order from standard language as being a result of contact with English. Consider the following example:

Example 3

a) D. Schmidt: ... **dass wir hatten** ein so guten Tanzboden ...
b) D. Schmidt: Und als ich in die Schule **bin gegangen** ...
c) C. Schmidt: **dass er ... soll** der [F. Schmidt] [....] Französisch lernen, Englisch und Deutsch

Examples 3a and 3b are likely syntactic transfer phenomena[43] – the word order is clearly English. Although example 3c looks very similar, it is more likely that the speaker does not transfer an English word order and fill it with German lexical items. Particularly if one takes into consideration the interruption noted by the dotted pause, 3c is a normal occurrence in spoken discourse.[44]

Between English and German, word order transfers are most common at the syntactic level, but instances of levelled case marking or gender marking (or both) have been reported – for example, dative and accusative forming one oblique case, the frequent use of *es* with non-neuter antecedents, or the overgeneralized rule in the example below (in which all nouns ending in –e are feminine).

Example 4

D. Schmidt: Ich denke, **die** Interesse ist dort ... Wenn er **die** Interesse noch zeigt ...

We talk about semantic transfer when the meaning of a word in one language is transferred to a word in the other language whose form is similar. In example 4 above, *dort* is a transfer from English *there*. The German equivalent would likely be *da*.[45] In the example below, s*tark* is used in a similar way to an intensifier in English (as in *to strongly object*), certainly not with the meaning *strong*.

Example 5

D. Schmidt: mein Lehrer, der war **stark** streng.

In our interviews we also found examples of phonological transfer in cognates: words like *Radio* and *Kanada* were pronounced in accordance with Canadian-English pronunciation [reɪdɪou, kænədə]. Such examples as well as the other transfer types discussed above are a good indication that language acculturation has been taking place. The participants make appropriate use of structural resources from both languages. They also successfully alternate these two codes, as we show in the next section.

Code Switching and Code Mixing: A Conversation-Analytic Perspective

Code switching refers to the speakers' juxtaposition of two or more languages (codes). Code switching is a resource for bilingual speakers to make salient selected aspects of the communicative situation, speakers' attitudes, and preferences. Thus, bilinguals are able to use code switches where monolinguals would use other means of communication such as volume, pauses, intonation, voice colouring, and non-verbal behaviour. The speakers in the interviews use code switching for different purposes. One such purpose is to mark a quote, as in the following example:

Example 6

D. Schmidt: Die [T. Schmidt] hat gesagt, sie hat gleich gesagt, '**I'm going to take German. You're not going to talk in front of me. I've got to take German.**' In der High School jetzt.

In such instances of switches to English, it does not matter whether the quote's original language was the same as the language used in the quote. In fact, as Alfonzetti has found, it is often the case that bilinguals switch into the other language to mark the stretch of discourse as a quote, while the quote's original language was different.[46] A similar case is the following:

Example 7

D. Schmidt: Mein Vater und ich, wir haben jetzt geschwäbelt, haben unseren Dialekt gesagt, und dann haben uns umgedreht, **and then said something in English**. Und dann wieder zurück zum anderen.

In this example, the speaker uses the code switch into English in support of the content of the message: when talk is about saying something in English, the speaker switches into English and then back into German when she is talking about a switch back into German.

In the following example, the speaker's code switch into English marks the onset of a change in footing,[47] indicating that the words uttered in English are not necessarily those originating from the speaker himself – that is, he is not the author but the animator.

Example 8

Interviewer: Das Geschäft, wo Sie gearbeitet haben: Haben Sie dort deutsche Kunden gehabt?
A. Meier: No. Nein. Das war **strictly English**.

In this example, A. Meier contextualizes his code switch into English (*strictly English*) with a preceding pause and a smiling voice. In this way, the English phrase – which could also be understood as an order in a context where only English ought to be spoken (e.g., by German Canadians to their children at home) – becomes a statement. The strictness of the order becomes weakened by the pause and the smiling voice, while the code switch indexes this phrase as originally coming from another speaker.

Yet another function of a code switch is to mark something as additional information or an aside, as in the following example:

Example 9

C. Schmidt: Haben sie die Jagd Klub gegründet. **He's a founder**.

The switch into English in this example separates *He's a founder* from the preceding utterance in German. One could imagine the phrase being introduced by a 'by the way' in monolingual discourse.

In all the examples above, code switching has a discourse-related function: 'participants search for an account for "why that language now?" within the development of the conversation.[48] This relates to 'the use of code-switching to organise the conversation by contributing to the interactional meaning of a particular utterance.'[49] In other contexts, code switching can also be participant-related, meaning that 'they [participants] search for an account within the individual who performs this switching, or his or her co-participants.'[50] Sometimes the code switch may serve both functions at the same time, depending on how participants interpret the code switch of the speaker. In the following example, the switch into English has a participant-related function, while at the same time it may be discourse-related.

Example 10

D. Schmidt: Zum Richter gehen und zahlen, weißt du? Das war für Spaß, gell? **It's like a fundraiser**.

Very similar to example 8 above, the discourse-related function here could also be to mark that which is said in English as additional information or an aside. At the same time, the switch could relate to how participants in the interview perceive each other. In particular, D. Schmidt may want to make herself better understood to the interviewer, whom she may perceive as not having the same background knowledge about life in the German club; she may want to help the younger interviewer understand the situation. She thus uses widely understood English vocabulary (*fundraiser*). This interpretation is probable, considering the introduction of the noun phrase by *it's like*. The switch may also be related to the fact that the English *fundraiser* is linguistically more economical than describing this concept in a German paraphrase.

For both discourse-related and participant-related switches, the juxtaposition of the two languages has meaning beyond the information expressed through the words themselves. The juxtaposition functions as a contextualization cue. The notion of a 'contextualization cue,' which comes from Gumperz,[51] refers to the interactants' use of verbal and non-verbal elements to signal how they want their message to be interpreted.

Participants – speakers and listeners – might not even notice the use of a different code. Auer argues that analysts should take this into account[52] and make the distinction between code switches and mere code mixes; also, he defines a mixed code as a code in which elements from two or more languages are mixed so that bilinguals perceive these elements as part of a new code rather than as functional code switches.[53] This is exemplified by a quote from one of our participants (D. Schmidt), who reflects on her language use: '*Wir sagen 'fridge' und 'garbage.' Man denkt gar nicht mehr daran ... Das wa'n englisches Wort und das haben wir gar nich gemerkt.*' Schmidt is asserting that she mixes between German and English – more specifically, that she inserts English words into the German. Furthermore, she says that she does not notice this process of mixing any more, which means that from her perspective, the boundaries between German and English have been lost and a mixed code has emerged, even though an outsider recognizes the English or German origin of words.

Typical for a mixed code is the borrowing of discourse markers from one language into another (see examples 11 below and 2c above). The insertion of discourse markers from one language into another is prevalent in many language-contact situations, including in German-English bilingual communities in the United States.[54] Auer discusses discourse markers as evidence of mixed codes and of advanced bilingualism. Competent bilinguals seamlessly insert discourse markers into stretches of discourse in the other language. Following are examples of discourse marker use from the data:

Example 11

a) A. Meier: Verstehen tun sie ja, nur Sprechen kommt ihnen, *halt*, **you know**, schwerer.

b) B. Meier: Ja, **but** lesen können sie ja nicht so gut wenn's Bücher sind.

c) F. Bauer: Ich bin nur Mitglied da. Ich mach, **well**, wenn man Hilfe braucht und so, ja, aber meistens sind sie Angestellte jetzt.

d) D. Schmidt: Und da waren wir die Dummen **because** er hat Englisch und wir haben Deutsch.

e) C. Schmidt: **Anyway**. Zurückzukommen zu der Müllabfuhr.

In Example 11a, A. Meier uses both a German and an English discourse marker (*halt, you know*), which shows that he, like other bilingual speakers, is equally competent in both languages. In fact, most use discourse markers with identical meaning from both languages. In some cases, a German equivalent is difficult to find or requires much more conversational effort. This is the case with *anyway*, where the reason for the borrowing of the English discourse marker may have been linguistic economy. The examples selected from the data show that similar processes can be observed with all five speakers. However, the number of insertions of English discourse markers into German is very different across the three interviews. While F. Bauer shows only one use of an English discourse marker (the discourse marker 'well'), A. and B. Meier employ a higher number and different kinds of English discourse markers. C. and D. Schmidt exhibit the highest use of English discourse markers. This somewhat corresponds to how relaxed the speakers seem in the interview process. In the interview, C. and D. Schmidt discuss their mixed use of German and English as something that came naturally and that is part of their identity now, rather than as something they do not accept and try to subdue. They seem very relaxed during the interview and do not treat it as a test situation in which an unmixed standard German is required. In contrast, the Meiers and F. Bauer may be striving to show 'good' German in the interviews, feeling that their perceived competence in German is at stake during an interview by a university representative.

Comparing the interviews, one also notices that among all the speakers, C. and D. Schmidt use code switching most often as a functional strategy. This is not surprising, considering that they state that they are comfortable alternating languages. All the speakers heavily use German tags, such as *gell*, *ne*, and *ge*, which indicates a typical conversational ability in German. In fact, the interviews are evidence that the participants can sustain a conversation in German.

Conclusion

In this chapter we have discussed results from a linguistic analysis of interviews with five participants of German-speaking background who live in Kitchener-Waterloo. To situate the linguistic results in the sociocultural context, we have presented information on their cultural background and on general immigration patterns of German-speaking people to Canada. Our analysis of the language these speakers use in the interviews has revealed linguistic phenomena of transfer, code switching, and code mixing.

The results of our analysis are best interpreted within the framework of language acculturation, which takes into account that bilingual speakers converge the two contact languages by making them more similar to each other and thus diverge from the standard of either of these two languages. Both convergence and divergence are processes that are part of our speakers' construction of their identity as German-English bilinguals in Canada. Although there is no simple, universal one-to-one relation between sociocultural identity and linguistic behaviour, phenomena in language use are often rooted in sociocultural identity and this identity is in part constructed through linguistic activities. Our analysis reveals that the speakers do not see a need to keep English out of their German or vice versa. This is in contrast to what participants report in the interviews about their language use in the German-language island – Transylvania and the Danube Basin – where they used to live. This language use was characterized by a stable diglossia. The analysis of the interviews has shown that there is no such diglossic situation for these speakers in Canada; both English and German are used in domains such as home, work, and German social clubs.

The linguistic phenomena discussed in this chapter are a result of the speakers' resourceful use of the contact languages involved. The influence of one language on the other, as seen in the analysis of the phenomenon, often happens without the intention of the speaker. The analysis of the language use of the German-speaking participants in our study has revealed that they make use of their high competence in both German and English. They speak a German variety that is influenced by English. In addition, we have pointed to the possibility that the participants speak a mixed code, though some of the differences among the speakers in that regard may have been due to how they perceived the interview in terms of formality and how familiar they were with the interviewer. A mixed code is considered in the literature on language contact as indicating an advanced stage of bilingualism. It shows that speakers are comfortable with this kind of mixing and, therefore, with the merging of their old and new sociocultural identities into new and creative forms (as expressed through language), so as to allow for others to perceive of their language expression as alluding to a merged identity. The acceptance of such a merged identity in society can be seen in the coining of hyphenated labels such as German-Canadian. Interestingly, the diverse cultural and linguistic backgrounds of our speakers are important when it comes to their labelling of the language they speak at home as either *Sächsisch* (Transylvanian Saxon) or *Schwowisch* (Danube Swabian). However, in the interviews it was more their German-Canadian identity that transpired, as evidenced by the language contact phenomenon. Also, the speakers call themselves German-Canadian in response to the question of their ethnicity, because there are no such labels as Danube Canadian or Transylvanian Canadian.

In summary, we noted that all participants exhibit typical language contact phenomena in their language use. In that regard, their cultural and linguistic environment outside of Germany has influenced their language use and, at the same time, influenced their sociocultural identity, which can be associated largely with the label 'German-Canadian.' While (language) acculturation is the process of adopting and adjusting to the new environment, this process is never unidirectional; rather, it is a complex interrelation of two (or more) languages and cultures. In our data, we have seen ample evidence of the results of such acculturation processes in the construction of something new based on the bilingual resources available to the speakers.

NOTES

1 For a discussion of the terminological difficulties (What *is* German?), see the Introduction in Joachim Born and Sylvia Dickgießer, *Deutschsprachige Minderheiten. Ein Überblick über den Stand der Forschung für 27 Länder* (Mannheim: Institut für deutsche Sprache im Auftrag des Auswärtigen Amtes, 1989), 9–13.
2 Nancy C. Dorian, 'The Problem of the Semi-Speaker in Language Death,' *International Journal of the Sociology of Language* 12 (1977): 23–32.
3 For the terminology discussed here (language death, language loss, language attrition), see Donald Winford, *An Introduction to Contact Linguistics* (Oxford: Basil Blackwell, 2003).
4 See also Monika S. Schmid, *First Language Attrition, Use, and Maintenance* (Amsterdam: John Benjamins, 2002).
5 Braj B. Kachru, 'The Second Diaspora of English,' in *English in its Social Contexts: Essays in Historical Sociolinguistics*, ed. T.W. Machan and C.T. Scott (Oxford: Oxford University Press, 1992), 230–52 at 235.
6 Language acquisition processes are observed predominantly with the descendants of the immigrants.
7 Kachru, 'The Second Diaspora of English,' 235.
8 Ibid.

9 See, for example, Michael G. Clyne, *Dynamics of Language Contact: English and Immigrant Languages* (Cambridge: Cambridge University Press, 2003); and Lesley Milroy and Pieter Muysken, *One Speaker, Two Languages: Cross-Disciplinary Perspectives on Code-Switching* (Cambridge: Cambridge University Press, 1995)

10 Katherine Stenger Frey, *The Danube Swabians: A People with Portable Roots* (Belleville: Mika, 1982), 19.

11 *Die Flucht der Deutschen. Die Spiegel-Serie über Vertreibung aus dem Osten (Spiegel Special 2/2002)* (Hamburg: Spiegel Verlag, 2002), 60.

12 Rick Heli, *Deutsche Genealogie: Donauschwaben im Banat, einschließlich Arader Land*, 2000, accessed 5 April 2012 at http://www.genealogienetz.de/reg/ESE/dsban-d.html.

13 Stephan M. Horak et al., *Eastern European National Minorities, 1919–1980: A Handbook* (Littleton: Libraries Unlimited, 1985), 228.

14 Fritz Wieden and Michael Benzinger, *Canada's Danube Swabians. Kanadas Donauschwaben* (Windsor: St Michael's Church, 1992), 58.

15 Elemér Illyés, *Nationale Minderheiten in Rumänien: Siebenbürgen im Wandel, Ethnos; Bd 23* (Wien: Braumüller, 1981), 7.

16 Horak, *Eastern European National Minorities*, 198.

17 Karl Schlögel, 'Völkerkarussell Mitteleuropa. Bugwelle des Krieges,' in *Die Flucht der Deutschen*, 92.

18 Frey, *The Danube Swabians*, 26. We are quoting to provide some evidence for the existence of such contact phenomena. We do not, however, always concur with the linguistic interpretation of the authors. What is described here as a lack of competence might be an indication of advanced bilingual competence.

19 Horak, *Eastern European National Minorities*, 222.

20 Born and Dickgießer, *Deutschsprachige Minderheiten*, 232.

21 Horak, *Eastern European National Minorities*, 197.

22 For a discussion of levelling and shift processes in Transylvanian dialects, see, for example, Anton Schwob, 'Zu Problemen der Sprecherbewegung und Sprachbewegung. Historische Begleitumstände des Sprachausgleichs in südostdeutschen Sprachinseln,' in *Zur Rechts- und Siedlungsgeschichte der Siebenbürger Sachsen*, ed. Siebenbürgisches Archiv (Köln und Wien: Böhlau Verlag, 1971).

23 Born and Dickgießer, *Deutschsprachige Minderheiten*, 176.

24 For example, 'Nicht gib das Buch auf den Tisch.' 'Steh ein wenig auf die Seite.' Walrus Schuller, *Die Mundart der Siebenbürger Sachsen* (1999), accessed 5 April 2012 at http://www.siebenbuerger-sachsen-bw.de/buch/sachsen/12.htm.

25 Patrick Ongley and David Pearson, 'Post-1945 International Migration: New Zealand, Australia, and Canada Compared,' *International Migration Review* 29, no. 3 (1995): 765–93 at 767.
26 Ibid., 770.
27 Louis Parai, 'Canada's Immigration Policy, 1962–74,' *International Migration Review* 9, no. 4 (1975): 449–77 at 455.
28 Donald Avery, *Reluctant Host: Canada's Response to Immigrant Workers, 1896–1994* (Toronto: McClelland and Stewart, 1995), 145, 158, 166; Citizenship and Immigration Canada and Statistics Canada, *Profiles Germany: German Immigrants in Canada, Immigration Research Series* (Ottawa: Statistics Canada, 1996).
29 John English and Kenneth McLaughlin, *Kitchener: An Illustrated History* (Waterloo: Wilfrid Laurier University Press, 1983), 246–7.
30 Klaus H. Bongart, 'Deutsch in Ontario, II: Deutsche Sprache und Kultur in Kitchener-Waterloo,' in *Deutsch als Muttersprache in Kanada. Berichte zur Gegenwartslage*, ed. Leopold Auburger and Heinz Kloss (Wiesbaden: Franz Steiner Verlag, 1977), 26. Wolfgang G. Friedmann, *German Immigration to Canada* (Toronto: Ryerson Press, 1952), is an example of how German immigration to Canada was viewed at the time.
31 Statistics Canada, *Census of Canada: Profile of Languages in Canada: English, French, and Many Others* (Ottawa: Statistics Canada. Cat. no. 96F0030XIE2001005, 2002).
32 Ibid., 20.
33 Ibid. 'Allophone' is the term used by Statistics Canada for persons with a language other than French or English.
34 Lori Theresa Heffner, 'Heritage Languages: The Case of German in Kitchener-Waterloo,' MA thesis, University of Waterloo, 2002.
35 German here refers to the matrix language that is the dominant language of a discourse; see Carol Myers-Scotton, *Contact Linguistics: Bilingual Encounters and Grammatical Outcomes* (Oxford: Oxford University Press, 2002).
36 We use pseudonyms consisting of initial and an invented surname to identify the interviewees.
37 Dirk Hoerder, 'German-Speaking Immigrants of Many Backgrounds,' in *Austrian Immigration to Canada: Selected Essays*, ed. Franz A.J. Szabo (Ottawa: Carleton University Press, 1996), 14, 18.
38 Traude Horvath and Gerda Neyer, 'Austrians Abroad: Austrian Emigration after 1945,' in ibid.; Gunther Beyer, 'The Political Refugee: 35 Years Later,' *International Migration Review* 15, nos. 1–2 (1981): 26–34 at 29.
39 Clyne, *Dynamics of Language Contact*, 76. We find that the one term 'trans-

fer' is sufficient to capture both process and result. Consequently, we do not use 'transference' as Clyne does.

40 Clyne, *Dynamics of Language Contact*, 103–58.

41 Myers-Scotton, *Contact Linguistics*.

42 Deborah Schiffrin, *Discourse Markers* (Cambridge: Cambridge University Press, 1987), 31.

43 For a discussion on German word order in subordinate clauses, see, for example, Christoph Kuper, 'Is Subordinate Clause Order Being Lost in German? On the Pragmatic Function of Word Order in Main and Subordinate Clauses,' *Deutsche Sprache* 19, no. 2 (1991): 133–58.

44 Johannes Schwitalla, *Gesprochenes Deutsch. Eine Einführung* (Berlin: Erich Schmidt Verlag, 2006).

45 Thanks to an anonymous reviewer for pointing this out.

46 Giovanna Alfonzetti, 'Conversational Dimension in Code-Switching between Italian and Dialect in Sicily,' in *Code-switching in Conversation: Language, Interaction, and Identity*, ed. Peter Auer (London: Routledge, 1998).

47 Erving Goffman, 'Footing,' *Semiotica* 25, nos. 1–2 (1979): 1–29.

48 Alfonzetti, 'Conversational Dimension in Code-Switching,' 8.

49 Peter Auer, 'Introduction: Bilingual Conversation Revisited,' in *Code-Switching in Conversation*, ed. Auer, 4.

50 Ibid., 8.

51 John Joseph Gumperz, *Discourse Strategies* (Cambridge: Cambridge University Press, 1982), 131.

52 Peter Auer, 'The Pragmatics of Code Switching: A Sequential Approach,' in *One Speaker, Two Languages: Cross-Disciplinary Perspectives on Code-Switching*, ed. Lesley Milroy and Pieter Muysken (Cambridge: Cambridge University Press, 1995), 117.

53 Auer, 'Introduction: Bilingual Conversation Revisited,' 15.

54 Emily L. Goss and Joseph Salmons, 'The Evolution of Bilingual Discourse Marking: Modal Particles and English Markers in 19th Century German-American Dialects,' *International Journal of Bilingualism* 4, no. 4 (December 2000): 469–94; Joseph Salmons, 'Bilingual Discourse Marking: Codeswitching, Borrowing, and Convergence in Some German-American Dialects,' *Linguistics* 28, no. 3 (1990): 453–80.

12 Reimagining German-Canadians: Reflections on Past Deconstructions and Literary Evidence

MYKA BURKE

Too often the damaging mirror of reality is banned,
because it tends to tarnish the 'ideal image.'

Georg K. Epp

A review of scholarly literature on 'German-Canadians' reveals that a German-Canadian cultural identity is considered by some to be a 'verifiable historical phenomenon'[1] and by others to be impossible.[2] Indeed, several scholarly articles and essays broach the thorny subject of categorization. For example, in 1983, David Artiss wrote an article titled 'Who Are the German-Canadians – One Group or Several?' In the same volume, Manfred Richter's article looks at the Canadian census and social sciences to answer this question: 'Who Are the German-Canadians?' K.M. McLaughlin's 1985 *The Germans in Canada* traced the diverse origins of German-Canadians. In 1998, *A Chorus of Different Voices* featured several articles that addressed the seemingly pivotal question 'One group or many'?[3] Many publications have sketched the countless paths that Germans have followed to Canada.[4] Several other publications have focused on the German presence in specific cities or regions in Canada and during specific time frames. Scholars have presented various arguments to back up their views on what German-Canadian excludes or includes. What we *know* is that German – in a Canadian context – has been used to refer to people with diverse citizenships, regional identities, and religious affiliations and with, outwardly, only one common characteristic – the German language as their mother tongue.

Poignantly, Canadianist and literary scholar Enoch Padolsky has suggested that these kinds of difficulties regarding categorization, and their accompanying limitations and ambiguities, may be 'necessary stages in the development of ideas.'[5] He recommends an overt examination of the categories as well as an analysis of how they have failed to correspond to the complexity of the lived realities of those in question. Accordingly, an attempt to anthropomorphize and contextualize German-Canadian cultural identity is behind this exploration, which looks to the realm of creative writing by German-Canadians to humanize the notion of a German-Canadian cultural identity, and which attempts to transcend the 'name game' in order to examine the complexity of elements and dimensions involved when cultures merge, evolve, and change.

These writers' reflections on their 'life projects' from their 'transcultural spaces' – as historian Dirk Hoerder terms them – serve as material for researchers' investigations of different aspects of the immigrant experience, of the processes involved when cultures evolve and merge, and of reflections on the world at large during specific periods of time from unique points of view. Literary critic Maya Dutt summarizes as follows: 'Literature reflects the times, and immigrant literary texts serve as major points of reference for the dual purpose of exploring and evaluating the different racial, cultural, religious, and value orientations that are in the process of evolving and merging with one another and with mainstream culture. The texts are in fact authoritative cultural studies.'[6]

Poet and visionary scholar Smaro Kamboureli[7] would certainly add that 'particular communities and individuals resist being subsumed into a single narrative; instead, they demand that we address their cultural, historical, and ideological specificities.' Thus, it is my conviction that our understanding of German-Canadian cultural identity can only benefit from the authoritative insights provided by German-Canadian writers in their creative writing. Their views on German and Canadian, themselves, others, the past, the present, cultural identity, place, race, gender, sexuality, language, age, class, and time will augment any study of what German-Canadian may be – provided that context and processes are recognized and considered.

In this chapter, the literature by German-Canadians is situated in the context of all ethnic literature in Canada. This is followed by contrastive and comparative treatments of discourse and literary subject matter, and then by a brief sketch of the interconnected nature of discourse on German-Canadian identity and the treatment of their literature by researchers. The empirical evidence that follows focuses on three main issues: the new diaspora, language, and Canada and Germany. Welcoming the categorically disruptive, I read these texts for their critical comment on the conceptual categories that conventional scholarship has used to 'manage' the disorderliness and ambiguity of German-Canadian narratives of experience.

Ethnic Literature

> Writing is translating from inside out.
> It is listening to what is already known and written inside the mind.
>
> Verena Stefan

There are many paradigms for contextualizing ethnic literature. Hungarian-Canadian literary critic Georg Bisztray's five dimensions for literature not written in one of Canada's two official languages provides several useful trajectories for its study: it belongs to world literature, to the literature of the country of origin, to the national literature of the new country, to the other immigrant literatures of the new country, and to the literature of the same language group in other countries. In this treatment of German-Canadian literature, the most significant dimension will be its belonging 'to other immigrant literatures of the new country.'[8] With this in mind, it is interesting to consider the broad *Canadian Encyclopedia* definition of ethnic Canadian literature: it includes all creative writing both in non-official languages and in translation; writing by those who consider themselves part of an ethnic minority and who write from this perspective; and literary texts by non-ethnics that deal with 'the' ethnic or immigrant experience.[9] It has often happened that multicultural studies of Canadian literature embrace more restricted schemes and only consider those texts by writers not considered members of the dominant anglophone or francophone culture. What, then, can German-Canadian literature be?

For many reasons, German-Canadian literature is a difficult body of writing to discuss. Sociopolitical approaches to German-Canadian and Canadian literary categorization have loaded the analytical tools being used to describe this kind of writing. Scholars have used this category to refer to all types of writing in various German dialects, in High German, in English, and in French – sometimes even by the same writer – when written in Canada. The term German-Canadian has often been used generously to refer to those whose native language is German, regardless of country of origin, and whose permanent residence is Canada. As noted above, for example, 'Germany,' writes literary scholar John Considine, is 'shorthand for all the communities of German-speaking Europe.' But even this inclusive definition is restrictive. It does not account for those writers who grew up in two languages, like Uta Regoli, or those who grew up outside of Central Europe (e.g., in the United States) before coming to Canada. In an effort to be concise, the definition would have to be broadened to include those people with German as one of their native languages. Furthermore, people of 'German' descent who cannot speak or write German are also often considered to be German-Canadian.[10]

A peripheral glimpse at Arabic-Canadians and their literature shows that the problems arising from this kind of categorization are not unique to German-Canadian literary discourse. Research on Arabic-Canadian writers has focused on thirty-five writers from six countries. These writers are often trilingual; also, they have various religious backgrounds and multiple ethnic origins, and they remain relatively isolated from one another in Canada. What they do share are similar professions: almost all of these writers hold public functions – five have taught at or headed departments at Canadian universities.[11] The parallels with German-Canadian writers are dramatic. For example, albeit over a much longer period of time, German-Canadian creative literature has been written by professors and teachers like Elisabeth von Ah, Angelika Arend, Walter Bauer, Henry Beissel, Hermann Böschenstein, Hans Eichner, Wolfgang Franke, Abram Friesen, Hans-Jürgen Greif, Konrad Haderlein, Helga Kleer, Petra von Morstein, Ernst Loeb, Elisabeth Mann Borgese, Suzette Mayr, Walter Roome, Hartwig Roosch, Kurt Schleiermacher, and Verena Stefan.[12] These writers, too, have various religious backgrounds and multiple ethnic origins, and they remain more or less isolated from one another in Canada.

With regard to Italian-Canadian writing, writer and literary critic Joseph Pivato has noticed that this 'literature is different from mainstream Canadian writing because it demonstrates not only a consciousness of another country, Italy, but also an attachment to it.'[13] The same can certainly be said for German-Canadian writing with reference to the writer's particular country of origin. Yet what may be different with German-Canadian texts is the new evaluation of their old world from a distance.[14]

It is imperative to mention that cross-minority literary research of Canadian ethnic literature is gaining momentum but is not quite at the stage where conclusive remarks can be made. The reasons for this are varied. Ukrainian-Canadian literary critic Jars Balan, for example, regarding research on Ukrainian-Canadian plays, states that investigations of primary sources are usually only superficial, which makes it difficult to draw authoritative conclusions.[15] And as noted by historian Christiane Harzig in her contribution to this volume, this type of result is not necessarily due to a lack of interest but may be due to 'different research trajectories.' Nevertheless, it must be asked why the various scholars interested in German-Canadian cultural identity have continually overlooked these writers as authoritative mediators of their own cultural identity.

Nonetheless, the existence of German-language writing from Canada can no longer be debated.[16] Even a cursory survey of early German-Canadian literature renders untenable the position that it is a recent phenomenon. Questions regarding the quality of this literature may be another matter. There are, undeniably, academics who would argue that there are at most only a few good writers writing creatively in German in Canada, that the bulk of their texts do not warrant study or collection, and that the same standards applicable to 'Germanistik' (e.g., methodology, theory) should be applied here. There are, indisputably, other academics who recognize the importance of collecting these texts and making them available for literary, linguistic, and cultural study regardless of their supposedly insignificant 'literary' value to Germanistik (German Studies) – which is not to deny that many of these texts do possess high 'literary' value. This is in keeping with the premise that in order to anthropomorphize and humanize the idea of German-Canadian cultural identity and transcend questions of categorization, more research should be devoted to and incorporate this creative writing.

German-Canadian Identity and Literature

> In a sense, we haven't got an identity
> until somebody tells our story.
> The fiction makes us real.
>
> Robert Kroetsch

The enigmatic elements of any Canadian cultural identity have prompted a plethora of comments on what is 'Canadian.' Comments range from ambiguity[17] to not American or British[18] to the geopolitically subjective.[19] In 1983 and 1998, German-Canadian scholars Walter Riedel and Matthias Zimmer noted that both components of German-Canadian bring with them their own demons that render complex and difficult any attempt to study these people. Germanist Peter Liddell, also in 1983, observed: 'German Canadian (with or without the hyphen?) is controversial enough ... to need constant definition.'[20] A label like German-Canadian suggests many things in addition to being Canadian (e.g., born in Germany, Austria, or someplace where German is the predominant language, or being of German descent or a native speaker of German).[21] Furthermore, the evasive and seemingly interchangeable labels 'Germans in Canada,' 'Canada's Germans,' 'German Canadians,' and 'German-Canadians' make it much too easy to 'emphasize one identity to the near exclusion of the other.'[22] Granted, with multiple identities and varieties of identities becoming the norm, the idea of dichotomous symmetry becomes increasingly problematic.[23] Moreover, the seemingly innocent Canadian hyphen, as in 'German-Canadian,' creates a vague place that both 'compounds difference and underlines sameness.'[24] In his essay 'Half-Bred Poetics,' Canadian writer Fred Wah further reveals the implication of the Canadian hyphen: 'Though it is in the middle, it is not in the center. It is a property marker, a boundary post, a borderland, a bastard, a railroad, a last spike, a stain, a cipher, a rope, a knot, a chain (link), a foreign word, a warning sign, a "head tax," a bridge, a no-man's land, a nomadic, floating magic carpet, now you see it now you don't.'[25]

Wah concludes that the hybrid writer must work at creating poetic tools of 'disturbance, dislocation, and displacement' in order to become audible and visible.[26] Or, as German-Canadian writer Uta Regoli formulates it: 'a language / that has an echo,'[27] *audible* and *visible* being other words for being heard, understood, 'taken seriously' or 'counting.' In essence, these writers are telling us that 'labels hide as much as they reveal'[28] and that it may be more pertinent to listen to or hear what 'they' are trying to tell us before we attempt to categorize them.

Through their poetry and prose, these writers also help mutate conventional concepts of Canadian and world history and institute a 'multitude of alternative versions'[29] of the past and the present. For example, as the two dissentient renditions of 'O Canada' below illustrate, the German-Canadian experience (Klassen) can be very different from the African-Canadian experience (Bailey):

Oh Canada, my homeland
To you I make my pledge

[...]
to be your loyal citizen
With word and deed and life
[...]
Your freedom after heavy chains,
How do I praise the day
When I made that glorious gain:
Here I am free to pray [...]

                    Peter J. Klassen, *Mein Bekenntnis* [30]

        You can keep your English bigots!
And your dumb Frenchmen too!
[...]
Oh Canada!
I will not stand on guard
for thee
You treat your native Blacks
and Indians like they have leprosy
or some other bad disease [...]

                    Peter A. Bliss Bailey, *Oh Canada* [31]

Yet German-Canadian ethnic experiences can also overlap, as these quotes from Ulrich Schaffer and Suzette Mayr demonstrate:

Our deepest yearning is nothing else
than to be meant
by someone, somewhere,
– and to finally count. [32]

All about choices and having no choices. All about shouting your presence to the world. I am not invisible. I deserve eye contact and to be taken seriously. [33]

'O Canada,' the Canadian national anthem, has often been reinvented by German-Canadian writers over the years. [34] Their sentiment that Canada has provided them with safety and freedom is not echoed by Bailey's version. Schaffer, a successful German-Canadian writer, and Suzette Mayr, a successful Caribbean-German-Canadian writer and professor, express the same sentiment in their writing: that they/their characters deserve a place in the arena of importance.

Georg K. Epp, in reference to Mennonite writers in Canada, stated that the Canadian ethnic writer will have to 'contend with critics who frequently do not understand him, and only too often the author's severest critics come from his own background.'[35] This certainly holds true for the group deemed German-Canadian. Statements such as the following are quite common: 'a colourful array of writings ranging from some good poetry to rhymes by amateur-poets and immigrants snivelling about their lost homeland or singing the praises of a newly found one.'[36] The first rendition of 'O Canada' quoted above would seem to be one such example. However, an understanding of how much literature has been produced and what these people write about has often evaded scholarly focus.[37] Instead, scholars have focused on those writers who have published most of their literary texts in English, with Felix Paul Greve (alias Frederick Philip Grove), Robert Kroetsch, and Rudy Wiebe in the lead. The essay collection *Refractions of Germany in Canadian Literature and Culture* (2003), for example, included essays on Virgil Gheorghiu's *The Twenty-fifth Hour*, Rudy Wiebe's novels, A.M. Klein's works, Henry Kreisel's *Betrayal*, Leonard Cohen's Holocaust poetry, Mavis Gallant's fiction, Suzette Mayr's *The Widows*, Jane Urquhart's *The Stone Carvers*, and Goethe's *Faust* in Canada. Robert Kroetsch contributed an essay on his own situation, and there is also a section on Jack Thiessen's 'Mennonite Dictionaries.' References to writers of German-language creative writing and creative writing in French by native speakers of German were largely absent. The spectrum of study of German-Canadian literature also includes works by many Mennonite writers as well as by Walter Bauer, Else Seel, Carl Weiselberger, and Charles Wassermann.[38] Literary texts by women have only recently been the focus of a few studies,[39] and most texts by authors writing in German have remained completely unstudied. A list of Canadian writers who have written creatively in German and had their works published since 1970 would easily top sixty and include the *Wie Gottlieb Hauptmann die Todesstrafe abschaffte Erzählungen*[40] by Thomas Mann's daughter Elisabeth Mann Borgese as well as the award-winning Swiss-Canadian playwright Kurt Hutterli, the wildly successful Ulrich Schaffer, and the legendary feminist/lesbian writer Verena Stefan – to name only a few.

According to Heinz Kloss, the misguided alienation of German writing in Canada by literary critics Kühn, Guthke, and others may perhaps be a matter of applying inappropriate (*Germanistik*) categories to this literature.[41] Also, the study of immigrant literature in Canada seems to have taken a detour around German-language literature and halted at partly acknowledging its existence. The manner in which these writers weave the elements of their lives and their identities into their stories and draw from here and there, then and now, this language and that language, to create truly insightful stories reveals the complex processes involved in forming a new cultural identity.

Margaret Atwood reminds us of the importance of place (and time) in literature: 'Literature is not only a mirror; it is ... the product of who and where we have been.' She further states that 'we need to know about here, because here is where we live.'[42] German-language Canadian literature does read like a geographic dictionary, one in which places and their meanings are defined. Cultural expression, like art, arguably cultivates a more discerning and dimensional sense of place and region than scientific geographical methods.[43] The subjective and emotionally charged awareness of place among the displaced automatically incorporates an element of time, because this awareness is part of their cultural inventory and colours their perceptions of here and now. For example, the Klassen rendition of 'O Canada': 'Your freedom after heavy chains, / [...] / Here I am free to pray.'

But what about those who have not been displaced? In Regoli's 'New Immigrants' cycle of poems, it is the 'spiritual paralysis of our contemporary world'[44] that the new immigrants search to overcome. For example:

> What kind of people are they
> who are free
> and not hungry,
> who shun reckless adventures
> and yet leave their native land?
> Do they think DISTANCE?
> Do they think NEW or MORE?
> Or do they think GLOBAL VILLAGE? [...][45]

From the many odes to Canada, Canadian cities, lakes, rivers, and unique regions, these 'new immigrants' are voicing critiques of local, national, and global environmental disregard and of societal and cultural imbalances. For example, Loeb's poem 'Natur und Kunst, 1985': 'But Art remains: a flamingo, / it replaces, what has been stolen. / Nature (even Goethe's Gingko), / is demystified and leafless.' Or Regoli's poem: 'Art has become merchandise – in over-supply.' And again in 'Montreal': 'A stone growth / composed of monoliths of longing, / encased in glass and coffins, / an obstacle to the wind, / [...] / three days of walking / to cross poor rich poor poor rich.'[46] The search for more human compassion in a globalized world continues to feed their writing.

German-Canadian writing, despite societal and cultural critique, often also has a leitmotif of spiritual rebirth for those who persevere. Some examples: In 'New Start,' Regoli simply becomes 'nova' (new). In Weiselberger's 'Kain und Abel in Kanada,' Abel is reborn, like the phoenix, in the embers of the Northern Lights. Walter Bauer claims that he was born when he came to Canada. Clotilde in *The Widows*, after going over Niagara Falls in a space-age barrel, says that 'one minute I was dead, the next minute I was alive.'[47] In some stories, however, the characters do not make it. Their past kills them. For example, in 'Die Zauberinsel,' Ernst's violent past is objectified as an old revolver that he uses to commit suicide.[48] The gap(s) between their worlds, rare though they are, sometimes just cannot be bridged.

The New Diaspora

No matter where I am
On our planet
the edge is also the centre.
–Uta Regoli

Most communities in Canada today, indeed in the world, include diasporic elements. Clifford lists as diasporic elements 'a history of dispersal, myths/memories of the homeland, alienation in the host (bad host?) country, desire for eventual return, ongoing support of the homeland, and a collective identity importantly defined by this relationship.' The mechanisms employed to expose and explore the 'asymmetrical relations of power' in a framework of 'cultural and social displacement, transnational dialogues and diversified forms of cultural contacts' often fail.[49] Diasporic dimensions of experience can be felt and revealed in many ways. For the women writers in this survey, the body serves as a vessel on and through which the 'new diaspora' is felt and revealed. The contradictory role played by Canada in the creation/abolition of diasporic elements has been the subject of several German-Canadian narratives. To problematize the traditional, accepted, and forgotten, these writers draw attention to their own unique experiences. Beyond the literary strategy employed by Uta Regoli in *Briefe auf Birkenbast* and Suzette Mayr in *The Widows* – a strategy that itself displays a mesh of the past and the present – both writers frame their work with quotations from authentic reports. Regoli selects quotations from Margaret Atwood and poetically 'writes' to Susanna Moodie. Mayr chooses reports about actual (vs fictional) attempts to go over Niagara Falls and concentrates on Annie Edson Taylor's life. In both cases, the real women of the past become part of the story. Their texts distil female experiences. For example: 'You are a free woman, Hannelore lied.' And of being an old woman, Mayr says: 'No one wanted to pay eighty dollars to see an old and bitter woman tell the world like it was, how she had no place because no one would give her any room.'[50] These writers also draw attention to the treatment of women and older women in Canadian society by playing with the chronology of events in their texts. 'Prolog '85' by Regoli, for example, is a reference to 1885 and 1985 – 1885 is the year Susanna Moodie died, and 1985 is the year Regoli wrote the poems of *Letters on Birchbark*. Mayr, besides jumping back and forth between the time within the story and actual attempts to go over the Falls, also presents multiple narratives like streams of consciousness flowing down the page together – much like the water of the Falls – while the women are in the Niagara Ball going over the Falls. Their voices are those of the marginalized: old, lesbian, and immigrant. Furthermore, fact and fiction collide to problematize the accepted versions of the past.

German-Canadian – Language Wor(l)d?

> I spent more than four fifths of my life in and between two languages.
> I did not know, that one day language and metaphors would become a home for me.
>
> Ulrich Schaffer

The term 'Canfusion' (Canada, fusion, and confusion) helps describe the ambiguity that permeates German-Canadian discourse. As noted earlier, a German-Canadian cultural identity is considered by some to be a 'verifiable historical phenomenon' and by others to be impossible. Indeed, many articles, essays, and studies broach the subject. In the 1990s, the exploration of literature, history, the social sciences, and the Canadian census by Artiss, Richter, and McLaughlin was expanded to an even broader range of disciplines by Angelika Sauer, Matthias Zimmer, Dirk Hoerder, and a group of younger scholars.[51]

Increasingly, such studies have problematized the notion of dichotomous symmetry; in reference to the group deemed German-Canadian, perhaps this has always has been so. We know that 'German' – in a Canadian context – has been used to refer to a diversity of people whose mother tongue is German. The range of external German markers, from the visibly invisible to the flamboyantly flagrant, seems to undermine any attempt to refer to these people as one group.

The German language has been considered by many German-Canadian writers and scholars[52] to be a significant factor in the maintenance and evidence of a German-Canadian cultural identity as well as an avenue through which loss of this identity can be at least partly avoided. Over the past few decades, German-Canadian writers have been particularly interested in the significance of the German language and in language in general. In Wiebe's novel *Peace Shall Destroy Many*, we are constantly reminded that the main characters speak Low and High German; use of English and Cree signals persons 'outside' the group.[53] Neuendorff's play *Und keiner hört hin* (*And Nobody Listens*, 1982) presents a family divided by the English and German languages.[54] Many poems attest to how torn these people are between languages as well as by time and place. Schaffer, for example, writes:

I don't have what I once had.
All shapes have shifted.
Words have dissolved,
the wisdom, the rules, the systems,
the various gospels – they have all gone.
[...]
In the process I myself am ground to fine flour
between the two large stones
of the mill I have chosen.[55]

Or, as Uta Regoli in *Letters on Birchbark* wrote: 'we're always only half here. / We eat from at least two tables: / comparisons never end. / The heart halved /. the head somewhere else than the foot.' Being torn between languages and place can certainly be considered one common sentiment these writers express. It is interesting that these writers do not ponder the question, 'One group or many?' For example, Robert Kroetsch begins his essay 'Occupying Landscape We Occupy Story We Occupy Landscape' with this sentence: 'I am a Canadian writer. I am of German descent. We live as well as write in just such middles. That is our predicament. And our good fortune.'[56] Whether in command of the

German language or not, these writers feel and express their German-ness and Canadianness. Robert Kroetsch's family made their way to Canada from southern Germany through the United States some 150 years ago. Uta Regoli's parents were German and Dutch. Neuendorff was born in Estonia and moved to Canada by way of Germany. The question begs to be asked: Have we researchers been focusing on a peripheral question for too long?

For these writers – many of whom have been completely ignored by critical investigations – their provocative focus on language as experience and on process as complex and contradictory serves to challenge the conventional ways we imagine them and read their poetry and prose. Moreover, it suggests that the use of the German language is more than a relic feature of their cultural landscape, that it transcends traditional religious and political divisions and is a vital component of their complex cultural identity.

Canada and Germany

Two solitudes thrown together by chance[?]

Uta Regoli

It has been observed that *being* Canadian is much easier than *defining* 'Canadian.' Writer Lawrence Hill calls Canada 'the true north, proud and vague.' The existence of ambivalent elements of Canadian cultural identity can also be witnessed in the winning phrase 'as Canadian as possible, under the circumstances.'[57] This is not to say that many have not tried – even profitably – to be more transparent on the subject of Canadian cultural identity. For example, the particularly successful 'I Am Canadian!' Molson beer commercial, besides promoting the *'consume ergo sum'* / consuming nations philosophy, paralleled the Canada/U.S. Siamese-twin syndrome: Canadian patriotism equals anti-Americanism.[58] Yet on a deeper level, the frustration expressed in the 'rant' did, and perhaps still does, echo the not uncommon sentiment that Canada and Canadians are being forced to take the back seat while Americans drive. With this in mind, this section focuses briefly on a few defining moments and aspects of American influence on Canadian, 'German,' and German-Canadian culture and history to illustrate some parallels of experience and to reveal some decisive and thus far quite unstudied factors in reference to the German-Canadian case.

In Washington in 1969, Canadian Prime Minister Pierre Elliott Tru-

deau expressed his view on the subject of Canada's geopolitical proximity to the United States: 'Living next to you is in some ways like
sleeping with an elephant; no matter how friendly and even-tempered
is the beast, if I may call it that, one is affected by every twitch and
grunt.' And in 1987, Margaret Atwood expressively described the
Canadian 'survival' of the cultural penetration from the south:

> Canada as a separate but dominated country has done about as well
> under the U.S. as women, worldwide, have done under men; about the
> only position they've ever adopted towards us, country to country, has
> been the missionary position, and we're not on top. I guess that's why the
> national wisdom vis-à-vis Them has so often taken the form of lying still,
> keeping your mouth shut, and pretending you like it.

It is noteworthy that as global opinion divides into 'with the Americans
or against the Americans,' many nations, regardless of their stance, continue to embrace American pop culture and have internalized so many
elements of America that the pre-emigration effects of this long-standing American presence likely play a role in post-immigration behaviour.
For example, the American Declaration of Independence was the most
often quoted document in German legal documentation after the Second World War, and other aspects, such as German TV programming,
fast food restaurant choices, and vocabulary ('Anglizismen') would
seem to make it more difficult to differentiate between American and
German.[59] Therefore, as with 'Canadian,' any questions of what 'German' is today must also consider American influences and elements.

Though relatively few references to the United States can be found
in German-Canadian literature, it may be more imperative to consider
the fact that references are from a German *and* a Canadian perspective.
For example, Suzette Mayr's character Clotilde in *The Widows* refers to
Americans from a German point of view: 'Americans, says Clotilde.
She remembers how when the Americans arrived a lot of people waved
from the windows and the great wave of amnesia descended forever.'
Mayr, again in *The Widows*, from a Canadian point of view: 'friendly
tourists in American flag leather jackets'; 'My daughter is half American. Don't you slag Americans.' Regoli's poem cites a Canadian perspective: 'A glance at the map shows / that we cling to an invisible line
/ seeking to be protected by our neighbours to the south.'

In summary, the cultural influence of the United States on Germany
and Canada may differ only in geographic proximity yet still have pre-

emigration and post-immigration effects that, though they have not been the major focus of scholarly research, nonetheless exist. German-Canadian literature, albeit minimally, does reflect the global presence of America; and most important, it does so from more than one geographical or historical perspective.

Conclusion

> The leap across the ocean
> brought about a mutation.

Uta Regoli

German-Canadian literature has a long history with a recent crystallization. It is considered a distinctive canon by this researcher, for it draws upon a variety of cultural (and 'national') traditions, accents, and languages. Though I have not discussed themes in this article in great detail, the literature probes identity issues surrounding gender, sexuality, language, race, class, and religion. Perhaps its most persistent quality has been its tendency to appropriate the autobiographically inspired and to transubstantiate it into narrative forms.

Through their stories, German-Canadian writers transform, reinvent, and reimagine themselves, engage in linguistic metamorphosis, and negotiate and mediate their many identities. Their literary texts are their instruments and vehicles and, therefore, authoritative cultural reports that successively need to be incorporated into mainstream (non-literary) German-Canadian discourse on identity. Furthermore, the reference to 'reimagining' in the title of this contribution intends to both acknowledge the imagination of these writers and recognize how they imagine themselves in their literary texts.

Political science professor David Cameron could not have encapsulated the Canadian situation any better: 'To live in Canada, to live as a Canadian, is to experience multiple loyalties and in some measure to inhabit different spheres of identity.'[60] For German-Canadians, the unique nature of their cultural and social displacement, with both internal and external factors, has initiated dialogue between these people and the scholars studying them. The manner in which they inhabit different spheres of identity is largely a result of the diverse processes affecting their multiple identities. We know that diversified forms of cultural contacts affect members of different groups differently. The numerous examples from their literature have made it possible to explore previously hidden or buried elements of their existence and facilitate a more anthropomorphized and contextualized exploration of the factors affecting these processes. Furthermore, the questionable reliability of reference documentation when dealing with the marginalized and victimized in general as well as regarding ethnic Canadians, and to some degree German-Canadians, would seem to validate the need for their poetic efforts; by problematizing 'accepted' versions of the past and present (e.g., Mayr's The Widows, Regoli's Letters on Birchbark, Klassen's 'Oh Canada,' Schaffer's poems, and so on), these writers are helping create lasting stratagems that will ensure their visibility and audibility. As they help articulate new identities in the midst of cultural shifts, they are opening up new venues through their writing through which they can discuss issues of gender, race, sexuality, class, identity, and culture. Their writing can be characterized as documents of cultural protest and mediation that give voice to a complex and multidimensional group. They remind us that 'the immigrant experience is an ongoing process in which we all participate.'[61]

NOTES

1 Gerhard P. Bassler, 'German-Canadian Identity in Historical Perspective,' in A Chorus of Different Voices: German-Canadian Identities, ed. Angelika E. Sauer and Matthias Zimmer (New York: Peter Lang, 1998), 85–98 at 86.
2 Matthias Zimmer, for example, claims that a distinct German-Canadian identity does not and cannot exist. Matthias Zimmer, 'Deconstructing German-Canadian Identity,' in A Chorus of Different Voices, ed. Sauer and Zimmer, 21–39.
3 David Artiss, 'Who Are the German-Canadians – One Ethnic Group or Several?' in German-Canadian Studies: Critical Approaches, ed. Peter G. Liddell (Vancouver: CAUTG, 1983); 49–55; Manfred Richter, 'Who Are the German-Canadians?' in ibid., 42–8; K.M. McLaughlin, The Germans in Canada (Ottawa: Canadian Historical Association, 1985); Sauer and Zimmer, A Chorus of Different Voices.
4 See, for example, the following by Dirk Hoerder: 'German-Speaking Immigrants [in Canada]: Co-Founders or Mosaic? A Research Note on Politics and Statistics in Scholarship,' Zeitschrift der Gesellschaft für Kanadastudien 14, no. 2 (1994): 51–65; 'German-Speaking Immigrants of Many

Backgrounds and the 1990s Canadian Identity,' in *Austrian Immigration to Canada: Selected Essays*, ed. Franz Szabo (Ottawa: Cambridge University Press, 1996), 11–31; and 'The German-Canadian Experience Viewed through Life Writings, 1850s to 1930s,' in *A Chorus of Different Voices*, ed. Sauer and Zimmer, 99–117.

5 Enoch Padolsky, 'Italian-Canadian Writing and Ethnic Minority/Majority Binary: Paci's *Black Madonna* and Atwood's *Lady Oracle*,' in *Social Pluralism and Literary History: The Literature of the Italian Emigration*, ed. Francesco Loriggio (Toronto: Guernica Editions, 1994), 248–68 at 249.

6 Maya Dutt, 'The Multicultural Wheel: The Texture of Canadian Society and Literature in the Twenty-First Century,' in *The Canadian Distinctiveness into the Twenty-First Century*, ed. Chad Gaffield and Karen L. Gould (Ottawa: University of Ottawa Press: 2003), 183–96 at 184.

7 Kamboureli quoted in Sandra Regina Goulart Almeida, 'Transcultural Fictions in the Americas: Women Writers in Canada, The United States, and Brazil,' paper presented at the ICCS Transculturalisms Conference, Montreal, May 2003, 4.

8 George Bisztray, *Hungarian-Canadian Literature* (Toronto: University of Toronto Press, 1987).

9 'Ethnic Literature,' *The Canadian Encyclopedia*, 2007.

10 Liddell, *German-Canadian Studies*.

11 Elizabeth Dahab, 'Voices of Exile: The Trilingual Odyssey of Canadian Writers of Arabic Origins,' *Canadian Review of Comparative Literature* 28, no. 1 (March 2001) 48–69.

12 In addition to works mentioned throughout, see also Wolfgang E. Franke, *Über die Schwelle vom Hakenkreuz durch den Roten Stern zum Ahornblatt* (Toronto: self-published, 1997); and Abraham Friesen, *Aus Gottes linker Hand: Stimme eines Irrenden* (Toronto: GCHA, 1995);

13 Joseph Pivato, 'What Is Italian-Canadian Writing?' accessed 17 April 2007 at http://www.athabascau.ca/cll/research/hisitcan.htm#what.

14 Myka Burke, 'From Kanada to Canada: Translating Canada in German-Canadian Literature,' *German-Canadian Yearbook* 18 (2005): 153–60.

15 Jars Balan, 'Old World Forms, New Settings: The Emergence of Ukrainian-Canadian Plays on North American Themes,' in *Cultural Identities in Canadian Literature*, ed. Benedicte Maugière (New York: Peter Lang, 1996), 5–23.

16 In Canadian literary studies, it was not until recently that a shift in focus toward non-English and non-French Canadian literature could be felt. For example, Tamara Seiler contends that Canadian Literature is becoming more 'inclusive of diverse voices' – making them a foremost concern of literary studies in Canada; 'Stories From the Margin: "Insider" Fictions

of Immigrant and Ethnic Experience in Canada,' PhD diss., University of Alberta, 1998, 2.

17 For example, 'As Canadian as possible, under the circumstances.' Margaret Atwood quoted this 'catchphrase' in Havana in 1996.

18 For example, 'Canadians have been so busy explaining to the Americans that we aren't British, and to the British that we aren't Americans, that we haven't had time to become Canadians.' Helen Gordon McPherson.

19 For example, 'Canada is above all an idea of what a country could be, a place of imagination.' John Raulston Saul.

20 Peter G. Liddell, 'Introduction,' in *German-Canadian* Studies, ed. Liddell, 7.

21 Manfred Prokop, 'Defining German,' accessed 17 April 2007 at http://www.ualberta.ca/~german/PAA/DefiningGerman.htm; Richter, 'Who Are the German-Canadians?' Leo Driedger, in 'In Search of Cultural Identity Factors: A Comparison of Ethnic Students,' *Canadian Review of Sociology and Anthropology* 12, no. 2 (May 1975): 150–62, identifies language use, endogamy, choice of friends, religious denomination, parochial schools, and voluntary organizations as components of cultural groups. Alan B. Anderson and James S. Frideres, in *Ethnicity in Canada: Theoretical Perspectives* (Toronto: Butterworths, 1981), 40, define cultural groups by ethnic origin, ethnic-oriented religion, and folkways. Artiss, in 'Who Are the German-Canadians,' suggests four tests of 'German-ness': historical, linguistic, cultural, and geographic. See also Gerhard P. Bassler, 'German Overseas Migration to North America in the Nineteenth and Twentieth Centuries: Recent Research from a Canadian Perspective,' *German-Canadian Yearbook* 7 (1983): 8–21; and Walter Riedel, 'The Study of the Literature of the German-speaking Canadians: A Thematic Approach,' in *German-Canadian Studies in the 1980s: Symposium 1983* (Vancouver: CAUTG, 1983), 254–63.

22 George Elliott Clarke, 'Treason of the Black Intellectuals?' Working Paper of the Third Annual Seagram Lecture, presented 4 November 1998 at McGill Institute for the Study of Canada, Montreal, 1999, 5.

23 Gordon Bailey and Noga Gayle, *Ideology: Structuring Identities in Contemporary Life* (Peterborough: Broadview Press, 2003).

24 Fred Wah, *Faking It: Poetics and Hybridity* (Edmonton: NeWest Press, 2000), 72–3.

25 Ibid.

26 Ibid.

27 See Uta Regoli, *Letters on Birchbark*, trans. Henry Beissel (Manotick: Penumbra, 2000), 15.

28 Henry Beissel, personal interview, Leuna, 4 November 2004.

29 See Gordon Bölling, 'Acts of (Re-)Construction: Traces of Germany in Jane

Urquhart's Novel *The Stone Carvers*,' in *Refractions of Germany in Canadian Literature and Culture*, ed. Heinz Antor et al. (Berlin: de Gruyter, 2003), 295–371, 295.

30 Translated by Epp, in Georg K. Epp, *Unter dem Nordlicht: Anthologie des deutschen Schrifttums der Mennoniten in Canada* (Winnipeg: German Society of Canada, 1977), xvi.

31 Peter Bliss A. Bailey, 'Oh Canada,' in *Fire on the Water*, vol. 2, ed. George Elliott Clarke (Lawrencetown Beach: Pottersfield Press, 1992), 113–14.

32 Ulrich Schaffer, *Herz Arbeit – Heart Work: zweisprachiger Gedichtband* (Stuttgart: Kreuz-Verlag, 1998), 24.

33 Suzette Mayr, *The Widows* (Edmonton: NeWest, 1998), 148.

34 Another German-language version of *Oh Canada* is F.P.J. Rimrott, 'Die Nationalhymne,' in *German-Canadian Yearbook* 2 (1975): 251.

35 Epp, *Unter dem Nordlicht*, ix.

36 Riedel, 'Study of the Literature,' 255.

37 For example, Karl J.R. Arndt and May E. Olson, *The German-Language Press of the Americas 1732–1968: History and Bibliography* (Pullach bei München: Verlag Dokumentation, 1973); Hartmut Fröschle, 'Deutschkanadische Bibliographie. Eine Auswahl,' *German-Canadian Yearbook* 1 (1973): 327–44; and 'The Germans in Ontario: A Bibliography,' *German-Canadian Yearbook* 8 (1984): 243–79; John Miska, 'Austrian' and 'German,' in *Ethnic and Native Canadian Literature: A Bibliography* (Toronto: University of Toronto Press, 1990), 29–32, 83–120.

38 Georg K. Epp and Heinrich Wiebe, 'Select Bibliography of Canadian German Mennonite Writing,' in *Unter dem Nordlicht*, ed. Epp, 290–2; Walter Bauer, *A Different Sun*, trans. Henry Beissel (Toronto: Oberon Press, 1976); Angelika Arend, *Documents of Poetry and Compassion: The Poetry of Walter Bauer* (Montreal and Kingston: McGill–Queen's University Press, 1999); Helfried Seliger, 'Charles Wassermann: Life and *Oeuvre* in the Service of Mutual Understanding,' in *The Old World and the New: Literary Perspectives of German-speaking Canadians*, ed. Walter Riedel (Toronto: University of Toronto Press, 1984), 124–43.

39 For example, Rodney T.K. Symington, ed., *Else Seel: Ausgewählte Werke, Lyrik und Prosa* (Toronto: GCHA, 1979); Angelika Arend, 'Verführte, Hexe, Hure, Weib: Frauenbilder aus der Hand der Dichterin Else Lübcke Seel,' *German-Canadian Yearbook* 17 (2003): 47–58.

40 Elisabeth Mann Borgese, *Wie Gottlieb Hauptmann die Todesstrafe abschaffte Erzählungen* (Hürth bei Köln: Edition Memoria, 2001).

41 Heinz Kloss, 'Bemerkungen zur deutschkanadischen Literatur,' *German-Canadian Yearbook* 3 (1976): 188–92 at 190–1.

42 Margaret Atwood, *Survival: A Thematic Guide to Canadian Literature* (Toronto: House of Anansi, 1972), 18–19.

43 S.J. Squire, 'Ways of Seeing, Ways of Being: Literature, Place, and Tourism in L.M. Montgomery's Prince Edward Island,' in *A Few Acres of Snow: Literary and Artistic Images of Canada*, ed. Paul Simpson-Housley and Glen Norcliffe (Toronto: Dundurn Press, 1992), 137–47.

44 Beissel in Regoli, *Letters on Birchbark*, 2.

45 Regoli, *Letters on Birchbark*, 10.

46 Ernst Loeb, *Fussnoten sind wir. Gedichte* (Toronto: GCHA, 1986), 35; Regoli, *Letters on Birchbark*, 20, 55.

47 Regoli, *Letters on Birchbark*, 88; Carl Weiselberger, *Carl Weiselberger. Eine Auswahl seiner Schriften*, ed. Peter Liddell and Walter Riedel (Toronto: GCHA, 1981); Eugen Banauch, 'The Third Reich and Its Aftermath: Exile Literature of German-Speaking Canadians,' Diplomarbeit, Universität Wien, 2001, 118; Mayr, *The Widows*, 236.

48 Weiselberger, *Weichselberger*, 111–22.

49 Quoted in Almeida, 'Transcultural Fictions in the Americas,' 6.

50 Mayr, *The Widows*, 176, 123.

51 Zimmer, 'Deconstructing German-Canadian Identity.'

52 Wsevolod W. Isajiw, 'Identity and Identity-Retention among German Canadians: Individual and Institutional,' in *A Chorus of Different Voices*, ed. Sauer and Zimmer, 67–83.

53 John Considine, 'Dialectology, Storytelling, and Memory: Jack Thiessen's Mennonite Dictionaries,' in *Refractions of Germany*, ed. Antor, 145–68.

54 Gert Neuendorff, *Und keiner hört hin / And Nobody Listens* (Toronto: GCHA, 1982)

55 Schaffer, *Herz Arbeit – Heart Work*, 44.

56 Robert Kroetsch, 'Occupying Landscape We Occupy Story We Occupy Landscape,' in *Refractions of Germany*, ed. Antor, 23–9 at 23.

57 This famous phrase, quoted by Margaret Atwood, was the winning entry in a contest where people were asked to complete the phrase 'As Canadian as … ' It is interesting that the reason for the contest was to create a catchphrase like the American 'As American as apple pie.' See Lawrence Hill, *Black Berry, Sweet Juice: On Being Black and White in Canada* (Toronto: HarperCollins, 2001).

58 'I Am Canadian: Hey … / I have a Prime Minister, not a President. / I speak English & French, not American, and I pronounce it "about," not "a boot." / I can proudly sew my country's flag on my backpack. / I believe in peace keeping, not policing, diversity, not assimilation, / … / A toque is a hat, a chesterfield is a couch, and it is pronounced "zed" not "zee,"

"zed." / Canada is the second largest land mass, the first nation of hockey / and the best part of North America.' Quoted by Monique Bégin, '"I am Canadian!" From Beer Commercials to Medicare: In Search of Identity,' in *Canadian Distinctiveness*, ed. Gaffield and Gould, 173–81 at 177–8.

59 Paul Mog and Hans-Joachim Althaus, *Die Deutschen in ihrer Welt*, 5th ed. (Berlin/München: Langenscheidt, 1996).

60 David Cameron, *Taking Stock: Canadian Studies in the Nineties* (Montreal: Association for Canadian Studies, 1996), quoted in John D. Blackwell and Laurie C.C. Stanley-Blackwell, 'Canadian Studies: A Guide to the Sources,' accessed 18 April 2007 at http://www.iccs-ciec.ca/blackwell.html.

61 Leuba Bailey, *The Immigrant Experience* (Toronto: Macmillan, 1975), 2.

Contributors

Kerstin Boelkow studied history, German, and Canadian studies at the University of Trier and the University of Manitoba. She holds a Master of Arts and a *Staatsexamen* (graduate certificate in teaching). She worked for the Embassy of Canada in Germany and at high schools in Lauterbach (Hessen) and Moers (North Rhine-Westphalia). Currently she works as a teacher in Southern Germany.

Myka Burke has studied at Carleton University, the University of Vienna, and the University of Leipzig, where she is a doctoral candidate at the Herder Institute and was a lecturer at the Institut für Germanistik. She is co-editor of the *German-Canadian Yearbook* and won the University of Leipzig DAAD Preis in 2005. Recently, she translated *Deutsche Welle – Deutsch Interaktiv*, ed. E. Tschirner (2006; online: http://www.deutsche-welle.de/dw/0,2142,9572,00.html) into English. Her PhD thesis is entitled 'Literature, Language and Cultural Identity: Using the Example of Contemporary German Language Canadian Literature.'

Ross D. Fair is an adjunct professor in the Department of History at Ryerson University in Toronto. He is the author of '"Theirs Was a Deeper Purpose": The Pennsylvania Germans of Ontario and the Craft of the Homemaking Myth,' *Canadian Historical Review* 87, no. 4 (December 2006), which received the Ontario Historical Society's Riddell Award for the best article on Ontario's history published during the award year.

Patrick Farges is an assistant professor (Maître de conférences) in the Department of German Studies at the University Sorbonne Nouvelle in Paris (France). He is the author of *Le trait d'union. Itinéraires d'exilés ger-*

manophones au Canada après 1933 (2008). His current research interests include gender and migration, as well as masculinity studies.

Alexander Freund iş an associate professor of history and holds the Chair in German-Canadian Studies at the University of Winnipeg. His recent publications include 'Representing "New Canadians": Competing Narratives about Recent German Immigrants to Manitoba,' *Journal of Mennonite Studies* 30 (2012); 'A Canadian Family Talks About Oma's Life in Nazi Germany: Three-Generational Interviews and Communicative Memory,' *Oral History Forum d'histoire orale* 29 (2009); and, with Alistair Thomson, *Oral History and Photography* (Palgrave 2011). His current research includes a SSHRC-funded study of refugees in Manitoba since 1945 and a project on digital storytelling and oral history with children of survivors of Residential Schools, funded by the Aboriginal Healing Foundation. Dr. Freund is the co-director of the Oral History Centre, co-president of the Canadian Oral History Association, and co-editor of its online open-access journal, *Oral History Forum d'histoire orale*.

Christiane Harzig, Arizona State University, taught women's and North American history as well as the history of global migrations of domestics and caregivers. She published *Einwanderung und Politik. Historische Erinnerung und Politische Kultur als Gestaltungsressource in den Niederlanden, Schweden und Kanada* (2004); with Danielle Juteau and Irina Schmitt, eds., *The Social Construction of Diversity: Recasting the Master Narrative of Industrial Nations* (2003), and the co-authored *Peasant Maids – City Women: From the European Countryside to Urban America* (1997), as well as 'Women as Global and Local Agents: New Research Strategies on Gender and Migration,' in Pamela Sharpe, ed., *Women, Gender and Labour Migration: Historical and Global Perspectives* (2001).

Dirk Hoerder, Arizona State University and Universität Bremen, Germany, taught North American social history and historiography, Atlantic economies, global migrations, borderland issues, and sociology of migrant acculturation. His publications include *Cultures in Contact: World Migrations in the Second Millennium* (2002), the co-edited *The Historical Practice of Diversity: Transcultural Interactions from the Early Modern Mediterranean to the Postcolonial World* (2003), and *Geschichte der deutschen Migration vom Mittelalter bis heute* (2010), among others.

Grit Liebscher is a professor in the Department of Germanic and Slavic Studies at the University of Waterloo. Her current research on German-Canadians is captured in a forthcoming co-authored book entitled *Language, Space, and Identity in Migration, and Aspects of Language Attitudes* and in the article 'Language Attitudes, Migrant Identities, and Space' (with Jennifer Dailey-O'Cain), *International Journal of the Sociology of Language* 212 (2011). She has also published on language and identity in Germany after 1989, including the book chapter 'Identity and Positioning in Interactive Knowledge Displays' (with J. Dailey-O'Cain) in *Style and Social Identities: Alternative Approaches to Linguistic Heterogeneity*, ed. Peter Auer (2007). Her publications on language use in the classroom include 'Learner Code-Switching in the Content-Based Foreign Language Classroom' (with J. Dailey-O'Cain), *Modern Language Journal* 89, no. 2 (2005).

Barbara Lorenzkowski teaches at Concordia University in Montreal. She is the author of *Sounds of Ethnicity: Listening to German North America, 1850-1914* (2010). Her current research project is a FQRSC-funded study on childhood, space, and memory in wartime Atlantic Canada – 'The Children's War, 1939–1945' – which is based on close to one hundred oral history interviews.

Pascal Maeder is an assistant professor at the University of Basel, where he is affiliated to the chair in Modern and Contemporary History. He is the author of *Forging a New Heimat: Expellees in Post-War West Germany and Canada* (2011) and recently co-edited the book *Wozu noch Sozialgeschichte? Eine Disziplin im Umbruch* (2012).

Manuel Meune is a professor in the Department of Modern Literatures and Languages at Université de Montréal. He is the author of *Les Allemands du Québec. Parcours et discours d'une communauté méconnue* (2003) and 'Die DDR und die "Bürger deutscher Herkunft" in Kanada: die Rolle der Gesellschaft Neue Heimat (1980-1990),' *Forum Deutsch* 1 (2008) (www.forumdeutsch.ca).

Angelika Sauer is a professor of history and chair of the Department of History at Texas Lutheran University. Her most recent publications include two chapters in *Migrants and Migration in Modern North America: Cross-Border Lives, Labor Markets and Politics*, ed. Dirk Hoerder and Nora

Faires (2011) and a chapter in *Transnational Networks: German Migrants in the British Empire, 1670-1914*, ed. Stefan Manz et al. (2012).

Mathias Schulze is an associate professor of German at the University of Waterloo and the director of the Waterloo Centre for German Studies. His research interests are in applied linguistics. He is the editor of the *CALICO Journal*, a journal on Computer-Assisted Language Learning, co-editor of *German Diasporic Experience: Identity, Migration, and Loss* (2008) and the author, together with Trude Heift, of *Parsers and Pedagogues: Errors and Intelligence in Computer-Assisted Language Learning* (2007).

Hans Werner is an associate professor in the Departments of History and Mennonite Studies at the University of Winnipeg. He is also the executive director of the D.F. Plett Historical Research Foundation. His publications include *Imagined Homes: Soviet German Immigrants in Two Cities* (2007) and a forthcoming study of the autobiographical memories and stories of a Soviet German-Mennonite soldier.

Index

Upper Canada: bill on right to hold lands, 93, 96; Church of England domination in, 91; marriage laws, 91–2, 104n42, 104n48; militia laws, 85–91, 99; naturalization act (1828), 80, 97–8; Pennsylvania Germans relocation to, 9, 79–81; right to use affirmation and declaration in, 94–5, 98–9; Simcoe's land proclamation, 82–5

Valverde, Mariana, 153
Vogt-Moykopf, Chaim, 202
Volksdeutsche, 29, 32, 237

Wah, Fred, 273
Waldstein, Gerd, 193
Waldstreich, David, 108
Waller, Harold M., 203
Wanka, Willi, 230–1
War of 1812, 9–10, 89, 95–7, 99
Warschauer, Heinz, 199
Waterloo County: choral societies, 129; collective memory of, 126; French-origin migrant population, 113; German cultural patterns in, 54; middle class of, 128; as Ontario's German heartland, 124; Pennsylvania German (Mennonites) settlement in, 10, 79, 96–8, 99n3. *See also* Berlin (Kitchener)
Weinmann, Heinz, 181
Weisbach, Henry, 229–31, 235
Weiselberger, Carl, 275; 'Kain und Abel in Kanada,' 277
Welt, 197
Werner, Hans, 13–15
West Germany: displaced persons in, 238; economic miracle (*Wirtschaftswunder*), 32; expellee population in, 227–8; homeland

societies in, 14, 229, 231–4, 236, 240; immigrant population from, 4; war compensation legislation (1952), 234
West, Roxroy, 158n34
'whiteness,' 8, 53–6
Widows, The (Mayr), 275, 277–8, 281, 283
Wiebe, Rudy, 275; *Peace Shall Destroy Many*, 279
Wilhelmy, Jean-Pierre, 181
Wittke, Carl, 124
women: Canadian literary writers, 275, 277–8; in civil service, 140–1, 154; family duties/relationships, 55, 141; groups and charity work, 52–3; historiography and studies of, 7–8, 44–8, 55–7; middle-class, 139, 142, 144, 152–3, 155; and migration trends, 23, 31; Moravian mission sisters, 66–7; movements, 48, 52, 56; protection societies for, 148–53; roles in peace jubilees, 10, 118–19; rural American, 48–9; salary discrimination, 142; Soviet-German, 217, 223–4; transatlantic migration network for, 11, 138–9, 143–52; urban American, 8, 49–53
Women's Emigration Society (WES), 151–2, 161n90
Wong, Lloyd, 30
Würtele, J.C.S., 168

'Yekkes,' 197, 202
Yiddish speakers, 23, 26, 29, 199
Young, James, 113, 126

Zimmer, Matthias, 273, 278, 283n2